The Horror of Life

The *Horror of* Life

ROGER L. WILLIAMS

The University of Chicago Press

THE UNIVERSITY OF CHICAGO PRESS, CHICAGO 60637
WEIDENFELD & NICOLSON, LONDON SW4 7TA
© 1980 by THE UNIVERSITY OF CHICAGO
All rights reserved. Published 1980
Printed in the United States of America
85 84 83 82 81   5 4 3 2 1

ROGER L. WILLIAMS is Distinguished Professor of History at the University
of Wyoming. His previous books include *Gaslight and Shadow; Henri Rochefort,
Prince of the Gutter Press; The Mortal Napoleon III;* and with C. Warren Hollister
et al., *River through Time: The Course of Western Civilization.*

LIBRARY OF CONGRESS CATALOGING IN PUBLICATION DATA

Williams, Roger Lawrence, 1923—
    The horror of life.

    Bibliography: p.
    Includes index.
    1. French literature—19th century—History and
criticism. 2. Despair in literature. 3. Decadence
in literature. 4. Authors, French—19th century—
Biography. 5. Syphilis—France. 6. France—
Civilization—1830–1900. I. Title.
PQ295.D47W5   840'.9'008 [B]   79–26641
ISBN 0-226-89918-7

To Henriette,
in appreciation and affection

Contents

Preface
ix

1 *Charles Baudelaire*
1

2 *Jules de Goncourt*
63

3 *Gustave Flaubert*
111

4 *Guy de Maupassant*
217

5 *Alphonse Daudet*
275

Notes
313

Bibliography
357

Index
375

Preface

WE SEEM TO BE RECONCILED THESE DAYS TO THE ALIENATION OF MANY artists and writers. We accept their posture as outsiders, expect from them forecasts of impending deluge, anticipate their nostalgia for the more virtuous past, and note their penchant for drastic solutions to those contemporary problems they are alleged to see or feel more acutely than the rest of us. We expect art to be a medium which denounces, forgetting that it has served to decorate and celebrate; and our guilt for having failed to erect that other Eden, when so many infallible theories have offered the hope, has often left us victims of the claim that the artist alone is competent to diagnose the health of society.

Our distinguished writers between 1910 and 1930, the period called the second renaissance in American literature, who also dominated the literary scene for the next thirty years, had in common the conviction that America was a cultural wasteland. We had reached the machine age, something forced upon us by the vile greed of capitalists. It became fashionable to despise science and technology as incompatible with the humane and aristocratic values artists represented, and to despise the democracy which prized the humane uses of technology. The language of those recoiling from technology and capitalism was usually laced with radical political jargon which gave the impression of a profound concern for people, whereas the preoccupation with the supremacy of art over ordinary life with its plebeian concerns canceled out compassion. Indeed, the rightist and leftist solutions they were apt to espouse have converted much of the world into states little better than concentration camps: the more utopian, the more tyrannical.

The language of those hostile to technology also carried hints of paranoia: a conviction that philistines plotted to convert the world into a place uninhabitable for people of taste. The paranoid loses the ability to distinguish between real and imaginary threats, between real and imaginary grievances. Such myopia may account for the tendency of those critics of America, so certain that true merit was appreciated only abroad, to revere the literary giants of nineteenth-century France. It is ironic that they saw as their spiritual home that very land that had been denounced for its philistinism hardly two generations before by Flaubert and Company.

The hatred of the bourgeois by all right-thinking people in the nineteenth century has been so often and sympathetically studied that we are prone to forget that, throughout the history of our civilization, the commercial classes have always been suspected of not sharing its highest values. What gave that suspicion distinction in the nineteenth century was its affiliation with despair for the future, the conviction that excellence and virtue are bound to be exterminated by gadgets. So effective were the literati in propagating that conviction that it has come down to us as an article of faith, indeed, as the only faith left. One almost hates to remark, as an intrusion upon private religion, that the nations most fervently denounced remain the last, if imperfect, practitioners of liberty; and that the suffocating uniformity predicted to be the product of Babbittry and gadgetry has flourished most richly where the philistines have been liquidated to enable social architects to set their hands to the noble task of remodeling mankind.

Historians have advanced a variety of tenable explanations to account for the peculiar philosophical and literary gloom of the nineteenth century. We know of the disenchantment after the apparent failure of the French Revolution; we can sense the moral dismay over the decline of legitimacy and the birth of utilitarianism as principles of authority; and we still can be moved by the descriptions of sordid life in the new factory towns. On the other hand, does any historian give us a world, before 1789, so celestial and sanitary that we would unhesitatingly opt for it ahead of the nineteenth century? For that matter, did the French Revolution really "fail" to a degree that would justify the pessimism that followed? Did not the Industrial Revolution offer hope for the future, if perhaps too soon, and not merely horror? And were there not ample alternatives to utilitarianism—given the will to prefer them?

The writer Jules Romains, born in 1885, noted the extraordinary contrast between the vigorous advance of European civilization in the nineteenth century—its social and political progress, the benefits of science and technology—and the writers' tendency to see the period as a time of decadence. In his words, such a distortion "is certainly the most phenomenal misinterpretation ever committed by literature. There was a kind of collective schizophrenia, the meaning of which was probably not negligible." And A. E. Carter has since observed that the nineteenth century looks amazingly massive in retrospect, "an accumulation of steam, cast iron and self-confidence," an age of astonishing vigor at home and abroad. It remains equally astonishing to see the number of writers, philosophers, and critics who devoted entire careers to deploring the decadence of their age.

Even if one continues to insist that those writers had extraordinary cause for pessimism, there remains the matter of their literary duty to their fellow men. Some of us remember the moving words of William Faulkner as he accepted the Nobel Prize in 1950, when he said that it is a writer's duty "to help man endure by lifting his heart and reminding him of the courage and honor and hope and pride and compassion and sacrifice which have been the glory of his past." In the passion of that moment, it escaped us how much of the work of the twentieth-century literati he implicitly indicted, including his own. And the indictment was equally applicable to their French predecessors whose message had been a hatred for life.

Jean Carrère, who loved their novels and poetry, called them "the bad masters" and deplored their influence on subsequent literary generations. He saw Baudelaire not as immoral, but as a demoralizer and a coward in his confrontation with life. Throughout Flaubert's novels he found a horror of man and society. The ruthless ridicule of Homais in *Madame Bovary*, for example, enabled Flaubert to vent his scorn of mankind with its limited knowledge, to make mankind's hopes and pretensions absurd. There was no charity in that outlook: no compassion for those who live and labor in obscurity, who struggle on in half-knowledge and aspire to know more. Carrère concluded that Flaubert had been a great writer with the brain of a woman, lacking a sense of history and politics, imagining that he could separate art from life.

What follows are not full-length biographies, but rather biographical studies, medical studies of five distinguished French writers, illustrious in their own century and still read in ours. I began the study with the understanding that all five had been syphilitic, and with the suspicion that disease had blackened their outlook on life. My medical inquiry soon revealed that four of the cases were far more complicated than anticipated, Daudet's being the exception; but the very complications lent credibility to the initial assumption of an association between disease and cultural destiny in the later nineteenth century.

I had known at the outset that, as geniuses tended to become outsiders in the nineteenth century, it became customary to think of them as degenerate or decadent. That attitude has been attributed to the philistine public, meaning the bourgeois—people so smugly satisfied with convention that they find eccentricity unbearable. We know that many men of genius may be eccentric or warped in various ways; and we have come to recognize that the warped or the mad may play an important social role, especially in unsettled times. Watching a mob invade the French National Assembly on 15 May 1848, the liberal cabinet minister Dr. Ulysse Trélat cried out: "I recognize them, I have taken care of them: Blanqui, Barbès, Sarbier, Huber. *All* of them are mad. They belong in the Salpêtrière, not here!"

But we also know that geniuses have no monopoly on neurosis or deformity. Both are widespread throughout the population without relation to talent or intelligence. Not only is the notion that the artist or writer is degenerate now medically intolerable, but the classical ideal, common to both the Renaissance and the eighteenth century, had celebrated the complete man. Then poetry or painting would not have been identified with weakness, but as qualities of a man's completeness. This enables us to understand why it was easy—too easy as it turns out—to attribute the change of attitude in the nineteenth century to the triumph of the bourgeois.

Much of that change in outlook can be attributed to the literati themselves, some of whom were sadly demoralized by illness, most of whom were far from aspiring to the classical ideal, much less approaching it. In rejecting romanticism as well, they turned their backs on its command to strive for greatness, no matter what the odds. And in the sterility of the world left to them, they found their worst suspicions about life, or their lives in particular, confirmed by the latest medical science.

Historians have long been familiar with the tendency of the nineteenth-century intelligentsia to link private cosmic despair with the presumably inexorable laws of thermodynamics and evolution. We know already of the association of decadence and degeneration made by racial theorists in the nineteenth century—about the presumed mongrelization being hatched by political democracy. But it is less well known that fashionable psychiatric theory in that century held gloomy predictions for intellectuals and writers, confirming what they were quite prepared to believe. They have been repeatedly quoted on the decadence of their age, railing against the drift of civilization into barbarism, often with considerable justice and insight, for which we have revered them. We have overlooked how deeply decadent they often felt themselves to be—not to speak of the medical wellsprings of that despair.

In the course of my research, I have accumulated many debts. I benefited, first of all, from the availability of distinguished studies of my cast of characters: by Enid Starkie and Marcel Ruff, by André Billy, by Benjamin Bart and Francis Steegmuller, by René Dumesnil and Paul Ignotus, and by Murray Sachs. I have pestered not only Professors Bart and Sachs with questions by mail, but also Professor Robert Niess, who sat on my dissertation committee eons ago and from whom I have continued to learn. My footnotes and bibliography attest to the wealth of expertise that has been at my disposal: historical, literary, and medical. The responsibility for interpretations, of course, is mine alone. I am already aware of instances where I have differed from the established authorities whose work has been of such value to me; and differences, no doubt, there will continue to be. The translations from French editions of correspondence, diaries, journals, novels, and poetry are my own.

As so often in the past, I am again indebted to the staff of the Bibliothèque Nationale in Paris for their indispensable and courteous service. I am grateful to the librarians of the University of California at San Francisco, who graciously put the latest medical literature at my disposal. Thanks to the friendly cooperation of the Interlibrary Loan personnel at the University of Wyoming, I was able to read a vast medical literature not otherwise available to me in Laramie, in journals drawn from a remarkable number of American libraries and research centers. I also acknowledge, with thanks, several travel grants for research from the University of Wyoming.

Finally, I express my gratitude to those colleagues who have given me counsel and encouragement.

·I·

Charles Baudelaire by Etienne Carjat. Courtesy of the Art Institute of Chicago

Charles Baudelaire

Life is a hospital in which each patient is consumed by the desire to change beds.

Baudelaire, Paris Spleen

IN HIS LATER YEARS, THE ANGUISHED BAUDELAIRE ATTRIBUTED HIS temperament to bad heredity. His notion that only something freakish could have resulted from the mating of parents thirty-five years apart in age was in fact quite consistent with the teaching about heredity in his day, though such a marriage was not unusual in that era. François Baudelaire, a widower with one son, was sixty at the time of the marriage in 1819; the bride, Caroline Defayis, was only twenty-five. Today we would not believe that the disparity in age could be accountable for physiological defects in the couple's offspring.

On the other hand, the disparity in age can account for Caroline's lack of passionate attachment to her husband; and though we know little of Baudelaire's first years of life after his birth in 1821, his mother does indeed seem to have lavished her heretofore stifled affections upon him. Moreover, the heredity was tainted, if not in the manner supposed by Baudelaire. Unbeknown to him, he was predisposed to paralytic disease. His father died in 1827 from a paralysis of uncertain origin; his half-brother, Alphonse Baudelaire, would die in 1862 of a cerebral hemorrhage with hemiplegia on the left side; and his mother, who would outlive him, died both hemiplegic and aphasic. Little is known of prior generations, but Baudelaire's heredity appears to have been tainted on both parents' sides.[1]

In later years, Baudelaire enjoyed remarking that he was the son of a priest. His father had been reared in the austere Jansenist tradition, trained for the priesthood, and ordained. That career came to an end during the Revolution, and he married for the first time in 1797. Under the Consulate he became an official at a substantial salary and retained his post until the fall of the Empire. Out of office thereafter, but with a respectable income, he devoted his leisure to sketching and painting. When he died in 1827, he left a widow of thirty-four, her child of six, and a son by the previous marriage who was then studying law.[2]

The following year Caroline Baudelaire married Major Jacques Aupick, a glamorous officer only four years her senior. It was a love

1

match from the start, and they remained devoted until his death. The marriage meant a radical change for young Charles. Until then, he had basked in the near totality of his mother's affection. He suddenly had to share that affection with an army officer whose rapid promotions in the service were proof of his success. He was a firm and busy man, never to have children of his own. Though no student of Baudelaire has ever suggested that Aupick was hostile to his ready-made son, his career demanded frequent reassignment, disruptive of normal family life, and he had little time for his stepson. As a result, the boy attended a series of boarding schools.

In his later years, Baudelaire looked back at his mother's second marriage and his subsequent childhood years with bitterness. "When one has a son like me," he said to a friend, "one does not remarry." In 1850, he referred to his mother as a "guilty" woman;[3] and in 1861, he wrote her at great length to review their association, a letter that has been regarded by some as evidence of an Oedipus complex: "I loved you passionately in my childhood; later, under the influence of your injustices, I lacked respect for you, as if a maternal injustice could justify a lack of filial respect. I have since often repented that, although, as is my habit, I said nothing about it. I am no longer the ungrateful, furious child . . . [Before your remarriage] you were mine alone. You were simultaneously an idol and a comrade." Then came the dreadful period of boarding school ordered by Aupick.[4]

On the other hand, most of Baudelaire's biographers have regarded such recollections as his inventions of a later day, reflecting the grievances of adulthood, not childhood. Apparently, Baudelaire had been regarded by his friends as a normal, happy child, and his youthful correspondence with members of the family was affectionate in tone. The late Enid Starkie, who had a pronounced aversion to medical and psychoanalytic interpretations, insisted that there is no evidence that Baudelaire—as a child—felt antipathy to Aupick, adding that "much nonsense" has been written about Baudelaire's sexual jealousy of General Aupick.[5] Starkie's ire was aimed in particular at René Laforgue, a Freudian. While Laforgue did write of Baudelaire's Oedipus complex, he thought that his conflicts with Aupick were the consequence of a neurosis rooted in infancy.[6] The mother's second marriage, in other words, did not *cause* the trouble, but came as a shock to a child whose Oedipal attachment had not been resolved in the normal manner. Claude Pichois, however, saw no conflicts with Aupick and argued that the two remained on good terms at least until Baudelaire was twenty, when a shocking attack of syphilis produced a sharp change in his destiny[7]—of which more later.

A superficial reading of Baudelaire's youthful letters would indeed lead one to think that he had been a normal, conventional child. When he was eighteen and preparing for the *baccalauréat* examination, he wrote to his mother in a manner that suggests no hatred for either boarding school or family. Yet, he did seem to miss being at home to enjoy his mother: "There is such an understanding between a mother and her son; they live so congenially along side each other."[8] A month later, he wrote a cordial, entirely proper letter to Aupick to congratulate him on a new command and his promotion to brigadier general.[9] But as Marcel Ruff suggests, the picture of the youthful Baudelaire as the happy conformist is probably an inaccurate portrait,[10] despite surface impressions. What Baudelaire later saw in Edgar Allan Poe's childhood tells us more about Baudelaire than about Poe: "The hours of imprisonment, the discomfort of the puny and deserted child, the terror of the enemy who is our master, the hatred of tyrannical companions, the lonely heart, all the tortures of early age," are words that expose the secret life of the hypersensitive child.[11] Even if one wishes to avoid the Oedipus-complex issue as something insubstantial, the pathetic letters between mother and son in later years remain as proof that she played too large a part in his life, that there was something equivocal or dishonest in their relationship, that both were aware the second marriage had been a catastrophe for Charles.[12]

As this opinion contradicts that of several eminent scholars, it need be added that about one hundred additional Baudelaire letters, most of which fall between the years 1832 and 1841, have since come to light. It seems, moreover, that the biographers did not suspect the deliberate destruction of some letters, for the purpose of distorting the record, or rather of providing a sterilized record for posterity. It seems probable that Baudelaire's early letters were preserved because the family recognized their unusual quality. At some point, however, Alphonse Baudelaire put the letters in good order and began to keep copies of his own letters to Charles—letters, incidentally, that unmask Baudelaire's later claim that he had never really known his half-brother. A great share of the newly found letters were written to Alphonse, by then a lawyer, and the tone is affectionate.

Alphonse had married Félicité Ducessois, and it was the Ducessois family who retained and passed on the Baudelaire letters and who also endeavored to conceal them as containing shocking and embarrassing information, offensive to religious sentiments in particular. One of the heirs, Marie-Anne Ducessois, a prudish spinster, burned some of the letters she held to be especially hideous before releasing the files to Jacques Crépet, editor of the five volumes of Baudelaire's *General Correspondence*. The special file containing the hundred juvenile letters escaped her censorship, because they had been hidden, for reasons unknown, and were only discovered when a badly bombed house was being reconstructed ten years after World War II.[13]

These juvenile letters might tend to confirm the traditional view of the happy schoolboy, afflicted with petty miseries to be sure, but showing none of the extreme sensitivity that Baudelaire would later claim for his youth. It is possible to read into them, however, evidence of the personality characteristics of his later life; and if that is a fair reading, then the notion of Baudelaire as the normal, unblemished child, suddenly converted through a crisis into the incorrigible young man is less convincing. Away from his family, he developed a penchant for putting off letter writing, and then apologized repeatedly for his laziness. A letter to the Aupicks, when he was twelve, is that of the dutiful child, confessing the errors of his ways, promising he will improve and struggle against his admitted sloth and thoughtlessness; but he also pleads with them to visit him, to give advice and encouragement.[14]

Another letter reveals the seventeen-year-old Baudelaire's interest in painting, already enhanced by a penchant for criticizing art. His class had been invited by King Louis-Philippe to visit the apartments in the château at Versailles. Among the many marvels, he singled out a painting by Delacroix, the *Bataille de Taillebourg*, as superior to the other scenes in the Galerie des Batailles.[15] This admiration reemerged when the twenty-four-year-old Baudelaire published his first art criticism: "M. Delacroix is decidedly the most original painter of both ancient and modern times. That is a simple truth, like it or not."[16]

Those of us who have suffered through the five volumes of Baudelaire's published correspondence—for all too many of his letters make for painful reading—are only too keenly aware of his indebtedness and his appeals for money. One is necessarily struck, therefore, to discover that the first such appeals were delivered in November and December of 1839, and coincided with an apparent venereal infection. The tenor of these letters was an accurate forecast of what was to come in later life: He has been thoughtlessly running up bills for books and clothes (and in this case, for medicine, too), so that he must have additional cash. But he will mend his ways and will not ask his half-brother for anything more in the future. Baudelaire was then eighteen.[17]

Meanwhile, Baudelaire the schoolboy, as Enid Starkie has related in detail, was a puzzle to his teachers. They found him insufficiently serious about his work, undisciplined and often uncivil, given not simply to frivolity and levity, but to falsehood if the need arose. Yet, they knew he had a good brain and that he undoubtedly had talent for prose and verse. Whereas his teachers feared they were witnessing the signs of premature depravity, we would in all probability define his behavior as that of the disturbed child or adolescent who has been removed from the heart of the family. At seventeen, on a holiday with his stepfather, he composed a poem that he called "Incompatibilité," the title alone reflecting his awareness that he was becoming an outsider.[18]

Despite expulsion from school in 1839, he prepared privately for, and passed, the examinations for the *baccalauréat* that year. General Aupick had been recommending that Charles prepare for a career in diplomacy, and he did enroll in the Ecole de droit in November of that year. But the truth is that he had made up his mind to pursue a literary career. Instead of attending lectures, he was settling into the bohemian life of the Latin Quarter, breaking with his bourgeois background and moving toward a poetry in which *le mal* would provide the fundamental insights and themes. It has been argued, therefore, that this "sudden change" in Baudelaire's life was related to his recent syphilitic infection, and that he had thereby acquired a pariah's destiny.[19]

Ingenious as that argument may be, especially when applied to a young man of Baudelaire's evident sensitivity, it has fatal flaws. In the first place, clear evidence of adolescent rebellion against authority and convention disposes of the notion of "sudden change" in Baudelaire. In the second place, the idea that Baudelaire felt irremediably stained by adolescent venereal infection is sheer conjecture, and can hardly be squared with his well-known comment that "on the day when a young writer corrects his first proof, he is as proud as a schoolboy who has just caught his first pox."[20] Nor could he have feared, as Pichois would have it, the dreadful physical outcome of syphilis, "the rotting of his bones" and so on; the tertiary stage of syphilis was yet unknown.[21] In fact, Baudelaire quite accepted the popular belief that "no one is more hale and hearty than one who has had the pox and has been quite cured."[22] We must, in short, look elsewhere for the sources of Baudelaire's preoccupation with *le mal*.

During 1840, members of the family were increasingly distressed by reports of Charles's unconventional comments and behavior, though his letters to the family gave the appearance of propriety.[23] Under French law, Charles had been an orphan since the death of his father, giving the *conseil de famille* not merely a moral, but a legal obligation to oversee his affairs. By early 1841, Alphonse, the attorney in the family, was endeavoring to ascertain the true state of Charles's finances and obtained from him a long list of his debts, mostly for clothing. Charles asked for Alphonse's financial assistance, promising to be reasonable in future purchases if he could be extracted from his dilemma. He specifically asked that the Aupicks not be apprised of his situation,[24] which suggests he had no inkling that Alphonse had been cooperating with the family in preparations to bring him to heel.

His list of debts had been far from precise, and Alphonse suspected the worst. As best he could calculate, the debt amounted to at least 3,270 francs—for Alphonse a shocking figure. He had not the slightest intention, he wrote Charles, of sacrificing his own inheritance from their father to settle the debts; his own income as an attorney permitted no such largess. The burden, he concluded, would have to fall upon General Aupick, a responsibility that would be highly unfair to the man who had done well by him as a son. He demanded more precise information about which debts were owed to whom.[25]

The upshot was that General Aupick settled the debts out of his own pocket and convened the *conseil de famille*.[26] It was agreed that Charles should be removed from the unsavory influences of the Left Bank by sending him on a long trip abroad; the funds for this were to be withdrawn from his patrimony, still held in trust as he had not reached his majority. Earlier biographers, having no conclusive evidence that the family was aware of Charles's venereal infection, believed that the family acted primarily for financial reasons and to prevent moral disaster. We now know that Alphonse had learned directly from Charles of the infection in late 1839; and we may deduce from a later letter from Charles to his mother that he understood the family had known the details: "You know that I had a syphilitic infection when very young."[27]

In explaining the family action to Charles, Alphonse endeavored to emphasize that the family as a whole wished him well; yet, their fondest hopes for his success in life had been disappointed. They had watched him grow from a charming and pleasant child into a difficult and suspicious young man, invariably ready to rebel when someone wanted to impose some salutary check upon him. "Your friends have taken you among loose women, whom you have chosen as the models for life in a state of freedom. You have no thought for tomorrow, you disregard all social restraints, and you are at war with all those who do not see your manner of living as you do." Alphonse's letter was long, very firm, and fair and wise in a conventional way. He reiterated his expression of the family's good will, promised that all would be forgotten if Charles could manage a change in his ways, pledged his own friendship, and urged him to write often while abroad.[28]

The prescribed remedy could have little chance of success unless a seedbed of trust and regard had been prepared much earlier in Charles's life. Nothing so much demonstrated his earlier sense of rejection and alienation than his hostile reaction to the voyage. That he had not been consulted about the family decision was a minor matter compared to his role as outsider for over ten years. An old story, this, but nonetheless sad in its retelling: the sincere attempt to repair that which had long since become irreparable; the injuries that no one plotted, but for which everyone must now feel undying guilt. Henceforth, Baudelaire's letters would be crammed with recrimination and sarcasm, the tardy surfacing of his anger at having been pensioned off as a child.[29] Packing him off to India exposed him as a solitary gardener, and the exquisite crop would be flowers of evil and illness.

The voyage to and from Calcutta, anticipated to require twelve to fifteen months, was a fiasco. The young man made himself disagreeable at every opportunity and, in fact, never reached India. Having left Paris on 9 June 1841, he regained France on 15 February 1842, having traveled no further than Mauritius and Réunion. Within two months after his return, on 9 April to be exact, Baudelaire attained his majority and inherited his patrimony, about 100,000 francs, a very large sum for that day. Having already revealed a modest capacity for living beyond his means, he was now offered the opportunity to perform on a grander scale without family restraint. He not only left the Aupick residence, but removed himself from the filth and noise of the Latin Quarter and established himself on the Ile Saint-Louis. News of his bonanza enabled him easily to buy on credit, and he plunged into the task of setting himself up as a dandy.[30] This included the acquisition of a mistress, the mulatto Jeanne Duval

—the Black Venus of his poetry—who entered his life in 1842.[31]

This era of rash spending and borrowing lasted until 1844, when Baudelaire was brought up short by news that his family was on the verge of reestablishing judicial control over his finances. Over 44,000 francs of the inheritance had been spent, and the *conseil de famille* determined to put the remainder in trust so that he would not become destitute.[32] Baudelaire protested that this would deprive him of his proper liberty. He was especially dismayed that his mother had passed judgment on him—had condemned him. By participating in this offensive action, she might as well be breaking his arms and legs. "Although I be merely your son, you must respect my person enough so as not to subject me to an arbitration by outsiders." To her claim that she was participating with the rest of the family for his own good and out of affection for him, he answered that he was quite prepared to give her any legal instrument through which she could take care of him; he was willing to allow anything but what the family was planning to do. Abandoning himself to her control would be acceptable, because that would be a *free choice* on his part.[33]

But in the summer of 1844, the family proceeded to go to court, and the trust was established on 21 September with the attorney Narcisse Ancelle, an old family friend, as the *conseil judiciaire* (administrator). In effect, Baudelaire was once again managed against his will by the family, and this time for life; for old Ancelle was still performing his duties when Baudelaire died in 1867. He was to have a small annual income, too small on which to live; on the other hand, he avoided destitution and died still owning a substantial part of his capital.

Thus began the era when bills became due that Baudelaire could not meet, and Baudelaireans ever since have debated the wisdom of the family decision. One's verdict in the matter depends upon whether one looks at the facts as they were known in 1844; or whether, with the advantage of hindsight, one is aware that Baudelaire's next twenty-two years were to be plagued with debt and continual financial bickering. Consequently, Starkie and Ruff have condemned the settlement, the latter believing that Baudelaire's own proposal was reasonable, the former believing that it would have been preferable to use the remaining capital to pay off the debts and let him start afresh with no income at all.[34] Turnell called the establishment of the *conseil judiciaire* "a cruel and stupid" business that reflected a "narrow middle-class outlook."[35] Such condemnations, in fact, transcended mere concern for Baudelaire's financial welfare, as they implied that the settlement was responsible for the appearance of his spleen, his bitterness, his subsequent inability to cope with life as a mature person.[36] Porché has speculated, with a somewhat more sophisticated insight, that Baudelaire's immediate appeals for help, to the Société des gens de lettres in particular, in which the "beaten child" confesses his defeat and incompetence, were meant by him to be discovered by the family.[37]

Some have argued that one effect of the *conseil judiciaire* was to turn Baudelaire toward literary forms that could make money, thus delaying the development of his poetic career. In truth, as Starkie has pointed out, Baudelaire had already been more interested in painting—and in art criticism—than in poetry, which he considered to be a pastime.[38]

The fact that neither aid nor financial success came quickly to Baudelaire possibly contributed to his attempt at suicide in June of 1845. It took place in a cabaret in the rue de Richelieu in the presence of Jeanne Duval, his mistress; he dealt an ineffective knife-blow to his chest, after which he was carried off to his mother's house. Some of his debts were thereafter settled by the startled Aupicks, and he remained in their home for nearly half a year. Because of his quick recovery, and because he later made fun of the incident when describing it to his friend Louis Ménard, the attempt at suicide has been deemed a fake, cleverly designed to mislead everyone, including Jeanne.[39] Others, impressed by the sincerity of the letter Baudelaire gave Jeanne to be delivered to Ancelle, the *conseil judiciaire*, have seen it as a genuine attempt, an admission of failure and despair.[40]

Jeanne did not know its contents. It was both a will and an explanation for his act. He set aside a portion of his estate for his mother, leaving everything that remained after the settlement of his debts to his mistress. Fearing that his mother and half-brother would try to have his will set aside on grounds of his mental incompetence, he proceeded to explain his association with Jeanne Duval and the reasons for his suicide in the hope that this would help Ancelle protect the integrity of the will. He included a list of his debts to be paid, but protested that he was not killing himself because of them. As he put it, not being like other men, he could not be disturbed by financial matters. He was killing himself because he could no longer tolerate life. "The fatigue of going to sleep and the fatigue of waking up have become insupportable. I kill myself, because I am useless to others—*and dangerous to myself.*" If he leaves almost everything to Jeanne, that is because she is the only person in whom he has found any peace. He has hardly known his half-brother; and his mother, who has unwittingly but continually poisoned his life, has no need for money. What is more, "She has a *husband,* she possesses a *human being,* an affection, a *friendship.* I have only *Jeanne [Duval].*" Jeanne being the only woman he has loved, he cannot endure the thought that she might be dispossessed by the family, for she has nothing. He would, himself, have tried to explain the "deep humiliation of his spirit to his mother had he believed she would understand."[41] But he did reside in her home for the next few months, his debts were reduced, and some manner of reconciliation, if only temporary, was achieved with the Aupicks.

The Dandy

Baudelaire was not only an admitted dandy, but his definitions of dandyism help to reveal the neurotic roots of that phenomenon in the nineteenth century. Dandyism is too often perceived as an amusing extremism in fashion; and since fashions continually change, from the yellow gloves of the July Monarchy to the insolent sportsmen of the Second Empire, for instance, the study of their change becomes an exercise in superficiality. Baudelaire was one of those who understood that dandyism characterized the man himself and his perception of life, that dandyism was style rather than fashion. Most of us, more or less, are the victims of fashion, whereas the dandy is acutely conscious of being the victim of life. Consequently, dandies will possess common moral characteristics that changes in fashion will tend to obscure. Misfitted for society, they adopt the psychology of the regal outcast; and their manners or mannerisms, though infinitely varied, are unrelated to any need or utility. They do not seek to please, but to astonish; and as outcasts, they are subject not to social regulation, but only to self-imposed demands. They deny this to be self-indulgence, regarding it, rather, as a noble duty, a struggle for loftier values than those worshiped by the culturally bankrupt society of their day; in short, dandyism is for them a gilded monasticism where values are sheltered from barbarism.[42] If we recall, however, that Baudelaire advanced his lack of utility as one reason for his suicide, we shall be reminded that the dandy's heroic posture masks profound distress.

As Baudelaire's sense of his rejection by the family dated from school days, and was related to his first irresponsible spending for clothes, his own avowal of infantile dandyism was insightful: "I used to confuse the smell of furs with the smell of women. . . . Indeed, I loved my mother for her elegance. Thus, I was a precocious Dandy."[43] At twenty-one, he possessed both the flair and the

10

equipment to astound lesser mortals. Exhibitionism of any nature is calculated to mislead observers; and some, like Jean-Paul Sartre, have seen Baudelaire's dandyism as concealment of his timidity, his shyness, his fear of being seen as he really was. Perhaps Baudelaire did not hate General Aupick for having separated him from his mother as much as he envied him his fine military and diplomatic career and the regard he enjoyed in high society. So much has been made of Baudelaire's alleged hostility to everything Aupick presumably represented, that the very idea that Baudelaire secretly aspired to a comparable level of success—as the leading personage of the realm, and not simply as the first poet of his era—will likely offend most Baudelaireans.[44]

"There are only three respectable human beings," Baudelaire wrote, about 1860: "the priest, the warrior, the poet. To know, to kill, and create."[45] The equation suggests an admiration for Aupick's profession and hints that Baudelaire had sought Aupick's esteem. In 1853, in fact, he had written to his mother about his translation of Poe with biographical notes. The manuscript had been *promised* to a publisher, but it lay *unfinished* on his table and was causing him anguish. The delay was causing him double torment, he explains, as he was anxious to send a fine copy, printed on choice paper and handsomely bound, to General Aupick. He knows that although any affection between them is impossible Aupick would recognize such a gift as a token of his esteem and as proof "that I desire his."[46] Yet, when Baudelaire embarked upon the life of a dandy in defense of his own ego, he cultivated the very traits that guaranteed a total defeat in society, shunning the path taken by the disciplined and puritanical Aupick.

Baudelaire's friend Charles Asselineau protested that, even though Baudelaire gave the appearance of hoping to become rich from his publications, he was too refined and had too much self-respect to ever become "a money-making author." It is curious how those with private means, like Asselineau, can attribute an indifference to money to those who lack it. Far from being indifferent to money, poor Baudelaire was to spend the remainder of his life devising stratagems to obtain it and to flee from creditors. One of the reasons he would be attracted to Belgium toward the end of his life was his realization that large sums were being paid to literary lecturers abroad. Asselineau knew very well of his inclination to capitalize on such an opportunity.[47]

In defining dandyism, Baudelaire clearly stated the dandy's need for time and money. But the hidden qualification was the importance of seeming to have wealth without exerting oneself for it as the common herd does. All dandies, Baudelaire insisted, live by a rigid code which is beyond the ordinary law. Their purpose is to cultivate the idea of the beautiful in their own persons, to satisfy their own desires, and "to feel and to think." That requires leisure. What is more, "without leisure and money, love can be nothing but a plebeian orgy or the fulfillment of a conjugal duty . . . a loathsome utility." Contrary to popular notion, the dandy is not primarily concerned for personal appearance or material elegance. These only serve to signal the luckless plebes the superiority of the dandy's person. He has a burning need to acquire originality; he delights in causing astonishment; but he *never*, himself, appears to be astonished. His strength is visible in his extravagance, as there is a certain grandeur in a life dedicated to follies. The code requires a self-discipline as rigorous as that of a monastic order. It must be aimed at opposing all that is trivial: "The last gleam of heroism in times of decadence," a heroism, Baudelaire predicted, that would soon be submerged by the rising tide of democracy.[48]

As Baudelaire understood, the dandy's pride does not accommodate itself to external discipline or to submission to external authority. He must have had some inkling, therefore, that he, as a dandy, had little comprehension of conventional obligations: not to society, to family, or to friends. Which is to say that his cult of *soi-même* meant that he never really attained male maturity. Jean-Paul Sartre quite rightly saw Baudelaire as the eternal minor, the middle-aged adolescent, existing in a steady state of hatred and anger, yet surviving under the benevolent protection of others, a protection he could not bear to forgo, despite his pride of independence.[49] If anything, Baudelaire exalted the absence of maturity, saying that the child is always exhilarated, that everything is new for him: "Genius is simply *childhood* rediscovered by an act of will."[50] We know that he had friends, meaning close associates, but he never had real comrades or intimates. The idea of marriage was evidently utterly foreign to him. He never considered it. And as for public affairs, though he occasionally pronounced on politics, he was fundamentally indifferent.

It will be argued to the contrary that he threw himself into 1848 on the side of the revolutionaries. Perhaps he did so in the hope of seeing General Aupick shot, as he claimed; for there can be no doubt that he had a profound contempt for the intellectual quality of the revolutionary theorists and leaders, a contempt he would reiterate after 1848. Later that year, he undertook the direction of a newspaper in Châteauroux, showing himself quite unable to select and support one cause or political line.[51] Not principle, but the spirit of revolt led to his engagement. "My intoxication in 1848: What was the nature of that intoxication? Liking for vengeance. *Natural* pleasure in destruction."[52] His enthusiasm for a democratic republic? "Can you imagine a Dandy speaking to the people, unless to scoff at it? The only reasonable and settled form of government is the aristocratic."[53] Toward the end of his life he added: "All of us have the Republican spirit in our veins, like syphilis in our bones; we are democratized and syphilitic."[54]

It should come as no surprise to learn that Baudelaire, as the middle-aged adolescent, lacked the mature person's discipline. He not only wrote slowly and painstakingly, as Asselineau recorded, but in fits and starts, so that he was never able to grind out work in the routine manner necessary for commercial success. He would repeatedly calculate the literary output needed to make the money to cover his debts, and when that requirement was met he devoted his energy to formulating reasons to justify his procrastinations. An exception was a brief period, beginning in 1852, when he commenced work on the Poe translations. Since, as we shall see, life with Jeanne Duval was never conducive to productivity, it seems no mere accident that this "bout of energy," as Starkie called it, coincided with Baudelaire's decision to leave her in March of 1852. The translations that began appearing in 1856 brought him the only substantial money he ever earned. Unfortunately, his diligence had already flagged by 1855, the year he resumed living with Jeanne.[55] The key to Baudelaire's appalling poverty and debt was not, in fact, in the establishment of the *conseil judiciaire*, but in his character and personality; and we must ultimately account for why his biographers have been so ready to fix the blame elsewhere.

Baudelaire was no conventional dandy, and his exhibitionism and eccentricity were seen by his contemporaries more as marks of a charlatan than of a literary genius. Told that Baudelaire had taken residence in a small hotel near a railroad, where his corridor was always full of travelers, the Goncourts remarked that Baudelaire always kept his door wide open so that the multitude might see genius at work.[56] Even the kindly Asselineau once revealed that Baudelaire had slept under the bed at the Hotel Pimodan for no other reason than to astonish his friend.[57] Anecdotes about Baudelaire have to be suspect unless we are sure of the source. We must remember that he admitted inventing stories about himself to enhance his lurid reputation, and he felt certain that the worst would always be believed. He did not, for instance, live amid a hideous collection of lizards, grass snakes, and vipers.[58] One critic, aware of Baudelaire's inventions, was not entirely sure that he always distinguished between the true and the false;[59] but it may be that Baudelaire's provocative falsehoods were always ingeniously tinged with truth. In reading him, no matter what the literary form, we need to remind ourselves repeatedly that Baudelaire the exhibitionist meant to hide the truth about himself. At the same time, Baudelaire the artist cared for nothing but his vision of truth, which he rarely rendered in literal terms. Yet, the truth is always there—as he understood it—beneath and behind the lines.

Replying to the charge that Baudelaire was either mad or given to irrational eccentricities, Champfleury observed that, on the contrary, Baudelaire's eccentricities were always "touched with sincerity"; by which he meant that the bizarre actions were never frivolous but were, instead, excessively logical manifestations of his fundamental beliefs. During his early phase as a dandy, as an example, he required his tailor to make his clothes full of pleats on the grounds that "regularities horrified him." Whereas many eccentrics were seen to perform only for the astonishment of the bourgeois, Baudelaire's performance was designed for friend and foe alike. He confronted everyone with convoluted arguments and opinions; he could be straight and smiling one day, bent and scowling the next; as a young man he would sometimes suddenly shave his flowing locks to flaunt his gleaming skull. He wanted it understood, moreover, that he indulged in all manner of vices—proof, to be sure, that he was in no way a common mortal.[60]

The logic of his eccentricity was demonstrated to Alexandre-Louis Schanne, when Baudelaire offered lunch one day on a table set up for the occasion at the rear of a wine shop. The entire lunch consisted of a superb piece of Brie, accompanied by two bottles of vintage Bordeaux. When Schanne observed that it was unusual to begin lunch with the dessert, Baudelaire explained that he was a gourmet par excellence. When he found himself unable to afford a feast worthy of himself—a usual circumstance, thanks to his poverty—he always ate in this manner. He easily imagined that he had arrived at the last act of an excellent meal, which would reach its heights in the cheese and wine about to be served. After expounding to Schanne on the quality and the color of the wine, Baudelaire then proceeded to consume it with the greatest artistry.[61]

In the summer of 1852, he called on Maxime Du Camp in Neuilly, announcing upon his arrival that he was thirsty. Du Camp offered tea, beer, or a grog. Baudelaire politely explained that he only drank wine. Asked whether he would prefer Bordeaux or Burgundy, he said that he would like both. Two bottles were immediately brought to him, along with a carafe of water; but he asked to have the carafe removed, as he found the sight of water unpleasant.[62] He was making the point that water is *natural* and, therefore, abhorrent. With that equation we approach the very core of Baudelaire's unhappy existence. His dandyism was the outward sign of his rejection of nature or his acute consciousness that nature had rejected him, just as *maman* had done in opting for Aupick. "Woman is the opposite of the dandy," he wrote. "That is why she should be regarded with disgust. . . . Woman is natural, that is to say, abominable. Moreover, she is always vulgar, that is to say, the opposite of the dandy." And he would add, "I have always been amazed that women are allowed to enter churches. What manner of conversation can *they* have with God?"[63]

Baudelaire the dandy, yes, but hardly the salon dandy or a member of, or enthusiast for, the Jockey Club. From the early 1840s, when he had been regarded by his acquaintances as a dandy, he was unique among that tribe in his preference for black. From his black top hat to his glistening shoes he earned the tag given him by Catulle Mendès: His Eminence Monsignor Brummell. Later, he removed his short beard and wore his hair short to convey all the better his funereal outlook. In 1857, the Goncourts saw him supping alone at the Café Riche, noting with distaste his lack of tie, his bare neck, his shaved head, "dress appropriate for the guillotine," in contrast with his well-washed and manicured small hands,[64] the costume of the *spiritual* aristocrat.[65] His garb was the advertisement of Baudelaire's consciousness of evil [*mal*]. By that reckoning, either the perfect dandy becomes satanic, or, as one Catholic critic has put it, "In Lucifer, Satan becomes a dandy."[66] All Baudelaireans remark that Baudelaire was imbued with an awareness of evil and sin. But what is more he clearly saw himself as one of the fallen; he was aware quite early in life that he was doomed to an existence fraught with tension and anguish. "While still a child, I had in my heart two opposite feelings: a horror of life, and an ecstatic joy in life. Just the makings of a neurotic idler."[67]

The general reader with a limited knowledge of Baudelaire will likely identify him with *Les Fleurs du mal* and recall that after the publication of the poems in 1857, when he was thirty-six, he faced, in court, charges of obscenity and blasphemy.[68] It will come as some surprise, therefore, to learn that a great portion of the poems had been written before the end of 1844, during those moments of luxury at the Hôtel Lauzun on the Ile Saint-Louis. Thus they were in fact written before the establishment of the *conseil judiciaire* that has been condemned for "devirilizing" Baudelaire morally and leaving him either a child or a woman,[69] and at a time when he was seemingly carefree and happy with Jeanne Duval. The collection was first announced for publication, in 1845, under the title *Les Lesbiennes*. One view is that the title was deliberately chosen to be sensational.[70] A far more subtle interpretation would claim that Baudelaire had discovered, to his dismay, that his sexual desires were for women, but that he could not perform as a male.[71] The *conseil judiciaire* was appointed too late to be blamed for that. In 1848, the still unpublished poems were reannounced under a new title, *Les Limbes*, meaning *Limbo*—a title reflecting, according to Starkie, the spiritual crisis of contemporary youth.[72]

But surely the title was a clear sign of his own crisis, of the void in which he found himself. In his suicide note of 30 June 1845, he had written of his mother: "She has a *husband*, she possesses a *human being*, an affection, a *friendship*. I have only *Jeanne Duval*."That last phrase meant, as the suicide attempt attests, that "I have nothing at all." He still claimed Jeanne as a mistress, but his hopes for a passionate liaison had long since been disappointed, and for a reason that could give him little hope for an amorous future. After the suicide failure, he was carried to the Aupicks' house for recuperation, remaining there until approximately the end of 1845, when he evidently slipped away without warning. He needed solitude, he wrote his mother, in order to pull himself together and recover his strength. He did not intend to return until both his financial and mental states had improved. Moreover, as he could not convert himself into the sort of man General Aupick wanted him to be, it seemed fraudulent to remain in his home.[73]

Thus, at age twenty-four, Baudelaire was truly in limbo. He had no home, no family, no love, no promising career. It was a period from which he would never emerge until death took him, a period during which his most characteristic sentiment would be spleen—that is to say, ennui in its most profound sense: a feeling of disgust for everything and for himself in particular.[74] Within two months of his flight from the Aupicks, he inaugurated the appeals to his mother for money that would also characterize the remainder of his life, signing himself Baudelaire-Dufays, one spelling of her maiden name, as if to remind her of their attachment. Since most of his letters to her would involve requests for money, the cynic might conclude that his feelings for her had become entirely mercenary. After reading dozens of such letters, however, one should be convinced that she remained in his mind as the last best hope for companionship.[75]

The word *spleen* did, indeed, suggest profound weariness and disgust as Paul Bourget defined it. But since that does not exhaust the definition of the word, and because Baudelaire used the word in titles for both verse and poems in prose, we must consider his intentions further. Just as hysteria was historically linked to the *uterine genesis*, thus to gynecologic disease, so was hypochondria believed to be the male counterpart, though it was not linked to a sex organ. Beginning in the seventeenth century, the abdominal viscera—especially the spleen—were regarded as the seat of hypochondriacal troubles. In the later eighteenth century, the French began to use the word *spleen* to describe morose sadness or melancholia, thus relating that temper to hypochondria. In Baudelaire's century, therefore, the splenetic was a hypochondriac, a person suffering from a specific disease. J. U. Bilguer had defined it in 1767: "Hypochondriasis is a prolonged lingering disease in which one rarely feels ill and never really feels well."[76] Consequently, when Baudelaire used the word *spleen*, he would have understood its mental depression to be the outward sign of actual disease. Today, we would no longer use the terms *hypochondria* or *hypochondriasis* as if they were specific diseases. Rather, we use the adjectival form, *hypochondriacal*, to qualify syndromes.[77]

Since a substantial amount of what came to be *Les Fleurs du mal* had been written by the time Baudelaire was twenty-three, it must be deduced from the erotic and satanic or blasphemous poems which were included that Baudelaire, if pathetically immature in person, was astonishingly mature in experience and expression.[78] That is not to say that he had experienced literally those things that became his subject matter, but that he had been dreadfully scarred by life. The poems did not appear as *Les Limbes*, as announced in 1848; and when, in 1852, Théodore Véron published a book of poetry under that very title, Baudelaire necessarily abandoned it. The title *Les Fleurs du mal*, suggested to Baudelaire by Hippolyte Babou, seems to have been adopted about 1855. It seems clear from the preface, as Marcel Ruff has noted, that Baudelaire by then saw his work to be founded on the distinction between Good and Evil, hence *mal*—though it was hardly a celebration of *mal*, as was so readily believed.

At the time of his trial in 1857 he stubbornly denied having outraged public morality in his poetry;[79] and by 1861 he would insist that his volume had been grounded in Catholic ideas.[80]

On the other hand, given the history of the title, one can say, without impugning Baudelaire's integrity, that the metaphysical implications of his work came late to him. *Les Fleurs du mal* became a most serviceable title because it at once suggested both the poems of evil—in the medieval sense in which certain plants or flowers were the emblems of sins or vices—and the youthful flowering of his illness, since *mal* means both evil and malady. In the century since the Second Empire, critics have increasingly dwelt upon Baudelaire's spiritual vision and message, which were surely there. And as that dimension of his work became clearer, their outrage at the charges of obscenity and blasphemy became shriller. How could so many of his own generation have missed the purity of his intent, the innocence of his mission? The answer is that *some* of them, at least, knew him.

Among the immediate reviews of *Les Fleurs du mal* in 1857, the most snide came from Baudelaire's former schoolmate, Louis Ménard. However limited Ménard's poetic perceptions may have been, he sensed that Baudelaire's satanic pose was ludicrous. Baudelaire had "babbled interminably about vice," he recalled; but the truth of the matter was that Baudelaire really had the "salacious imagination" of those who lead secluded lives. His passion for decay had been caused by living in an imaginary world peopled by phantoms. He called Baudelaire a schoolboy suffering from arrested development.[81] The remark struck home, spiteful as the attack may have been. It may be risky to recall, given the prejudices of his milieu, that Henry James had little taste for Baudelaire as a person. Perhaps that enabled James to sense that, when Baudelaire used the word *mal* in his title, he had not necessarily meant *evil* at all. "This is not Evil," James wrote; "it is not the wrong; it is simply the nasty." He acknowledged Baudelaire's technical zeal but thought him to be of vicious sentiment.[82] Such reactions do not eliminate the accepted metaphysical interpretations of Baudelaire's thought, but they do remind us that some of Baudelaire's contemporaries viewed him as warped.

Baudelaire and his defenders, in 1857, had argued that his poems had been designed to expose the horror of vice and corruption. Four years later, when a revised edition of *Les Fleurs du mal* was ready for press (thirty-five poems were added and many of the older ones had been reworked), he told his mother that the volume would stand as witness to "my disgust and my hatred of everything."[83] A subsequent letter, indeed, gives us the true source of Baudelaire's poetic vision: *"I have a horror of life.* I repeat it: I am going to flee from the sight of the human face, above all from the French face."[84] His disenchantment had come early; it reflected his shattering discovery that, with his particular intelligence and sensibility, he could not bridge the gap between dream and reality:

> —*Certes, je sortirai, quant à moi, satisfait*
> *D'un monde où l'action n'est pas la soeur du rêve.*[85]

One of the additional poems, written in 1859, which contains what surely must be among the most lacerating lines in modern poetry, should permit us no doubt of Baudelaire's defeat:

> *O Mort, vieux capitaine, il est temps! levons l'ancre!*
> *Ce pays nous ennuie, ô Mort! Appareillons!*[86]
> [Oh Death, old captain, it is time! let us weigh anchor!
> This country wearies us, Oh Death! Let us set sail!]

With this poem he ended the second edition of *Les Fleurs du mal.*

Women and Drugs

The popular image of Baudelaire in France today is not the man of spiritual despair but the man of sexual and narcotic excess. It is this intemperance that is said to account for the bizarre in his literature and for his early death; Baudelaire, ever the exhibitionist, was largely successful in veiling the truth about himself. He did, indeed, like women, and he liked the things they like, recognizing that the love of feminine elegance is one of the roots of dandyism. Yet, he recorded his misogynist views—especially in *Mon coeur mis à nu*—with unmistakable venom, regarding women as accomplices of the serpent that engineered the fall of man.[87] If real women make works of art of themselves, they do so only to enhance the natural and to promote a natural purpose; and Baudelaire had found the natural repugnant. The dandy also turns himself into a work of art, but only on his exterior, whereas the poet—the spiritual dandy—endeavors to turn his whole life into art, to abandon entirely the natural for the artificial.[88] He has a love for the feminine, in other words, but a hatred of women. Woman is natural, vulgar, the opposite of the dandy: "The dandy must aspire to be sublime, continually. He should live and sleep in front of a mirror."[89] Such a man could only have been an enigma to the women he aspired to love.

We know surprisingly little about Jeanne Duval, Baudelaire's mistress for many unhappy years, and his biographers differ substantially in their evaluation of her. Maxime Du Camp believed that

19

Baudelaire found her in South Africa during his trip to the Orient in 1842, but we know that she knew neither English nor Dutch.[90] It seems probable that she was of West Indian origin—a mulatto—and that when Baudelaire met her about 1842 she was an aspiring actress. It has been conjectured that he found her acceptable because of her "infected blood," meaning her mixed blood, which accorded with his own syphilitic past and would have included them both in the world of pariahs. Such an argument required a knowledge of the tertiary stage of syphilis (which Baudelaire could not have had), and thus it is not convincing.[91]

Some of Baudelaire's contemporaries asserted that Jeanne was not beautiful, that she was a woman of low cunning rather than intelligence, and that she saw him as an inexperienced lad with a bank account. Others, however, have insisted that a man of Baudelaire's sensibility would never have tolerated a stupid and wretched creature or have celebrated her in poetry.[92] Though it is true that he never abandoned Jeanne even when he ceased to live with her, his fidelity, contrary to the assertions of some biographers, is not necessarily proof of his devotion or gratitude. Some men require punishment, and the observation that Baudelaire made in later years is noteworthy: "The strange thing about women—her preordained fate—is that she is *simultaneously* the sin and the Hell that punishes it."[93] As Michel Butor remarked, there is enough evidence of her coldness and his impotence to assert that "in the hell of their bed, the sexes were reversed."[94]

Being well-to-do in 1842, Baudelaire established Jeanne in a separate apartment in the rue de la Femme-sans-Tête, now the rue le Regrattier, near his residence on the Quai d'Anjou.[95] But after the appointment of the *conseil judiciaire*, when poverty became the rule, he could no longer afford either the Hôtel Lauzun or separate quarters for Jeanne. To be precise, they began to share quarters only after Baudelaire's passionate hopes had been thwarted and he was entering his limbo period. The "hell" of their life together was pathetically described in a letter to his mother in 1852, when he had decided on a separation. To have any peace and quiet, and to avoid "Jeanne's insupportable interference," it had become necessary to work at night. She had become an obstacle to his happiness and to the improvement of his mind. Her good qualities had vanished; she did not understand his work; she was impeding it; she had no desire to learn anything and took no interest in his studies, being totally ignorant of literature and politics. She did not "admire him," regarding him as her servant and property; and she would throw his manuscripts into the fire if that would bring in more money than publishing them. She had disposed of his cat—his sole distraction in the apartment—and brought in dogs, because she knew that the sight of dogs made him ill. "I have tears of shame and rage in my eyes as I write this to you."

Before turning to the subject of money, inevitable in a letter from Baudelaire to his mother, he told her that he had reached the conclusion, after his experience with Jeanne, that only the woman who has suffered to bring forth a child is the equal of a man. "To beget is the only thing that gives moral intelligence to the female." He had postponed getting rid of this childless one, because he could not condone leaving her without giving her a substantial sum of money, and he was unable to do so. He went on at great length about his deplorable financial situation, the object being to wheedle money from his mother that would enable him to make the break and clear up his debts. He had wasted ten years of his life in his battle with Jeanne, "but I shall never see her again."[96] Mme Aupick did send him money for this good cause, and he did leave Jeanne.[97]

Subsequently (evidently in 1852), he paid court to the actress Marie Daubrun, who had been rejecting his protests of love. "It is undeniable that I love you, Marie, but the love I feel for you is that of the Christian for his God." He wanted her to be his guardian angel, his muse, his Madonna. In fact, he used the phrase "a chaste attraction" to describe his feelings and intentions.[98] The cycle of love poems in *Les Fleurs du mal* celebrating the Green-Eyed Venus was inspired by his infatuation for Marie. He seems to have renewed his pursuit of her in 1854, but to little avail, though Starkie insisted that they were lovers for a brief time.[99]

Meanwhile, he had also been smitten by Mme Sabatier, originally Aglaé-Joséphine, later known as Aglaé-Apollonie. The artists and literati who frequented her renowned salon in the rue Frochot called her "La Présidente." Beginning in late 1852 Baudelaire wrote to her anonymously, dedicating love poems to her (as the White Venus of *Les Fleurs du mal*), guarding his anonymity for over four years—though she had long since been aware of his secret.[100] In his third letter, he sought to explain his anonymity: "I am an egotist like all children and the sick. I think about those I love when I am suffering. Usually, I think about you in verse, and when the verses are written, I cannot resist the urge to have the person, who is their object, see them. At the same time, like anyone who has an extreme fear of ridicule, I conceal myself."[101] Two years later, he was calling her "not only the most attractive of women, but also the dearest, the most precious of superstitions."[102]

In August of 1857, when Baudelaire was facing legal action against *Les Fleurs du mal*, he wrote to her openly, sending her a copy of the book and identifying those poems that "belonged" to her, two of which had been found offensive during the legal inquiry (*instruction*). He asked his "chère Idole" to pardon his past "folies et enfantillages," appealing for her patronage in that hour of legal trouble. "Flaubert had the Empress for him [and *Madame Bovary*]. I am lacking a woman."[103] It would appear that she offered him more than support, and he was sent into a panic. The following day he wrote that he was having great trouble composing a suitable letter, as he was suffering from "an abominable nervous ailment" and had awakened with "the inexplicable mental disturbance that I had when leaving your house yesterday evening."[104] After his long courtship, she was baffled by the rebuff, complaining not only that he had fled from her embraces but that she felt "humiliated and diminished." Yet, she finally accepted defeat, and they remained friends.[105]

In the meantime, he had not banished Jeanne Duval from his life as he had promised his mother in 1852. He called on her every month to give her an allowance and tormented himself with the idea of resuming life with her. Toward the end of 1854, smarting from debts and in need of clothes, he startled his mother with a threat to return to concubinage, explaining that he must have *a family*, no matter what the cost; it was the only way to work and to spend less.[106] *Maman* authorized Ancelle to send three hundred francs.[107] Her investment only postponed the resumption of concubinage for a few months. Before the end of 1855 Jeanne developed an illness that served to bring them together under the same roof.

Their reconciliation happened to coincide with an unusually difficult period in Baudelaire's relations with publishers and reviewers,[108] which was the tacit reason, perhaps, for his unwise decision to resume cohabitation. The literary wrangling made him unusually difficult at home; and after nine months, Jeanne left him. Thus ended the fourteen-year liaison, broken at her initiative, Baudelaire admitted, after a two-week struggle on his part to prevent her departure. Worse, she had seemed unperturbed, remarking that he would someday be thankful for her decision. But she had been his "sole distraction," he wrote his mother, his "sole pleasure" and his "sole comrade." No matter that their life together had been stormy; the idea of permanent separation had never entered his head. He was obviously crushed, "wounded," as he put it. For ten days he had not slept, he had vomited frequently and often wept. No more family! A life alone without family or friends. He used the occasion to plead for additional money,[109] and his mother sent it in short order.[110] He had been wounded, yes, but not to the point of refusing Jeanne further financial aid. In the spring of 1859, she suffered a minor attack that left one arm paralyzed. He struggled at once to provide funds for institutional care,[111] and was humiliated to discover that on one occasion she had denied receiving a payment in the hope of receiving a second.[112]

She evidently left the institution without warning, and he responded by renting an apartment for her welfare in rural Neuilly. Because of the financial burden, he joined her there, only to discover that her worthless brother was moving in to enjoy Baudelaire's largess.[113] After a few incredible weeks of quarreling, Baudelaire left the house, tortured by the notion that the man might well not be Jeanne's brother at all. Though Baudelaire still did not abandon her financially, they were never again to live together.[114] The only woman who remained was his mother.

One physician who has studied the literature available on Baudelaire's health and suspected the true poverty of his love affairs, has wondered if his amorous failures could be attributed to the sedation of drugs.[115] Baudelaire had, after all, written extensively about the effects of drugs, and, after his death, writers and physicians debated whether he had been a moderate user of narcotics or an addict. But this physician did not ask the reverse side of his question: namely, could Baudelaire's sexual distress have led to his use of drugs?

At age twenty-eight, Baudelaire reported a mild stomach upset that he attributed to the use of laudanum, a tincture of opium, adding that he had had similar results in the past.[116] In the nineteenth century, laudanum was a specific for ailments of the digestive tract; and we know by inference that Baudelaire suffered from hemorrhoids. In 1902, an undated letter came to light in which Baudelaire, signing himself Doctor Medicus Parisiensis, passed on his personal remedy for hemorrhoids to a correspondent. Though no physician would have prescribed such a remedy, the wording of the letter revealed Baudelaire's familiarity with the ailment.[117]

In 1860 he published *Les Paradis artificiels*, one of the major works on drug addiction in the nineteenth century. Yet, the major portion of his analysis of the mental effects of hashish had been written in 1851, when Baudelaire was thirty, and allegedly reflected personal experiences of his youth. However, his abridged translation of Thomas De Quincey's *Confessions of an English Opium Eater* and *Suspiria de Profundis*, which comprised the second half of *Les Paradis artificiels*, presumably did not reflect Baudelaire's own experience with opium, which has instead been deduced from scattered poems, notebooks, and letters.[118]

In his "Poem of Hashish," Baudelaire set out to analyze the mysterious affects and the morbid delights induced by hashish, to note the inevitable dangers of its prolonged use, and to emphasize the essential immorality inherent in such pursuit of a false ideal.[119] When describing the effect of hashish upon a group that had taken it, he called them "sick men" when under its influence. One of the "sufferers" rejected help scornfully. How could one "sick with joy" want to be cured, Baudelaire asked? His intent was absolutely clear: to warn against the ultimate "rotten fruits" of such a diet, to catalog hashish as a poison.

As for the moral implications of its use, Baudelaire distinguished between the natural dreams of ordinary sleep—which are made of the stuff of our own lives and can reveal ourselves to us—and the artificial dreams of intoxication—which are supernatural, unreal, distorted, and uninstructive. And in a striking passage, he wrote of the addict as an enchained or enslaved creature: "an appalling thing, the marriage of a man to himself!"[120] Opium and hashish, he concluded, are the surest means at Satan's disposal for the recruitment and subjection of deplorable humanity. "It is a fact that any man who does not accept the conditions of human life," the drug addict in this case, "sells his soul." The drug addict is immoral in that he creates a private universe in which he, himself, is God, and in which he seeks the riches of this world passively. Such riches are only legitimate and genuine when earned by "assiduous seeking."[121] Whether these words are those of the reformed user or of the innocent onlooker, they define damnation; and they inform us what Baudelaire understood when he asserted that he had a horror of life.

The letters of his later years were consistent in deploring the use of drugs, of alcohol, even of stimulants. He knew a woman who had reached a state of apathy and melancholy because she and her husband had drunk champagne with both lunch and dinner as if it were *vin ordinaire*. After several years, she could not reach a normal state without champagne—an innocent corrupter compared to Indian hemp, laudanum, or morphine. "I have taken any stimulant with repugnance because of the [resulting] exaggeration of time and the enormity of the character that a stimulant gives to anything. One cannot be either a businessman or a man of letters if one indulges in an *orgie spirituelle continuée.*"[122]

To deplore, however, was not necessarily to abstain. During his last few months in Belgium before the seizures that led to paralysis, Baudelaire began to experience what he called severe head neuralgia. For two weeks he avoided the pain-killing pills that were available, believing them to contain quinine, cocaine, and morphine.[123] Finally, in desperation, he summoned a physician, who prescribed doses of opium, quinine, digitalis, and belladonna for his relief. Because this physician was unaware that Baudelaire had formerly taken opium over a period of time, the prescribed doses were ineffective; and Baudelaire doubled and even quadrupled them.[124] He did get relief from his migraine, but felt that his senses were dulled.[125] Shortly thereafter, he had a series of dizzy spells and vomiting. His mother suggested that these spells might be attributed to the drugs he had been taking for his migraine, but he disagreed, saying that he had taken only very small amounts of belladonna. As for the opium, "you well know that for several years I regularly took up to 150 drops of it without any danger."[126] Yet, to Ancelle, he admitted that the spells he had been experiencing in January and February might mean that he had been poisoned by the digitalis and belladonna he had taken in December for neuralgia.[127]

We also know that during those last few months in Belgium Baudelaire began to drink brandy in unaccustomed amounts to abate his suffering, to the great distress of his friend and publisher, Poulet-Malassis. Shortly after the onset of Baudelaire's paralysis in March of 1866, Poulet-Malassis sent word of Baudelaire's condition to Jules Troubat, Sainte-Beuve's secretary, attributing the paralysis to alcoholism.[128] In literary circles, consequently, Baudelaire's fatal illness was ascribed to alcoholism and drug addiction.

In the preface to a posthumous edition of Baudelaire's works (1868), Théophile Gautier endeavored to destroy the rumor of Baudelaire's intemperance. He recalled the celebrated sessions of the Club des Haschischins at the Hôtel Pimodan in 1849, when the literati had experimented with hashish before finally renouncing its use. Baudelaire had tried the drug no more than once or twice, coming to the sessions rarely and only as an observer; he was certainly not a habitual user of the drug. On the contrary, Gautier remembered Baudelaire as temperate—as all workers must be.[129] Inasmuch as Gautier was writing nearly two decades after the demise of the Haschischins, the accuracy of his memory has been challenged.[130] On the other hand, it has been repeatedly noted that Baudelaire's analyses of the effects of drugs seem to be secondhand, derived from a study of medical treatises on the hallucinations and mental alienation experienced by drug addicts,[131] from the descriptions given by literati in describing their symptoms when using hashish or opium, and from his reading of Edgar Allan Poe and Thomas De Quincey.[132] One writer, in fact, did not heed Baudelaire's warnings about the deleterious effects of drugs, because he had been told by an old hand from Cochin China that Baudelaire's writing on opium was pure bunk, that to the contrary the smoking of opium produced a charming sense of well-being.[133]

No real evidence has ever been mustered to prove that Baudelaire used hashish other than during a brief period of experimentation in 1849. The experience taught him that no great intellectual benefits were to be derived from its use, and that it could destroy one's will.[134] Wine, he believed, elevated the mind; but Nadar, who often ate with him, insisted that Baudelaire rarely drank a half-bottle at a meal.[135] He was no alcoholic; indeed, he was considered unusually sober for a man of letters.[136] But there remains convincing evidence that he used opium occasionally over many years and was fearful of both the physical and moral consequences. It would appear that his original need for opium had been medicinal. Five of the six letters in which he mentioned the drug either stated or implied it was being used to treat an ailment.[137]

The sixth letter, however, suggested his use of opium to combat depression: "I am quite low, my friend, and I did not bring any opium. I had no money to pay my pharmacist in Paris."[138] In addition, when struggling with his abridged translation of Thomas De Quincey, he explained to Poulet-Malassis that he wanted "to blend [his] personal sensations with the views of the original author."[139] On the basis of such evidence, several physicians have declared Baudelaire to have been an opium addict. One of them, fully aware that Baudelaire sought neither to glorify the use of drugs nor to recruit disciples for the drug cult, attributed Baudelaire's personal inability to abstain from opium to his instability and low morale. Yet, he retained sufficient integrity not to try to convince others of the possibility of an artificial paradise.[140]

A second physician, agreeing with the diagnosis of drug addiction, emphasized that Baudelaire had been a depressed personality. Unlike De Quincey, whose habit was rooted in his need to quiet physical pain, Baudelaire used opium to cope with emotional disorders—that is, periods of anxiety and a profound sense of emptiness. As Baudelaire suspected, the use of opium may indeed have been responsible for the gastric pain, the vomiting, the feeling of heaviness or dullness in his head, the lethargy. But use of the drug had been a response to, rather than a cause of, mental depression.[141] And he knew that the artificial paradise he was creating had been bought at the price of eternal salvation.[142]

As for actual addiction, however, let us return to Baudelaire's words, written from Honfleur, to Poulet-Malassis: "I am quite low, my friend, and I did not bring any opium. I had no money to pay my pharmacist in Paris." This reminds us of Baudelaire's poverty; and one physician, familiar with the price of the drug in France and abroad, declared that true opium addiction would have been a very costly habit in Paris. Financial reasons alone would have prevented him from being a regular user.[143] Moreover, Baudelaire had been in Honfleur approximately three weeks when he complained about the lack of opium. No true addict, in our sense of that word, could have tolerated such a separation from his crutch.

Thus Baudelaire's use and abuse of opium, for body and for mind, was actually hypochondriacal—or splenetic—behavior. And because it has become common to interpret the use of drugs as the perversion of the instinct for survival, some have argued that Baudelaire's abuse of opium was suicidal behavior, and that his periodic talk of suicide was sincere.[144] Surely that is why he understood that the user of drugs had become Satan's ally and denied himself salvation. He knew that to have a horror of life was blasphemous. He also feared the unpleasant bodily effects he associated with opium (the colic, the vomiting, the lethargy). Given his ultimate paralysis, it must be suspected that his abuse of drugs, when combined with his abuse of alcohol during those final months, contributed to arterial damage.[145]

Mother and Son

After Baudelaire's flight from the Aupick residence at the end of 1845, mother and son were virtually estranged. She could not approve his manner of living, and he bristled at her disapproval. His infrequent letters were dedicated to abusing her for his financial distress; and though meaning to be firm, she occasionally fed him small sums.[146] However embittered, he missed his mother and endeavored to arrange meetings with her, in public gardens in good weather, in museums in winter. She concealed such meetings from General Aupick.[147] His appointment as ambassador to Turkey in 1848, where the Aupicks remained until 1851, enhanced the estrangement. Through Ancelle, Baudelaire learned of their return from Constantinople and of his mother's wish to see him. Refusing to enter Aupick's house,

Baudelaire met her elsewhere. She failed to appear for a second rendezvous and was shortly off to Madrid to join her husband at his new post.[148]

As we know, he informed her in detail of his separation from Jeanne Duval in 1852, and he reminded her now and then of her part in the horror of his life. Had she thought of him on 9 April (his birthday), "that fatal day" that so cruelly reminded him of the event thirty-three years before?[149] And, of course, he complained of the establishment of the *conseil judiciaire*, which he wanted to challenge and destroy. He knew he would have no chance of success, however, since "I believe that my life has been damned from the beginning, and that it will remain so forever."[150] His wretched existence, he wrote his mother, had affected his stomach for months; "and moreover I have insupportable nervous troubles, exactly like women."[151] In fact, his letters to her would increasingly convey alarming medical details as an accompaniment to reports of his deplorable financial condition.

Toward the end of 1855, a year in which she had refused to see him, Baudelaire made a strong bid for reconciliation. He called their estrangement totally abnormal and absolutely humiliating. He knew that she viewed him as an eccentric, but she must not think that he took an unhealthy pleasure from his solitude, from their estrangement. "I am not old at the moment," he warned, "but I can soon become so." Not only that, but "one of us could die," and how intolerable to think of such a fate without having seen each other. For a long time, he told her, he had been fairly sick in mind and body; and as he watched the years pass, without any improvement in either, he was driven to seek an instant renewal of youth. He was sick to death of cheap restaurants and furnished rooms; weary of colds, fevers, and migraines; fearful above all else that such a life would cause him to go to seed, would cost him his admirable poetic faculty, his clarity of vision, even the power to hope. He must have the means for a regularized existence—a life without petty cares—if he is to create the art that is within him. Yet he lacks everything that might make that life possible in his own home.

His drive toward reconciliation with his mother was aimed quite frankly at reestablishing himself in an attractive and tranquil residence. With her aid, he could lead the secluded, chaste, and sober life of "un honnête homme." It could be done for 1,500 francs.[152] Mme Aupick was sufficiently touched to authorize Ancelle to make such a payment to Baudelaire, but she had been too offended in the past to desire reconciliation, and she had no faith that her financial sacrifices would essentially alter his horrible life.[153]

Though perhaps General Aupick's death on 28 April 1857 removed an obstacle to the reconciliation of mother and son, the widow was reduced to the limitations of a general's pension, a gloomy prospect for both of them. To provide some additional capital, she soon sold her Parisian possessions and prepared to make her vacation cottage in Honfleur a permanent home. Baudelaire promised to do everything possible to make her happy. Since she attached so much importance to the *success* of his literary projects, he said that he would be working for her in working for himself. "Remember," he concluded, "that I belong totally to you, and that I belong to you alone."[154] Aupick's death spared him the scandal of *Les Fleurs du mal*, published several months later; but the devout Mme Aupick felt dishonored by what she heard of the poems, telling Baudelaire to abandon any hope of returning to live with her.[155]

Rebuked by both the court and his mother, Baudelaire felt his solitude all the more and protested that he was unable to work. He found himself in such a pitiful state of mind and body that he pleaded for his mother's indulgence. "If ever a man was sick, without it concerning medicine, it is indeed I."[156] He spelled out his symptoms: "an immense discouragement, a sense of insupportable isolation, a perpetual fear of a vague misfortune, a total distrust of [his] powers, a complete lack of desire, an impossibility to find any sort of amusement"—in short, a serious state of mind for someone whose business it was to invent and flesh out fictions: "The true *esprit de spleen*." Add his perpetual poverty, his worries about money, and we are not surprised when he reports of a month of stomach disorder with colic.[157] Two weeks later he notes that his stomach is somewhat better, thanks to the use of ether; but though he has brought the colic under control by taking opium, he fears the side effects.[158]

Meanwhile, Mme Aupick, having been for some months influenced by friends not to risk contamination from *Les Fleurs du Mal*, had at last opened the book. If she was still offended by some of its words and images, she recognized the admirable literary qualities in her son's poetry. "He possesses the art of writing to an eminent degree," she wrote her stepson, indicating that she had also been struck by the excellence of his Poe translations.[159] She sent her compliments to Baudelaire in late January 1858, delighting him with her apparent change of heart in which he perceived her desire to have him near her. In reply, he told her that he had been preoccupied with the notion that "my mother does not know me, she has hardly ever known me; we have not had the time to live together. We must, however, find some years of happiness in common."[160]

After receiving his mother's compliments, Baudelaire called on the attorney Bernard Jaquotot, who had participated in the *conseil de famille* in 1844 when the *conseil judiciaire* had been established. Baudelaire sought his assistance in obtaining Mme Aupick's consent to their living together. Five or six meetings with Baudelaire convinced Jaquotot of his sincerity; and it was agreed that Baudelaire should put his proposals in a letter to Jaquotot which the attorney could show to Mme Aupick. Baudelaire noted, correctly, that he had not asked his mother for any money since her husband's death. His motive in seeking reconciliation, therefore, was not money but a desire to take responsibility for her. But since she had earlier said that she would not live with him, he must wait until she changed her mind. She had, on the other hand, recently expressed a desire to see him, and only pressing commitments in Paris had prevented him from going to Honfleur. The possibility of reconciliation had inspired him to make money quickly in order to clear up his debts in Paris.

If, however, his mother could be persuaded to authorize Ancelle to advance one year of income, 2,400 francs, to be repaid in one year, he could then pay off his debts immediately and be free to spend some time in Honfleur. He pledged to repay by not taking anything more from Ancelle for a year, meanwhile cutting down on his expenses in order to live on his literary income. In his desire to live with her, he was emulating another writer (obviously Flaubert), who had lived in a retreat with his mother, where he had found the peace of mind to produce a fine book "and become celebrated." Though he had formerly made fun of his mother's passion for order, he had come to understand that "liberty is created by the spirit of order," and he hoped that the spirit might be contagious.[161]

After waiting a few days for these proposals to bear fruit, he wrote to his mother in anticipation of their reconciliation and the beginning of a new life: "For I believe I am sick, and a sick man, even if the sickness is imagined, is a sick man. What else could be these perpetual fears, these palpitations, and this breathlessness, especially during sleep?"[162]

His mother, in the meantime, had been sufficiently impressed by his message through Jaquotot that she consulted Ancelle about the advance payment. Evidently wanting assurance that the money would not fall into the hands of either Jeanne Duval or Marie Daubrun, she asked Ancelle to visit Baudelaire at his residence, then the Hôtel Voltaire. Ancelle arrived unannounced. Baudelaire was out, but a few indiscreet questions to the hotel staff satisfied him that Baudelaire was living alone. Upon his return, Baudelaire was informed of Ancelle's call and construed it as an attempt to spy out of mean curiosity. Ancelle was wrong, of course, not to have waited to discuss the proposed advance with Baudelaire, at which time he could have satisfied himself that Baudelaire was living alone. As it was, Baudelaire felt bitterly humiliated; and he fired a series of five letters at his bewildered mother, all written on 27 February 1858. They were utterly and ridiculously furious, threatening all manner of violence to Ancelle. But none of the threats was carried out.[163] His anger brought on neuralgia and fever that lasted all night, but in the morning some violent vomiting somewhat relieved him.[164] Jaquotot was enlisted to mediate the quarrel, and Baudelaire sought to save face by refusing further negotiation about the money.

Thus his plans to go to Honfleur were shelved, though he repeatedly wrote to his mother to anticipate his arrival and sent some packages of books and belongings as evidence of his intentions. Only eleven months after his fracas with Ancelle, in January 1859, did he manage to go to Honfleur. He had obtained a loan of 3,000 francs from Poulet-Malassis as a substitute for the advance from Ancelle.[165] With the understanding that he would not ask his mother for money if they were to resume life together, he remained with her until June. Consequently, he borrowed also from Nadar.[166]

It has been said that these six months amounted to the last happy and peaceful period in Baudelaire's life.[167] Mme Aupick did exert herself to please him and to provide an atmosphere favorable for his work, and he did respond by composing a number of poems. Yet, his increased indebtedness was a cloud; and, in any case, Baudelaire was not constituted for happiness. Can we ignore those lines from "Le Voyage," written in Honfleur: O Mort, vieux capitaine, il est temps! levons l'ancre!

Gustave Courbet and Alexandre Schanne tell a curious story about meeting Baudelaire by chance in Honfleur. He insisted that they come to dinner to meet his mother, after which he not only escorted them to the boat for Le Havre, but boarded their train to accompany them to Paris before returning home. It may be that the story was not true in every detail, but its critical point was that the occasion gave Baudelaire opportunity to escape from his mother. He told his guests that he was on a forced vacation with her and that he hated the countryside, especially in good weather. He longed to be back in Paris and away from the stupid realm of cereals. "I tell you that I find unconfined water [the sea] insupportable." To please him, water had to be imprisoned within the geometrical confines of a *quai*. When he bathed, he wanted to be in a bathtub. A music box, he insisted, was preferable to a nightingale, and the fruit from the garden could only reach perfection in a fruit dish. To submit oneself to nature, he concluded, was to take a step backward toward our original savagery.[168]

When Baudelaire went to Paris in late June of 1859 to attend to publishing matters, Mme Aupick expected him to return. In the autumn, she began pressing him to come home, finally offering him money if that would make his return possible. "I must take into account," he replied, "that over a period of seventeen years you have given or lent me several thousands of francs; and it is high time, not only that I not borrow more from you, but that I pay it back."[169] He paid her a brief visit in mid-December, but the truth is that they were never again to live together, though their rapprochement would endure.

On 13 January 1860, Baudelaire—then thirty-eight—suffered a strange seizure somewhere on the streets of Paris. He had had little to eat, so he ruled out indigestion and described the attack as being similar to a cerebral congestion. An elderly woman had come to his aid; but after apparently recovering, he had experienced a second attack. His weakness, nausea, and giddiness made the stairs to his room an agony, and though he did not faint again, he feared that someone might think him drunk.[170]

These seizures were probably indication that the tension of Baudelaire's existence was becoming more than he could tolerate. In particular, his financial situation, though never sound, was far from improving; and we become aware that in 1860 it was threatening to engulf him for the first time. His mother had belatedly discovered that he had acquired debts while in Honfleur, and now they were being brought to her door for payment. She wrote: "Charles, despite the fact that you are good and that you can earn money, I am afraid that you are ruining me." Whereupon he had to confess that two more bills were about to fall due, which she would be obliged to cover, though they would be the last. Then followed his customary avowal that she must not be bled for him, that he must not become her financial burden. She must, however, recognize his great suffering; that he feared he would die before accomplishing his work and she might die before he could make her happy, "you, the only human being with whom I can live quietly, without tricks, without lies." Saddest of all, he feared never to be able to cure his vices.[171]

By mid-summer, he seems to have lost all hope of coping with his debts by himself; though he had found life with mother less than ideal, he knows he cannot survive without her. He will have to return to Honfleur, he tells Poulet-Malassis, assuring him that *Mme Aupick and he* will be able to settle his debts before winter's end.[172] He prepares the ground with letters about his increasing indebtedness and his deteriorating health, certain that such news is bound to make her ill. He includes word of his usual bad stomach, his inability to sleep, a body that might be sound if his soul were well—though he knows that his soul will never be well, that he is incurable. Frequent vomiting even when he has not eaten, when he has not been angry, fearful, or anxious. Yet, he often *was* angry, fearful, and anxious.[173] In October he listed an absolute flood of troubles, including the accusation that the establishment of the *conseil judiciaire* had ruined his life. Suicide, he concluded, would be the most rational act of his life. "I can die before you do, despite this diabolical courage that has so often sustained me. What has restrained me for the past eighteen months is Jeanne. (How would she live after my death, since you would have to pay out all that I would leave to meet my debts?) Other reasons, too: To leave you alone! and to leave you this awful jam and to embroil you in a chaos that I alone can understand."[174]

Four days later, October 15, he arrived in Honfleur, discovering that landslides from the cliffs adjoining his mother's garden had also been eroding her purse as she struggled to have her property protected. She could spare him only 400 francs, not the 3,000 he needed to repay Poulet-Malassis. He was by then indebted to her alone for 23,000 francs—a sum, given his income, far beyond any reasonable expectation of repayment.[175] Sending her a New Year's greeting several months later, he revealed his despair and perversity: "For the first time in my life I am nearly happy. [The second edition of *Les Fleurs du mal*] is *almost good,* and this book will remain as witness to my disgust and hatred of everything."[176]

He continued to mention the possibility of suicide to those from whom he wished to borrow money; to Poulet-Malassis, for instance, who had been generous in the past, but whose publishing reverses threatened bankruptcy and left him powerless to respond to Baudelaire's financial appeals. Suspecting that both Mme Aupick and Poulet-Malassis believed him guilty of exaggerating his woes, Baudelaire underscored them by speculating that suicide was his only remaining resource. Pride alone had prevented him from leaving his affairs in such a tangle.[177] With his fortieth birthday hard upon him, he summed things up: "If ever a man knew, while still young, both spleen and hypochondria, it was I. Yet, I desired to live,

I wanted to have a bit of security, fame, and self-contentment. Something terrible tells me *never,* but something else tells me *try.*" But as he had fallen into persistent nervous terror, marked by frightful sleep and frightful awakening, all action was impossible and suicide tempting.

Before killing himself, however, he had the duty to provide the detailed information necessary to pay off his debts, a task he could not accomplish immediately, as he had left the necessary documents behind in Honfleur. Moreover, he was reluctant to be finished with life before completing publication of at least his works of criticism, especially of a great book he had been planning for two years, *Mon coeur mis à nu,* which would be a compilation of his angers, a book that would make Rousseau's *Confessions* pale stuff. All this prefaced a request for 200 francs. She sent him 300 francs.[178]

A month later, he returned to that theme, but with variations. Would they ever see each other again? He has told her of his woes, of his health, of his horror of life, yet has been invariably fearful that such news might destroy her feeble body. He believed that she loved him.

> *I* loved you passionately in my childhood; later, under the influence of your injustices, I lacked respect for you, as if a maternal injustice could justify a lack of filial respect. I have since often repented that, although, as is my habit, I said nothing about it. I am no longer the ungrateful, furious child. . . . We are obviously destined to love each other, to live for each other, to finish up life properly and calmly as possible. On the other hand, in my dreadful circumstances, I am convinced that one of us will kill the other, and that finally we shall be the death of each other. After my death, it is clear that you will no longer live. I am the sole object that keeps you alive. After your death, especially if you should die of a shock caused by me, it is beyond doubt that I should kill myself.

He recalled the time of her first widowhood, no doubt a bad time for her, but a period of maternal tenderness and attention for him: "You were mine alone. You were simultaneously an idol and a comrade." He needed her loving care in order to be saved and appended a grandiose plan to obtain money that would solve all problems for them both.[179] She immediately sent him 500 francs. His first impulse was to return the money because of his shame, but he quickly overcame the impulse on recalling that another note was coming due in a week.[180]

In retrospect, it seems evident that Baudelaire, however anxious for home and money, however sincere may have been his desire for reconciliation with his mother, did not seriously expect to return to Honfleur for that "proper and calm" existence he had experienced for six months. His perplexed mother invited his return and complained of his neglect, but he pleaded the press of work, again raising the option of suicide as the easiest solution to the horror of his life.[181] When she relayed to him a report that he seemed to be very well, he assured her that none of his ailments had vanished: his rheumatism, his nightmares, his anxieties, his terrible sensitivity to noise which upset his stomach, and especially his fears: the fear of dying suddenly, the fear of living too long, the fear of seeing her die, the fear of going to sleep, the horror of waking up.[182] By 1863 he was considering leaving France, further indication that Honfleur did not attract him as a refuge. To his list of ailments he added his suffering from solitude and from the want of comfort; and he was feeling guilty for having abused his life, health, and talent. He expressed disgust for his gift for procrastination, a tendency to postpone even the most agreeable duties, a dreadful vice.[183]

Since Baudelaire's blasphemous poems had deeply offended Mme Aupick's devout Catholicism, and because he did not become a practicing Catholic despite the spiritual concerns of his later years, religion remained a barrier to Mme Aupick's understanding of her son. The question of Baudelaire's religiosity was first raised at the time of the trial by the aristocratic Catholic dandy Barbey d'Aurevilly, who saw Baudelaire as the potential Catholic, grasping in *Les Fleurs du mal* for religious values. T. S. Eliot, decades later, would give a similar interpretation, seeing Baudelaire's religious values as contrary to the bourgeois ethic and to political liberalism and its philosophical underpinning.[184] Recently, Marcel Ruff has portrayed the youthful Baudelaire as humane and democratic. His sympathy for the poor and suffering, in Ruff's view, was expressed by his approval of the February Revolution, yet he became disillusioned with politics after the events of 1848 and 1851 and became increasingly Catholic.[185] One might better say that Baudelaire, early in life, became a seeker, and that the salvation he sought eluded him to the bitter end.

In his quest he did, indeed, adopt the language of Christianity; and in his frequent rejection of this world, which went considerably beyond hostility to the bourgeois ethic, one might see the mystic or the ascetic. Yet, the Brie and the Bordeaux, the passion for elegance, the pursuit of the varicolored Venuses, his thirst for celebrity, his distaste for poverty, did not reveal an implacable hatred for the things of this world. Instead, he despised nature, including human nature, an attitude which, we must suppose, derived from insight into himself. In 1856, when much of *Les Fleurs du mal* had been completed, he read Alphonse Toussenel's *Les Monde des oiseaux, ornithologie passionnelle*. It stirred in him dormant ideas about original sin. *The* great modern heresy, he remarked, the foundation of all other modern heresies, was the substitution of the doctrine of the natural goodness of man for the idea of original sin. Nature was not a state of goodness, for, as Baudelaire put it, nature had *participated* in original sin. "The *naturally* good man would be a *monster*, I mean a *God*."[186]

In denying the goodness of nature, he was not asserting that nature is a nonmoral state or realm, but rather associating nature with *le mal*. That view permeated his life and was central to his work. Most errors about the nature of beauty, he wrote in 1863, derive from a moral fallacy of the eighteenth century: that nature is the foundation of the good or the beautiful. "The denial of original sin had not a little to do with the general blindness of that period." Since nature compels us to work for our survival, for our self-interest, he felt, that which is instinctive should be condemned. What is natural is abominable—woman, for example; whereas everything beautiful and good is the result of reason and thought and is thus artificial. "Evil arises, of itself, *naturally* and by predestination. Good is always the product of a creative skill."[187]

In defining Baudelaire's religiosity, one must begin with the generally accepted view that he became a profoundly religious man, an understandable evolution in a man who came to believe he had been damned from birth, who regarded atheism as scandalous. He wrote of "My tendency to mysticism, since my childhood. My conversations with God."[188] On the other hand, when it comes to Christianity or, more specifically, orthodox Catholicism, theological tests must be applied before determining an individual's membership in the community. One critic has properly noted that, aside from "Châtiment de l'Orgueil" [The Punishment for Pride] and "La Reniement de Saint Pierre" [Saint Peter's Denial], Baudelaire's entire work contains about twenty allusions to Jesus; and none of them focuses on His redemptive role.[189] Baudelaire's hatred for his mother's curé in Honfleur symbolized his hatred for the Church as an institution; and as for prayer, the very idea that she was offering prayers for the success of his literary affairs struck him as "very comical."[190] A year later, it is true, in a moment of woeful unhappiness, he did ask her to pray for him vigorously if she believed prayer could have any efficacy; but even though he was not twitting her, his very request revealed his own lack of faith and a dependence on hers.[191]

The truth is that for all Baudelaire's belief in original sin and his apparent acceptance of some of the beliefs of orthodox Christians, his view of nature itself and his belief that evil is incurable, with Eden lost forever, make it impossible to regard him as a true Christian. No saints appear in his work; and in the competition between the Bad Angel and the Good Angel, the latter remains passive or impotent.[192] Finally, the true Christian does not merely believe in the possibility of salvation and work toward that end, but he believes that he must also work for the salvation of his community. No doubt Baudelaire was touched by human suffering and outraged by injustice. Yet, he was incapable of envisioning any improvement, nor could he have worked for the general salvation. For he was a man locked within himself, incapable of the slightest exit; his religious life, if sometimes intense, was always strangled.[193] It could not have been otherwise in a man who had, as Baudelaire often claimed, a horror of life.

That pathetic vision of reality—his sense of alienation and damnation—came very early to Baudelaire. As Pierre Emmanuel has put it, Baudelaire wanted himself damned after being deprived of his mother; and his debate with God began in childhood. He became instinctively susceptible to the myth of Paradise lost, of original sin, of man driven out by God. Such a God he could not love; such a mother he could no longer really love; and he was doomed, in his relations with other women, to the absence of a sense of love, to the life of the exile.[194] During those final dreadful years of his self-exile in Belgium, when he was sinking into utter impotence and indignity, he would not go home again. He had long since insisted on limbo.

His Perversity

At a moment of exceptional despair about money and his unfulfilled career, Baudelaire cried out, "Why is it that, having so upright, so spotless, an idea of duty and of the useful, that I always manage to do the contrary?"[195] Eight years later, that theme reappeared: "I spend my life giving myself sublime, irrefutable sermons that have never healed me. I am, and I have always been, at once reasonable and vicious."[196] He also put that observation into verse in the last two stanzas of "L'Héautontimorouménos":

37

Je suis la plaie et le couteau!
Je suis le soufflet et la joue!
Je suis les membres et la roue,
Et la victime et le bourreau!

Je suis de mon coeur le vampire,
—Un de ces grands abandonnés
Au rire éternel condamnés,
Et qui ne peuvent plus sourire![197]

[I am the wound and the knife!
I am the slap and the cheek!
I am the limbs and the rack,
Both the victim and the headsman!

I am the vampire of my heart,
—One of those forsaken and
Condemned to eternal laughter,
And who can smile no more!]

Because Enid Starkie knew that a French psychoanalyst, Dr. René Laforgue, had typed Baudelaire as a masochist, she specifically denied that those lines from "L'Héautontimorouménos" illustrated masochism: "From contemplation of the human heart, he grew to hate himself as well as others, and became his own tormentor."[198] In other words, having found the world perverse, he saw his own perversity. Unfortunately for that position, there remains too much evidence to the contrary: Baudelaire knew early of *le mal* within himself, and he saw the world as himself written large.

Baudelaire believed that his dreams were a hieroglyphic language to which he did not have the key, but he was struck by the fact that the material of his dreams was quite foreign to his actual experience, especially his amorous life. He evidently recorded the material of only one dream, in a letter to Charles Asselineau, but it powerfully suggests the symbolic richness of his dream life. In this dream, he was walking the streets of Paris alone at two or three o'clock in the morning when he met Hippolyte Castille, the historian and Republican of 1848. Baudelaire wanted to take advantage of Castille's carriage to accomplish an errand. He had just published a book and felt obliged to offer a copy to the madam in charge of a large house of prostitution. The book was obscene, which explained the reason for offering it to such a woman; but he was also aware in the dream that this gift really served as a pretext for entering the house for sexual purposes, since otherwise he would not have dared enter such a place.

Immediately upon entering the house, he realized that his penis was exposed through his unbuttoned trousers, and he felt that it was indecent to present himself in such a manner even in a house of prostitution. Moreover, he sensed that his feet were wet and noticed that they were bare. He had evidently waded through a puddle at the bottom of the stairs and knew he would have to wash his feet before sexual intercourse and again before leaving the house. He went up the stairs, and from that moment on, his book was absent from the dream.

He perceived a series of large galleries, badly lighted like old cafés, old reading rooms, or gambling dens. The prostitutes were scattered about talking to men, among whom he saw some schoolboys (*collégiens*); and he felt very sad and intimidated. He feared that someone would see his feet. Looking down, he saw that one of his feet wore a shoe. A bit later, he noticed that both were shod. The walls of the large galleries were covered with sketches of all sorts, all of them framed. Not all were obscene. He saw some architectural drawings and remembered some Egyptian figures. As his discomfort was increasing and he dared not approach one of the prostitutes, he gave himself to the sketches on the walls. In particular, he noted a strange group of pictures in one of the more obscure parts of a gallery—small pictures of highly colored birds, whose eyes were alive. Some of the birds were only partially formed; grotesque, monstrous, nearly amorphous images. Down in the corner of each picture was a note: "Such and such a prostitute, aged——, gave birth to this fetus, on such and such a date." In the dream, it occurred to him that an art of that genre was little conducive to thoughts of love.

At that point in his dream, he became aware that the funds to establish the bordello, with its medical museum, had been put up by the publishers of *Le Siècle*, the only newspaper in the world stupid enough to forge such a combination. He could account for it by remembering that *Le Siècle* had a mania for science, for the spread of knowledge, and for progress. This caused him to recognize that stupidity and modern foolishness do have their utility, that what is often done for evil reasons turns out for the good, thanks to some spiritual mechanism.

He next approached an object that was alive, a monster, born in the bordello, perched on a pedestal as part of the collection in the museum. Even though the beast was obliged to squat in a strange and contorted position, it was not entirely ugly. The face was almost pretty, of a tanned or Oriental hue, with some pink and green in it. But a large black object, rather like a snake, was wound around its body and limbs. The monster explained to Baudelaire that this object was an enormous appendage that emerged from its head, rather elastic in character, but so dreadfully long and heavy that the head alone could not support it. Hence, it had to be coiled around the body. Baudelaire chatted at length with the monster about its annoyances and grievances, discovering that its principal problem involved having to sup with the girls of the establishment. Getting the burdensome appendage to the supper room and arranging it so that eating was possible necessitated quite a struggle. Baudelaire dared not touch the monster, but he was fascinated.

At that moment, he was awakened from his dream by the sound of "his woman" moving a piece of furniture. He found that he had been sleeping in the contorted position of the monster on its perch, and he felt weary and exhausted.[199] He transcribed the dream immediately upon awakening, which would have been the morning of 13 March 1856. It has been variously interpreted by some Baudelaireans, and ignored by others; Michel Butor devoted a book to it. In the dream, Baudelaire considered it a duty to offer the madam a copy of his new book. In fact, on the preceding day, 12 March 1856, he had published his first book, *Les Histoires extraordinaires* of Edgar Allan Poe, translated and prefaced by Baudelaire. At the moment of the dream, he had not yet received his author's copies; but by the fifteenth he had three. Two of them were sent to Ancelle, one of which was for Mme Aupick.[200] We may deduce, therefore, that the true identity of the madam was Baudelaire's mother, and that her role in the dream revealed Baudelaire's opinion of her remarriage to General Aupick.

As for the duty to present the book, we already know that Baudelaire had been borrowing money from his mother in the expectation that literary success would enable him to repay her. Since an author may be pardoned for supposing that publication is merely the prelude to financial success, the presentation of the book not only symbolized the obligation to repay, but the rather pathetic assertion of his manhood and his anticipated independence from her. We notice, too, that Baudelaire entered the bordello anticipating sexual intercourse, not with the madam, but with one of the girls. Yet, the dream informs us that his virility, supposedly reconquered through publication, proved inadequate to the occasion.[201]

This verifies what Baudelaire's friends said of his private life. He often went with Nadar and others to the Folies Bergères or the Casino Cadet, but he was never known to choose a girl and disappear with her. They knew that he haunted bars and cafés frequented by prostitutes, watching others who were happy in their love, but rarely speaking to anyone. The girls simply knew him as the sinister man who prowled about at late hours—and in no other way.[202]

The bordello as picture gallery is another striking feature of the dream, as the dreamer was an art critic; but the equation may have meant nothing more than the gallery or museum as the secret meeting place of mother and son while General Aupick was still alive, as he was in 1856. On the other hand, Baudelaire left an account of a visit to the Louvre with Louise Villedieu, "a five-franc whore. She had never been there before, and began to blush and cover her face with her hands, repeatedly pulling at my sleeve and asking me, as we stood before deathless statues and pictures, how such indecencies could be flaunted in public."[203] *Louise's* reaction, presumably, not Baudelaire's; yet, it may be that the nudity offered by the Louvre was, in its artificiality, the only nudity with which Baudelaire felt comfortable; the Louvre was converted into the bordello he could visit in safety. Sartre has noticed that women evidently excited Baudelaire only when they were clothed. He hated their nakedness.[204]

No matter that Baudelaire claimed ignorance of the hieroglyphic language of his dreams; he subtly indicated otherwise by identifying his posture upon awakening with the contorted position of the monster on its perch. *He* was the monster born in his mother's house; alive, he was condemned to the sterile existence of the museum— thus to neither life nor death, but to limbo. As if that were not bad enough, he had as an appendage, Jeanne Duval (the black, snakelike bonds in the dream) to make a torment of daily existence.[205] The dream had occurred midway through their brief cohabitation in 1856.

The case for sexual abnormality does not rest, of course, entirely upon evidence dredged from a dream. Baudelaire did not believe, on the basis of his experience, that there could be any genuine mutuality in love. He likened love to torture or a surgical operation. One of the partners must be either torturer or surgeon, the other either victim or patient. "Do you hear those sighs, preludes to a tragedy of shame, those moans, those screams, those rattles in the throat? Who has not uttered them, who has not irresistibly extorted them? . . . I should for certain think it blasphemous to apply the word *ecstasy* to this kind of collapse into rottenness. A dreadful game, in which one of the players must lose self-government! . . . *I* say that the unique and supreme pleasure in love-making lies in the certain knowledge that one is doing *evil*."[206] He represented copulation as ersatz, as inferior to the poetic act:[207] "The more a man cultivates the arts, the less randy he gets. . . . Only the brute is good at coupling, and copulation is the lyricism of the masses. To copulate is to aspire to enter into another—and the artist never emerges from himself."[208]

Indeed, a number of Baudelaire's acquaintances, including Nadar, Félicien Rops, Théodore de Banville, Emile Deschamps, and Louis Ménard, believed that he died a virgin despite the evidence of his liaisons, despite his statements about bizarre sexual fantasies and desires. In the presence of friends at a bar, for instance, Baudelaire told a blond woman how he would like to make love to her: that he wanted to bite her, to tie her hands and suspend her by the wrists from the ceiling, which would enable him—on bended knee—to kiss her bare feet. The dismayed woman fled. Though some have seen such incidents as proof of Baudelaire's sadism, there remains no evidence that he put such desires into practice; and their expression was further example of his exhibitionism and his wish to astonish conventional society.[209] On the other hand, the fact that the threat to the blond woman was idle is hardly proof of sexual normality. At the time of Baudelaire's trial for obscenity, Prosper Mérimée's appraisal of the poet was considerably more perceptive than his appraisal of the poems. He found them to be mediocre, not at all dangerous, works in which a few sparks of poetic talent could be seen, but little more than might be found in the poems of any poor lad who knows nothing of life and is weary of it because some flirt has deceived him. "I do not know the author, but I would bet that he is a virgin and quite decent; and that is why I should prefer that they not burn him."[210]

The truth about Baudelaire's sexuality lies somewhere between the extremes of the interpretations that have been put forth. He was no more the saintly virgin than he was the voluptuary given to all manner of sexual depravities, and the wonder is that the legends of his venereal infection and his virginity could have coexisted so long. But this is not to deny that his sexual life must have been "poor," as one physician blandly put it, and poor from an early age.[211] Sartre has asserted that physical possession was too natural to have attracted Baudelaire, though one might better argue that his repugnance for physical possession was the key to his aversion for everything natural. Sartre was on firmer ground in noting that sexual intercourse, being a form of intimate communication, was antipathetic to the artist who never goes out of himself. Consequently, if Baudelaire had ever had coitus, it would have been as a solitary, as an onanist. "The woman one loves," Baudelaire wrote, "is the one who does not get any fun out of it." She must, in other words, be frigid; and he cannot, must not, give her any pleasure. He can only have sexual relations with himself—which is masochism in association with sadism.[212]

Some Baudelaireans, shrinking from the stark language of medicine, have found the phrase "sexual timidity" adequate to describe Baudelaire's dilemma. The necessary word is *impotent*, though the word merely describes the manifestation of the dilemma rather than its cause. Everything suggests his total impotence with women of respectable station; and even as a late adolescent, he sought out the lowest, ugliest, dirtiest prostitutes, the most likely to cooperate in those acts of perversion that he could tolerate, and with whom at the same time he could be reasonably sure of concealment. For the perversions were the shame of his life, and he did not dwell upon them for the edification of his contemporaries or posterity. The venereal infection came as a blessing, because it facilitated the sham. His eroticism was strictly in his head, and he might well have lived in near chastity had he not been driven to feel that which passed through his head, to bridge the awful gap between dream and reality.[213]

This interpretation goes far to account for Baudelaire's long toleration of Jeanne Duval. It is well not to be misled by Théodore de Banville's favorable description of her, for one of his most attractive qualities was his inability to see anything or anyone in true light. But the picture of Jeanne given us by others, not to speak of some drawings of her by Baudelaire himself, is that of a vicious and insatiable prostitute, a lecherous animal, experienced in all manner of sexual indulgence. She had neither mind nor heart, and if not a prostitute in title, she had the appropriate professional skills and instincts. She easily would have recognized his perversions and known how to cope with them, and she would thereby have assured herself the money that was her only concern. She did not, and could not, love him, much less understand him; and his letters in reference to her never made any claims to the contrary. Always calling him Monsieur rather than Charles, referring to him as "strange," she held him in the trap of his sensual needs, his anger no match for his shame, just as she also served as his cover. Far from being the cynical debauchee of legend, he was a tormented and frustrated soul, experiencing a martyrdom and believing himself damned. One must not say, of course, that his condition was her fault. She merely knew how to exploit his condition, and he knew no other solution for the satisfaction of his base appetites. Thus it fell to that "stupid, obscene, alcoholic guttersnipe," one uncharitable characterization of Jeanne Duval,[214] to inspire literary masterpieces for which she had no understanding or respect. As Baudelaire put it, she had given him mud, and he had fashioned gold of it.[215] In the end, it was she who left him—to his enormous distress, since he needed her for protection.

In diagnosing Baudelaire as a masochist, Dr. Laforgue had not relied solely on the evidence of Baudelaire's sexual abnormality, but took note of the many actions of his life which amounted to an unconscious aim to provoke blows or counterstrokes: the disordered mode of his daily life, his tendency to lie, his use of language to give hurt, and even his candidacy for l'Académie française.[216] When he gave notice of his intention to present himself for election to the Académie, his letter was couched in the most modest terms, perhaps appropriately for the circumstances; but as the letter contrasted so sharply with Baudelaire's usual tone and assurance about his literary merit,[217] any reader would conclude that this wordly success meant much to him and would agree with Starkie that Baudelaire's candidacy was a serious attempt to secure recognition, which could bring financial benefits and please his mother. Consequently, Starkie ridiculed Laforgue's assertion that Baudelaire had been indulging his masochistic tendencies in finding a new occasion to suffer failure. He received ample friendly advice about the hopelessness of his application, but argued that acceptance was merely uncertain.[218] The hub of the disagreament would seem to have been Starkie's ignorance of the fact that masochistic actions are neither deliberate nor conscious.

The necessary campaign to win election contributed to his nervous fatigue, and he was morally offended to have to seek the support of all the "old goats" already selected for immortality. He knew, moreover, that his fellow poet, Théophile Gautier, would not sully *his* reputation by seeking a chair in the Académie. Yet, Baudelaire persisted.[219] After two months, he abandoned the humiliating campaign and asked that his name be withdrawn. His polite withdrawal made a favorable impression, about which he was informed; but he never again stood for election.[220]

His life, therefore, was a punishment, because he was driven to actions where he would meet rebuff, because he had a genius for making himself odious and repelling others. He even had a penchant for circulating rumors about himself, such as the rumor that he was a pederast, which he hatched in Belgium, where he had gone in desperate search of literary and financial success.[221] His second public lecture in Brussels, in 1864, on the subject of Gautier, was largely attended by women and girls. He began by thanking his audience for his kind reception at the first lecture, adding that "it was with you that I lost my virginity as a speaker, a virginity no more to be regretted than the other kind." The schoolgirls were promptly ushered out, leaving him with a nearly empty hall. This performance cost him his nerve; he could only stammer during the third lecture, and the series from which he had expected so much ended in fiasco. "All through his life," wrote Starkie, "some demon prompted him to strange actions which he always afterwards bitterly regretted when he found himself ostracized."[222] That demon was masochism, which Starkie could recognize, if not define.[223]

Immediately before the trial for obscenity in 1857, Champfleury told Baudelaire that he would surely be accused of *realism*. The idea horrified Baudelaire, not because he feared the hostility of those who hated or feared the realist movement (he wanted that!); but because he insisted on receiving the court's brickbats *all alone*. Champfleury, who could not have known the term *masochism*, called Baudelaire's peculiarity "monomania."[224] In fact, the well-known anecdote of Baudelaire and the dog bears repeating as symbolic of his life. Baudelaire, who did not like dogs, once persisted in stepping on a dog's tail, until the animal finally turned on him and knocked him down into the mud. He went to a friend's house nearby to clean up. Asked who had put him into such a state, Baudelaire replied, "A dog. I seriously offended him."[225]

Baudelaire not only arranged a life of punishment for himself, he wanted it for others. In his view, because we are all evil, we ought to suffer in search of expiation. He believed that the death penalty must never be repealed, and wrote of both the utility and the fertility of pain as spiritual treatment. "In politics, the true saint is the man who whips and kills the people for their own good."[226] Suffering, he wrote, is a divine remedy for our impurities. To refuse someone pain is to deny him what Heaven has decreed, to stand between him and Providence, to reduce his chances of salvation. Thus, on moral grounds, he questioned the use of anesthetics during operations.[227]

One must be careful, of course, never to take Baudelaire too literally, but to look behind the shocking lines to glimpse the psychological realities he meant to display. The tale of the "Le Mauvais Glacier," one of Baudelaire's poems in prose, has been repeatedly cited as a literal example of his sick behavior, of his cruelty and misanthropy.[228] Asselineau was right to complain of the inability of readers to recognize Baudelaire's "rhetorical artifice";[229] but he was also too charitable to perceive that Baudelaire meant to describe faithfully the mania for punishment that was part of his hatred for life.

In the poem, Baudelaire notices from his window a glass peddler in the street six stories below and is seized with an arbitrary loathing for the poor man. He beckons him to mount the six flights of stairs, delighted by the thought of the difficulty the man will have in supporting his heavy and fragile wares. Having examined the peddler's stock item by item, Baudelaire is outraged to discover no colored panes. What do you mean, he shouts at the poor man, going through poor neighborhoods without a single pane to make life beautiful! And he pushes him out the door and down the stairs. Going to his balcony, he selects a flower pot; and when the peddler appears at the entrance below, he drops his missile, knocking him down and shattering his stock. Then, drunk with madness, he shouts in anger: "Make life beautiful! Make life beautiful!" He knows that one often pays dearly for such pranks, but asks, "What is an eternity of damnation compared to an infinity of pleasure in a single second?"[230]

We have already noted Baudelaire's financial tangles, which reached a crisis in the summer of 1860 when he could not repay Poulet-Malassis the 3,000 francs borrowed the previous year for the sojourn in Honfleur. Some of Baudelaire's other creditors were also presenting overdue bills at Honfleur, aware that Mme Aupick was more likely to pay than Baudelaire. When she would write to express her fear of being ruined, he would beg her to be kind and not add to his miseries, making reference to the horror of the *conseil judiciaire* as her invention, but confessing his terror at not being able to cure himself of vices. We might expect, as a normal, conscientious reaction to that crisis, an eagerness to earn the money necessary to meet his obligations; but the masochist's conscientiousness must find a self-destructive mode. In 1860, Eugène Crépet invited Baudelaire to write commentaries on some of the poets whose work Crépet was putting into an anthology, and he paid him an advance of 600 francs for the work. After the copy was delivered, Crépet asked for certain revisions. Baudelaire refused to make them, saying he preferred to pay back the advance even though he had already spent it and would have to borrow additional money.[231]

The primacy of sadomasochism in Baudelaire's personality, and the consequent impotence, did not exhaust his list of psychological quirks. In many letters to his mother, he wrote of the obsessions that dogged him, of the fears that haunted him. Beyond his obsession with sexuality and his fear of the love act, he was obsessed with death, with suicide, and with personal hygiene. It always took him two hours to accomplish dressing for the day, and he had an obsession for clean hands, those small, well-manicured hands the Goncourts had noticed.[232] In the dream, he had fretted about the necessity to wash his feet before and after sexual intercourse, a ritual that became unnecessary when he found himself gradually shod as he moved away from the girls toward the museum. One analyst has seen evidence of paranoia in these fears and obsessions, as well as in Baudelaire's alleged desire to kill General Aupick.[233]

A curious aspect of Baudelaire's sensibility has been underscored by several investigators on the assumption that it provides insight into his psychology and sexual constitution. It is known that some writers are strongly visual-minded, whereas others are more auditory-minded. Some combine those sensory characteristics, though one sense usually predominates. Baudelaire had well-developed visual and auditory senses, but was especially sensitive to odors; and he remarked that his soul soared on perfumes, as other men's souls soar on music. He was olfactory-minded; for him odors were a fourth dimension, which enriched his poetic possibilities. On the other hand, the olfactory temperament is quite rare and suggests an abnormal sensorium[234]—indeed, a finicky sensibility which, in Baudelaire's pathetic case, served a disillusioned mind.[235]

The Pox

The reader is by now aware that Baudelaire experienced a venereal infection in his youth, and that the recent discovery of his youthful letters has enabled us to date that infection more precisely: at age eighteen rather than at twenty or twenty-one as previously believed. The reader has also been introduced to the proposition, advanced by Claude Pichois and others, that the infection was a moral shock to Baudelaire which altered his destiny and was the foundation of his preoccupation with *le mal*. We have not only challenged the validity of that proposition,[236] but have endeavored to show that Baudelaire's consciousness of his destiny as a pariah dawned with the shocking discovery of his perversity.

Pichois's proposition was based on his assumption that, for the literati of the nineteenth century, the impact of syphilis was more psychological than physiological; not because they had powerful remedies for syphilis—which they did not—but because these men of powerful imagination felt themselves stricken to the core of their being and feared the consequent reduction in their vitality.[237] Pichois may be right about certain individuals, but there remains no evidence of such an association in Baudelaire's correspondence. In

1859, he cautioned Poulet-Malassis to take care of his pox as he, Baudelaire, had had varied symptoms of the disease after an apparent cure.[238] About nine months later, Baudelaire again cautioned Poulet-Malassis to be careful and not to be misled by the appearance of a cure. However, he added a very optimistic note: "You have just given me the exact description of the symptoms I once had. Be assured, however, that no one is more hale and hearty than one who has had the pox and has been quite cured."[239]

We have already noted that Baudelaire mentioned the matter again, in 1861, in a letter which revealed that Mme Aupick had long since known about the youthful venereal attack. He had believed himself to be cured, but the symptoms had reappeared in 1848; and now, in 1861, he was experiencing a new manifestation of the disease: spots on his skin and an extraordinary lassitude in all his joints. Since he added that he needed a rigorous regimen that was impossible under the circumstances of his current life in Paris, his complaints may have been just one more instance of appeal for her sympathy and help.[240] At the same time, the chronological evidence he gave in this letter bears no resemblance to the classic course of syphilis.

Be that as it may, Baudelaire obviously believed that he had had an attack of syphilis, but he did not return repeatedly to the matter as if it were a mortal stain and the curse of his existence. He reserved that honor for the *conseil judiciaire*. As for all those friends who believed he had died a virgin, either they did not know of the alleged infection, or they dismissed it as the product of his poetic imagination. To generalize, furthermore, about the horrors of syphilis, as Pichois did, is to read into the nineteenth century a comprehension of the true nature of the disease that only the twentieth century possessed. For Baudelaire's generation, as for those of prior generations, an attack of syphilis may have been incapacitating and uncomfortable, embarrassing or humiliating to those who had a secret life to conceal, even a source of pride for those who had something to prove; but *no* association between a syphilitic infection and what we now know to be the tertiary stage of untreated syphilis, such as general paralysis or tabes dorsalis, had gained medical acceptance. What is more, syphilitics of Baudelaire's day could have had no knowledge of the uselessness of the treatment they were given.

In the primary stage of syphilis, the infection becomes systemic within a few hours after exposure, the spirochetes passing through mucous membranes and abraded skin into the bloodstream and, hence, into every organ of the body. The primary lesion, a chancre, will develop at the portal of entry within three or four weeks, though the time may vary from ten to ninety days; it will persist up to five weeks, and then heal.

About six weeks later, though that time can vary from two weeks to six months, the patient will experience the secondary stage of syphilis: a cutaneous eruption, either localized or generalized. A loss of hair can be another secondary manifestation; but if the scalp is infected, the baldness will be patchy and irregular. A spontaneous healing of the secondary manifestations will then occur after two to six weeks. In some cases, even after the secondary lesions regress and disappear, they may be followed by fresh lesions; thus the final disappearance of the secondary stage may take as long as nine months.

At that point, the patient has reached the latency stage, and clinical examination will reveal no evidence of an active disease. Not only is the patient apparently healed, but an immunization has taken place. That is why Baudelaire's assurance that Poulet-Malassis would be more "hale and hearty" after his cure reflected popular optimism about the eventual outcome of the nasty infection, albeit a total ignorance of the terrible possibilities. In approximately 25 percent of these cases, further cutaneous relapse occurs until the immunologic changes are completed—practically never after the fourth year of the disease, however.[241] In any case, when Baudelaire related ailments in 1848 and 1861 to his venereal infection of late 1839, we must deduce that those later maladies had nothing to do with syphilis.

To challenge Pichois's estimate of the profound psychological impact syphilis had upon the literati of the nineteenth century is not to deny the immense consequences of the disease for the population as a whole. Dr. Alfred Fournier estimated that the Parisian population was 15 percent syphilitic at mid-century. Since he did not have a serologic test to detect latent syphilis (for only a blood test, either the Wassermann, the Kahn, or Price's Precipitation Reaction, can establish a diagnosis of latency), we must suppose that the incidence was higher than 15 percent. Aside from the temporary incapacity or possible sterility resulting from the infection, we now know that about one-third of those in the latency stage would have ultimately developed the destructive lesions of late syphilis; and that about 23 percent of *all* cases ultimately died as a result of the original infection.

Treatment of syphilitics in the nineteenth century could not have affected these statistics, inasmuch as the standard specifics during the primary and secondary stages amounted to no treatment. Mercury in small doses, the most conventional prescription, had been used since about 1497. William Wallace introduced the use of potassium iodide as a therapeutic in 1836, and it was popularized in France by the famous syphilographer, Dr. Philippe Ricord. But neither remedy could have had any significant effect upon infectiousness. By our standards, therefore, all nineteenth-century victims of syphilis were untreated. The known decline in the incidence of syphilis in the Western countries between 1860 and 1910—the year that arsphenamine or "606" was developed by Paul Ehrlich as a therapeutic agent—has to be attributed to social factors, such as the Industrial Revolution, which raised the general standard of living and made widespread public education possible.[242]

In 1839 Baudelaire did not specify the medicine he was purchasing to treat his infection, nor did he mention a physician. In fact, until the approach of Baudelaire's fatal illness in Belgium, only one reference to a physician can be found in his correspondence. He evidently never had a personal doctor, and the remedies he sometimes mentioned or urged on others were self-prescribed.[243] It makes one wonder whether Baudelaire's syphilis of 1839 had been diagnosed by a physician—but the facts remain obscure.

On the other hand, even if a reputable doctor had diagnosed syphilis in 1839, we still might not know what to make of it. For several centuries there had been a debate as to whether syphilis and gonorrhea were different diseases. In 1838, Dr. Ricord did insist that the two diseases were distinct; but unless we could know that Baudelaire's physician knew of, or accepted, the new distinction, we could not surmise what he might have said of Baudelaire's symptoms. And, in any case, the specific etiology for syphilis was not known until 1905 with the discovery of the spirochete named *Spirochaeta pallida* by Hoffman and Schaudinn of Berlin.[244]

The accepted notions about Baudelaire's syphilis remained predominant through the first third of the twentieth century. Some have seen it as almost a concomitant of the bohemian student life of the Latin Quarter, where Baudelaire lived at the time of his alleged infection. It has been conjectured that the infection may have made him pathologically timid—impotent—and that it led to his death in the form of cerebral syphilis, not to speak of accounting for his depression and lack of will long before the end. The evidence of syphilis that Baudelaire himself gave in letters is taken as credible.[245] Dr. Laforgue, the psychoanalyst, argued that Baudelaire the masochist deliberately sought infection as self-punishment—therefore, that the neurosis was the father of the infection, rather than the reverse.[246]

During the second third of the twentieth century, the Baudelaireans were inclined to equivocate about Baudelaire's syphilis. That is, they tended to accept the fact of syphilis with its mortal implications in his case, while registering their doubt about the reliability of the evidence. The date of the infection was then obscure; the source of the infection, a Jewish prostitute named Sara, was a matter of myth; there remained no proof that he had ever undergone specific treatment for syphilis; and Baudelaire's tendency to exaggerate his medical symptoms in letters led one physician, Dr. Caubet, to wonder if Baudelaire had merely perceived an eruption of herpes on his penis and had jumped to horrendous conclusions. Still, it was hard to abandon a time-honored diagnosis that had for so long sufficed to account for Baudelaire's life and death. One could recognize that his symptoms of 1848 and 1861 probably had nothing to do with syphilis without denying the possibility of the original infection.[247]

In 1966, the publication of Baudelaire's youthful letters provided a legitimate exit from the equivocation, though equivocation did not entirely cease. The two critical letters in the collection had been written to assure his half-brother that the money lent for medication had been spent for medication. He acknowledged, moreover, some improvement in his condition: he was sleeping much better, his stiffness had vanished, and his headaches had nearly disappeared; but his digestion was still unsettled, and he was experiencing a "painless but continual discharge."[248] As Dr. Christian Dedet put it, Baudelaire had succinctly described the symptoms of a simple gonococcal urethritis, namely, gonorrhea. The date of the infection would have been the early autumn of 1839, as we already know; but in view of Baudelaire's later letters about syphilis, Dr. Dedet was unwilling to rule out the possibility of a later syphilitic infection.[249] In fact, however, the only substantial evidence of venereal infection points to gonorrhea alone, though Baudelaire believed he was suffering from syphilis.[250]

Poor Belgium

On 13 January 1860, Baudelaire suffered a strange seizure on the streets of Paris that he likened to a cerebral congestion.[251] By midsummer, his financial tangles were reaching unresolvable proportions; and by then he had had good reason to believe that Honfleur was no longer an acceptable refuge or the answer to his

51

financial impasse. In retrospect, it appears that an irreversible decay had taken hold by the age of thirty-eight or thirty-nine. He was painfully aware of the erosion: "I have cultivated my hysteria with enjoyment and terror. I always have vertigo now, and today, 23 January 1862, I have experienced an unusual warning: I felt pass over me *the wind of the wing of madness.*"[252]

He tried to raise immediate money by offering publishers new editions of his books for substantial outright sums, but they preferred to pay him royalties on the basis of sales. It began to appear as if his only salvation lay in abandoning his country.[253] He applied to the government for a grant to enable him to study the art galleries of Belgium, proposing to write a book on them, but he was turned down.[254] Meanwhile, he told his mother that he could go to Belgium to earn money through lectures, to write articles for *L'Indépendance belge,* and to finish up books interrupted by his Parisian tribulations. Were it not for her, he would never return—such was his horror of Paris and France.[255] He successfully arranged a series of lectures to begin in November 1863, but was checked in his hope to write for the Belgian publication.[256] Desperate to acquire money for the trip, he signed a contract with Michel Lévy on 1 November 1863, giving Lévy outright ownership not only of the three published volumes of Poe translations but of the two yet to be published—all for 2,000 francs.[257] In time, Baudelaire came to recognize the folly of the sale and to resent Lévy's opportunism bitterly, as the published volumes had been bringing him between 400 and 600 francs a year.[258]

Since it was Baudelaire's nature to procrastinate, he did not manage to get to Brussels until 24 April 1864. He began his lectures in early May and was dismayed to discover a misunderstanding about his lecture fees. Moreover, even his reduced financial expectations were erased by the swift collapse of the series, and he early concluded that the Belgians were beasts, liars, and thieves.[259] There remained, however, the opportunity to sell a collection of articles on art criticism to the publisher Lacroix at the highest possible price, which Baudelaire now admitted had been the true motive for the trip to Belgium,[260] and which may well account for his otherwise incredible decision to surrender five titles to Michel Lévy. When Lacroix declined to enter into contract, Baudelaire's mission to Belgium had totally failed; yet, he could not simply return to Paris and the tangle of debts from which he had fled.

His mind had previously dwelt upon the horrors and injustices of his past; by the summer of 1864, his energy went into worry and anxiety about his future, and his recitals of continual illness no longer had a theatrical ring. He knew himself to be both "physically and morally sick," and was compelled to ask his mother for more money, complaining that the Belgians had been stealing from him.[261] He was suffering from palpitations of the heart, a nervous stomach, and continual diarrhea,[262] though he noted that the diarrhea was periodically interrupted by insupportable constipation, which he fought with cold enemas and laudanum.[263]

As in the past, Mme Aupick sent several small sums of money out of pity for his plight; but when she proposed, out of worry for his condition, to pay him a visit, his basic health instantly rebounded. All French visitors to Belgium, he assured her, experienced the same intestinal troubles in Belgium because of the bad climate, and he protested that he did not suffer from any "specific illness."[264] But to Ancelle, Baudelaire continued to complain of illness, though he cautioned him not to inform his mother. A "fever" had now seized him, awakening him at one or two in the morning, preventing all sleep before seven, and resulting in great fatigue; but at least the nocturnal fever had replaced the diarrhea. He knew perfectly well that he could not assign to Belgium the responsibility for his ailments—that he had been sick before leaving France.[265] In the autumn, he announced that he was sufficiently acclimated to eat normally, but that the rheumatism season was at hand.[266] He used his New Year's greeting to his mother to expose a mind loaded with "funereal ideas," dwelling upon his preoccupation with imminent death, adding that he feared to return to Paris even for a moment, that he would return only when he could go "gloriously."[267]

In early 1865, he listed for Ancelle his ailments since arriving in Belgium (the stomach and intestinal upsets, the nocturnal fever), but added that he had recently been suffering from either neuralgia or rheumatism, and that his eyes had been clogged because of a cold.[268] A week later, he dined out for the first time in ten days, indulging in what he called a small orgy: oysters, beefsteak, and a half-bottle of wine. He paid for his indulgence with piercing pains.[269] Three weeks later, he still complained of an aftereffect, a dull pain over his right eyebrow.[270]

Meanwhile, his financial agony also deepened. In May, he applied to his mother for a substantial sum to settle overdue rent in Brussels, so that he might be free to go to Paris for urgent meetings with publishers. The poor woman provided him with 700 francs as of May 12, but he postponed departure, first citing his revived neuralgia and abdominal pains, then the succession of diarrhea and constipation.[271] He finally slipped into Paris for several days during the first week of July, where he learned firsthand of Poulet-Malassis's financial desperation. By then, Baudelaire owed Poulet-Malassis 5,000 francs, and the latter told him frankly that the note would have to be sold to a moneylender, who would inevitably hound Baudelaire for the money. He reached Honfleur on 7 July 1865 to plead again for assistance, and his mother arranged to borrow 2,000 francs from Ancelle so that Baudelaire could reduce his debt to Poulet-Malassis. Baudelaire took the money to Paris on the tenth and was back in Brussels by the fifteenth.[272]

His letters throughout the summer and autumn expressed his desperate desire to sign Parisian contracts for new manuscripts, which included *Le Spleen de Paris* and a new edition of *Les Fleurs du mal*. If he could only pay off his remaining Belgian debts, including the 3,000 francs to Poulet-Malassis (who had crossed the border to avoid his creditors), it might be possible to return permanently to France. Yet, at the same time, he tried to borrow additional funds for living expenses and for another business trip to Paris, which he would never make. He told Ancelle that merely waiting for money made him "physically ill from impatience," and that his bitch of a landlady made him ill out of annoyance and shame. His irritation had reached a point of martyrdom, and he could barely tolerate any society at all. "I prefer absolute solitude to insensitive, stupid, or ignorant company."[273]

In December, he again developed persistent "head neuralgia," but was avoiding the pain-killing pills available because of his horror of drugs.[274] He was finally driven to summon a physician, Dr. Oscar Max, who prescribed doses of opium, quinine, digitalis, and belladonna for his relief. Baudelaire found that he had to double and even quadruple the prescription to make it effective.[275] In a few days, his migraine lessened; but he expereinced a sense of dullness,[276] and he was occasionally bedridden. Evidently Dr. Max suggested that he might be a hysteric, which led Baudelaire to dispense with his services.[277]

He next called in Dr. Léon Marcq on 20 January 1866 and was asked to supply a written list of his symptoms, information that he later duplicated in a letter to Asselineau. He informed Dr. Marcq that he was never hungry and could go several days without feeling a desire to eat. He had experienced dizziness and severe head pain, and along with a feeling of heaviness and congestion his head seemed unclear. He had experienced falls, when both standing and sitting. After regaining consciousness, he would be nauseated, in a cold sweat, with his head very hot. His vomit could be either yellow, watery, glaireous, or spumous. If he failed to vomit, he would experience belching. Though conscious, he would be in a stupor.[278]

He also informed Ancelle of the falling spells, the vertigo, and the vomiting,[279] but the description given to Asselineau was somewhat more graphic. One evening in January, before he had eaten, he began to knock about and to experience falls as if he were drunk, grabbing the furniture for support and dragging it along with him. Subsequent seizures followed an identical pattern. He would feel perfectly well and be ready to eat. Suddenly, he would feel himself becoming vague, distracted, stupefied, whereupon he would get a frightful pain in his head. Unless he happened to be reclining, he would be obliged to fall. Finally, there would be the vomiting, the cold sweat, and the lethargy. The pills for his migraine had been composed of quinine, digitalis, belladonna, and morphine, but he also mentioned having taken valerian and ether, plus mineral waters for his constipation. The physician told him to walk extensively for exercise, a suggestion that Baudelaire found as absurd as the prior mention of hysteria.[280]

Consequently, he sent his symptoms to his mother in the hope that her physician, a Dr. Lacroix, might make a diagnosis and give a more acceptable prescription. On the one hand, Baudelaire claimed he did not know what was wrong;[281] yet, he also seems to have suspected that he might be on the verge of either apoplexy or paralysis. He had noted also that he could induce the onset of the vertigo simply by thinking of vertigo—after which the attack would run its course. That distressed him, as he feared he would be classified as a *malade imaginaire* if he should admit the evidence to a physician. Still, he thought it might be useful to consult Dr. Charles Lasègue, then a practicing psychiatrist, the next time he went to Paris.[282]

In the meantime, he was asked from Honfleur whether the attacks had been induced by the drugs he was taking for migraine. He ruled out belladonna, saying he had taken it only in small amounts, and opium, saying that he had formerly taken it without adverse effects.[283] But the suspicion that he had been poisoned by his treatment for migraine did, in fact, seem possible to him.[284] In any event, he seemed to improve later in February, and the doctor was no longer calling at the hotel. That is, the violent attacks of vertigo and vomiting had ceased when he abandoned the drugs he had taken in December and January; but the headaches persisted, and he was lethargic, awkward, and timid—disinclined to be seen in public.[285] It would seem, therefore, that the drugs had produced intoxication,[286] whereas the migraines and the diarrhea were related to his chronic anxiety and tension.

There is a notable gap in Baudelaire's correspondence between 5 and 20 March 1866. That had to be the period during which Félicien Rops paid his last visit to him. On 18 March, Baudelaire, Rops, and Poulet-Malassis visited the Church of Saint-Loup in Namur, where Baudelaire fell on a step. While he insisted that he had merely slipped, his consequent exhaustion and subsequent deterioration indicate that his fall was a prodrome of his fatal disease.[287] We note, too, that this fall was different in character from those in December and January, as it was not accompanied by vomiting.

Back in Brussels, Baudelaire dined with the photographer Neyt, and besides being taciturn and glum, he gave occasional indication of confusion. After the two parted, Neyt suddenly regretted not having accompanied Baudelaire back to his hotel, the Grand Miroir, and set out to find him. Baudelaire was finally found in a tavern, drunk from brandy and despair. Neyt assisted him back to his hotel, but the furious Baudelaire ordered him to leave. Returning in the morning, Neyt found Baudelaire stretched out on his bed and partially paralyzed.[288] The precise dates of these events are uncertain, but we do know that the last letter in Baudelaire's hand was written on 20 March 1866. Dr. Oscar Max, the house physician whom Baudelaire had earlier consulted, was summoned to his bedside on 30 March 1866, the very day that Baudelaire had dictated his last letter. He found him without movement or speech. We may deduce, therefore, that Baudelaire must have suffered a series of attacks that progressively reduced his powers. Dr. Max diagnosed hemiplegia of the right side (paralysis) with aphasia. It was thought that the patient's lucidity was unimpaired.[289]

Dr. Max, who died prematurely in 1870, did not leave any written record of his treatment of Baudelaire, though he talked about the case to his brother, Dr. H.-E. Max, who provided what information he could some thirty years later. According to him, Dr. Max believed that the poet had suffered a slow progressive paralysis over a number of years, but that the paralysis was not accompanied by madness. He had advised notifying the family and friends that Baudelaire would have to be removed from the hotel to a *maison de santé* (nursing home). It fell to Poulet-Malassis to write to both Mme Aupick and Ancelle as delicately as possible, and the dutiful Ancelle set out at once for Brussels. Max recommended the Institut Saint-Jean et Sainte-Elisabeth in the rue des Cendres; and on 3 April 1866, Baudelaire was taken to the home by Ancelle, with the assistance of Poulet-Malassis and Arthur Stevens, the Belgian painter. The diagnosis of aphasia was confirmed on 7 April by Dr. Lequine, the head physician.[290]

Two days later, Poulet-Malassis took it upon himself to describe the situation for Jules Troubat, Sainte-Beuve's secretary, so that the Parisian literary world might be informed of Baudelaire's dreadful fate. Poulet-Malassis claimed that Baudelaire's decline had been evident to his friends for six months, as he had been abusing his nervous system with stimulants and had been drinking brandy in unaccustomed amounts. At Poulet-Malassis's home, brandy was no longer brought to the table, since Baudelaire showed no power to resist it. When the initial attacks produced ataxia on the right side, Baudelaire had rather heatedly rejected Poulet-Malassis's offer to take him either to Paris or to Honfleur; and by 30 March, the paralysis of the right side was accompanied by a softening of the brain.[291] By not stressing the prior tensions and despair that had finally reduced Baudelaire to intemperance, Poulet-Malassis inadvertently implied that Baudelaire had ruined himself with drink and drugs. Such a phrase as "softening of the brain," moreover, suggested idiocy; but in fact, though Baudelaire may have been paralyzed and mute, his eyes revealed that his intelligence had not failed.[292]

The episode in the nursing home proved to be short. The institution was operated by the Sisters of Charity, who soon came to learn that Baudelaire was not of their faith. Since we know that Baudelaire was able to mutter only one phrase after being stricken with aphasia, and that the phrase was "cré nom," understood as a common French curse, "sacré nom," it seems probable that the nuns, for all their good intentions, were dismayed by the blasphemy uttered in their midst, since Baudelaire had to use it to express all manner of meanings. No doubt, that is what the superior had in mind when she wrote Mme Aupick that it would be difficult to keep a man without formal religion in the home.[293]

Far from being a deliberate attempt to insult their sensibilities, the expression was all Baudelaire could muster. His behavior was quite in line with the studies of Hughlings Jackson on aphasia, especially the preservation of what he called a "leitmotiv" word that was most frequently a curse. We do not know if Baudelaire ever again endeavored to write with his unaffected hand. But studies of similar cases would suggest that, even if a partial recovery of speech and writing had been achieved (and Baudelaire was able to learn a few words before his ultimate dotage), his artistic activity could not have been resumed. The disability would have had nothing to do with a deficiency in memory, reasoning, or judgment, or even with a loss in aesthetic taste. Rather, it would have been an expected function of the aphasia, a disease which converts the artist or "subtle grammarian" into an agrammatist.[294] The sacred fire had vanished forever.

When Mme Aupick was informed that Brussels contained no alternative nursing home, she went there, despite advancing age and infirmity, and took charge of Charles herself. On 19 April 1866, she removed him from the nursing home, and they returned to the Hôtel du Grand Miroir, where she had already settled his back rent. There seemed to be no improvement in his speech; and his mother, recognizing that she could not cope with him at Honfleur, made preparations to establish him in a nursing home in Paris. The original plan had been to take him to the famous nursing home of Dr. Blanche, who had known Baudelaire as a visitor to his patient, Gérard de Nerval. For reasons unknown, Mme Aupick took him instead to Dr. Emile Duval's nursing home in the rue du Dôme, just off the Etoile in the Sixteenth Arrondissement. The date is uncertain, but it was about 2 July 1866.[295]

Mme Aupick remained in the neighborhood, but evidently worrying and wearying all concerned and treating Charles as an incompetent child. Dr. Duval concluded that it would be better for the patient if she were to return to Honfleur, and he encouraged her to go by telling her that Baudelaire was improving. She had, meanwhile, consulted Dr. Charles Lasègue, the psychiatrist Baudelaire had mentioned he might see on a trip to Paris; and Lasègue also urged her to return to Honfleur.[296] Consequently, she returned to her home at the end of July, paying him a visit in early November.

Dr. Emile Duval, when later interviewed by Dr. Augustin Cabanès, was unable to provide much precise information about his distinguished patient. In fact, Duval was not a physician, but what the French called an *officier de santé*, a public-health officer licensed by the government. Thus the medical information about Baudelaire's final year is both limited and dubious, either recorded by those who had heard the literary gossip or provided by Mme Aupick, by then seventy-four, in letters to Charles Asselineau. It may be that Baudelaire did manage to pronounce a few additional words clearly, as claimed, and that he was not bedridden until the spring of 1867. He could make himself understood with signs, yet there could have been no substantial improvement, and he died on 31 August 1867.[297]

Ancelle, correct and devoted to the end, took charge of all ar-

rangements. The funeral took place 2 September at the Church of Saint-Honoré in Passy; and at the cemetery funeral orations were given by Théodore de Banville and Charles Asselineau, whose grief made them barely audible. Mme Aupick then returned for the last time to Honfleur, where she died in 1871 at the age of seventy-eight. As for Jeanne Duval, no one knows what happened to her. Mme Aupick had made no effort to find her and give her money, as Baudelaire would have wished (though she scrupulously paid off his debts). Nadar claimed to have seen Jeanne in 1870, on the streets of Paris, dragging herself along on crutches.[298] Her end was as obscure as her origin.

The debate in medical circles about Baudelaire's illness and death began thirty-five years later, stimulated perhaps by a subscription for a monument at Baudelaire's grave in the Montparnasse Cemetery.[299] Dr. Michaut, recognizing the invalidity of much of the gossip, put out an appeal for reliable facts. He noted in particular that, though there seemed to be general agreement that Baudelaire had died aphasic with hemiplegia on the right side, his intelligence had remained nearly intact. In other words, this could not have been a case of general paralysis (or paresis), which terminates in madness, such as Jules de Goncourt experienced.[300]

After it became firmly established, in 1913, through the work of Hideyo Noguchi,[301] that paresis was a late manifestation of syphilis, the dispute about Baudelaire's fatal illness inevitably focused on his admitted infection and the manner in which it had contributed to his death. One graphologist contributed to the confusion by lecturing and publishing on Baudelaire's handwriting. He saw clear signs of mental disorder in Baudelaire's script as early as 1858: the unconscious omission of letters or words, mistakes in spelling surprising for a literary man, the blurring of oval letters, and persistent erasures. Baudelaire had, as an example, written the word Honfleur with two *f*'s. Noticing the error, he had crossed out the word, but repeated the error in rewriting it, the second time even writing *Honfleur* with a small *h*. An unfortunate example, perhaps, considering Baudelaire's ambiguity when it came to Honfleur, and perhaps nothing more than indication of the tension that plagued him; but the graphologist diagnosed from such errors the onset of general paralysis.[302]

Most of those who published on Baudelaire's death took the syphilitic infection for granted. The issue was whether the infection reached the tertiary stage, cerebral syphilis; or whether syphilis was merely one of several factors that led to a softening of the brain and to endarteritis of the left cerebral artery—an inflammation of the inner coat of the artery wall—and, thus, to a cerebral hemorrhage or stroke. Because a majority of the disputants were aware that Baudelaire never exhibited periods of mental confusion, megalomania, or the ultimate madness of general paralysis, they reached a rough agreement in the 1930s that Baudelaire's paralysis and aphasia had resulted from a cerebral hemorrhage.[303] Had they known of the letters that indicated gonorrhea rather than syphilis, their confidence in that diagnosis could only have increased.

No one has subsequently seen fit to challenge that diagnosis, and for good reason. Yet, to speak of a cerebral hemorrhage as being the *cause* of Baudelaire's death might lead us to forget that the cerebral hemorrhage, itself, was an *effect*. In the first place, a hereditary predisposition to stroke was indicated in the deaths of Baudelaire's father, mother, and half-brother, who died at the ages of sixty-eight, seventy-eight, and fifty-seven respectively, all partially paralyzed, with some degree of aphasia in both mother and half-brother.[304] Baudelaire's own death at age forty-six, however, attested to the existence of unique factors in his case which led to premature decay: not the alcoholic, narcotic, or sexual orgies of Baudelairean mythology, but a life of almost unrelieved tension and anxiety. Consumed by shame and hatreds, imbued with a sense of damnation from an early age, he came to have a horror of life, not simply of his own life, but of life itself. Given such circumstances, and remembering his many suicidal temptations, some might conclude, with some relief, that his premature demise had been a blessing. But no euphemistic refuge should be allowed to conceal the terror that was his daily bread, or to prettify the legacy of despair woven into the beauty of his words.

Jules and Edmond de Goncourt by Nadar. Arch Photo. Paris.

Jules de Goncourt

*The normal effect of nervous disorders of the body is to destroy all sense
of proportion in human joys and sorrows so that they are only experienced in their extreme forms.*

Edmond and Jules de Goncourt, *Germinie Lacerteux*

THE ORIGIN OF THE GONCOURT FAMILY IN LORRAINE HAS BEEN
clearly established, but its claim to nobility was unfortunately
vague and, to the immense irritation of the Goncourt brothers, it
came to be contested during the Second Empire. Their father,
Marc-Pierre Huot de Goncourt, had been born in 1763 in the Bourmont district of what came to be Haute-Marne; their mother,
Annette-Cécile Guérin, born in 1798, was his second wife. She was
only twenty-three at the time of their marriage in 1821, he being
thirty-five years older than she.

The financial details of their marriage are not entirely clear. Marc-
Pierre had been a professional army officer, but had been forced to
retire prematurely on half-pay in 1818, apparently for political reasons. Yet he had saved a substantial amount of money and had
inherited two farms, one at Brainville in the Bourmont district, one at
Breuvannes in the Clermont district, both of which produced good
yields of grain. Annette-Cécile, moreover, brought him a very respectable dowry of 30,000 francs.

They lived briefly in Nancy, where Edmond was born 26 May 1822.
Eighteen months later they moved to Paris, to 22 rue Pinon, now the
rue Rossini, where their remaining three children were born. The
second child, a daughter, died in infancy. Emilie, known as Lili, was
born in 1827 and struck down by the cholera in 1832. Jules, the last
born, came into the world on the morning of 19 December 1830. Thus,
when the young mother was widowed in 1834, she was left with two
sons, one eleven and one three; and she did not remarry.

It would seem that Mme de Goncourt found it difficult to cope with
widowhood, and some have attributed her trials to a sudden loss of
income. The deceased major's retirement pension was cut down to a
pension of 500 francs for his widow; but her dowry would have come
back to her, and she inherited the productive farms in Haute-Marne.
Because she moved in with her brother, Alphonse Guérin, the most
reliable of the Goncourt biographers has proposed that the major
may have mismanaged the dowry or that the income from the farms
was unreliable for some reason. In 1838, Mme de Goncourt moved in

with a friend, Françoise Mangin, remaining there until the latter's death in 1842, when she received a legacy of 2,000 francs.[1] But the financial information is very imprecise; and if Mme de Goncourt had, in fact, been reduced to poverty, it would be impossible to account for the substantial legacy she left her sons. By their own admission, they had an income from capital of approximately 10,000 francs a year,[2] four times that of Baudelaire, a sum sufficient for independence if not a definition of wealth. It may be, therefore, that they were able to extract from the farms the sums their mother's agent had been withholding from her.

The Goncourt brothers were jealous of the particle *de* in their father's name, but were painfully conscious that the indisputable claim to aristocratic connection came from their mother's side, with family names they could not wear. Through her, they were related to the Le Bas de Courmont and the Laurent de Villedeuil families. Nephtalie de Courmont, the Goncourt brothers' aunt, was the woman who most influenced the development of Edmond's sensibility and taste. Even before his father's death, Edmond had been sent to boarding school, which meant that he could be home only on Sundays; and he went on to the Lycée Henri IV for his secondary instruction. His orbit centered more on Aunt Nephtalie than on his mother; and from Nephtalie, a refined and delicate woman with a passion for antiques, Edmond drew his lifelong mania for collecting art.

Jules, the last-born, an extremely pretty child, of delicate construction, was adored and absorbed by their mother. He was sent to day school, the Collège Bourbon, so he lived at home. Mme de Goncourt withdrew from society entirely to devote herself to an indulgent supervision of his studies, trying to spare him the hardships of school, where he was disliked by most of his fellows, who on several occasions even endeavored to disfigure his face. Jules did, however, befriend Louis Passy at school and spent much time at the Passy home in Gisors. His favorable opinion of the Passy family persisted into later years; it was evidence of a positive attitude about people that would be rare in either brother.

Mme de Goncourt died on 5 September 1848, in Jules's eighteenth year; and it comes as no surprise to learn that he had given little thought to a career. Even the elder Edmond had reached no professional decision. Along with their comfortable inheritance came their mother's servant, Rosalie Malingre, known to them as Rose, who took charge of their home as their mother would have wished.[3] They had retained, from an earlier trip with their mother, a pleasant image of the literary life: At an inn at Gondrecourt, a man had ordered, in their presence, a bottle of champagne, a pen, and ink. But this idyllic scene of a man on a trip, writing on a table in an inn, while sipping champagne was one they later came to rue as the very contrary of literary reality.[4] In 1848, however, the life of art seemed to be their obvious destiny, and they planned, for 1849, the trip to Italy that was then the prerequisite to the artist's life. The political unrest in Italy deflected them to the south of France and, briefly, to Algiers, from whence they returned to Paris on 17 December 1849. They selected a new home, a dark, ground-floor apartment at 43 rue Saint-Georges, in the neighborhood of their childhood; but they soon moved upstairs to a brighter flat on the fourth floor, which they would occupy for the next twenty years.[5]

For good reason, the literary world has remembered the Goncourt brothers as if they had been one person, and that is as they would have wanted it. Until Jules's premature death in 1870, they were not merely inseparable, but produced their literary work together as one man. So close were they that it was an event to see one brother alone; and some saw them separated for the first time in the funeral procession that conveyed Jules to the Montmartre Cemetery, a particularly harrowing occasion for those onlookers who understood the frightful personal and literary consequences for the survivor. Each brother had sacrificed his individuality to form one person, and neither ever betrayed the secrets of their collaboration.[6] Zola saw in them a unity of temperament and passion unique in literature, so that when death carried off Jules, it was supposed that Edmond's literary talent had been severely undermined.[7] While it is true that Edmond exposed the wound of his grief for at least eight years, Zola's observation reflected the common assumption that Jules had been the more talented writer of the two. In fact, some of the finest passages in their *Journal,* which they began jointly in 1851, are to be found on pages written after Jules's death.

It may be that Edmond decided to write the story of a fraternal collaboration in order, finally, to put the past behind him. He sketched out the theme for the new novel late in 1876. It featured two acrobatic clowns, "two brothers loving each other as we loved each other, my brother and I. They will have combined their spinal column and will seek, throughout their lives, to perform an impossible feat which will be, for them, like the solution of a problem in science." He meant to include many details about the childhood of the younger brother and the elder's fraternal affection—infused with a bit of parental love. They would sacrifice everything for their muscles (meaning for literature), thus abstaining from women or anything else that weakens a man's strength.[8] This, indeed, became the theme for Edmond's *Les Frères Zemganno,* which he completed on 10 March 1879 and dedicated to Mme Alphonse Daudet. He even included, from his own experience in 1848, a scene in which the dying mother places the younger brother's hand in the elder's, transferring the maternal duty to the elder brother; and he did not conceal the mother's preference for her younger son.[9]

That novel was no exaggeration. Writing from the Hôtel de Normandie in Rouen in 1859, one of them, probably Jules, had noted that for the first time in their lives a woman had separated them. By which he meant nothing more sensational than that he had gone alone to Rouen to examine a bundle of letters, dating from the eighteenth century, written by the duchesse de Châteauroux to the maréchal duc de Richelieu, which were then in a private collection. Because of this momentary separation he wrote, "I understand perhaps today what love must be, if it exists. Remove its carnal side, the joining of the sex organs, and it is that which exists between us. So that when one is not with the other, there is a splitting as in a pair of birds who can only live together. Separate one from the other, and half of ourselves is missing. It leaves us with only half-sensations, a half-life; we are incomplete as a two-volume book of which the first volume is lost." He recognized not only the fusion of two hearts, but the fusion of two minds—a complete marriage of the entire moral being, perhaps unique, theirs alone. Indeed, "I was flattering love by comparing it to our fraternity."[10] This merger only deepened with the years. In 1866 they wrote: "We are now like two women who live together, whose health is identical, whose periods come at the same time. Even our migraines develop on the same day."[11]

The original manuscript of the Goncourt *Journal,* now in the Bibliothèque Nationale in Paris, fills eleven notebooks. Nearly all of the first five are in Jules's tiny script. After Jules's death, we find Edmond's more regular and aristocratic hand. Despite the evident collaboration of the early years, Jules was the sole author of many entries, including accounts of dreams that never appear in the *Journal* after his death. None of their friends was aware that the fraternal collaborators spent many evenings each week recording their impressions of the day.[12] The secret helps to account for the frankness and indecency of comments made in their presence, for the purveyors of gossip could have had no knowledge that their confidences were systematically put in storage by these two literary squirrels. Not until 1883, thirteen years after Jules's death, did Edmond decide to break the secret. On 12 July, he invited the Alphonse Daudets to lunch and considerably astonished them with the news of a diary kept for over thirty years.[13]

Three years later, he arranged for the serialized publication of the *Journal* in *Le Figaro*. The indignant outcry was immediate, and publication was halted after seven installments. Recognizing that he must be more prudent, Edmond began editing out the most indiscreet materials before resuming publication in book form in 1887, with a new volume appearing every year. The unfriendly reaction to the publication of what had been spoken in confidence was so great that Alphonse Daudet again advised that publication be suspended; but Edmond persevered, suspecting that Mme Daudet had found his published praise of her literary talent insufficient. In fact, she feared that the "real" *Journal*, the unabridged manuscript, would be published after Edmond's death, and that it would contain cruel references to Alphonse and her. Edmond insisted that the Daudets were the only people he loved, and that he was putting into his *Journal* only evidence of his warm feelings for them (an assurance which on the whole proved to be true). But he did not permit them to see the original manuscript, and some members of the family thought his unwillingness was grounds for suspicion. The anxiety would most likely have ruptured their friendship with Edmond had he lived much longer.

At the time of his death, 16 July 1896, nine expurgated volumes of the *Journal* had been published; and Alphonse, at least, still liked Edmond profoundly.[14] Edmond's will contained evidence that he had pondered its terms at length after Jules's death, committing it to paper only on 16 November 1884, and that it amounted to *their* will, not just his own. On the grounds that all members of the Goncourt family had financial means, the entire estate was left to establish a literary foundation that would grant an annual prize for a literary work. The self-perpetuating board of directors was to be composed of ten prominent writers who had scorned membership in l'Académie française, a bastion, in their view, of middle-class morality and taste. Edmond named eight of the ten in the will, but seven predeceased him and had to be replaced through codicils. He later removed Zola from the list for having stood for election to the Académie and dropped Maupassant when he became insane.

Edmond's clear intent was the creation of a rival academy independent from the state and from politics, and indifferent to the whims of the mighty. He asked that all his properties be sold for the foundation's support, and that his royalties, including those from an unexpurgated edition of the *Journal* that could be published by the foundation twenty years after his death, should also be part of the endowment. When the terms of the will were known, Edmond's relatives fought unsuccessfully to set it aside, but the courts upheld the will and Alphonse Daudet, the executor. The first meeting of the Académie Goncourt took place in 1900.[15]

The literary world has been substantially indebted to the Goncourt brothers, not simply for having provided a generous annual prize for literary merit, but for having assiduously kept a record of the literary scene from 1851 to 1896, a record that was finally published in full—in twenty-two volumes—between 1956 and 1958. Their novels, plays, and histories were never popular in their own time—or since—and are all but forgotten. The *Journal*, on the other hand, in both truncated and unabridged editions, has been an invaluable source for literary historians; for it would seem that the brothers had known everyone worth knowing, as well as a good many, in their opinion, not worth knowing. But while we all read, use, and value the Goncourts, virtually no one emerges from the reading with a fondness for them.

We can sympathize with their indignation at the systematic in-comprehension of their work, we can understand their consequent bitterness, we can even agree with many of their views; but we do not warm up to them as beloved or admired writers. The trouble is that, except for a few superb pages written by Edmond about the death of Jules, the pages of their *Journal* revealed no sense of, or compassion for, humanity. They deliberately isolated themselves from the world, and the desiccation of their lives flowered in their novels during the daytime and was more explicitly spelled out in their *Journal* at night. The Goncourt isolation and pessimism, if not rooted in their bizarre brotherhood, can only be explained by factors that made their association both necessary and possible. We sense their inhumanity and the desolation they felt, and we cannot avoid their preciousness; but we do not pity them.[16] It is surprising that no biographer has portrayed them as the emotional cripples they were, as sick, pathetic men, in retreat from existence. And of the two, Jules was the sicklier.

Despite the intimacy of their minds and spirits, the brothers were different in notable respects and respected the differences. Edmond was dark, the taller and more rigid of the two, with the military bearing of their father. Jules was blond, and his fair hair and skin and pale gold moustache made him seem more youthful than he actually was. He was the livelier of the two, more delicate and polished in society, the more Parisian; whereas Edmond had the tone of the intelligent country squire. They dressed alike, both wearing a square monocle on a black cord. Yet, in conversation with others, Edmond always said *we*, Jules always said *I*. Most of their letters were signed with both names.[17] They never walked arm in arm or even side by side, as Jules always walked several steps ahead; they looked like two fashionable Benedictines lost in thought.[18] In fact, Edmond was the more reflective, with a firmer will and a greater dedication to work. Jules had a penchant for idleness which was overcome by the mysterious psychic bonds of their collaboration. Consequently, though they seemingly lived only to write, accepting the privations and demanding routine of a literary asceticism, pushing self-analysis to the point of vivisection, turning their scalpel on themselves before employing it on their contemporaries, it remains hard to imagine that Jules—had he been the survivor in 1870—would have had the fortitude to carry on alone, faithful to their routine and outlook, as Edmond was.[19]

For all their pride in their merger, they knew their differences and discussed them one night at table after dinner, with Jules recording the conversation. He found in himself the lymph of the nineteenth century, meaning the disenchantment with his century so common to the literati; and he admitted that there was a streak of depravity in himself which had never been fully developed, and that his aspirations were not the same as Edmond's. He could envision Edmond happily married to a sentimental woman, and at home as the ideal bourgeois. But he saw himself as an eighteenth-century ecclesiastic with an inclination toward malice, with a touch of sixteenth-century Italian deviousness, though he had a horror of blood, of cruelty, and of bodily ills. "I am a Latin of Paris." He put Edmond in a more favorable light, as a more disciplined Germanic type, reflecting his birth in Lorraine. And yet, for all their differences in temperament, in taste, and in character, they had achieved absolute identity in their ideas, in their antipathies and friendships, and in their judgments and intellectual perspective. They used the same brain and the same eyes.[20] Two days after that entry they added, "Between us we are complete: Edmond is determination, Jules, the will."[21]

They left us only hints as to why they had chosen to collaborate in literature rather than in art, as they had had instruction in painting and Jules, especially, showed some talent. The choice *seems* to have been Edmond's, and the diary they kept of their travels in 1849 served as their literary apprenticeship and provided the idea for the *Journal* begun in 1851. When Jules lay dying in 1870, Edmond reproached himself for having made the literary option: "Perhaps without me he would have been a painter and could have made his name without destroying his brain."[22]

That there is no hint of Jules's resistance to Edmond's choice of art form suggests not merely passivity or affection for Edmond, but a fundamental indifference. On the other hand, one may assert that, once they were at work, the tone of the *Journal* was established by Jules. A certain caustic and obscene vocabulary largely disappeared from its pages after his death, as did the delineation of erotic dreams; and pessimistic sentiments in his early correspondence were echoed in the pages of the *Journal*. Edmond, of course, shared Jules's view of reality and maintained the pessimistic mood of the *Journal* after his death. But we can understand what Jules had meant when he contrasted the streak of depravity in himself with the image of Edmond settled into domestic bliss. Edmond, in other words, became the dedicated and indulgent mother; Jules remained the dutiful but spoiled child.

To Love and To Loathe

One may divide the books the Goncourts wrote before Jules's death into two categories. Their histories of eighteenth-century personages and painting were their works of love. The *Journal* and their novels—which were not so much fiction as they were portraits of contemporary reality—were works of hatred. For them, the nineteenth was the loathsome century.[23] Their aristocratic connections, no doubt, had steeped them since childhood in respect for talent and privilege. Even so, we are surprised to discover the depths of Jules's reactionary sentiments after the June Days in 1848 when he was only seventeen. He saw that uprising not simply as an episode in the age-old warfare between the classes, in which attacks upon the rich, the noble, or the superior were disguised as the defense of a principle, of a king, or of a pretender; in 1848 the assault had been undisguised, "revealed in its monstrous nudity," an attack upon quality by the mediocre, who were demanding to govern themselves, *for themselves*. The very idea that aristocrats, under the circumstances, ought to throw themselves into politics to provide guidance or leadership for those who sought to rise, was quite beyond his sight. "Down with politics," he wrote; "long live literature!"[24]

After the legislative elections of 1849, which gave France an Assembly anything but radical, we find him writing of "220 socialists in the Assembly . . . and of 12 million citizens stricken with this social cholera," figures so overblown as to suggest hysteria. "Quite clearly we are done for," he continued. "France will be socialist and Europe republican. It is annoying, but I am convinced that I see the situation as it is."[25] A month later, visiting his cousin's charming château near Bar-sur-Seine, he recalled the elegant and delightful life that "1789 had guillotined."[26]

By some astonishing quirk of fate, the first novel on which they collaborated, *En 18 . . .* [In the Year 18——], had been scheduled for publication on 2 December 1851. As they tell us in the first entry of their *Journal*, the brothers had anticipated the event with great excitement and were dismayed to find themselves eclipsed by a coup d'état. They rushed into the streets to find the posters advertising their book and found only notices of troop movements. In fact, there *was* no novel that day. Their printer's office had been scoured by troops, and their posters had been burned as too suggestive of the 18th Brumaire. The book did appear on the fifth, but without the advertisements, and it sold only sixty copies.[27] President Bonaparte had stolen their show, and they were never to find forgiveness in their hearts. Politics had triumphed over literature.

Jules's early prediction that the masses were on the verge of suffocating civilization was a recurring theme in the *Journal*, and that preoccupation made Jules the enemy of every enterprise which promoted the advancement of the common people or, more particularly, defined the advances of contemporary life as progress. Science, whether pure or applied, was high on his list of humbuggery: "Every morning we are promised a miracle, an element, or a new metal by these jokers, promises which lead to the Institute, to decorations, to influence, to salaries, to high regard by serious people. Yet, the cost of living continues to rise, and basic commodities are still lacking. The bargain remains the worst buy in the world."[28] At dinner, in 1869, the brothers heard that the chemist Marcelin Berthelot had predicted that physical and chemical science—in a hundred years—would know of what the atom is constituted; and that, as a consequence, we would be able to moderate, extinguish, or relight the sun as if it were a lamp. The physiologist Claude Bernard had allegedly commented that, in a hundred years, man would have mastered organic law so completely that life could be created in competition with God. "We raised no objection. But we believe that when that moment arrives in science, the good Lord, in his white beard, will descend to earth, swinging His keychain, and say to humanity, as they say at the Museum at five o'clock: 'Closing time, gentlemen.' "[29]

The charm of that image should not cause us to overlook its essential despair for the future. The disaster envisioned was imminent, whether from the intervention of a wrathful God or from the more likely triumph of the illiterate and unwashed. "When stomachs are full and men can no longer copulate," Jules wrote, "they have fallen to six-foot barbarians from the North. But now that Europe contains no more savages, the workers will do the job of revitalizing civilizations in about fifty more years. It will be called the Social Revolution."[30]

Though such remarks have been cited as evidence of political and social insight, they reflect, in fact, a melancholia, a pessimism, a discouragement, an indolence, a lethargy of mind and body, profoundly felt and admitted by the brothers. Returning home after six months in Italy, they found that nothing had changed for the better: "We resume our stagnant life in the same place." Then the pronoun changes, a signal of Jules's authorship: "When one is away, he comes to believe that some change will have taken place by the time of his return—but nothing. Everything around me is the same old thing and fills me with an insupportable sensation of insipidity. . . . The people, too, are exactly the same as I left them; and they bore me as much as I bore myself. None of my acquaintances even died during my absence. I am not simply unhappy; it is worse than that."[31]

The melancholia may have been insupportable, but it was also revered as the outward sign of superiority. Having defined advances in knowledge as humbug and the new social revolution as the next barbarian invasion, the Goncourts defined true progress in civilization as the advance in sensibility. Thus, as humanity advances, it becomes increasingly neurotic and hysterical; and those who have nothing left but nerves are the finest of our flowers. This explained the melancholia they found not only in themselves, but in their literary circle.[32] Nothing could be done—not even an eternal trip to Italy—to alleviate this suffering, as it was the reward for being the outpost of civilization. But at least the brothers knew, with the outer defenses in such hands, that the future of civilization could not be bright. Thus was the vanguard not even a rear guard, but in full psychic retreat. For Edmond and Jules, the eighteenth century became the haven, that happy moment before 1789, before mankind embarked upon the vulgarization of life and culture, when life had been charming rather than hateful.

For them, the Old Regime made sense: a government founded on divine right and tradition, a nobility with genuine noble blood, a rational, sensible order, where people knew their place. In contrast, they saw the Second Empire as a democratic regime with a fictitious emperor at the helm and a bogus nobility in power, a regime founded on a cult that raised one man *above* the principles of 1789: "Equality licking Caesar's boots! Stupid and odious!"[33] Their political insights would have been contested by both Napoleon III and the intellectual critics of the Old Regime could they have known of such opinions; but the literati lived in that private world of the unhappy few where factual precision lost out to epigram and passion.

They mourned the eighteenth century as a time when men of letters were welcomed into "what one properly calls society." The real aristocrat, aware and proud of his station, was not jealous of the man of letters and could be on familiar terms with him, as talent could neither intrude upon his rank nor undercut his vanity. He could take pleasure in the company of a Voltaire or a Diderot. The man of letters, indeed, was seen as having "reigned" in society. But, with the destruction of hierarchy by the establishment of equality, the men of letters had been pushed aside. The Goncourts knew not a single man of letters, in their own time, "who moves in what one properly calls society." Flaubert, who came to Paris briefly every year, went nowhere and saw only a few friends: he led "the life of a bear that all of us writers lead." The bearishness had been forced upon them by the bourgeoisie, who could not endure the proximity of men of talent. And in any case, given its humdrum activities, the bourgeoisie required nothing more than a newspaper.[34]

Flaubert did indeed proclaim his bearishness, but he would have bellowed indignantly at the suggestion that he had been ostracized by the bourgeoisie. It was *he* who could not endure the bourgeoisie and its morality, *he* who chose a rural den and came to Paris only of necessity, a withdrawal beyond the ken of the citified brothers. It was *they* who aspired to the drawing room, *they* who brooded on the death of "what one properly calls society." Though they called Flaubert a friend and recognized him as a man of talent, they found him wanting as a man and writer. Having heard him complete a reading of *Salammbô*, they found in him the very quality to which they objected in Homer: he had written a novel of the flesh rather than of the soul, of physical suffering rather than mental suffering.[35] The superiority of the contemporary novel, theirs for example, lay in its focus upon spiritual agony.

They disliked not merely Homer but Greek art in general, for to them it celebrated perfection, the sublime, the absolute in beauty. They saw it as impersonal art, "decapitated" art, a photographic deification of the human body, reflecting the perception of a materialistic culture. Aside from exposing a rather feeble grasp of Hellenic civilization, this Goncourt attitude explains their conviction that advanced, sophisticated art, being the work of neurotics and hysterics, portrays decadence rather than perfection. What is more, classical art represented to them the conventional standards taught at school, and the distinction and salaries of those (unlike themselves) who adhered to convention.[36] Classicism, in other words, was the opiate of the mediocre.

It is a wonder that the Goncourts found their salvation in the eighteenth century, an age with some claim to classicism. That it had been an aristocratic society was its primary attraction for them; and when they championed eighteenth-century painting, their favorites were those artists whom they called "wonderful, charming, free decadents, adventurous in line and color, mixing everything together, risking everything, leaving their particular, corrupt, and rare mark on everything." They might even be muddlers; but if they painted with exuberance and imagination, or if they revealed a melancholy disposition, one of individualism rather than convention, the Goncourts found them kindred spirits. They saw Fragonard as the most innovative among painters, Watteau, the painter of melancholy cast.[37]

There can be no doubt about the formulas which became conventions for the Goncourts: Democracy equals mediocrity and means barbarism; science deflects us from a true perception of reality; reality is boredom, as only superior writers know; and the superior human being is the decadent. To define decadence as vitality, to find mental disease as the root of vigor, is surely to define life as hateful. To hate life, moreover, will be to hate nature; after which the final formula asserts that art is superior to life.

The Goncourts were not oblivious to the beauty of nature, but they much preferred the city; and they believed that their kind had become much too civilized, too refined, too corrupt, too learned, too artificial, to find happiness in foliage and sky.[38] After a walk in the country, they described nature as the enemy, the green earth seeming to be an enormous cemetery waiting for them, grass feeding on man, trees rooted in rotting bodies. For them, nothing in nature was comparable to a woman's dress or face, or to something a man had to say.[39] At the beach in Trouville, they noted: "The true horror of nature consists in sincerely preferring paintings to countrysides and preserves to fruit."[40]

Since the Goncourt brothers thought rather poorly of Greek civilization as materialistic, one should not assume that they, themselves, were entirely free of that very characteristic. Their own materialism simply took different forms, and they would have been affronted to have been told that it was a good deal more obvious than that which they professed to see in the Greeks. The brothers accompanied Flaubert on a visit to the Parisian catacombs in 1862, where they saw "bones so well arranged that they recalled the wine cellars of Bercy . . . a library of skills." After seeing all those remains, all those people of bone, Jules noted: "Why this lie about immortality, the skeleton?"[41] As to the question "What is life?," they answered that it is the "usufruct of a conglomeration of molecules."[42]

It did not follow that the Goncourts' preference for the city meant that they liked people. Their *Journal,* if read from beginning to end, gives the unfortunate impression of a systematic denigration of everyone else, living or dead. The more scurrilous the anecdote, the more certain they were to record it, the vocabulary of the entry generally revealing Jules's particular touch. In 1855, they learned of the late Honoré Balzac's great aspiration: "The most enormous ambition to enter the head of a human being since the beginning of time; the most impossible, the most unrealizable, the most monstrous, the most olympian of ambitions; something that neither Louis XIV nor Napoleon had ever had, that Alexander could not have achieved in Babylon; an ambition forbidden to a pope, to an emperor, to a dictator, to the master of masters: namely, Balzac's ambition, which was to break wind in society."[43]

They were at pains to describe the appearance of others, and especially the furnishing of others' homes, as evidence of the quality of their minds and souls. After their first dinner at the home of Princess Mathilde Bonaparte, they noted that the house was not palatial nor were its furnishings princely. The standard was comfort, there were some flowers, but not one art object in its large rooms. They found the princess stout, the remains of a handsome woman—her features receding, her eyes very small, her skin a bit blotchy. She suggested the gay old girl making a comeback, the good-hearted child not entirely concealing a fundamental harshness. Naturally, her lover, Nieuwerkerke, was there, amiable and charming, easily assuming the role of master of the house. Two pugs followed her every step and were described as frightful. The food was indifferent, the conversation free and easy, as if in the home of a retired courtesan.[44] One would hardly imagine, after this introduction, that the brothers were to cherish regular invitations to such a house and to accept repeated kindnesses from such a woman.

Their social life also focused upon certain cafés frequented by literary people. Between 1851 and 1857, they haunted the Café Riche—a favorite of Baudelaire's—moving on to the Café du Helder in 1857 as the Riche had begun to attract too many common bohemians for their taste. The Moulin Rouge on the Champs-Elysées was also a favorite restaurant. Another regular meeting place was the Librairie Nouvelle on the ground floor of 15 boulevard des Italiens, where they might find Théophile Gautier, Gustave Flaubert, Gustave Doré, Charles Edmond, or Arsène Houssaye.

In 1862, the year the Goncourts joined Princess Mathilde's salon, they became regular members of the Magny circle, a group of writers who dined at the Magny Restaurant. The first dinner took place on Saturday, 22 November 1862, and dinners thereafter were scheduled fortnightly on Mondays. The legend that the dinners fell on Fridays, especially on a Good Friday, to permit the diners to affront Catholic opinion by eating meat publicly, is an amusing, believable, but erroneous anecdote. The freedom of the conversation amounted to a bonanza for the Goncourt *Journal*, where every indelicacy was relished and embellished, a reminder that *that* literary generation did not traffic in daffodils, but in the brutal, the gross, the vicious, in rascality, and in the adulterous—its vision of reality.[45]

Though accepted in literary circles, the Goncourt brothers were not much liked; a dismal outlook, eternal discontent, and hypersensitivity are not endearing qualities. After attending a Magny dinner on 12 February 1866, George Sand wrote that she had liked Flaubert best of all, but that she had found the Goncourts, especially Jules, simply too sure of themselves.[46] Moreover, they made their bitterness as unappreciated authors too manifest, reflecting their belief that they merited a greater public esteem than their fellows who enjoyed it. Their conviction of a general hostility toward them, which runs as a theme throughout the *Journal*, suggests pathology. They endeavored to account for that hostility by asserting that the world was jealous of their love, their brotherhood, their style of life, "particularly of our calm, our simplicity, the absence of any pose in us, not to speak of our home and our name."[47] Indeed, how hostile life is, they added, for anyone who does not live in the ordinary way, for those who either escape or resist it. In other words, for all those who are neither functionaries, bureaucrats, married, nor heads of families, who will be punished in a thousand large or small ways.[48] Their lot, in sum, was to be respected but hated.[49]

The hatred that they gave in return, their hostility to their own era, and their pessimism about the future were enunciated in a poisonous vocabulary that became, in the twentieth century, the lingo of bigotry and fanaticism. Jules's contempt for all that ordinary mortals must do to sustain life—his contempt, in other words, for everything but art—explains his youthful rejection of advice from his uncle, Jules de Courmont, and from his friend, Louis Passy, about the necessity of a career. Despite the likelihood of family criticism, he was firmly resolved, by the age of nineteen, "to do nothing at all." No such conventional existence for him![50] Once the literary life was launched, once Edmond had succeeded in imposing a discipline that guaranteed a routine production of prose, then, indeed, Jules did work hard, sometimes to a point of exhaustion. But he was sustained by the conviction that his was a higher calling, and that the rewards would be quite beyond the grasp of the vile multitude. "Paradise will be for those who have worked for posterity, where they will see themselves live on. Hell is for those who have done nothing for posterity—the bureaucrats, the bourgeois, cretins, pawns, and so on—where they will see themselves dead, dead, dead."[51] In the meantime, the brothers expected the lower orders of society to harass their betters, noting that they, along with Baudelaire and Flaubert, the purest of craftsmen and the most consecrated to art, had at one time or another found themselves on the benches of a police court.[52]

"The more I study the eighteenth century," Jules wrote, "the more I see that its principle and its goal was amusement and pleasure, as the principle and goal of our century is money, to get rich."[53] While we may well share the Goncourts' disapproval of money as an end in itself, we can also be staggered by a myopia that awarded moral ascendancy to the spenders of that which had been previously amassed, especially as that money was seemingly sanitized by being committed to amusement. The theme is repeated in the Goncourts' writing: "To spend money was life in the eighteenth century. To amass it is modern life."[54] In *Renée Mauperin*, they devoted a substantial passage to depicting the proper standards of a young Parisian, Denoisel (standards which were, of course, also their own), contrasting them with the debased manners of the bourgeoisie of the nineteenth century.[55]

To sympathize with the Goncourts' strictures about acquisition is to forget that their moralizing had not been inspired by a social conscience. Had the bourgeoisie bought canvases with nary a quibble over price, had they besieged bookstores to buy out a Goncourt first edition, the Goncourts' world would have been restored and mankind saved. Their snobbery, in fact, led them into self-congratulatory observations about the nobility which they had good reason to know were untrue. Having paid a New Year's Day call on their elderly cousin, Cornélie, in her tiny fifth-floor apartment, where she survived on very limited means, they noted that one of the finest aspects of the nobility is that it does not flee from poverty, but closes ranks against it. In middle-class families, we are told, one recognizes no relatives below a certain income—or above the fourth floor of a house.[56] We are left to wonder why, in a family of substantial wealth, Cornélie is perched on the fifth floor with insufficient chairs to accommodate her swarming well-wishers. Later, we find Jules furious because no one in the family but Edouard Lefebvre de Béhaine, a cousin, has congratulated Edmond upon receiving the cross of the Legion of Honor, or even responded to invitations to attend a housewarming after they had enlarged their apartment. "The family is a pleasant invention. It is composed of people who sometimes get together at your burial, but never for your joys."[57]

Some will argue that the brothers had a social conscience. André Billy, for example, notes the remark in the *Journal* that the sight of a poor man's face "saddens me for the rest of the day."[58] But the *Journal* is so remarkably free of similar comments that one is moved to tag this an aesthetic statement. For men inclined to judge a man's soul by his house and garden, the sight of the poor man, the man without the means for art objects, was the sight of a man without soul.[59] We would think, in fact, that men with serious social conscience would have been identified with a political or social movement. They made no such alliance; and aside from their hatred of Napoleon III, which was a personal matter, and their hostility to Bonapartism as a form of socialism, they were nonpolitical. They firmly opposed the government's policy of extending public instruction by confiding it to lay teachers, calling such instruction "schools for socialism";[60] and the very idea that people should seek to better themselves through education was in their view *the* modern disease.

One day in 1857, they visited the Librairie France, a favorite bookstore of the period, whose owner they respected as upright and independent. But they were offended to learn that his thirteen-year-old son had been sent away to school, which meant, to them, that instead of becoming an honest bookseller like his father, he would become a bureaucrat at 1800 francs a year, once his studies had been completed. Schooling was the disease that led to the modern plague of officialdom, to the creation of too many official places, and to the inevitable crash of swollen ambitions and expectations. When privilege had been abolished in 1789, competition had taken its place; and the day was not far off when every man would be able to read and every woman would play the piano. At such a moment, they concluded, pride and presumption would have entirely replaced obedience.[61] Even if we should concur that a nation of pianists was an infernal prospect, it remains difficult to discern a social conscience in such reactionary opinions. (The thirteen-year-old son, away at school, was Jacques Anatole François Thibault, whom we know as Anatole France.)

Goncourtian diatribes about the bourgeoisie, about the world of commoners in which everything of value is presumably for sale, had an occasional stain of anti-Semitism. For the brothers saw Jews as buyers and sellers, as intermediaries and procurers, producing nothing themselves. In Alsace, they remarked, not one cow can be sold without some Jew becoming involved between cow and peasant for a profit.[62] In sneering at the popular theater, Les Bouffes-Parisiens, as "the *Figaro* of theaters," the Goncourts neatly linked sensational journalism and the bogus aristocrat Villemessant (publisher of *Le Figaro*) with the librettists Hector Crémieux and Ludovic Halévy and the composer Jacques Offenbach, all three of them Jews. The equation was extended to include the duc de Morny as amateur musician and patron of Offenbach, and as chief architect of the coup d'état of 1851 (the event that consumed the broadsides announcing their first novel). A world with cheap journalism on one end, a dilettantish minister at the otheriend, and corrupt Jewish vaudevillians in the middle—"all the decadences but the great ones."[63]

Their interest in the case of Jules Mirès, a banker of Jewish origin indicted for fraud in 1861, seems not to have touched upon his innocence or guilt, but to have been simply one more example of the commercial morality of the nineteenth century. After Mirès was acquitted on appeal in 1862, they noted that his attorney, Aurélien de Sèze, bore the same name as one of Louis XVI's defense attorneys, Romain de Sèze (or Desèze), an indication that "God seems to measure the great lawsuits by the standards of the day."[64] And they were subsequently outraged to see, in the Bois de Boulogne, a carriage belonging to Mme Mirès so dazzling that they found it insolent. "Money speaks today as Louis XIV could have spoken to the Grand Dauphin."[65]

For them, the Jew was superbourgeois, the most hideous flower of a corrupt civilization. In their eagerness to attribute abnormality to Jews, they fell upon the idea that "the Jewish fixation on money" is at least in part the result of circumcision, which they believed either killed or greatly diminished sexual pleasure with women.[66]

It is a good bet that the offensive anti-Semitism in the *Journal* was more Jules's contribution than Edmond's, not only because Jules set the tone, but because late in life, he was guilty of a gaffe that revealed his dislike of Jews. In 1869, the brothers had begun to complain about the deterioration of the quality of Princess Mathilde's guests, calling them a servile claque and fearing that she might have wearied of courageous, independent men like themselves. The matter came to a head one morning before lunch as Jules listened to the princess praise Jewry in general and, in particular, Adolphe Franck, a professor at the Collège de France. Jules, who had found Franck distasteful on repeated occasions, suddenly snapped: "Well, princess, become a Jew!" Others in the room were shocked by his remark, and Jules instantly regretted having made it. On going to lunch, he drew the princess aside and apologized, expressing his great affection for her and breaking into tears as he kissed her hands. In turn, she held him close and kissed him on both cheeks, assuring him of her own affection and confessing that she, too, had been in a highly nervous state.[67]

And so, loathing so much of the nineteenth century and its creatures, a hatred shared with us through their novels, the Goncourts took refuge in the cloister of their home. In a eulogistic piece written about Jules for *La Liberté,* Paul de Saint-Victor described him as having been armed against life's illusions and lies from an early age. Art had then become his only faith—"a cult."[68] As the years went by, the brothers came to believe that, from the beginning of time, they were unexampled. Never had there been two men living as they lived, submerged in the things of the mind and in art. Books, drawings, engravings had become their entire life. They claimed no passion for scholarship, for contemplation, for an idea or a line; and political ambition was utterly foreign to them. By being submerged, they meant "to leaf through, to look at," to savor the art objects for which they had spent money unearned in contemptible enterprise. As for women, they had reduced their need for them to the simplest possible expression: "To weekly possession."[69] In fact, they reached a moment when they boasted of having very nearly substituted painting for both women and nature. "For us, anything which is not revealed as art is like raw meat."[70] The passivity of their enjoyment is as striking as its moral vacuity; and the wonder is that, in their passion for enjoyment without responsibility, they summoned the energies to produce the numerous volumes of their collaboration. It would appear that their hatreds overcame their loves, that their determination to sicken us with reality overbore their preference for inaction.

Moreover, they would have rebuffed the charge of nonmorality. They had risen above their personal cares, above life itself; they had eliminated from their lives the worries and concerns of ordinary mortals, that they might conceive and create in a free and untrammeled way and thus assume the greatest moral authority.[71] Their morality, in other words, was not that of their country or their time, but a standard binding only those who put art above all else. By such reckoning, a book well-written or a canvas well-painted was a moral piece of art, no matter that the language or subject was offensive to ordinary taste or injurious to established propriety.[72] Indeed, to outrage the bourgeoisie became a moral imperative, the good works necessary to promote mankind's salvation by art alone.

No missionary ever embarked upon a more hopeless crusade, and contempt for the heathen was the least of the guarantees of failure. For what those misanthropes hated more than people was life itself. During a discussion about life at a Magny dinner, only three of those present—the "melancholiacs," Flaubert and the Goncourts—would have asked not to have been born.[73] They noted that Buddha, a prince and a noble, had founded his religion on a disgust for life, evidence for them of a precise perception of reality.[74] They seemed unaware of the Buddha's alleged compassion for humanity. The many others whom they so regularly castigated in their *Journal* were really appalling examples of what life does to us all; a truth they recognized because of what life had done to them personally. From there, it was a mere step to place art, which they created, above life. But the prescription of physicians unable to cure themselves was bound to fall on deaf ears.

Women and Dreams

Biographers of the Goncourts have been baffled by their love life, and the confusion has been enhanced by their use in the *Journal* of the plural pronoun. Even in its unexpurgated edition, it provided only bits and pieces of information; and the frankness with which they related the affairs of others faded into obscurity when it came to the intimacies of their own lives.[75] Their views of women and marriage, however, have never been in doubt; they were repeatedly expressed in the *Journal* and in their novels, the literary works reserved for their expressions of contempt. Let us begin, therefore, with the assumption that their misogyny was *one* key to the puzzle.

Or perhaps we should say it was a key to *Jules's* love life, since the misogynous tone pervaded the pages of the *Journal* during his lifetime; and it was he who found it possible to envision Edmond happily married, though explicitly denying that possibility for himself. Edmond, approaching fifty at the time of Jules's death, did not thereafter marry; and later in the century a groundless rumor circulated to the effect that he had been impotent. Neither brother had been capable of passionate love; for Jules especially it was nothing more than a physical necessity. It is not tyranny, they noted, but passion which destroys the tree in order to enjoy its fruit; "and there is no durable liaison except with women that one does not love."[76]

In 1856, they had a curious argument with the writer Alexis-Xavier Aubryet—not about marriage, but about what kind of amorous activity is most suitable to men of letters. Should a man be primarily a man or primarily a man of letters? Aubryet supported the former position, the Goncourts the latter. In their view the proper mistress was a woman already married but on the loose, like Mme Arsène Houssaye;[77] a bordello did not provide the ideal setting. Better yet was the woman of little background or education, the woman of light heart and natural spirit, the woman who charms and pleases as does a pleasant animal. But let her be touched by a bit of art, a bit of literature, or a bit of society—let her want to talk to them of such matters on an equal footing, to become their companion in their work and life—and she was bound to become as insupportable as an out-of-tune piano, an object of annoyance.[78] Though they were not given to alcohol, they considered the bottle a superior distraction. When it is empty, it is finished. It asks neither a visit nor a memory from you, nor consideration, love, or even gratitude; and it cannot make a child for you.[79]

During the winter of 1854, when the brothers were hard at work on their study of French society during the revolution, they gave away their evening clothes and neglected to order any new ones so it would be impossible for them to accept invitations: no women, no pleasures, no distractions.[80] The claim was no doubt an exaggeration, but it was meant to illustrate their argument that any writer worthy of the name devotes himself entirely to his work, that a woman must not matter to him in any way. In their novel *Charles Demailly*, the hero can never forgive himself for having made the mistake of marriage. His wife forever advises him to lower his literary standards in the name of material benefits, forcing him into wretched and petty compromises that lead to mediocrity and meanness. The theme was reiterated in *Manette Salomon*, but sharpened by making the female agent of ruin a Jewess: Woman achieves her domination of man by making herself an accomplice of that which is basest in us all, until the day arrives when the man is deprived of his talent and his life ends in madness. Not only was celibacy advanced as the only state that guarantees the artist his brain, his conscience, his liberty, and his literary powers, but the artist was warned against domination by a mistress.[81]

Immediately after the death of their maid Rose, in 1862, the faithful Rose whom they had known since childhood, the Goncourts learned the horrifying details of affairs that had been going on under their roof, of a nymphomania that had driven her to the most sordid means to gain relief—to no avail. She had stolen from them, lied to them, and all the while successfully concealing from them the depravity of her existence. The shock of the revelations forced them to wonder if Rose's consummate genius for lying was typical of all women, whether women in general could have integrity; and, worst of all, it made them wonder whether the memories they cherished of their mother, as a woman pure of heart and entirely devoted to them, had any validity. They tried to find it in their hearts to pardon Rose, recalling the long years of her devoted service; but the incident gave their misogyny a new tone of bitterness,[82] and offered them the theme for the finest and most popular of their novels, *Germinie Lacerteux*.

André Billy confessed that he had searched the brothers' lives and the *Journal* in vain for an explanation of their misogyny, concluding that it must have been "congenital." Yet, he also correctly noted their understanding of feminine psychology, for they made psychological observations in their novels and *Journal* that were exact and penetrating. For example: "When a woman, no matter what her background, goes out to eat in a restaurant with a man, whether he is her husband or her lover, she always has herself seated to face the public and the man with his back to the public." Billy knew, moreover, that women occupied the brothers' attention in most of their novels, and that there was something quite feminine in their preoccupation with interior decoration, with dress, with knickknacks. But it was a preoccupation with the feminine rather than with women personally.[83]

One hastens to add that they both had sexual affairs, but the imprecise confidences planted in the *Journal* suggest deliberate deception. We have it from Edmond himself, just after Jules's death, that there had been some overindulgence in women in Jules's youth, but never later in his life.[84] What Edmond's measure of overindulgence was we are not told. His remark, however, contributes to the impression gained from the *Journal*, that, of the two, Jules had been the more sensual, the more ribald, the more misogynous.

Most of their mistresses are unknown to us, but Marie Lepelletier and Maria M**** were acknowledged as mistresses on the pages of the *Journal*. It is a pity we know so little of their roles in the Goncourts' lives, as the little evidence which remains provides intriguing hints of the brothers' character. Edmond claimed to have discovered Marie when he was twenty-four and she sixteen or seventeen, roughly 1846; but he did not record the incidents of the affair until 1889 and admitted that his memory was fallible. He did not remain her lover long as she passed into the arms of a friend. In about 1848, Edmond again found Marie Lepelletier, but gave her over to Jules as his first mistress. Jules, in his final year or so as a schoolboy, would have been seventeen or eighteen. He dropped her after what Edmond called a torrid passion of several weeks.[85] Marie then faded from the picture until the beginning of 1855 when Jules rediscovered her living with an Anglo-American photographer named Thompson, whose chief characteristics seem to have been hemorrhoids and a fixation on dominos.[86] Two years later, they actually visited her in Thompson's apartment and were astonished to find her quite domesticated, even aiming at marriage![87]

In 1857, we find them enjoying an unnamed mistress who made no secret of her former lovers, but they were confident that she would not play them false. For a time, she had struck them as an ideal mistress, the "femme bon garçon"; but it remains unclear whose mistress she was—and the suspicion dawns that she may have accommodated them both. She also persisted in being a woman, and that became in time a source of annoyance. She read trash, that is, the novels of Ponson du Terrail and Paul de Kock, exclaiming over their virtues and even reading aloud from them. She was mad for cards—more lower-class time-killing—confirming their belief that there could be no intellectual companionship between men and women. So convinced were they that genius is exclusively a male quality, that they believed that an autopsy of Mme de Staël or of Mme Sand would reveal "une construction un peu hermaphrodite." The true woman, they had learned, was entirely dedicated to the superficial. Even in a moment of deepest grief, a woman could not forget about her attire, her mourning dress. The tart, therefore, was only womankind exaggerated. What was insupportable, in this mistress as a woman, was not so much that she wanted to be heard, but that she insisted on being understood.[88]

In 1858, they ran across a former mistress, Maria M****. How much earlier they had known her, they did not say, but she had since become a professional midwife.[89] It would appear as if their renewed interest in her as a mistress had been at least in part excited by the desire to explore and exploit the gory treasury of her professional learning; and part of her life story, as Romaine, can be found in their novel *Soeur Philomène*.[90] It also appears that the brothers did share Maria as a mistress during her second intrusion into their lives, a remarkable expression of their brotherhood. That would seem to be the meaning of their comment that Maria had accepted their collaboration.[91] That is, they were using her for both physical and literary purposes.

Though the collapse of this enchanting triangle occurred in 1860, its unraveling was recorded in the *Journal* in paragraphs so oblique as to obscure forever what transpired. It may be that Edmond was the first to weary of the arrangement, and that he acquired a mistress for his exclusive use. In January of that year, for instance, they had noted that they were probably the only writers in the world to have published a book without telling "their mistresses" its title. Did that mean there were then two women on the scene, or was the plural merely the grammatical expression of their fraternal collectivity? In May, Jules wrote, "I am breaking with Maria, and I am enriching Monsieur Mothes."[92] Mothes was a member of the firm which produced a copaivic ointment, a medicinal oleoresin from the copaiva tree, the usual remedy for gonorrhea in that day. Are we to deduce that Maria infected Jules alone, precipitating the break? Or did the "I" mean that both brothers had been to the pharmacy? Whatever was the chronology of the collapse of the collaboration, it is clear that Maria later returned to Jules alone—in October of 1860.[93]

Marcel Thiébaut believed that a venereal infection contributed substantially to the development of the misogyny so evident in the *Journal*.[94] He referred not to the gonorrhea noted by Jules in 1860, but to an attack of syphilis ten years before. Jules had, in fact, been treated for both syphilis and gonorrhea in Le Havre in September of 1850, and he remembered that city as a sad and sinister place.[95] Unlike the diagnosis of syphilis in Baudelaire's case, the diagnosis of that local physician in Le Havre is one we can trust. His diagnosis revealed his belief that syphilis and gonorrhea were separate diseases; by now a dozen years had passed since the eminent Dr. Philippe Ricord had begun to teach their distinction.

In men as fastidious as the Goncourts, a venereal infection might well have been greeted as especially disgusting; and if they had seen women as the unique source of infection, that image could have contributed to misogyny. Thiébaut's suggestion, however, was offered as a probability, and necessarily so, as the Goncourts never described women as the carriers of disease, but characterized them as dishonest, superficial, and vacuous, forever conspiring against the genius in men. Even the remark, "I am always a bit startled to see [Dr.] Ricord in a woman's salon, in the same way that I should be startled to see a vile remedy on a woman's dressing table,"[96] was only a witticism; Ricord was infamous for sardonic humor and likely to be guilty of unseemly observations in the best of salons. He had advised rephrasing the first sentence of the Bible to read: "In the beginning, God created the heavens, the earth, man, and venereal diseases." Oliver Wendell Holmes called him "the Voltaire of pelvic literature, a skeptic as to the morality of the race in general, who would have submitted Diana to treatment with his mineral specifics and ordered a course of blue pills for the vestal virgins."[97]

However meager the amorous details in the *Journal* are, they surely convey, or were meant to convey, proof of sexual athleticism, of venereal calisthenics undertaken in a casual manner calculated to guarantee their literary independence while satisfying their physical needs. Yet, there remains a one-sentence entry in the *Journal* which provides a troublesome barrier to that image of casual, conscience-less lovemaking: "A man and a woman must have very little modesty to copulate without being drunk."[98] Since neither brother was given to drink, and since their oversensitivity was recognized especially by themselves, that one sentence must alert us to the probability that the brothers had discussed their sexual disappointments, inadequacies, or revulsions. If we can then comprehend that the philanderer, far from being the popular notion of a successful lover, is the pathetic failure in love, we shall suddenly be able to approach the source of Goncourtian misognyny, especially that of Jules, who had been an unmistakable Don Juan in his youth.

The dreams related in the *Journal* entries between 1854 and 1862 come from the period when Jules was doing the writing. In one dream he mentioned seeing Edmond, but otherwise Jules never indicated that all the dreams were his own. There is sufficient repetition of the symbols and subject matter in the dreams to suggest that they were the dreams of one person, and that the indecent language often employed to depict them should be attributed to Jules. Furthermore, the information that can be deduced from the dreams is consistent with personal information to be found in the *Journal*, and this should encourage us to accept them as having really occurred. They were not literary fabrication.

It is generally difficult to understand the symbolism of dreams unless the dreamer tells us what he thinks the dreams may mean, and Jules added very few comments that are of help. On the other hand, he took the trouble to record them, an indication that he thought they had meaning; and the personal information in the *Journal*, especially since it is in the form of dated entries, considerably facilitates analysis. Because we know, for instance, of Jules's venereal infections, and of his treatment for gonorrhea in 1860, the following becomes transparent: "I dreamt last night that a portrait of a woman in my room had the colic, and that *that* gave it to me."[99]

In August of 1854, the brothers spent a month by the sea at Sainte-Adresse, the resort adjacent to Le Havre. Rowboats were available for their recreation.[100] A dream in that setting was subsequently recorded: They were at the beach, and Jules got into a boat with Edmond. The boat had no oars, only a hook or grapnel, but it carried them along toward the open sea and the black horizon beyond. Fortunately, a hedge of trees extended into the water on their right, and the hook was long enough to enable them to grapple and make it to land. Whom should they find but Adolphe Thiers, walking along in a bizarre costume. Nearby a woman was spouting off against the government. Jules began to speak of his book to M. Thiers.[101] The first portion of the dream suggests Jules's helplessness after being deprived of his mother, and his subsequent rescue when Edmond assumed the maternal role and established the brotherhood. Since Adolphe Thiers was the most prestigious politician to oppose the policies of Napoleon III, the second part of the dream reveals the association between their first published book, the political crisis of 2 December 1851, and their subsequent hostility to the regime.

Most of Jules's recorded dreams, however, had nothing to do with politics, but are of particular interest to us as keys to the roots of his neurotic behavior and to his pessimistic view of life. Three principal motifs can be discerned: first, fixation on death, or, to be more exact, his association of birth and death, and his association of prostitution and death. Second, the grotesquerie of other people. Finally, the higher sexual pleasure to be achieved in the passive role (suggesting masochism). There is one mention of a sadistic rape.

Jules dreamed of a shipwreck, with thousands of bodies rolling and whitening in the waves. Then he found himself on board a ship where he saw long rows of corpses. Before them a woman was standing, alive and entirely nude, and he took hold of her by the breasts. Next, he was in a dining room, chatting and drinking with several friends. The night was ending, daylight breaking through the small curtains; but the dawn was indistinguishable from a twilight, "a boreal day." Many people began to run around the house in circles, seizing and breaking art objects, bringing them into the room where he sat. He remembered in particular a little Dresden figurine and some tapers that belonged to him. As there were some claymores (Scottish swords) on the walls, he took one down in a fury and struck an old man a heavy blow. The man sprouted a second head. Several women behind the old man moved into view, their heads blossoming into the grotesque masks that clowns wear. From there he moved into a large salon, feeling as if he were in a madhouse, surrounded by people whose faces were partly green. Other men and women appeared, wearing gold clothes and pointed hats. Finally he reached another salon, ornate in the style of Louis XV. "There I pressed my mouth to the mouth of a woman, and I married my tongue with her tongue. An infinite pleasure came over me, as if my entire soul rose to my lips and was breathed and taken in by this woman. A peculiar pleasure in the dream quite beyond real pleasure. Ideal coition."[102]

A year later, he saw three statues of death in a dream. One was a skeleton; the second had the body of a consumptive with a ridiculous, oversized head—the clown at the fair; and the third was a figure in black marble. All three were standing on a pedestal in a room, and in the background he could see vague human forms that seemed to be arguing and in some fear. One after the other, the three statues descended from the pedestal and sought to catch him, to take him by the arms and pull him close, "fighting over me like streetwalkers on a sidewalk."[103]

In another dream, shortly thereafter, he found himself looking for a hotel. He entered a large building, at the end of which was a conservatory, where an old woman sat surrounded by "a Decameron of frightful old men," grotesque phantoms. He apologized to the old woman for having mistaken her house for a hotel, but she assured him that the building belonged to all of the people there, and he was then introduced to them. He recited the titles of his literary works, was accepted by the group, and was taken into the dining room where each table was set in isolation, surrounded by an arbor. He could see one old man serving himself wine from a bottle labeled "Wine of 1682," in seventeenth-century script.[104]

Six years passed before Jules recorded more dreams in the same vein as those between 1854 and 1856. He dreamed of going to England with Edmond and their friend Gavarni, from whom he got separated as they went with a throng into a public garden. When he awoke from the dream, he had a vague sense that many scenes and extraordinary sensations had transpired during his sleep, but he could remember only one elaborate sequence of events. In a large room, he was lying on what seemed to be a bed, the covering for which was made of two large faces similar to the grotesque masks he had seen on clowns' huts at the fair. This figured coverlet rose in the air and fell back over him. Soon the figures dissolved into the faces of a man and a nude woman, surrounded by a large bed of flowers. Both the flowers and the couple moved about on him, and over his entire body he felt "a delicious titillation as if thousands of tongues were pecking at me." Then, in another room, narrow and high like a tower, he found himself strung up by the feet, head down, naked, suspended under some sort of glass bell. Masses of luminous sparks of a greenish color began to fall on him, smothering his skin, giving him the same sense of freshness that one gets from bathing the temples with eau de cologne. He was then thrown high in the air, experiencing the thrill of a roller coaster, "a delicious anxiety." It was as if he were passing through an initiation into a secret society, greeted with surprises that were delightful rather than fearful. The pleasure was comparable to the experience of danger when one knows beforehand of a safe outcome, a "frisson de plaisir," a paradisiacal torture. In recording the dream, Jules speculated that opium might well induce sensations identical to those in his dream; and if so, he would be very fearful of the drug, as it could make real life even more intolerable.[105]

A few weeks later, Jules was suffering from a migraine and took to his bed during the day. He dreamed that he went to see Lord Hertford, and that they talked about some Boucher sketches and about Hertford's collection of clocks. Richard Seymour-Conway, fourth Marquess of Hertford, who spent considerable time in France, possessed great properties, including the Bagatelle Park and its eighteenth-century pavilion, as well as a celebrated art collection. He worried endlessly about his inability to keep his nearly 250 clocks synchronized. He has often been confused with his brother, Lord Henry Seymour, a founder of the Jockey Club, and with his illegitimate son, Sir Richard Wallace, who embellished Paris with fountains for horses.

In the dream, Hertford was garbed as a courtier in the time of Louis XV, and Jules and he passed through a series of rooms filled with grotesquely costumed people. Finally, they reached a large amphitheater, an outdoor concert hall with a lawn. Jules could hear gusts of music and a woman singing, and he recognized the song as well as the singer, the duchesse de Berry. He found himself seated on a bench with Lord Hertford, and between them was a small woman dressed in white, so small that she was like a statuette. "I nudged her, and she looked at me with lizard-like eyes, finally saying to me,

'Don't lift my skirt.' But I was carried away and entered her passionately, while Lord Hertford kept time by slapping me gently on my bare rear."[106]

Jules's indifference to women, which is recorded in the *Journal*, his lack of respect for anything associated with women, his inability to love, his description of sex as nothing more than the mechanical union of organs, tell us that his relations with women were onanistic; and that he never experienced in life the perfect coition of his dreams, which required a passive role. It would be extreme to call him impotent, but fair to claim that he never reached sexual maturity. The rape of the statuette raises a question about several other dreams which, out of that context, might seem innocent enough. He told Paul de Saint-Victor that he had dreamed of Mlle Claire, Saint-Victor's ten-year-old daughter, a charming child who had hugged him warmly, in a gesture that reminded Jules to write to Saint-Victor.[107] In a second dream, he found himself in hell. The devil gave him permission to return to earth for ten hours. In the guise of a bat, he visited the dormitory of a boarding school for girls.[108]

It has often been noted that the absorption of the son by the mother, as was Jules's fate, leads either to physical indifference to women or to promiscuity; and, indeed, promiscuity implies a certain contempt for women. It had been Jules's misfortune—and Edmond's, too—to be reared in an atmosphere too exclusively feminine; and as adults, they would describe themselves as living together like two old women. In 1864, Jules allowed his hand to be read by the palmist Desbarolles, who saw in him not only a pronounced desire to be notable, but a female nature: a highly nervous, feminine sensibility. To which Jules responded, "That is true."[109]

The Obsession with Illness

Both Goncourt brothers enjoyed poor health, or so it would seem from their *Journal*, where they took obvious pleasure in analyzing other peoples' maladies, as well as their own, in detail. Their collaborative novels were studies of pathological states and traits. In their *Soeur Philomène* we find descriptions of hospital life; and *Charles Demailly* was transparently autobiographical in its depiction of the struggle of the man of letters against encroaching madness. This obsession with illness, as André Billy has observed, was a manifestation of their own neurasthenia;[110] and though they drew upon their own experiences and observations for their novels, they also read extensively in medical literature.[111]

In an era when conventional medicine paid little heed to emotional stresses as antecedents to physical disease, the Goncourts were prepared by their preoccupation with nerves to accept the teaching of the pioneers in what we would call psychosomatic medicine; and they acknowledged in particular the work of Dr. Joseph Moreau de Tours. Moreau knew perfectly well that since the earliest times and in most civilizations physicians have been aware that the body is greatly affected by emotional condition or state of mind; but he thought that such knowledge was too imprecise, too theoretical or general, to be utilized in the actual practice of medicine. His own research, therefore, was designed to establish direct association between specific illnesses and disturbed mental states, and he had become convinced that the association was far more frequent than was generally suspected. In fact, he aimed his medical teaching, not simply at his medical colleagues, but at all those people whose leadership in society presumably rendered them more vulnerable to emotional disorder.[112]

He claimed that the nervous system itself is fundamental in the marvelous association of mind and body, "a center of life" of which the brain alone is the center, but from which radiate the stimuli which activate each bodily organ and enable it to perform its unique function. The state of mind, therefore, is necessarily communicated to all parts of the body by way of the vast network of nerves and the spinal cord. He called the agent of that communication *nervous fluid*, describing its behavior as similar to electric current. When the current is cut off between the brain and any part of the body, that part becomes useless. A state of perfect health, in contrast, implies a perfect equilibrium in the association of all parts of the human machine; but since an equilibrium is rarely known in reality, we reveal substantial differences in sensibility and temperament.[113]

The Goncourts, sensible of their femininity and specializing in the horrors of feminine existence, could have found satisfaction in Moreau's assertion that women have innate predisposition to nervous disease, which becomes more evident after puberty because of its association with the female reproductive organs and processes. But everyone, he added, has a nervous system that is subject to the same laws of heredity as any other part of the body. Though he did not endeavor to define the mechanism of heredity, he believed that we inherit predispositions to states of mind and to physical ailments.[114]

In *Renée Mauperin*, the Goncourts give us a heroine whose fatal heart disease was foreshadowed in childhood through a tendency to emotional excesses, in this case precipitated by an abnormal grief over the death of a brother. The brothers may have been in advance of their time as to the genesis of cardiac disease, as one physician has claimed,[115] but they had borrowed freely from Moreau. And the likelihood of an abnormal grief over the death of a brother was a medical detail no one understood better than they.

In subsequent books, Dr. Moreau focused his attention more specifically on the neuroses, a new medical term used for the first time in the 1850s, and upon the inheritance of a tendency to neurosis and to madness. In the wing of the Bicêtre Hospital reserved for infant idiots, Moreau observed those cases where something was known of the parentage; for in those days idiocy meant no mental development at all after birth and was, therefore, regarded as entirely congenital in origin. His studies pointed overwhelmingly to pathological factors in the idiots' heredity. Of his fifty-six cases, insanity could be found in half the families; alcoholism was evident in one-fourth; epilepsy and hysteria had been reported in at least one-fifth; and there was evidence of a number of neurotic afflictions. What is more, his observations suggested an increase in nervous lesions as they passed from generation to generation, so that a degenerative evolution was obviously at work. Once he found insanity or epilepsy in a family, he was likely to find mere eccentricity a generation or two earlier.

It made little statistical difference whether the hereditary flaw came from the paternal or maternal side. On the other hand, his sample indicated that male children were more susceptible than female children to hereditary damage. And he challenged the traditional notion that hereditary insanity skipped generations—that is, that one is more likely to inherit from grandparents than from parents. Once emotional disease made its appearance in a family, the laws of heredity seemed to dictate an inevitable slide into neurosis, insanity, and idiocy.[116]

Moreau next set out to demonstrate that all psychological phenomena have hereditary antecedents, and he counted genius as a psychological phenomenon. He had found no evidence to support the claim of phrenology that intellectual superiority is related to the shape of the head; and he knew from postmortem examination of the brains of idiots and imbeciles that they are little different in weight from normal brains. Thus, he deduced that genius could not be a physiological phenomenon, but had to be psychological. In the second place, he detected no absolute or mechanical factors at work in heredity. Some children revealed the inherited abnormality; other children in the same family were spared. Moreover, those children who showed signs of inherited abnormality did not necessarily manifest it in the same degree or manner. Hereditary taint, in other words, did not mean predisposition to a certain abnormality, but simply to abnormality.[117]

By 1859, Dr. Moreau acknowledged an additional pathology that he had not noted in 1853: an apparent normality at birth that later degenerated into a form of idiocy initially characterized by intellectual brilliance. After a sound birth, the child reveals precocity and imagination, but is also hypersensitive, temperamental, and irritable. Parents not only sacrifice to advance such children, but *push* them, as the saying goes—only to see them grow into petulant, disoriented, hyperactive creatures, incapable of attention and given to destructive behavior. They become little maniacs, degenerating into either imbecility or idiocy.[118]

For the literati who read him avidly, Dr. Moreau had established that heredity accounts for most mental illnesses and had described one unpleasant association between intelligence and lunacy. It remained for him to specify the fate of the gifted who survived childhood, to define that association between intelligence and neurosis which gratified the unhappy few and gave them confidence that their horror of life rested on scientific foundation. "As in the case of child prodigies, those men whose brains are continually active will experience both physical and mental disorders, poor health in general, and death ultimately as merely the inevitable working out of the laws of life. The condition of nervous hyperexcitement, when it exceeds certain limits, must necessarily lead to functional disorder: to delirium and madness when the functions are of a mental nature; to spasms and convulsions when the functions involve motivity."[119]

Until madness inevitably strikes its intellectual victim, he should expect to suffer from all manner of physical and mental torments: neuralgias and nervousness, vague fears and indefinable ailments, insomnia, and anguish in the region of the heart. Moreau anticipated the argument that, if we are prone to such illness, and limit our activities, we can possibly avoid ultimate madness. His observations had taught him the impotence of free will in the majority of cases. Even if such a vulnerable individual receives wise medical advice, he will not feel free enough to exercise free will. He meant that such people are already prey to an illness that destroys the ability to make rational choices. In his view, only those who are already mad and completely alienated have a feeling of freedom. Moreau's one offer of hope to the intellectuals derived from his recognition that each intellectual's heredity is unique. Therefore, the limits of hyperactivity that the individual can tolerate will vary. What may produce ultimate madness in one, may produce only neurotic symptoms in another.[120]

Let us be clear that Moreau's views of abnormal psychology did not engender sickness in the literati. They gained from him, rather, the assurance that strength is not in muscles but in nerves,[121] that genius is necessarily a neurosis, and that excesses of sickly sensibility are the outward sign of superiority.[122] One must expect hypochondriacal behavior from men of genius. They will have a notable tendency to exaggerate everything relating to their health; they will be particularly critical of others, if remarkably self-indulgent; and they will be prone to see the worst in mankind, an outlook likely to become the focus of their studies. On the other hand, "though they may be cracked, the crack does let in light."[123] Dr. Moreau enabled the Goncourts to be convinced that their own illnesses, their neuropathy or neurasthenia, were fundamentally creative. If their visits to hospitals left them in a highly nervous state, so much the better for literature. If piecing together the appalling details of Rose's life for the story of *Germinie Lacerteux* plunged them into gloom and set their nerves on edge, so much the better for the novel.[124]

The social and political implications of Moreau's teaching, finally, were conservative and offered the Goncourts scientific underpinning for prejudices held long before they read him. Moreau was not indifferent to the benefits of education, but he feared that the nineteenth century, by following Rousseau's *Emile*, was too prone to take education for nature, to confuse the acquired with the inherited. Having demonstrated that mental disease is inherited, he denounced the ethical or environmental theories which were supposed to account for human behavior, just as he denounced the attempt to treat the alcoholic with moral suasion, on the grounds that he was on the route to insanity and predisposed to morbid activity. Moral exhortation, in other words, has no efficacy in combating mental illness. No amount of education or force can make musicians, poets, or mathematicians of children not born to become them; nor can education make lovers of virtue out of those whose hereditary flaws incline them otherwise.[125]

And so it was that the Goncourt brothers recorded their ailments and depression, not only to share their pain with posterity, but to leave us medical proof of their superiority, confident as they were that they were predisposed to the nervous abnormality that produced masterpieces and could lead to madness. Some of that evidence pointed unmistakably at Jules, especially in entries written during his later years when we read the symptoms of a fatal illness;

but on occasion the medical testimony is ambiguous, reflecting the brothers' desire to suffer in unison and to undergo identical treatment, no matter which one was genuinely ill.

A few weeks after Jules was treated in Le Havre for syphilis and gonorrhea, he apologized to his friend Louis Passy for not having answered a letter promptly, saying that he had been unwell, but neglecting to mention the nature of the ailment.[126] The following summer, approximately nine months after Jules's infection, just when the secondary lesions should have all but disappeared, both Jules and Edmond were taking a cure at the Swiss spa, Louèche-les-Bains. It seems likely that Jules sought "the lift," which was supposed to be the benefit of those particular waters, after his months of discomfort. In later years, Edmond and others were wont to mention Jules's good temper, his wit and charm, and those qualities he recovered during his cure in Switzerland. Their day began at five in the morning with a three-hour soak in waters of "Senegalese heat," followed by reading and dominos or other games. Beginning at two in the afternoon, they "marinated for another three hours, along with redominos, rereading, and reetcetera." A boring time for Jules, who feared he might emerge from the experience stupefied; and, unfortunately, neither brother was turning lobster-red, the sign that "lift" had been achieved.[127]

Between 1850 and 1857, when Jules reached the age of twenty-six, he had left the pages of the *Journal* free of medical information about himself. Even the reports of physical illness which began in 1857 were brief for the next decade and, therefore, so uninformative as to make a precise diagnosis risky. In March of that year, he experienced jaundice with intolerable stomach pains,[128] which, in conjunction with liver troubles he recorded that year, in 1858, and in 1860, might suggest a suppressed liver function.[129] Yet, the French penchant for ascribing all manner of digestive disasters to a liver attack leads us to wonder whether such a diagnosis was necessarily correct.

Depression, irritability, and bitterness, however, were more satisfactorily chronicled during those years, so that we would be surprised *not* to learn that the alimentary tract fought back on occasion. What the Goncourts did not record until 1857, however, though allegedly they had experienced such a loss from the start of their literary career, was a sense of the writer's terrible isolation or anonymity, when he so desperately seeks a public which continues to escape him. He is at war with his times, and to carry on the battle feverishly, impatiently, is "one of the great privileges of literature." And the fight is carried on alone, without friends, without family:

there is a conspiracy of silence against those who are beginning a career and who hunger to eat the cake of publicity. Even a small success would be healing and make the writer forget "the long and dreadful Golgotha."[130]

Several months later, the Goncourts attracted publicity with a scathing review by Barbey d'Aurevilly in *Le Pays* of their *Portraits intimes du XVIIIe siècle* and their *Biographie de Sophie Arnould d'après sa correspondance et ses mémoires inédits.* He called them the Sergeant Bertrands of literature (a nasty reference to a sergeant in the 74th Infantry Regiment who had been convicted in 1849 of exhuming and mutilating bodies in the Montparnasse Cemetery) and treated them in the review as the "vampires of history."[131] They initially feigned to dismiss the reviewer as an imperialist, for *Le Pays* was a newspaper favorable to the regime; but they had been painfully stung. Several days later they were debating whether the review required a duel; and having decided against that resolute solution, Jules was stricken with liver pains and feared a renewed attack of jaundice. "If only the public could know the price we pay for our little notoriety, they would pity us instead of envying us."[132]

Their bouts of depression could last indefinitely, as they were usually associated with the travails of publication. In 1859, having had a play, *La Guerre des lettres,* rejected by several producers, they converted it into a novel, *Les Hommes de lettres [Charles Demailly],* but fared no better with publishers. (They would be reduced to paying the expenses of publication to get it into print in 1860.) Everything seemed to be going sour, and Jules was "suffering from the association with others." The mere noise of words or people wounded and annoyed him. He found the maid and his mistress stupider than ever. Edmond joined him in "despair: the blackest most profound despair has seized us, to a point where we even are considering the idea of giving up being French, to begin life anew in Holland, in the free-thinking and free-speaking atmosphere of the seventeenth and eighteenth centuries."[133] They made no move toward Holland, but took their despair to the country: "A deep, desperate depression. Time seems to stop." The day before, Edmond had been seated at the end of a long table, Jules at the other end. Edmond was talking to a woman: "I heard nothing, but when he smiled at her, I smiled involuntarily and with the same inclination of the head. Never has one soul been put into two bodies to this degree."[134]

The Goncourts never sought to combat depression with alcohol; in fact, their preoccupation with poor health convinced them that they could not risk much drink, and a bottle of Bordeaux between them was rated "an excess."[135] They did, however, find solace in tobacco. A pipe after a meal, as a moment of deliberate inactivity, was cherished as a luxury; and to look at sketches through the haze of their opiated cigars was one of their greatest pleasures. They found tobacco a laudanum for the nervous system, a providence in that century of briskness, feverishness, and prodigious productivity.[136] They little recognized that they themselves, while celebrating genteel sloth, were formidable literary entrepreneurs. Twenty-five volumes were published in Jules's lifetime, that is, between 1851 and 1869. Another fifteen works on which they had collaborated appeared after Jules's death, not to speak of the material that went into the first eight volumes of the unabridged *Journal.*[137]

The humorous tone of Jules's letters had quite vanished by the time he was thirty-four, and the pessimism he had revealed about the future of the country in 1848 had expanded into grumbling about everyone and everything. Their books did not sell, their plays were rehearsed in maddening fits and starts,[138] yet they seem never to have considered fleeing the "hard life of letters" or "all the anxieties of art."[139] By 1867, even a vacation at the beach could not soothe them. They found everything in Trouville dreadful, from the people to their hotel accommodations; and Jules complained especially about the noise, which they could not escape even in their two cigar-box-sized rooms. They could hear horses in stalls beneath them, a child was cutting teeth in the room overhead, women were talking on all sides, and the sound of bells plagued them through the windows. To avoid the temptations of suicide, they plunged into work.[140]

Meanwhile, more stomach trouble, more liver trouble, their attacks coming at the same moment as gratifying proof of their extraordinary sympathy. Always in pain, at least never completely without pain, never one hour of the sound health that they saw in others. As perpetual convalescents, they found Flaubert's notable robustness an irritation to their nerves.[141]

The complaints about noise, unendurable noise, began in 1867 and became more frequent the following year. It is clear that Jules was the one afflicted (though Edmond necessarily adopted the symptoms and remedies) and that Jules's hypersensitivity to noise was the first indication that the latency of his syphilis was coming to an end. Even the noise in their own neighborhood for the first time seemed to be insupportable and was offered as the explanation for Jules's increasing inability to sleep. In May of 1868, desperately hoping for sleep, they went to the forest of Fontainebleau for a few days of quiet.[142] As a measure of his frustration, Jules dated a letter to Flaubert, *"Tuesday, I no longer know what day in May, 1868.* . . . Oh! the noise, the noise, the noise! I can no longer bear the birds, nor can Edmond either."[143]

In their search for quiet they would have to give up their apartment in the rue Saint-Georges, which they had occupied for nearly twenty years, and flee from the heart of the city. A charming cottage belonging to Jeanne de Tourbey was for sale in the Parc des Princes adjacent to the southern edge of the Bois de Boulogne; and in preparation for its purchase the Goncourts sold their farm at Breuvannes. The arrangements for the purchase having apparently been made, the brothers went off in July to take the waters at Vichy in the interest of their health.[144] But they found that life in Vichy was as flat as the water one drinks there, and were cast down upon receiving word that their cherished cottage had been sold to someone else.[145]

They soon fell upon another house, in Auteuil, the one that came to be known as "the Grenier" (the garret or loft), and they succeeded in buying it, though the price was double what they had expected to pay for Mme de Tourbey's cottage. The Grenier, at 67 boulevard Montmorency, was only a few steps from the Bois de Boulogne. Since one might expect that the Goncourts would have insisted on a house in the style of the eighteenth century, it seems important to admit that the Grenier was in the style of Louis-Philippe.[146] They moved in about mid-September with Jules plagued by pain and illness, feeling discouraged rather than elated, though by then he had cultivated a horror of Paris and did not regret the move to the suburbs. But the chores of moving had overwhelmed him and left him feeling very unsettled for several months, not to speak of his dismay at the prospect of permanent illness.[147]

In early February of 1869, the brothers had the bad fortune to be driven by an intoxicated coachman on their way to dine with the Princess Mathilde. He drove them at full tilt into a large van on the quai de Passy. They were given a terrible fright, and Jules suffered a blow on his forehead, which left no permanent mark. Edmond, however, hit his face against the cab's glass and was cut below the eye. Alarmed that the eye itself might have been punctured, they rushed to a pharmacist, who examined it and found it intact. Though badly shaken, they were able to proceed to their dinner. "Never take cab 170," Jules wrote to Flaubert.[148]

Flaubert soon complained that their letters were not very amusing, and Jules explained that it was because they were quite unable to feel droll. He identified his trouble as gastralgia, which was making a torture of his digestion and an insomnia of his nights. Edmond was suffering continually, and both of them had reached a point where they were incapable of work.[149] In fact, they had consulted with each other on the possibility that artistic overwork had at last caught up with them, that the fever or excitement of their literary efforts had led to consuming illness that would kill them.[150] Whereas all books are written with a pen, but also with an author's brain, imagination, and thought, their own books, in addition, had been written with their nerves and with their suffering. Consequently, each volume had been a loss—a nervous expenditure—an expenditure of sensibility and thought.[151] Given the impressive bibliography they had produced by 1869, the inevitable end, by their morbid reckoning, could only be close at hand.

Because of the true reason for Jules's increasing sensitivity to noise, the move to Auteuil could not have worked a cure; and we soon find him complaining that the racket around the house was making life a hell for them. Edmond joined in sharing his irritation. "Sick as we are at this moment, gastralgics, anemics, insomniacs, we are succumbing to the rack of our existence. We have come to believe that we are cursed, and that what one calls Providence has wished it upon us personally."[152] So, in June, off to Royat, the spa near Clermont-Ferrand, "the entire night writhing on the train, like a chopped worm,"[153] allegedly because of a liver attack after Jules had boarded the train. His letters dated from Royat leave no doubt that it was Jules who was ill, though both brothers underwent the cure. He found the town grim. It was rather like taking the waters at the Mazas Prison—"no casino, no music, nothing at all"—and the region a dreadful "country of savages."[154]

After a month of mineral water, mineral baths, hot and cold showers, they returned to Auteuil; and, for the first time, the handwriting in the *Journal* was Edmond's. The erasures became exceptionally numerous, a reflection, probably, of the emotional distress generated by Jules's failure to improve. Tormented by the stamping of a horse in the neighborhood and by the noise made by five children nearby, they sought refuge in the Bois de Boulogne "like some unfortunates who have no home." The same evening, they forced themselves to go to Saint-Gratien, where Jules thought he was coldly received by Princess Mathilde, "as princes do not like one to be sick." But he knew that she was preoccupied that evening by the labor unrest which threatened the regime,[155] and a few weeks later he took pains to acknowledge her gracious solicitude. They had gone to her home for dinner on a rainy evening, and she had insisted that they spend the night there because of the storm.[156] Flaubert, in the meantime, aware that all was not well, paid the brothers a call that July, which they found offensive. He was in such obvious good health, in their eyes, that it was in bad taste to exhibit it, and he was obviously indifferent to their wretchedness. "We find ourselves incapable of work, yet work has been our entire life. It takes almost heroic resolve to do even the slightest thing. Days are empty—or filled with nothing."[157]

In early August, Jules resumed the composition of the *Journal*, but an alteration in his handwriting appeared suddenly in September. His fine, minute script vanished, replaced by a heavy, square writing, with a minimum of erasures, which was quite readable; but he made relatively few entries in the *Journal* for the remainder of 1869.[158] He and Edmond paid a brief visit to Bar-sur-Seine in September and expressed their sadness at seeing, in illness, the river they had known in health. Toward the end of that month, and again in flight from noise,[159] they went to Trouville, from where Jules wrote his last known letter. He had put himself in the hands of a Dr. Helloco and was sleeping better, but now found himself assaulted by the sound of church bells.[160] After spending "the twenty worst days of our life" in Trouville, they retreated to Auteuil.[161] But as that was no escape from noise, Princess Mathilde prevailed upon them to occupy the pavillon de Catinat on her property at Saint-Gratien. They settled in just in time to be on hand for the testing of the bells that the princess had given to the local church. "The curé has them rung only ten out of every fifteen minutes!"[162]

On 14 December, they returned home to begin a regime of hydrotherapy. As the Goncourts could have had no knowledge of the tertiary stage of syphilis, and as the latest medicine had seemingly predicted nervous ailments and exhaustion for those in their profession, their decision for hydrotherapy was entirely consistent with the medical knowledge of that day. Its leading practitioner, Dr. Alfred Béni-Barde, to whom they went, directed hydrotherapy establishments in the rue Miromesnil in Paris and in the rue Boileau in Auteuil.[163] He made no claim to cure all diseases and, indeed, endeavored to distinguish between diseases that hydrotherapy could cure and those that it could merely attenuate. Organic diseases in general were declared beyond the province of his method; its greatest successes came from the treatment of nervous ailments or neuroses.[164]

When one went to a spa, it was to bathe in, or drink, mineralized waters, which reputedly possessed curative powers. Hydrotherapy, in contrast, employed ordinary water—cold water for stimulating or restorative effects; warm water for sedative or relaxing effects; but only moderately cold water in cases of nervous disorder. Water was administered in a variety of ways, including a variety of steam baths, various baths or soaks, or by shower. The shower equipment available was astonishingly complex, not only in the types of jets, but in their arrangement, which could shoot water at a patient from many or all directions, depending upon the illness. Hydrotherapy could also include postliquid treatment, either massage or exercise.[165] The Goncourts neglected to describe the hydrotherapy they received, dwelling rather upon the horror of going daily to "the little pavilion of suffering and torture" in the presence of a throng of ailing and misshapen creatures.[166]

On New Year's Day, 1870, there was nothing but "solitude and suffering," as no one paid them a call. Five days later, Jules noted that he had had a sleepless night, during which he had tried to distract himself with thoughts of his childhood; and on the tenth, when he was on the street, he was overcome by a sense of giddiness and fright, apparently induced by the confusion of the traffic.[167] His final entry in the *Journal* was dated 19 January; the collaboration had come to an end. A month passed before Edmond summoned the courage to write on alone.

Death at Thirty-Nine

Sometime in late February, the brothers were strolling in the Bois de Boulogne. Jules seemed unusually downcast, and Edmond sought to encourage him by remarking that, after all, Jules was only in his fortieth year. It might take a year or two for recovery, but there were many years ahead for book writing. To which Jules responded in a most emphatic tone: "I feel that I shall never be able to work again, never more!" The remark stunned Edmond as it recalled comments made by Jules the previous autumn, when they had been working on a book on Gavarni. At Trouville, where they had written the final chapter concerning Gavarni's death, Jules had composed the sentence, "He sleeps next to us in the Auteuil Cemetery," a sentence Edmond now realized had had a double meaning. The Goncourts, to be sure, had long believed that literary exertion led to nervous disease and then to death; but Edmond was now shocked, not merely by the fact that Jules might soon die, but by the belated recognition that he had long since given himself up as doomed.[168] In that state of dismay, Edmond resumed their *Journal* alone, perhaps as the only way he knew to cope with the impending separation.

For a brief moment thereafter, Jules proclaimed himself to be marvelously well and seemed overjoyed to be on the way to recovery, but the happy moment did not last. His depression returned; he revealed deep shame about his condition, did not want to be seen by other people, and resisted Edmond's efforts to get him out for diversion and exercise.[169] The momentary lapse at Princess Mathilde's the previous August, when his usual superb sense of tact gave way to an anti-Semitic outburst, seems to have been an early omen of his deterioration; for in March of 1870 his sense of tact and propriety began to erode. He also regressed to some of the pronunciations of his childhood, slurring the *r*, pronouncing *c* like *t*.[170] The mental deterioration was rapid. One afternoon in April, he sat facing a tree in the garden, refused to talk to anyone, pulled a straw hat down over his eyes, and was determinedly immobile for the entire afternoon. Another day, he found himself unable to spell the name Watteau, a name absolutely familiar to him.[171]

Changes in his personality were the most difficult aspect of the deterioration for Edmond to bear. Having always shown a great affection for Edmond, Jules began to exhibit "the fierce egotism of the child." He developed a mania for reading aloud from Chateaubriand's *Mémoires d'outre-tombe,* pestering Edmond from morning to night with it, requiring him to listen with interest. Certain that Jules was sliding into imbecility, Edmond became obsessed with a desire to kill him and commit suicide, but he failed to act. He continued to escort Jules on walks in the Bois de Boulogne, "among the joyous and the living," watching his aristocratic brother degenerate into animality. Jules no longer laughed or smiled, and, in his sullenness, was inclined to be contrary and indifferent to reason. His table manners also vanished, and he began to eat like a child.[172] A question had to be repeated three or four times, after which he would answer with an indifferent air.[173]

On 9 May 1870, Jules was reading aloud as usual from *Mémoires d'outre-tombe,* when he became angry because of an inability to pronounce a word correctly. A seizure caused him to stop reading, and he remained silent with his eyes fixed on the page before him. There were tears in his eyes. Edmond embraced him and tried to comfort him, but Jules could only respond with meaningless sounds. Nearly an hour passed before he could say anything but *yes* or *no,* and he seemed not to comprehend what was said to him. Suddenly, he took up his book to resume reading, immediately stumbling on the name "Cardinal Pa[cca]." He was unable to complete it and became highly agitated, to Edmond's enormous distress.[174]

Thereafter, though Jules experienced moments of lucidity, he

102

seemed reduced to a pathetic infancy, his attention occupied only with what he ate or wore. A dessert could please him; he could be happy with a new garment. But his immediate response to any question had become a *no*, "like the poor child who lives in perpetual fear of being scolded." Yet, on a day in early June when the two were seated near each other, with Jules apparently vacant and lost, Edmond said to him, "Where are you, my friend?" And he answered, "In space—empty."[175]

On the morning of 11 June, he could not recall a single title of their novels. When their cousin Edouard Lefebvre de Béhaine, Jules's childhood friend, arrived unexpectedly to invite them for lunch, Jules suddenly transformed. He not only began to talk, but recovered his memory for his books and talked of people and things out of the past. After Edmond saw their visitor to his carriage, he returned to find Jules seated in the garden, his straw hat pulled over his eyes, absolutely immobile. Edmond spoke to him. No answer. That evening they dined out. At the end of dinner, the waiter brought them finger bowls which Jules used sloppily, attracting some attention. Edmond spoke to him, somewhat impatiently, saying that he would have to be more careful or they would be unable to eat out in restaurants. "It is not my fault," Jules kept repeating, and he reached out across the tablecloth to grasp Edmond's hand and ask pardon. Both of them dissolved in tears before the astonished diners.[176]

On Thursday, 16 June, Edmond remarked that Jules seemed to be tired and was reading poorly from Chateaubriand, and suggested it might be well to take a walk in the Bois de Boulogne. Jules resisted the suggestion briefly, then gave way. But as he rose from his chair to leave the room, he tottered and fell into another chair; and Edmond carried him to his bed. In response to questions, he could only utter unintelligible sounds. When the frantic Edmond asked Jules if he recognized him, his only response was a loud, almost impertinent, laugh. In short order, however, he became calm, and a smile returned to his face. Then, without warning, he uttered such a loud, guttural cry that Edmond was obliged to close the bedroom window. Jules's face became convulsed, and the rest of his body was twisted by frightful contractions. Bloody foam oozed from his mouth. Edmond understood that the seizure was much more violent than that of 9 May; and, in this case, the initial seizure was followed by several less dramatic outbursts, each one preceded by a period of calm.

Dr. Béni-Barde was summoned, and Friday evening, the seventeenth, he frankly told Edmond that there could be no hope, that

103

Jules was finished because the brain was breaking down at the base of the cranium. Edmond hardly understood anything else the physician had to say; and, in the *Journal*, he finally confronted the appalling prospect of the coming separation. In the twenty-two years since their mother's death, the brothers had been apart only twice for as much as twenty-four hours. Could he survive alone after the loss of his other self?

Edmond shared the deathwatch with Pélagie Denis, their maid since 1868. When he relieved her at two o'clock on Sunday morning, Jules was awake despite three doses of bromide, his head rocking back and forth on the pillow, his breath coming in gasps, his attempts to speak unintelligible. At mid-morning Edmond wrote: "I curse literature. Perhaps without me he would have been a painter and could have made his name without destroying his brain."[177] According to the death certificate, Jules died at nine in the morning on Monday, 20 June 1870.[178] At nine-forty, Edmond wrote: "He has just died. His eyes have reopened with the appearance of his final suffering on his face."[179]

Edmond had known for some months that Jules despaired of recovery. On the day after the funeral, he learned from Marie, who had visited Jules several days before his violent seizure, that Jules had told her confidentially that he was incurable and that he would die.[180] On the very day of the funeral, 22 June, Edmond brooded about the cause of Jules's death, convinced that he had died from overwork on literary form, that is, from a striving for perfection of style. He recalled the many occasions in the past when Jules would work for hours without respite, rewriting, correcting, until he would be reduced to prostration and fling himself on the divan.[181] Théophile Gautier enlarged upon that thesis in his eulogy of Jules in the *Journal officiel:* Jules had died from overwork, from continual mental tension, from the neurosis given birth by the hypertension of civilized life; and against which medicine is powerless, because this modern disease is an affliction of the soul. One becomes irritable; the least noise is upsetting; and, too late, one seeks repose in the shade.[182]

Two days later, Emile Zola wrote to ask Edmond if he did not think that it had been public indifference to Jules's art which had killed him. Edmond replied from Bar-sur-Seine, where his Labille cousins had taken him, reiterating the phrases about the struggle for perfection of style that he had already confided to the *Journal*. When they were writing, they had often shut themselves indoors for three or four days at a stretch, seeing no one; but he admitted that the only proper way to produce a novel was hardly hygienic, adding that the originality of their literary work was rooted in nervous disease. Edmond believed, however, that he, himself, had been preserved by his diversions, especially his passion for collecting, which Jules did not share but tolerated out of deference. Moreover, Jules had taken no pleasure either in society or in the country, and avoided strenuous physical exercise or activity.

His mind, in other words, had been rarely diverted from literature, "and medicine sees in such a unique and fixed preoccupation the beginning of monomania." For such a person, a literary failure was exceptionally hurtful, and, thus, public indifference had contributed to his deterioration. Edmond knew of nothing else that might have promoted that decline. There had been some overindulgence in women in Jules's youth, but never later; he never drank a glass of liqueur, and his only excess had been his use of tobacco. All literary men, Edmond concluded, should take seriously Dr. Béni-Barde's assertion that "ten years of overindulgence in women, ten years of excessive drinking, will wreck a man less than one hour, one single hour, of mental excitement."[183]

André Billy has doubted the ingenuousness of Edmond's explanations. Had he not seen the entry of 2 August 1864 in the *Journal* where Jules confessed his syphilitic infection of 1850?[184] We must suppose that Edmond did, indeed, know the facts of Jules's venereal history; but in 1870 he could have had no knowledge of the tertiary stage of syphilis, no reason to associate an infection in 1850 with the dreadful destruction of Jules's brain in 1870. We can be confident that Edmond, as well as Gautier and Zola, had been perfectly sincere in attributing Jules's death to the eternal tension of his profession, as they were supported by the latest medical wisdom. Later in the century, it was accepted as gospel by other writers that the Goncourt literature had been infused with anxiety and morbidity of a pathological origin, that the brothers had cultivated neurosis as an illness of distinction, and that Jules had died of literary work.[185]

Even those physicians who took a historical interest in the case over thirty years after Jules's death differed as to its cause. A neurologist named Gélineau, who knew of Edmond's letter to Zola, and who had studied the limited medical information available in the censored edition of the *Journal*, thought that neurasthenia had been the key to Jules's demise. Neurasthenia, an archaism, meant an intense and lasting fatigue accompanied by mental depression. Gélineau thought it had been induced by frantic overwork, which had led to the exhaustion of both mind and body, to immobility and forgetfulness. Gélineau explained that Jules's ardent existence had exhausted his supply of phosphates, and had thus resulted in an insufficiency of red corpuscles. This, in turn, meant that the nervous centers had been inadequately flushed out and could not avoid misdirecting the body. Neurasthenia was the apparent result. Gélineau believed that both brothers had been predisposed by heredity to excessive nervousness, but that Edmond—the more vigorous and better built—was more able to resist the tendency to exhaustion. Finally, Gélineau saw in the alteration of Jules's temper and character the prodromes of general paralysis,[186] presumably the result of the neurasthenia.

A Dr. Scherb in Algiers, having read Gélineau's diagnosis, agreed that Jules had been the victim of a progressive general paralysis, but challenged the notion that neurasthenia had been its cause, no matter how neurotic Jules may have been. In other words, he sought the cause in an infection, in a meningoencephalitis (or inflammation of the brain and its membranes), which eventually would have led to general paralysis. Although his suggestion was certainly more medically sophisticated, Scherb was still a man of the nineteenth century, as he suspected that sensitive and productive writers were predisposed to the development of a variety of toxic infections and to the ravages of alcohol and drugs.[187]

The term *general paralysis of the insane* had been current in the early nineteenth century, until more precise observation of such cases suggested that it was misleading. That is, the paralysis was thought to always precede the alienation rather than being a consequence of insanity. In 1846, Dr. Achille-Pierre Requin proposed to rename the malady "progressive general paralysis," but physicians continued to debate the accuracy of the nomenclature because of a disagreement as to whether the general paralysis invariably led to madness. Or, to put it another way, was general paralysis *a malady* or merely the manifestation of a variety of diseases? Was it the result of mental illness (as Dr. Gélineau still believed in 1901), or the result of an infection (as Dr. Scherb asserted in 1901)? One of the characteristics of general paralysis that muddled the issue for nineteenth-century medicine was the irregularity of its development and symptoms, the irregular duration and intensity of its various phenomena. On the other hand, because general paralysis also exhibited some regular phenomena, some physicians were confident that the day would come when one fundamental cause of the disease would be discovered. A difficulty with words, for example, was an invariable early manifestation of the disease; it progressed slowly, not coming on suddenly like a cerebral hemorrhage, or progressing rapidly as in meningitis; and it was invariably a terminal illness.[188]

In 1894, the eminent syphilologist Dr. Alfred Fournier, after over a decade of study, sent a communication to the Académie de médecine to propose that syphilis was responsible for general paralysis. Fournier had noticed that general paralysis was rarely found in women, but when it was, the women were likely to have been prostitutes or courtesans. In the rural regions of France, he had rarely known of a case of general paralysis in a Quaker or in a secular or regular clergyman. In contrast, his observations had shown a remarkable frequency of prior syphilitic infection in cases of general paralysis when compared to other forms of madness.[189] By 1894, in other words, Fournier's clinical knowledge of syphilis was nearly complete, despite the absence of the laboratory tests that would not become available until after 1913, when general paralysis (or paresis) was established as a late manifestation of the disease.

Between 1894 and 1913, therefore, French medicine could only debate the probability of syphilis as the origin of general paralysis; and, as for Jules's case, there was no proof at that time that he had been syphilitic. With those handicaps, Dr. Pierre-Yves Even restudied the case in 1908 and agreed with his medical predecessors that at the time of his death Jules showed definite signs of general paralysis, but denied that the disease had reached its fatal stage. As for the causes of general paralysis, Dr. Even listed overwork, prolonged extreme emotion, alcoholism, and possibly syphilis. He was aware that it was, in fact, unknown whether Jules had had syphilis. In any event he believed that the violent seizure Jules had experienced on 16 June was an apoplectic stroke, which he called the immediate cause of death. The difficulty that Jules had experienced with breathing the day before he died suggested a pulmonary complication to Dr. Even, probably bronchial pneumonia.[190]

Dr. Paul Duplessis de Pouzilhac gave a curious twist to the case in 1910 by seeing veiled references to drug addiction in the *Journal*. Edmond had admitted that Jules had used tobacco excessively; and Dr. Duplessis, picking up the reference to opiated cigars in the *Journal* of 15 January 1865, proposed that, when Jules worked himself into a state of exhaustion and threw himself on a divan to find relief in smoking, he had customarily found it in opiated tobacco. Duplessis noted, furthermore, that hyperacuity, or extreme sensitivity to noise, is a frequent characteristic of drug abusers.[191] The thesis would be tenable if additional evidence of drug abuse could be found. Instead, we have Jules's remark that he would fear the alleged paradisiac effects of opium as making reality even more insupportable;[192] none of the brothers' contemporaries described them as intoxicated from any source; and the very volume of their literary productivity surely suggests an abstemious regime.

What is more, thanks to Edmond's painful compulsion to set down the details of Jules's final weeks, the nature of Jules's fatal illness is absolutely clear: its etiology (syphilis) was established in 1913; and proof that Jules had been syphilitic was published in 1957. The tertiary stage of syphilis manifests itself variously, but in Jules's case it was clearly neurosyphilis. The affliction has been called general paralysis of the insane, dementia paralytica, or syphilis of the brain; now it is most commonly called paresis. The more descriptive term is parenchymatous cerebral neurosyphilis.

We noted earlier that approximately one-third of the untreated cases of syphilis which reach the latency stage will ultimately develop the destructive lesions of late syphilis. It remains a mystery as to why the remaining two-thirds seem invulnerable, though it is known that tertiary syphilis is commoner in men than in women, and in whites than in the colored. Some suspect that late syphilis especially attacks the sedentary, those who use their brains.[193] If that suspicion should ever be verified, it would indicate that Edmond had been at least partially right in attributing Jules's death to intellectual overwork.

Tertiary syphilis virtually always appears ten or more years after the initial infection. The process is inflammatory and degenerative, chiefly a meningoencephalitis, which, if untreated as in Jules's case, grows progressively worse and ends in death. Its onset is revealed by mild personality changes which will gradually move toward psychosis. The victim becomes irritable; his memory and judgment are increasingly poor; he is subject to headaches and insomnia; and, as his behavior deteriorates, he becomes slovenly. There may be outbursts of aggression and moments of excitement, confusion, and delusion, especially alternate manic and depressive states—all evidences of the drift into psychosis. The patient will be prone to fainting spells or generalized epileptiform convulsions, as in Jules's case (which were erroneously diagnosed as strokes by several prior investigators); and he may seem to be suffering from a psychoneurosis. In fact, there has been severe damage to the cortex. As the mental power disintegrates, the victim is unable to concentrate, and his speech becomes slurred. He becomes, in other words, increasingly infantile; and, if he lives long enough, he will become incontinent and emaciated. The tertiary stage can last from a few months to as much as five years, and it ends in death.[194]

Jules evidently died before reaching emaciation, and, unlike most victims of paresis, he was quite aware of his decline. On the other hand, most victims of paresis have not spent a lifetime feeding on their nerves and anticipating—as a result of literary effort—an inevitable degeneration into imbecility. It may well be, therefore, that he could offer little resistance to the course of his appalling disease. In fact, death came to him in the cruel manner that only a man of his outlook would have anticipated, a death verifying his horror of life, a death confirming his belief that it would have been better not to have been born. The most critical disease in the life of Jules de Goncourt was not the syphilis which destroyed him at thirty-nine, but the neurosis hatched in his youth, the neurosis which left him an emotional cripple for the entirety of his abbreviated adulthood. By rationalizing that sickness into an enviable condition, he fashioned a measure by which health was plebeian and contemptible; or, as he would more likely have said, bourgeois. His novels written with Edmond were flowers of illness meant to sicken us with reality, in the hope that we might come to share the horror of life that could make paralytics of us all.

Gustave Flaubert by Mulnier. Arch. Photo. Paris.

Gustave Flaubert

She had had her love story, like everyone else.

Flaubert, *A Simple Heart*

FRENCH CRITICS AND WRITERS KNOW THE TERM *le bovarysme*, ALTHOUGH it has never been precisely defined for common usage. It reminds us at once of Flaubert's *Madame Bovary*, and yet, in fact, the term describes the pessimism about life that Flaubert wove into all his novels. At the root of that pessimism was Flaubert's conviction that we are all determined to see ourselves other than as we really are; and, consequently, to aspire to that which is not only unattainable, but which will bring us to ruin. The term implies a hatred for reality, which we seek to escape through the exercise of romantic imagination, the quest ending inevitably in grief.[1] *Le bovarysme* did not perish with Flaubert. We all know Emma Bovary, who slew herself at such length in Flaubert's novel, for she reappeared unhappily married to a country doctor, no longer in a dismal Norman town, but living on a hateful main street in what the French call *le corn belt*.

The brutal, if unmentioned, truth about *le bovarysme* is that it characterized Flaubert's hatred for life. Contrary to the logical assumption that so profound a pessimism could derive only from long years of bitter experience, Flaubert's biographers agree that his despondence was acquired early in life. Their debate has focused upon which morbid aspect of his childhood should be held primarily responsible for the desolation he felt. It is painful to realize that this most wonderful writer, whose literary craftsmanship remains one of the astounding achievements of his century, should have brought to that craft the mental equipment of a catastrophic youth, which he never outgrew. The themes, the anxieties, the issues of his youthful prose were, thus, reiterated in more sophisticated form in his later works. Indeed, he never permitted his early writing to be published, since he drew on it—as the record of his own experience—for his later books and stories.[2]

Flaubert's father, Dr. Achille-Cléophas Flaubert, was chief surgeon and director of the Hôtel-Dieu in Rouen when Flaubert was born late in 1821. As the family apartment was within the hospital, Flaubert spent his childhood in a place of suffering and death. He would claim

111

that the locale had failed to harden him, that he had remained throughout his life easily touched by the sight of physical pain, as his father had been.[3] Be that as it may, a letter he wrote at age fifteen requires us to believe that the sights of his childhood, when he played in the dissecting room, deeply influenced his sensibility and contributed to a premature pessimism about life. In this letter, where he expressed a youthful contempt for civilization and life, he remarked that "even the most beautiful woman is hardly beautiful on the dissecting table with guts on her nose, a leg with the skin pulled off, and half of a dead cigar resting between the toes of her foot."[4]

Dr. Flaubert, born in the province of Champagne in 1784, had not married until he completed his medical thesis in 1810. Mme Flaubert, born Anne-Justine Caroline Fleuriot in 1794, was from Pont-l'Evêque in Normandy. Their eldest son, Achille, born in 1813, lived to become a physician and, thus, earned his father's favor. Thereafter, two children were born who died in infancy. After Gustave, the fourthborn, came another son, who survived only six months; and, finally, Caroline was born in 1824. The infant mortality in the family, if shocking, was quite normal for that day; and the frequent explanation that Dr. Flaubert had been syphilitic is quite without foundation. What is more, the family lived in a hospital in a time when the most elementary prophylatic measures were unknown and when those ill with contagious diseases were not isolated.[5]

The nine years that separated Gustave from his older brother were unbridgeable for children, and they contributed to Gustave's alienation from the male members of the family. Instead, he had Caroline, who idolized him to a point where he became dependent upon her. It was once quite logically believed that Flaubert was denied a medical education because of his father's need to preserve his practice for his elder son. The second son, consequently, was marked for law. It now appears that differences in temperament between father and son produced conflict between them and marked Gustave for a world different from his father's. And that world, from beginning to end, was infused with his mother's spirit.

We ought to be struck by the fact that Flaubert's biographers give us portraits of Dr. Flaubert that are more clearly drawn than those they can provide of his wife. Yet he died in 1846, before Flaubert came to the attention of the literary world, whereas Mme Flaubert survived until 1872, living with Gustave when he became a personage and regularly serving as a topic in his letters. Both parents had known financial well-being before their marriage; and Dr. Flaubert, whose father had been a veterinarian, was financially successful in medicine and bought considerable property. Mme Flaubert brought a good dowry to the marriage and later came into a substantial inheritance. Flaubert, who knew his father to be successful, recognized him as a dedicated physician whose students revered, admired, and respected him; yet he also knew at an early age that a gulf separated them. To the son, such awareness amounted to a confession of deficiency.

Perhaps it was inevitable that a wife should have been overshadowed by a man so respected in the world of Rouen, but we should refrain from the easy assumption that such a woman is thereby cowed into a mean and mindless housewifery. There remains good evidence that Mme Flaubert was a willful woman, well-schooled in the art of getting her own way. The migraines and insomnias she experienced had a way of lessening when she accomplished a goal previously denied her.[6] Her tactics may seem to have been ignoble, especially with medical knight-errantry as the backdrop; life may have been cruel to her, as it can be to us all. But, to the degree that her character would allow it, she enjoyed her successes, among which must be counted the devotion of her son Gustave, who never married.

As we shall see, it would be superficial to conclude that Gustave Flaubert was ambivalent about his father and totally devoted to his mother; but no one would deny that he lived a difficult childhood in the gloomy atmosphere of the Hôtel-Dieu, that he became withdrawn, given to reading and living in fantasies, which formed his theatrical and literary bent. He later told a mistress that, as a child, he had delighted in imitating other people, in playing their roles, that he was by nature a showman, a clown, to a point where his father had endeavored to check such behavior as likely to get him into trouble.[7] He also confessed that he had been cowardly, fearful of the dark, unable to climb ladders, and that in his teens he had deliberately set out to become brave by slipping out to roam the courtyards at night and by climbing into church towers to walk on the balustrades—risking his neck.[8]

He had few friends, but offered them the excessive devotion that is characteristic of children uncomfortable at home. His earliest intimate was Ernest Chevalier, who was a year in advance of Flaubert at the Collège Royal of Rouen and the nephew of a man named Mignot (Flaubert called him "Le père Mignot") who encouraged the development of literary sensibility in both boys. It is regrettable that Chevalier, who became a magistrate loyal to the Second Empire, saw fit to destroy a portion of Flaubert's letters to him on the grounds that they were unseemly, for that is what he meant when reporting that they had unfortunately been lost.[9]

The more influential of Flaubert's youthful friends, however, was Alfred Le Poittevin, who was five years his senior. Alfred's father, Paul Le Poittevin, who owned cotton-spinning mills in Caux (the region around Le Havre), was a great friend of Dr. Flaubert's. Not only were the Flaubert and Le Poittevin families closely linked for several generations, but the Le Poittevins made two marriages into the Maupassant family, which will account for the later tie between Flaubert and Maupassant. Of the little group which included Gustave and Caroline Flaubert, Ernest Chevalier, and Alfred and Laure Le Poittevin, Alfred was the eldest and the leader. They formed a little stage company for which Flaubert did the writing. Alfred was apparently a seriously neurotic youth, sensitive to a point of frailty and decadence, convinced of the futility of life and antagonistic to conventional society. His association with Flaubert may have nourished Flaubert's juvenile literary ambitions, but his outlook was poisonous to a child already grappling with his unhappiness. Flaubert would turn out to have the courage of Le Poittevin's convictions, Le Poittevin (and Ernest Chevalier) would proceed to respectability through the successful study of law, and Le Poittevin would end up committing that ultimate act of bourgeois conventionality—marriage.[10]

We get a fair picture of Flaubert's juvenile attitude from the theme of a short story, *The Carthusian Monk*, which he wrote as a schoolboy, though its precise date is uncertain. He gives us an unhappy monk who is obsessed with the desire to possess a ring that had just been buried with a deceased monk. Everyone in the monastery knew that the ring was a memento of the happiness and love which the deceased monk had known in his youth, and the unhappy monk was convinced that possessing it would bring him love. In the dead of night, he crept into the crypt, opened the coffin, and removed the ring from the corpse's finger. But, in hastily renailing the coffin shut, he inadvertently nailed down the hem of his robe. This caused him to fall as he turned to leave, and he cracked his skull on the floor. Several years later, when the monks reentered the crypt for the burial of another brother, they found a skeleton with a ring on its finger. Flaubert then spelled out the moral of his story: The monk had wanted the ring in order to possess life. But he *had* lived, for to dream, to fear, to wait, to be consumed by agony, *is* living. For him, as for most of us, riches were in the grave, and his hopes were smothered in his shroud.[11]

Historians have long since recognized the fashionable pessimism which afflicted the sensitive for several generations after Napoleon's fall, when grandeur had been brought down and pettiness presumably restored. But even if one accepts that climate as contributory to youthful pessimism, it cannot have been entirely responsible for the black pessimism that engulfed Le Poittevin or Flaubert, or life could not have gone on. Alfred Le Poittevin, who would die at thirty-two, was a pathological case for the entirety of his brief life. The disgust for life he had represented to those in his circle reappeared in the nephew he never saw, in Guy de Maupassant.

In 1838, Flaubert completed his *Memoirs of a Madman*, the record of his first sixteen years. It included his recollection of two dreams of his childhood which had terrified him, and he related them to his unhappiness as a schoolboy when he would lie awake at night, often weeping until he would drift off into tormented sleep. In the first dream, he saw himself asleep in his father's house on a winter night, the snow reflecting whiteness into the bedroom. Suddenly, the snow melted, and the trees and grass took on a scorched, ruddy hue, as if a fire were lighting up the windows. He heard steps—someone coming up the stairs—when he was engulfed by hot air and a fetid odor. The door swung open, and seven or eight creatures entered the room. Some were tall, some short, but each one wore a heavy black beard and carried a steel blade between its teeth. They stared at him with large, fixed, but pupilless, eyes. He returned the stares, but could make neither a cry nor a movement. The house seemed to shudder, as if a lever had been pushed beneath it. After staring at him at length, each monster turned aside to reveal a face stripped of skin and oozing blood. They handled his clothing, leaving it bloodstained. They began to eat, and when they broke off pieces of bread, blood dripped to the floor. Their laughter sounded like a death rattle. Once they had departed, everything they had touched had been reddened, and the poor child was revolted, believing that he had eaten human flesh.[12]

In the second dream, Flaubert, as a child, walked with his mother along a river, which flowed through a green and flowering countryside. The mother fell into the water. He saw the water bubble, the circles enlarge and disappear, the river then resuming its normal course. He found he could no longer hear the water as it flowed through the reeds and made the rushes bend. Suddenly, his mother called out to him: "Help! my poor child, help me!" He stretched out flat on his belly on the riverbank to look into the water, but could see nothing as the cries continued: "I am drowning! I am drowning! help me!'' But the water flowed on, and the voice he heard from the depths of the river shattered him with despair and fury.[13]

The Freudian analyst, Theodor Reik, linked the two dreams in the *Memoirs of a Madman*, first published in 1910, to the neurotic patterns he had found in Flaubert's novels, especially in the *Temptation of Saint-Anthony*. For this orthodox Freudian, the dreams were complementary in that one reflected the father as the first object of a child's hate, whereas the other reflected the mother as the first object of the child's love. The frightful setting for the first dream, in Reik's opinion, was the operating table with the infant Flaubert as patient-victim. The surgeon-father, with his surgical tools, was threatening to punish the son for masturbation by snipping off his genitalia. Reik saw the second dream as the expression, and frustration, of the son's desire for sexual relations with his mother. The dreamer wished to rescue the drowning woman, that is, to make her a child, and believed that she was receptive to being rescued. But moral restraint kept him from plunging into the waters, the life-giving waters. The dreams also implied the desire of the son to kill the father.[14]

More recently, Jean-Paul Sartre came to comparable conclusions, though he ignored Freudian analysis and terminology. He argued that Flaubert developed a serious inferiority complex in regard to his father and brother and that he created, even as a child, a fantasy world in which his superior talents would be recognized. His aversion to the male members of the family led to emotional illness, which Sartre claimed amounted to asserting a desire for parricide, a desire of which Flaubert was perfectly aware.[15] However, in Flaubert's recently discovered *Intimate Notebook 1840–1841*, written before the appearance of his nervous troubles, we find the sentence: "I have loved only one man as a friend [Alfred Le Poittevin], and only one other, my father."[16] That does not have a ring of murderous intent.

Even if we prefer to ignore these interpretations characteristic of various schools of psychoanalysis, Flaubert's two dreams serve to reinforce the more conventional evidence of a difficult childhood; and it is pointless to quibble over whether the bed in the first dream was an operating table or a dissecting table, since we are informed, in either case, that the Hôtel-Dieu of Rouen was not the best of all possible nurseries for an acutely sensitive child. The dreams tell us, moreover, that Flaubert sensed very early that he was an anomaly in the family, remote from the two doctors and fearful that he could not reach his mother.[17] The inferiority complex, Sartre's term, does not adequately express the loneliness that Flaubert felt as a child, or its crippling effects on his outlook ever after. Forty years later, a visit to the Hôtel-Dieu of Rouen could plunge him into depression and upset his stomach, and the sight of his childhood home aroused his bitterness,[18] for it had been the seedbed of *le bovarysme*.

In the summer of 1836, when Flaubert would have been fourteen and a half, the family took its vacation at Trouville. On the beach one day he caught sight of a young and beautiful woman, who was evidently married—as she had a child with her—and he was overwhelmed, in love for the first time. Each day he returned to the beach to watch her from afar, and he learned that she was called Mme Maurice Schlésinger. We cannot know what Elisa Schlésinger, then twenty-six, thought of Flaubert's infatuation, which must have been evident even though he said not a word of it to her; but he thought he would die from being deprived of her love, and avowed that the unrequited passion had lasted until he was twenty.[19] In the meantime, at age sixteen, he undertook the description of his love in the *Memoirs of a Madman*. Convinced as he was of "the grotesquery of existence," he saw this most sublime sensation of love as the most ridiculous of all stupidities. Not only did it combine torment with joy, but it could lead the would-be lovers into that "grotesque coupling" which results in the production of one more imbecile on this earth, another unfortunate being doomed to imitate his progenitors.[20]

Flaubert's early disenchantment with love, however, did not merely mirror the torment of his unrequited passion for Elisa Schlésinger. At fifteen or sixteen (the date is uncertain, but before he began his *Memoirs of a Madman*), he had sought relief in the arms of a prostitute and had found the experience a disappointment. He tells us that he had been ridiculed for his chastity (by Alfred Le Poittevin?) to a point of embarrassment and shame, but that he had left his first encounter full of disgust and bitterness, as he had profaned his love for Mme Schlésinger.[21] We know that he would return to prostitutes from time to time to satisfy animal needs with a love that gave him no pleasure. Molière was right, he had concluded: a woman is to be compared to a soup. Many will taste of her and get their mouths burned.[22]

And so, at the age when others marry or make love without a qualm, he found himself "alone and naked," hopeless about the future, bereft of the aspirations of his childhood, unable to love anything at all, "a broken branch unable to bear fruit." On the other hand, he was aware that his disillusionment with life had not suddenly blossomed with his failures in love. He found in himself an unnatural aversion to other people and remembered that the first stirring of that distaste surfaced when, at the age of ten, he began to experience the cruel society of children at school. The taste for solitude, originally generated by his loneliness at home, served as his refuge at school; and he believed himself to have been despised, as a dreamer, by his teachers and classmates. The alienation had been profoundly tedious. He had become an outsider, what he called "a madman";[23] and the only moments of his previous sixteen years when he could recall not having been wearied had been the time spent with Alfred Le Poittevin.[24] What good had love done that poor imbecile Abélard beyond costing him "one of his testicles?"[25] All very sad and, one may say, very typical of the precocious adolescent; but the trouble is that the despair never faded with age.

We would think that most aspiring authors, no matter the tedium or agony of their origins, would anticipate success and glory, perhaps fortune with fame, as the necessary aftermath of their literary labors; but not Flaubert! He anticipated that his works would never be prizewinners, and that mothers would forbid their daughters to read his books. Indeed, he wondered if he had been wounded beyond repair, and if there would be no fame, no great works of any sort, no love.[26] In that frame of mind, he read a biographical article on the marquis de Sade, and asked Ernest Chevalier, gone to Paris to study law, to send him any of Sade's novels available, as they would be worth their weight in gold to him.[27]

The cherished object of Flaubert's thwarted love, Elisa Schlésinger, who haunted his literary imagination ever after, had been born Elisa Foucault. Though Flaubert would see her on occasion later in life, he evidently had no inkling of her own sad story, which was finally tracked down by Emile Gérard-Gailly and published in 1930. She had been married on 23 November 1829, at the age of nineteen, to a second lieutenant named Emile-Jacques Judée, who was then thirty-three. The marriage did not succeed, for reasons unknown. As divorce was then impossible, Judée simply left her for a military career in Africa and never reclaimed her. It may be, as some have surmised, that he "sold" his interest in her to Maurice Schlésinger, perhaps to clear up debts, for thereafter Schlésinger lived openly with Elisa as man and wife, though he kept her secret. On the other hand, he took advantage of her irregular position to have affairs with many other women, which she could not openly protest. A child, Marie-Adèle, the infant Flaubert would have seen on the beach at Trouville, was born to them on 19 April 1836. Judée died on 1 November 1839, and after the ten months required by law had passed, Schlésinger married Elisa on 5 September 1840. Subsequent financial difficulties forced the couple to leave France for Baden, where poor Elisa, burdened by the guilt of her premarital past, but loyal to Schlésinger for having legitimized her situation, began to experience emotional disorders. In 1862, she was committed temporarily to an asylum, and sometime after 1870 she took up permanent residence in an asylum in Illenau, where she died insane in 1888. Some literary critics have pointed to cryptic references in Flaubert's later letters as evidence that Elisa at some point did become his mistress, but the case is far from proven and such a liaison would seem most unlikely.[28]

In the summer of 1840, when Flaubert was eighteen, he was preparing for the examinations for the baccalaureate degree, which he received on 23 August, and also looked forward with considerable reservation to a trip to the south of France with Dr. Jules-Germain Cloquet; this was to be his graduation present. Dr. Cloquet, then fifty, was an old friend of Dr. Flaubert, a man of "excellent character and temper," as Gustave admitted, but not his choice for a traveling companion.[29] In the meantime, Flaubert had begun what we know as his *Intimate Notebook 1840–1841*. Though many of his entries in this journal were undated, it is possible to deduce which entries were written before, and which after, the trip to the south. Moreover, the tone of self-pity in the journal anticipated the tone in Flaubert's first novel, *November*, which he would complete in the autumn of 1842.

In the journal, he dreamed of lengthy embraces, intoxicating glances, and the sweet words that, given his age, should have been his long since: "I have such need of a mistress, of an angel!" But from his amorous wretchedness, he could suddenly switch to a paragraph on asceticism: "I would love to be a mystic.... The life of a saint is glorious, I should have liked a martyr's death; and if there is a God, a good God, a God who is the father of Jesus, let him send me His grace, His spirit, and I will accept it and prostrate myself. I well understand that people who fast regale themselves with their hunger and enjoy their privations. It is a much more refined sensualism than the other kind; these are pleasures, thrills, raptures of the heart."[30]

Thus, while the young Flaubert was yearning for love, for glorious nights and glorious hours, he also clearly understood the sensual, but masochistic, pleasure of martyrdom and defined that pleasure as "pleased with itself." He meant that sensual pleasure is exceptionally intense, because the subject and the object are the same; whereas love is a poorer thing, because it requires sharing. "Sensual pleasure is selfish and deliberate and serious. Such pleasures carried to the extreme are like orgasms of self-abuse, their self-contemplation and self-enjoyment are a kind of onanism of the heart."[31] He had come to believe, moreover, that everything the marquis de Sade had written was true, because he could not resist Sade's hypothesis of "limitless mastery and magnificent power," that is, the satisfaction felt by victims in surrendering to their tormentors, or perhaps the satisfaction felt by the tormentors when the victims surrender—but probably the former.[32] Such admissions by Flaubert at eighteen informed us that his despair about success in love cannot be blamed on the fact that Elisa Schlésinger had turned her back on him.

For Flaubert, the most memorable moment in the trip to the south with Dr. Cloquet was an encounter with a woman of about thirty-five, the fictionalized account of which Flaubert gives us in *November*. Having been in Provence and in the Pyrenees, the travelers reached Marseille, on their way to Corsica, on 29 September 1840.[33] They stopped in a small hotel. Returning from a swim in the sea, Flaubert, who was handsome and athletic in appearance as a late adolescent,[34] attracted the attention of the older woman and blew her a kiss. She came to his hotel room that night and introduced him to "an orgy of delights."[35] Her name was Eulalie Foucaud de Lenglade, and she was one of a party of women passing through Marseille, on the way home from a trip to Peru.[36] Flaubert's boastful account of the incident twenty years later omitted its unhappy aspects, which he more honestly confessed in *November*. We are given, it is true, a lengthy seduction scene ending in a divine coupling, a scene in which the woman is the accomplished lover and takes the lead. But afterward, the young man is overcome by sadness, feeling sated, weary, and full of disgust. There were subsequent letters between the two, but they never again met.[37] It seems likely that the sexual testimony also reflected Flaubert's prior disappointment with prostitutes, which contributed to the deep depression revealed in the novel. He would later claim that, between the ages of twenty and twenty-four, he had deliberately abstained from sexual relations.[38] Whether he remained absolutely faithful to that decision is less notable than the distress that led to the decision.

It had been expected that Flaubert would follow Alfred Le Poittevin and Ernest Chevalier to law school at the beginning of 1841, but he was somehow able to postpone for a year the career for which he had no taste. Asked what his hopes and plans for the future were, he answered that he had none, saying that he had adopted the old maxim, "Conceal your life and habits."[39] For the first time, he revealed a distaste for women, calling the whole species stupid, a coarse animal that men have mistakenly converted into a high ideal.[40] His emerging hostility, however, went quite beyond misogyny to encompass all mankind, who he believed existed primarily to suffer. He had grown to expect every possible evil from men and held that a woman's virtue is made possible by her "indifference, coldness, and vanity." In fact, at nineteen, he had reached the conclusion that art is superior to everything else.[41]

It should come as no surprise, therefore, that the youthful Flaubert was no democrat. His journal entries in 1841 go far to explain his behavior later on: his fundamental indifference to social or political engagement, an indifference rooted in self-pity and the need to put art above life. His maxims were painfully clear: "The future of humanity, the rights of the people—so much silly nonsense. . . . I often wish I could cut off the heads of people on the street whose faces I do not like. . . . I love to see humanity humbled. That spectacle cheers me when I am tired."[42] At the end of that year, when he knew that the dreaded law school was hard upon him, he proposed to spend New Year's Day quite alone; he would make no social calls, even though he would be criticized, for his guiding maxim was now somewhat altered: "Conceal your life and withdraw." He would leave the streets to the bourgeois, all decked out for the great occasion.[43] At nineteen, he had become Gustavus Flaubertus, Bourgeoisophobus, though only later on did he assume the title.[44]

Early in 1842, shortly after Flaubert's twentieth birthday, he at last began reading law, which meant taking rooms in Paris. His premonitions about total boredom were necessarily realized, as he found the subject intolerable and incomprehensible. "I see nothing more stupid than the Law, unless it is the study of the Law." The prospect of a legal career horrified him.[45] He did call on the Schlésingers occasionally,[46] which would suggest a determination, conscious or otherwise, to augment his unhappiness. After taking his first examinations in August, he fled to Trouville in September for a vacation with the family.

Some years later, Flaubert would confess that he had experienced, during his law studies, a strong desire to castrate himself, and that he had subsequently abstained from women for several years.[47] That masochistic urge has been logically associated with his dislike of Paris and his legal studies, though it would seem clear that the urge had been prompted by his sexual dissatisfaction and despair. At Trouville that summer, the Flauberts met the family of the British admiral Collier, whose two daughters, Harriet and Gertrude, fell in love with Gustave, later described as a "Greek god" by Gertrude.[48] Though Gertrude had evidently been seducible, Flaubert, instead, fell in love with Harriet, the semi-invalid. He reported the propriety of the vacation to Alfred Le Poittevin, who inquired: "Is the repose of your virile member due to the cold water? or to the age or the figure of the female bather? or to exhaustion due to too frequent masturbation?"[49] It may be regrettable that we do not have Flaubert's response, but his avowal of abstinence would seem to be verified.

Later in the fall, he returned to his work on the civil code and received word that he had passed the first year, which meant that he was eligible for a second round of legal unpleasantness. Recently published letters, however, inform us that Flaubert also began to suffer from dental problems in the autumn of 1842. He could only eat on one side of his mouth and feared he would have to have three or four teeth extracted.[50] Four months later, he still complained of dental trouble and an irritated mouth.[51] It was the beginning of a life of buccal maladies; and the well-known portraits of the mature Flaubert conceal the fact that he became nearly toothless. His dentist did not think that decayed teeth were the sole cause of his pain, suspecting a neuralgia that made his jaws ache. It made his legal studies all the more difficult.[52] He called them *merde* and dreaded the approach of his examinations, which were scheduled for 21 August 1843.[53]

There remain two conflicting pictures of Flaubert in 1843. One description is heavily based on unpublished letters to Flaubert from Alfred Le Poittevin and from Flaubert's new friend, Maxime Du Camp, an aspiring writer only a few months his junior. Here we see a Flaubert quite recovered from his recent abstinence, a Flaubert overindulging in prostitutes, coffee, tobacco, food, and drink, getting little exercise and taking on weight, encouraged in his overindulgence by Le Poittevin especially, whose obsessive dedication to sexuality was pathological.[54] The second picture must be deduced from Flaubert's own letters and Du Camp's memoirs. It presents the handsome Norman giant with booming voice and extravagant gestures, with blond hair, fair skin, and sea-green eyes, his beauty attracting women whom he disdained, a good friend but very demanding in his friendship.[55] It is the Flaubert frustrated by both dental pain and legal studies, who began to reveal an extraordinary need for sleep, going to bed two or three times a week for fourteen to sixteen hours at a stretch, yet still tired upon awakening;[56] and it is in this period that Flaubert would later claim to have abstained from women.[57]

To resolve the contradiction, we must first recall that Flaubert, from an early age, had developed a monkish image of himself. By the age of eighteen, moreover, he could define the sensual pleasure of martyrdom as superior to love; and later in life, he would identify himself as a virgin, sometimes in the very context of regaling his listeners with the sexual exploits of his past. He meant that he had never truly had sexual relations with women, but, that with all of them, he had gone to the mattress with the ideal woman of his imagination. He did claim, after all, that beautiful women were not meant for copulation.[58] At a Magny dinner, the usual forum for the literati to exchange indecencies, he would recall that, as a young man going to a bordello with friends, he would choose the ugliest of the girls and have intercourse with her in the presence of his companions without removing the cigar from his mouth. It had been done for the audience and gave him no pleasure.[59]

In 1853, he would subtly torment his mistress, Louise Colet, by trying to explain to her his liking for prostitution. The sight of a seductively dressed woman walking in the rain beneath gas lights had always excited him "in the very way that the sight of a monk in his robe with knotted girdle does, touching some ascetic, hidden corner of his soul." Both the prostitute and the monk represented to him the negation of human relationships, and he became filled with sadness. Whenever he had gone to a prostitute, he had felt the same loneliness that he associated with the ascetic monk. In fact, Flaubert told Louise, a man who has never awakened in an anonymous bed beside a face he will never again see, who has never left a brothel ready to throw himself into the river out of pure disgust for life, has missed something fundamental.[60]

The purist may protest that asceticism requires chastity, that the ascetic denies himself in his search for God. For Flaubert, however, asceticism was an expression of alienation, of a horror of life; and he went to prostitutes not in search of love or pleasure, but in the expectation of pain, as the celebration of what had been denied him, in those temples where the flesh might be mortified for the edification of the soul. For Flaubert, asceticism was not a personal quest for God, but an admission of sexual disorder and dismay. In 1843, therefore, it would have been quite consistent for him to be sexually active and yet to insist that he was abstaining from women. His angel had escaped him and left him a virgin.

Consequently, as Flaubert approached his examinations that August, he may have given the impression of a robust bohemian; but he was, in fact, suffering from both physical and spiritual pain. He not only failed the examinations, but apparently abandoned any idea he may have had of marrying the increasingly disabled Harriet Collier.

After a brief postfailure vacation with relatives in Nogent, he returned to Rouen to begin work on a long novel; but it was understood that he meant to return to Paris in November, where he would prepare intensely for a second try at the examinations. Alfred Le Poittevin, the perennial purveyor of dubious advice, urged him to frequent the studio of the sculptor James Pradier, where he might expect to find a mistress among the artistic hangers-on.[61] But that was an opportunity temporarily postponed. As the examinations were to be given shortly after Christmas, he did not return to Rouen but spent the day with the Colliers. He instructed his sister to decline all holiday invitations for him. "I am a bear and want to remain a bear in my den, in my lair, in my skin, in my old bearskin, quite undisturbed, far from the bourgeois and the bourgeoises."[62] It may be that he anticipated failing a second time, and he did not disappoint himself. He reached home on New Year's Day, 1844, to find his family preoccupied about the development of a property purchased in Deauville.[63]

What ensued that day—namely, Flaubert's first nervous seizure—became a medical and literary issue after his death: Where and when had it occurred? What was the nature of the malady? And what effect did it have on his subsequent life and career? The first published description of Flaubert's attack was written by his old friend Maxime Du Camp for the *Revue des deux mondes* in 1881, shortly after Flaubert's death. The account was republished the following year in the first volume of Du Camp's *Souvenirs littéraires* and, again, in *La Chronique médicale* in 1896. It remained the only account for a half-century; and, on the whole, it was a model of good medical observation. Du Camp had been invited to spend a few days in the spring of 1844 with the Flauberts in Rouen, where he witnessed several of Gustave's subsequent seizures, learned of Dr. Flaubert's opinion of the case, and drew some unwarranted conclusions of his own. Du Camp, however, was a physician's son, which may have contributed to a confidence in his own diagnosis. In recalling the details over thirty-five years later, Du Camp unwittingly antedated the initial attack about six weeks, placing it in October of 1843;[64] and the date went unchallenged for many years because of an apparent gap in Flaubert's correspondence during the autumn of that year.[65] Du Camp had also confused two Norman towns, Pont-Audemer for Pont-l'Evêque, in his account of the scene of the initial attack.

It is now established that the Flaubert brothers, Gustave and Achille, set out from Rouen on 1 January 1844 to investigate problems that had arisen concerning their father's desire to build a chalet on his new property near Deauville. They reached Pont-l'Evêque after dark, but decided to drive on to Honfleur for the night.[66] As they approached a country inn, the Porte Rouge,[67] whose lights they could see on their right, their cabriolet was passed on the left by a wagon. At the moment, Gustave, who was driving, fell to the floor of the cabriolet "as if stricken with apoplexy," as he himself later put it. "For ten minutes [Achille] thought I was dead."[68] Achille bled him in the hope of preventing another seizure, but Flaubert told Du Camp that he suffered four more attacks in the next two weeks.

At the Hôtel-Dieu, Dr. Flaubert undertook his son's care. He belonged to the school of Dr. Victor Broussais, who believed that such attacks revealed a bodily disequilibration caused by a plethora—an excess of blood in the system—which overstimulated the individual by giving him too much strength and energy. Consequently, Dr. Flaubert ordered Gustave to avoid "stimulants," meaning red meat, wine, liquor, coffee, and tobacco; and he bled Gustave periodically in the quest for bodily equilibrium. During one attempt to bleed him, the blood had not appeared readily in a vein in his arm, and hot water was poured on his hand to bring the blood to the surface. No one realized that the water was near boiling, and the result was a second-degree burn on the hand, which caused additional suffering. Flaubert also began to read about nervous diseases in his father's library, which inevitably increased his depression. At the end of the month, he told Ernest Chevalier that he had had a cerebral congestion, "which is to say, an apoplectic attack in miniature, accompanied by some nervous ills." He described his nerves as vibrating like violin strings, his knees, shoulders, and stomach fluttering like leaves. At twenty-two, he was afflicted by old men's diseases.[69]

In February, Du Camp witnessed several seizures, which were preceded by identical phenomena. Flaubert would suddenly raise his head and become quite pale. He had sensed the aura—the sensation preceding an attack of epilepsy or hysteria—and he would appear anxious. Several moments later he would say, "I have a flame in my left eye." Seconds later he would add, "I have a flame in my right eye; everything appears to be gold." (This coincides with Flaubert's own statement to Louise Colet: "I felt myself suddenly carried away in a flood of flame.")[70] After several minutes, he would hurry to his bed and stretch out on his back. He would then cry out, "I am holding the reins, here is the wagon, I hear the little bells, I see the inn's lantern." Then the convulsion would begin, and would be followed by deep slumber. He could be stiff for several days thereafter.

Flaubert suspected that the seizure near Pont-l'Evêque had not been his first. Several months earlier, when he was still in Paris as a student, he had awakened in a state of extraordinary lassitude which had persisted for nearly a week. He was convinced that he had had an attack during his sleep. The fear of seizures made him reluctant to ride in carriages or even take walks, as he felt secure only indoors. And so, Du Camp concluded, the disease broke his life, made him unsociable and a solitary. He would never mention the malady by name—epilepsy—but simply referred to his "nervous attacks." And Du Camp added the observation that would outrage the literati: "Gustave Flaubert was a writer of rare talent. Without the nervous disease, he would have been a man of genius."[71]

We know already, of course, that Flaubert was well on the road to being a solitary, an unsociable bear in his own idiom, before his illness struck; and we must ultimately reconsider Du Camp's motives when he gave the name epilepsy to Flaubert's nervous ailment in 1881. Meanwhile, he kept the secret to himself, but that did not prevent others from speculating about the nature of the illness. The writer and caricaturist Henri Monnier told the Goncourt brothers in 1860 that Flaubert was an epileptic. They were uncertain about the story, but thought that the fact that women left him after making the discovery of his epilepsy might account for his great grief in matters of the heart.[72] When his novel *Salammbô* received a hostile review at the end of 1862 in *Le Figaro*, the article concluded by calling the style "epileptic," which the Goncourts thought was an infamous reflection of a rumor widespread in literary circles.[73] In short, what Du Camp ultimately revealed was already widely believed.

It is reasonable to assume that, when Du Camp revealed Flaubert to have been an epileptic who had died during an epileptic seizure, he meant to describe Flaubert as a victim of *le grand mal*—the falling sickness—that form of epilepsy which had always attracted fearful attention because of its violent convulsions. In ancient times it had been known by various dreadful names such as *morbus lunaticus astralis* or *morbus demoniacus*. But the terms *morbus sacer* and *morbus divus* remind us that this form of epilepsy was once held to be a special infliction of the gods. Partial epilepsy, or seizures that were epileptiform, was first described by Dr. Hughlings Jackson in 1861 (hence Jacksonian epilepsy); but Du Camp could not have had that form of epilepsy in mind in 1844 when he convinced himself that Flaubert was epileptic.

Du Camp tells us that Flaubert never mentioned the malady by name. The fact that he refers only to his "nervous attacks" is easily verified in his letters and suggests, incidentally, that he may never have known of the gossip that he was epileptic.[74] Du Camp's remark, however, implied that Flaubert knew the truth of his malady and tried to conceal it out of shame. Du Camp also learned that Dr. Flaubert was quite affected by his inability to cope with his son's illness and was disinclined to talk about the case; his reticence seemed to be further evidence that the disease was humiliating for all concerned.[75] No one would deny that the attacks had been frightening, but the resulting despair did not necessarily derive from a diagnosis of *le grand mal*. Other cerebral or mental ailments, if suspected, would have been ample cause for alarm about Flaubert's future; and any uncertainty as to the nature of the disease would surely have distressed the physician in particular.

If the word epilepsy was never used by Flaubert in referring to his nervous attacks—if, in other words, he knew that he was an epileptic and that the word became taboo—would he ever have used it in a different context? It would seem improbable. Yet, one can find the word in his letters. At a moment of irritation with Louise Colet, he would inform her that their correspondence was becoming increasingly "epileptic."[76] And in 1871, he would describe conditions within Paris as "totally epileptic," a reference to a social and political milieu that he abhorred.[77] It has been generally agreed that, by 1844, physicians would have had no trouble distinguishing between an attack of apoplexy and an epileptic seizure, assuming that the epilepsy had been *le grand mal*. But there remains an unresolved debate as to whether the treatment Dr. Flaubert prescribed for his son gave clear indication of his opinion about the illness. In particular, were repeated bleedings and the implanting of a seton in Flaubert's neck (threads introduced beneath the skin by a knife or needle to provide a drainage wick) the conventional treatment for *le grand mal?* Those who have argued in the negative have seen that treatment as proof that Dr. Flaubert had seen the attacks as some sort of cerebral congestion or a minor attack of apoplexy, exactly as Flaubert himself reported.[78]

Dr. Gallet, on the other hand, has insisted that, since Flaubert's intelligence was not diminished by the attacks and there was no subsequent paralysis, Dr. Flaubert would have obviously known that he was not dealing with apoplexy. The treatment given, moreover, was common in epileptic seizures. Consequently, he conjectured that Flaubert must have been told that he was epileptic and subject to subsequent attacks. (The bromide medication that became standard for epilepsy in the nineteenth century was not utilized in France before 1866.)[79]

Both these opinions were partly right, but also partly wrong. Both Dr. Flaubert and Achille would have recognized attacks of *le grand mal*, just as they would have watched for the aftereffects of apoplexy. As for the treatment, given Dr. Flaubert's school of thought, it was not a specific but a general attempt to cope with bodily disequilibration. Thus, the treatment does not provide a clue as to Dr. Flaubert's opinion. Let us, therefore, look further into Flaubert's life with a supposition that Dr. Flaubert had been sincerely baffled by the symptoms in the case, and that he would have been able to tell his son only that he faced cerebral or nervous troubles that were potentially dangerous. And let us proceed with the expectation that Flaubert's later medical history might well indicate that the seizures in 1844 had been neither *le grand mal* nor apoplexy, thus justifying Dr. Flaubert's uncertainty and explaining Flaubert's imprecise description of his nervous troubles.

Saint Anthony of Croisset

Flaubert was wont to say that he had embarked upon a new life at twenty-two. He meant that the onset of his nervous troubles had brought his active, emotional, passionate life to an end. He now saw life through a new pair of glasses; and the skin on his heart, like that on one's hands, had become callused.[80] He revealed a profound desire to conceal the truth about himself which only deepened with age, and he established a life of withdrawal that would ultimately baffle his literary contemporaries. As part of that withdrawal, he took a private vow of chastity.[81] Though we may sympathize with Flaubert's perception of a great watershed in his life, the fact remains that the ascetic existence he embarked upon at twenty-two had long been foreshadowed. It was natural to see the attacks which struck him down as compelling, and accounting for, a secluded life, but in fact they were the culmination of years of youthful disappointment and despair.

When Du Camp visited his convalescing friend in the spring of 1844, he was struck by Dr. Flaubert's compassion and saw him as a man profoundly troubled by his inability to cope with Gustave's illness. That may account for the doctor's decision to purchase a country house at Croisset, several miles downstream from Rouen, which the family occupied that summer. It was a pleasant property along the Seine which served Flaubert as home and refuge for the remainder of his life.[82]

His recovery was slow, punctuated by renewed epileptoid seizures which became less severe in time; and the drainage wick was a continual bother.[83] He described each seizure as a kind of nervous hemorrhaging—like seminal losses, but from the colorful faculty of the brain: a hundred thousand images leaping up at once, as in fireworks. He had a dreadful sense of his soul being wrenched from his body.[84] These fiery images, variously related to Maxime Du Camp, Ernest Chevalier, and Louise Colet, bear a striking resemblance to Flaubert's definition of hallucinations many years later, suggesting that his seizures had been hallucinatory, but without the loss of consciousness that occurs in *le grand mal.*

By then, 1866, he would know the difference between the artist's interior vision and the condition of the hallucinated man. In the true hallucination, he put it, there always is terror: "You feel that your personality is escaping you, that you are going to die.... In poetic vision there is always a joy, as something is always entering you."[85] His own hallucinations had been preceded by a peculiar anxiety, a vague unrest, a sensation that something was about to happen, not unlike that experienced by a man in copulation when he begins to feel the sperm rising. Then, like a stroke of lightning, his memory "would be invaded." In fact, he defined his hallucinations as a malady of his memory, "a loosening of what the memory holds. One experiences the escape of images, like the loss of blood. Everything in one's head lights up at once like a thousand fireworks going off." On occasion, a hallucination would begin with a single image that would expand to a point where objective reality was veiled, "like a spark which flares and becomes a large flaming fire." During such occurrences, it was possible for him to think of something else at the same time.

It would appear that Flaubert came to believe he could exercise a considerable amount of control over his hallucinations. Though he had found himself unable to induce one, he claimed to have had considerable success in shaking off a hallucination by an act of will. In fact, though he took pains to distinguish between the artist's vision and the hallucination, he knew that his powers of imagination had been extreme since childhood. He could so easily induce images that it required effort to distinguish them from hallucinations. As a youth, for instance, when he went to a theater he saw skeletons rather than living people in the audience.[86] As a mature writer, his literary characters affected him deeply. He said that, when writing about the poisoning of Emma Bovary, he became so poisoned himself that he suffered two real attacks of indigestion and even vomited one dinner. We shall never know, of course, whether Flaubert's cook was responsible for that indigestion; but there is no reason to doubt that he was a man of immense and intense emotion and imagination.

The seizures evidently subsided during the summer of 1844. He had some sort of outbreaks on his skin that summer and wondered if he had contracted syphilis in the past.[87] Since his later medical history will show that he was prone to skin eruptions, we must doubt that this incident was a manifestation of syphilis, especially as we have no evidence of its primary stage. In the autumn, he said that he was neither better nor worse, but made no mention of seizures.[88] Nor was there any further thought of resuming his legal studies. By the end of the year, he admitted that his health had improved, but lamented the loss of three additional teeth and the large red scar on his right hand. Aside from Alfred Le Poittevin, he saw no one— "living like a bear," as he liked to put it.[89]

On the other hand, he had been far from idle. In February of 1843, at the time he had commenced his second year of law, he sought distraction in his first long novel, the first version of his *Sentimental Education,* a title that would make more sense to Americans if we had followed Francis Steegmuller's recommendation to translate it as *The Education of the Feelings.* Flaubert completed his novel on 7 January 1845, a year after his initial seizure near Pont-l'Evêque. The book was not published until thirty years after his death. Aside from being a literary curiosity as the precursor of the far more sophisticated *Sentimental Education* which Flaubert published in 1869, the version of 1845 is immensely revelatory of his psychological and medical condition at the time of his great crisis.

In the novel, Flaubert deals with the emotional education of two friends, Henry and Jules. We first meet Henry with a description of his first love, and the theme is already familiar: the older married woman, Mme Renaud, making the advances to the student, Henry. Having expressed her love for him, she then endeavors to spurn him, insisting that the flirtation has been a game. Ultimately, she comes to his room and gives herself to him. Henry is later treated to a scene which reveals to what extent Mme Renaud will go to deceive her husband, a despicable performance that suggests the youthful Flaubert's low opinion of female character. Henry, nevertheless, continues to sleep with her until her intense possessiveness begins to sour him. His blissful love is replaced by a sense of anxiety.[90]

In depicting the development of Jules's love for the young actress, Lucinda, Flaubert revealed an awareness of his own complicated sexuality. In the first place, he described Lucinda as "one of those daughters of Eve sent into the world for man's undoing," reminiscent of those royal mistresses in the past who were responsible for public calamities, and of perfidious but beloved creatures who will sell you for a kiss. In the second place, he offered the hint that we have love affairs not because we are driven by our passions, but because we grow up anticipating them, expecting them: "For everyone, the life of the heart begins with a serious passion, so [Jules] behaved like everyone else." Finally, Flaubert portrayed Jules as "nervous and feminine by disposition."

The contrasting stories of Henry and Jules have been legitimately interpreted as a novelized description of the sharp alteration in Flaubert's personal life, from Henry to Jules, and thus to a new outlook on life: the early, Henrician tendencies were abandoned for the life of Jules. It would be closer to the truth of Flaubert's youthful existence to say that he had housed both Henry and Jules from the beginning, and that the dualism had provoked intolerable tension, which finally ended in critical illness. From then on, his survival required living Jules's life alone, and thus being condemned to Jules's fate.[91] In discussing the novel later with Louise Colet, who had recommended that he separate the two stories into two books, Flaubert explained that he had originally planned only Henry's story, but found that he had to create Jules's story as a foil. He had, in fact, recognized two distinct personalities within himself, and the writing of the book had been a deliberate exercise designed to help him fuse these two tendencies. The effort had failed.[92] Other writers have recognized the dualism, as well as Flaubert's preoccupation with it, and have offered various interpretations.[93] In 1841, he had noted that there are moments when one wants to be an athlete, because one's muscles are primed for action. But at other moments, one longs to be a woman, because the flesh is yearning and afire.[94] In view of Henry and Jules, may we conclude that Flaubert had come to suspect that his juvenile affairs had been the product of convention; and that to proceed on that path, the Henrician way, would be emotionally ruinous, because he had been cut for the feminine role?

As the story of Henry's increasing troubles with Mme Renaud unfolds, we have already learned of Lucinda's betrayal of Jules, and of Jules's subsequent retreat to his study, "robbed of his illusions." His youth had begun as a love affair and had ended in despair. "Like a king who abdicates on the day of his coronation, [Jules] had voluntarily renounced, once and for all, everything that has to be earned and paid for: pleasure, honors, money, the joys of love, and the triumphs of ambition. He bade his heart forgo its storms and his flesh mortify its appetites."[95] This dismal decision led straight to a pronouncement about life itself: "Is it not always the same stale nonsense, the same everlasting tune, with the shrill notes in the treble piercing your ears, and the low, sustained notes in the bass keeping the time?"[96]

Henry, meanwhile, had taken Mme Renaud to New York; but, alas, the new locale did not preserve his affair. As Flaubert put it, "I know not what sadness it was that came over [Henry] next day, but he certainly experienced none of that serenity that accompanies the satisfaction of normal desires, and all his anxiety revived. . . . So amazed was he by the difference between his past love and the love he now felt, by the infinite distance that a single night had set between yesterday and today, between last night's transports and the horrifying calm of the present moment, that it seemed to him some inexplicable cause must be responsible for it." At which point, a letter from Jules concerning his own frustrations and unfulfilled love enabled Henry to sense his own disaster and to recognize that his passion for Mme Renaud was over. He could begin to think of returning to France.[97]

By the end of the novel, Henry had become the charming and conventional Frenchman, exactly what Flaubert had managed to avoid becoming; whereas Jules had turned to the unconventional life of artistic solitude, which had also become Flaubert's. Jules must live soberly and chastely, though he will be obsessed by dreams of love and orgies, and will hardly care whether he goes on living or dies. But he does, indeed, recognize the richness of his limited world, which is quiet and uneventful only on the surface. Beneath that surface, that world "glows with a magical light, blazes with sensuality, and is as drenched with sunlight as the azure skies of the Orient."[98]

Perhaps the most astonishing episode in the novel occurs in the twenty-sixth chapter, where we find Jules taking a walk after dark on a country road. He meets a dog whose eyes glow in the night, a wretched beast described so as to evoke disgust. Despite Jules's efforts to drive it away, it persists in following him. He reaches a bridge over a millrace, where his thoughts turn to death. He wonders whether he will see the body of Lucinda, the love of his youth who has betrayed him, at the bottom of the stream. Finally, he reaches the security of his home, only to brood over his encounter with the miserable dog. At last, he forces himself to go to the door to settle, once and for all, whether the dreadful experience has been real or a moment of madness. He finds the dog lying on the threshold.[99]

The incident was inserted without apparent reason or explanation, and would make no sense to a reader unfamiliar with the medical details of Flaubert's youth. But knowing them enables us to recognize a fictionalized description of Flaubert's emotional crisis in 1844, as well as a peculiar recollection of a childhood dream about the drowning of his mother and his inability to prevent it. Moreover, the episode makes it clear that Flaubert, at twenty-three, was quite convinced that the dog would remain on his threshold forever. He was necessarily bound to Jules's path, and the Henry within him was declared banished. Twenty years later, he would tell the Goncourts that there were two men within him: one, the traveling salesman with high spirits and a taste for vigorous exercise; the other, the puny recluse made for slaving at a table.[100] The latter was the visible Flaubert, but Henry still lurked in the shadows of his mind.

Flaubert had begun to write as a schoolboy, when he had first sensed that he was an outsider. As his literary ambitions increased, he evidently concealed them from the family, or so Maxime Du Camp later claimed. And it does seem probable that Dr. Flaubert would have been annoyed had he learned that his son was writing a novel while presumably reading law. With the novel completed in 1845, Flaubert decided to make a clean breast of his desire to be a writer. His father was not enthralled with the idea, but understood the futility, given the nervous ailment, of compelling his son to return to law school.

The perplexed man finally asked his son to read him something he had written. It was a warm summer day, just after lunch, when Dr. Flaubert sat down to listen to *Sentimental Education*. Within a few minutes he fell asleep, to Gustave's irritation. He awakened his father, observing that he had obviously heard enough. Dr. Flaubert tried to make light of the situation by stating that writing, as a distraction, is not a bad thing and certainly preferable to wasting time in cafés or losing money by gambling. But he did not see that literature was of any use. Gustave is said to have replied: "Tell me, Doctor, if you can explain the use of the spleen! You do not know anything about it, nor do I, except that it is indispensable to the human body as poetry is indispensable to the human soul!" Du Camp, of course, recorded that scene thirty-five years later, so we may doubt the accuracy of the quotation. But as the son of a physician himself, and one who had inherited the means to pursue his own literary ambitions, he would undoubtedly have found that scene memorable. His own father could not stand in the way; but he understood that Dr. Flaubert felt humiliated by his son's ambition since he had no comprehension of the literary life.[101]

Be that as it may, Flaubert had already chosen a new literary theme that would occupy him for much of his remaining life, the legend of Saint Anthony, which would permit him to explore the association of illness and the hermitic life. The context of that choice was Italy, which the Flaubert family visited in the spring of 1845. Flaubert's beloved sister, Caroline, was married to Emile Hamard on 3 March 1845; and it would seem that Dr. Flaubert envisioned the trip, which began a month later, as likely to contribute to his son's recovery, while ostensibly being a handsome gift to the newlyweds. They were to go first to Marseille—where Flaubert meant to look up Mme Foucaud, the woman who had educated his senses five years before—and then proceed to Genoa and Milan.[102]

Traveling *en famille* soon made him acutely conscious of his inability to live a conventional family existence. His relatives traveled with the outlook of grocers, and their companionship was as empty as he had previously experienced with Dr. Cloquet, who was uninterested in the historical sites of interest. In Marseille, he returned to the Hôtel Richelieu, site of his historic encounter, to find it abandoned and tightly closed down, a symbol of his own shuttered heart. No one knew where Mme Foucaud lived, and he abandoned his quest, overwhelmed by disgusting memories of the past.[103]

Somewhere along the Riviera, he saw a monkey in a garden which stimulated a bizarre dream that he subsequently recorded. In the dream, he was walking with his mother in a large forest full of monkeys. In fact, the farther they walked, the more numerous and larger the monkeys became. They were laughing and swinging on branches, but ultimately began to throng in their path, surrounding Flaubert until he became afraid. One tried to pat him and took his hand; but Flaubert shot him in the shoulder, causing him to bleed and to howl frightfully. His mother asked, "Why are you hurting him? What has he done to you? Don't you see that he likes you, that he resembles you?" The wounded monkey continued to stare at Flaubert, who became quite upset—and then woke up.[104]

It would seem that the dream, occurring during Flaubert's period of chastity when he had opted for the life of Jules, symbolized the dualism which had worked such emotional distress, and which he now sought to alleviate by destroying his sexuality or animality and embracing the ascetic life. It may be that Flaubert's conscious decision to withdraw from his prior sexuality was the intelligent response to the anguish it had brought him. But the dream reminds us of the price he paid for salvation, and the cruel truth is that he would never manage to reconcile himself to what had necessarily been lost. He was bent upon a life of suffering,[105] though, for the moment, that fate had not yet clearly focused in his conscious mind.

"The only way to avoid unhappiness," he wrote to Alfred Le Poittevin, "is to confine oneself to Art and to count everything else as worthless.... I have really been quite well since the moment I accepted being forever ill.... I long neither for wealth, nor love, nor the flesh ... and have said an irrevocable good-bye to the practical life. From now on, I ask only for five or six hours of peace in my room, a big fire in the winter, and two candles each evening for light." When he wrote that fatal formula, Art above Life, he had just seen, in the Balbi Gallery in Genoa, Brueghel's painting *The Inferno*, depicting the temptation of Saint Anthony. He immediately fell upon the idea of adapting it for the theater.[106]

The legend of Saint Anthony, in fact, had been familiar to Flaubert since his days as an unhappy schoolboy. The annual Saint Romain Fair, in late October, had always featured a marionette show, and its performance was invariably "The Temptation of Saint Anthony."[107] Now that his solitude was a conscious concealment of illness, he was quite prepared to associate illness with the hermitage; and the theme, perhaps more than any other, would preoccupy him during the rest of his life. (The third version of it was the only one he published, and that not until 1874.) Since we know from Flaubert himself that he was eminently autosuggestible, that he put himself into his literary characters, feeling and experiencing their sensations and illnesses, it would follow that he spent many more years as Saint Anthony than as Emma Bovary or Salammbô. *The Temptation of Saint Anthony* was to become the favorite of his own books, and he would be keenly disappointed that no one else would share that preference.[108]

From Genoa, the newlyweds were allowed to go their own way to Naples, while Flaubert and his parents went to Milan and Geneva. At some point—perhaps Geneva—he ran across three wretched idiots begging for alms. They were dreadful, ugly and feebleminded, quite unable to speak. Yet, they gave Flaubert affectionate signs, smiling at him and trying to blow him kisses. It brought to his mind some pasturage his father owned near Pont-l'Evêque. Its caretaker had an imbecile daughter, who had revealed a strange attachment for Flaubert the first time he saw her. "I attract animals and the mad," he wrote. "Is it because they divine that I understand them, that they sense I am part of their world?" A few sentences later, he was bemused by his withdrawal from women, and he used the word *fou*, as in 1838, to describe himself: the alien, the outsider.[109] He had experienced two nervous seizures while on the trip, which proved to him that he was not recovering quickly.[110]

Back at Croisset in the summer of 1845, Flaubert made a conscientious effort to put the best possible face on his new mode of existence. Having declared happiness impossible in the external world of passion and action, he would endeavor to find it in stagnation, in a calm and regulated regime where he might devote himself exclusively to literature and history. He professed not to regret his new regime, as he had been sensing in recent months a freedom unknown to him before the onset of illness. No doubt, his condition troubled the family, especially his mother; but he, himself, who knew what had been sacrificed for the new freedom, and what would continue to be sacrificed, was enjoying a sense of emancipation.[111]

This era of good feeling was unfortunately brief and came to an end with the death of Dr. Flaubert on 15 January 1846. Four days after the burial of that "gentle and lofty soul," as Flaubert characterized his father, Caroline Hamard gave birth to a daughter, Désirée-Caroline.[112] The young mother became critically ill thereafter and died on 23 March 1846. Caroline had been Flaubert's favorite and closest relative, and he was overwhelmed by her loss. When her funeral procession reached the cemetery, it was found that the grave had not been made large enough to receive the coffin. The gravediggers thereupon seemed determined to force the coffin into its place with as little enlargement as possible, and their crude methods sent Flaubert into a nervous attack or an emotional collapse. It would appear that the Flauberts had been discreet about Gustave's nervous ailment. After the wretched scene in the cemetery, Achille found it convenient to explain his brother's malady as resulting from his grief for Caroline.[113]

After those two deaths, Flaubert was left at Croisset with his mother and his infant niece, as it was understood that the baby would have to be reared by the grandmother. He claimed that the recent misfortunes, while paining him, had not actually surprised him, for they merely confirmed the black premonitions about life he had had as a child. His recent attempt to redefine happiness for himself came to an end,[114] and he used the word *ennui* to describe his state of mind. He did not mean boredom, but rather disenchantment with life: despair. "Ennui does not have any cause," he wrote. "To

want to reason about it, or to combat it with reasons, is not to understand it." He was convinced that life would never be otherwise for
him, and that brooding would do no good. He had found work to be
the only antidote, and he had begun to read and to write eight or ten
hours every day. If anything disrupted his routine, it could make
him ill. "I live alone, very much alone, more and more alone."[115]

Consequently, he cherished his few friends all the more, and said
so to Maxime Du Camp. Yet, he was obsessed by the fear that they,
too, would abandon him. Ernest Chevalier had entered the magis-
tracy and, the previous year, had assumed his first post in Calvi
(Corsica).[116] And now, in the spring of 1846, he was stung by the
news of Alfred Le Poittevin's impending marriage. Alfred was in
danger of abandoning Art and becoming bourgeois. With the announcement of Alfred's engagement to Louise de Maupassant,
Flaubert recognized that it was too late to interfere. Worse, his advice
had not been asked.[117] The wedding took place on 6 July 1846. It had
been understood that, after a wedding trip to Italy, the couple would
spend the winter in Paris.[118]

The threat of solitude had the immediate result of bringing Louis
Bouilhet into Flaubert's orbit. The two had known each other slightly
as schoolboys in Rouen, and Bouilhet had thereafter been one of Dr.
Flaubert's medical students at the Hôtel-Dieu. It may be that Dr.
Flaubert's death, which perhaps precipitated Bouilhet's decision to
give up medicine for a literary career, brought Bouilhet and Flaubert
together. In any case, he filled the place which Alfred had abdicated
and remained Flaubert's most intimate friend for over twenty years.

Despite Bouilhet's companionship, Flaubert treated Alfred's marriage as a personal affront, as if he had been scorned. His sense of
abandonment may account for his dubious decision, that summer of
1846, to allow himself once again to be enticed into an affair with an
older woman. The setting was the sculptor James Pradier's studio in
Paris, which Alfred had once recommended as the place to recruit a
mistress; but Flaubert went there to arrange memorials in stone for
his father and sister. There he met Louise Colet, a minor writer
married to a minor musician, and their correspondence began in
early August. She was then thirty-six, Flaubert not yet twenty-five.

Louise Colet: Round One

By all accounts, Louise was a beautiful woman. In fact, beauty may
have been her single virtue. Her husband, Hippolyte Colet, was a
professor of harmony and counterpoint at the Conservatoire, a post
he had obtained through the efforts of Victor Cousin, one of Louise's

former lovers, a list that had included the poet Alfred de Musset and the critic Abel-François Villemain. She had caused a stir in 1840 by attempting to plunge a carving knife into Alphonse Karr's back for witty but damaging words he had written about her in a gossip column. In retrospect, it seems clear that her literary reputation was not achieved by the pen; and it suffices today to scan one or two of her pages to recognize the blessing of her literary oblivion. It is incontestably a mercy that most of her letters to Flaubert have disappeared. His to her reveal only too obviously that he treated her shabbily, so that it is easy to overlook the extent to which she merited the treatment. The first period of their liaison, from mid-1846 into early 1848, amounted to six meetings, not everyone's measure of a torrid passion, including Louise's.[119]

It must be said that Flaubert recognized the grotesquerie of the affair from the start and sought to warn Louise of the unhappiness it would bring her, but she had no intention of admitting defeat. He had met her on 29 July 1846,[120] and they spent the night of 3 August together. The following day he left her, in tears, for Croisset, where his mother, also in tears, met him at the train. He was smitten with passion, he assured Louise, and proved it by writing long letters to her.[121] He failed, she complained, to note in his letters that he would love her forever. That, he explained, was because he knew the future: "I have never seen a child without thinking that he will become an old man, nor a cradle without thinking of the grave. To imagine a nude woman also conjures up her skeleton." When he had had a family, he had often wished to be free of it; now that death had robbed him of those close bonds, he had tied himself to the very walls that housed family memories.

Other men would be proud of the love that Louise had lavished on him, their male ego flattered, and they would be able to accept the pleasure easily—but not him: "She loves me; and *I*, who also love her, I do not love her enough. If we had never met, I would have spared her all those tears she has shed!" He warned that immense unhappiness was in store for her. His letters to her would inevitably be discovered and the truth uncovered. It might be different if he lived in Paris, where he could be near her every day; but, as they lived apart, they were destined to see each other rarely. "I am sick, and the sickness is you."

In a lengthy letter, he frankly characterized himself as an actor at heart, giving Louise ample evidence of his perversity and full warning that their affair could only be fretful and painful. An old witticism describes opera as an activity in which the principals, when stabbed, do not bleed, but sing. And Flaubert, when he allegedly fell in love, did not pursue the woman in question with ardor: he wrote. She must have no illusions about him. As a youth he had a passion for the stage. As an adult, he loves form above all else, providing that it is beautiful, and he does not believe that women can understand his religion of beauty. Physical love, that which touches most men most closely, is quite secondary for him.

Between the ages of fourteen and twenty, he explained, he had loved a woman without telling her of his love or touching her; and for three years thereafter, he had felt no sexual desire, a condition he came to believe would last his lifetime—and he thanked God for it. He did not deny having had sexual experience, but simply claimed that it had been associated with neither love nor pleasure. She, Louise, had been the only woman he had loved and also possessed. Now she is insisting on a letter every day, whereas the very demand will prevent him from complying. She must allow him to love her in his own way. At eighteen, he had written letters for six months to a woman he did not love (Mme Foucaud), in order to force himself to love her and to develop an amorous style that would be convincing.[122] Finally, he cautioned Louise not to love him too much *as it would make him ill.* "Do you not realize that loving too much will bring only misfortune to both of us!" Life is not made for happiness, and those who pursue it will be punished.[123]

He undertook an explanation of his condition—why he was different from other men. His youth had been terminated by a nervous illness that had lasted for two years. He had then become calm and stabilized; he saw things clearly again, including himself, and he entered a period of moral health. Others may have thought that he had reached a pitiful state, but he was enjoying a peace he had never before known. And now she, Louise, had entered his life to unsettle him again with a twist of her finger. Having been taunted by women as incapable of sex, he now found his savage instincts aroused. On the other hand, perhaps that is the opposite of love. "Perhaps it is only his heart that is impotent." Perhaps that explains why he has never understood the intensity of the pleasures experienced by other men; perhaps that proves he "had not been made to enjoy life." Consequently, he is bound to bring her unhappiness, and in due course they will separate.[124]

Moreover, there was the matter of his recently bereaved mother, who was having premonitions of death and needed him with her. Living in Paris was quite out of the question, though he might be able to go to the city sometime the next winter for as much as three weeks. He might, meanwhile, even arrange to be away for a day. Yet, what was the use of getting accustomed to seeing each other, of loving each other? Why feed on the luxury of affection if they must subsequently live miserably?[125] In the midst of this amorous agony, Flaubert wrote to his old friend in Calvi, compaining about not hearing from him, lamenting the tendency of old friends to marry or go away, while he remained sedentary and calm, his rear glued to a chair, pipe in mouth, working and reading, and reminiscing about the fine times they had had together.[126] Not one word about Louise, or a hint of personal distress!

At that very moment he was responding to Louise's entreaties, promising to come immediately to Paris for twenty-four hours. We find him still at Croisset three days later, suffering from a large boil on his right cheek, explaining that, were she to see him in that condition, "love would perhaps sulk." By the following day, the boils had spread, and he had taken to his bed. He had been wondering why his joy of anticipation—the thought of their parting and her tears—also brought him pain, and he asked her to be reasonable when the moment came. Two days later he was back on his feet bearing the scars of his recent disfiguration, and it would appear that he got to Paris for the promised meeting on 19 August.[127]

Upon his return to Croisset, he sent Louise a rapturous description of his twenty-four hours with her and informed her that he had just unpacked an engraving of Callot's *Temptation of Saint Anthony*, a work he had long wanted for his wall. "For me, the pitiful grotesque has a surprising charm, associated with the most intimate needs of my natural bitter clownery."[128] As Louise had begun to berate him for his swift departures, seeing them as proof he did not love her, he reminded her that he was in a vise, caught between Louise's love and his bereaved mother's pain.[129] A woman wiser than Louise Colet, confronted with that image, would have cut her losses and retired.

Indeed, in the early weeks of their correspondence, Flaubert exhibited a pessimism and a morbidity that ought not to have been lost on Louise; but she was too willful, too neurotic herself, to accept the hopelessness of an affair with such a man as this. His love letters remain a model of honesty, with never a forecast of happiness from either their affair or anything else. He confessed his alienation, explaining that he was rooted in neither time nor place: no more French than Chinese, no more modern than ancient. He described a brief excursion with Maxime Du Camp, then a houseguest at Croisset, to visit the Gothic ruins at Jumièges, a former abbey where Agnès Sorel had resided so happily with Charles VII and where her heart had been buried. Flaubert had known and loved the ruins since childhood, visiting them with those members of his family "who are no more." His thoughts, therefore, had been for the recent dead as well as for others he had never known. He saw the vegetation reconquer that place abandoned by men, and it gave him pleasure to realize that he would serve someday to enable tulips to grow. "Who knows!" his sentiment concluded. "The tree at whose foot they will put me may bring forth excellent fruit; I shall perhaps be a superb fertilizer, a superior guano."[130]

After a month of Louise's complaints and rebukes, Flaubert gave a hint of being wearied. Could she really love him if she found him such a deficient person? He had not been hypocritical, he added, but had told her from the beginning about himself and the life of seclusion he had commenced at twenty-two. As to her offer to cope with the separation by visiting Croisset, he found that quite impossible. Everyone in the neighborhood would know that he had been visited by a married woman, and there would be "odious stories." *Quite impossible,* but he mailed her a long kiss for having had the idea. Perhaps they could meet halfway between Paris and Rouen, at Mantes, where they could be together for "five marvelous hours." He even related a story (which he may have invented) of a love affair which evolved into a passionate and secret correspondence, laboriously concocted, that went on for seven years without the couple meeting. Finally, there came the long-anticipated rendezvous, and then no more. The writing tapered off until it ceased; she died, and he had other affairs. "And so it goes! Such is life. Everything passes."[131]

Louise was not amused and accused Flaubert of behaving like a sheltered maiden at Croisset. He replied that he did nothing more than to protect her name and honor.[132] He saw the wisdom, however, of arranging their third meeting, which took place during the day of 9 September 1846 in Mantes; and he warned her in advance that he would not spend the night. Even that short absence from Croisset distressed his mother, or so he reported to Louise. Upon his return, he had found her in a state of great anxiety. Not that she reproached him, but her face revealed her feelings.[133] It would seem that the affair had reached a point where Louise's insistence drove Flaubert to bend the truth. In his next letter, he portrayed his mother coming into his room, the infant Caroline in her arms, picking up an envelope (a letter from Louise) with curiosity about the feminine handwriting and what was inside. His duty to his poor mother, in short, became the constant excuse for his inability to see Louise frequently.[134] As we shall see, there is good reason to believe that Mme Flaubert was a willful and demanding mother. But at the very moment Flaubert was citing her as the reason for his immobility, he was planning a walking trip through Brittany with Maxime Du Camp, with her express approval. While it was understood that Mme Flaubert might meet them in towns along their route every week or two, she made no trouble about her son being away from home; and Flaubert assured Du Camp that they would be "totally free and alone."[135]

Louise, meanwhile, had not been placated by those few marvelous hours in Mantes and developed the notion that Flaubert was consorting with other women. On the contrary, he replied, he was quite capable of living in abstention for years at a time. The time was long past when he made it a duty to visit girls regularly; and even then, he had done so out of mania rather than the lure of pleasure.[136] His letters to Louise, indeed, began to take on a sadistic tinge. Having assured her, for a disquieting reason, that he had not been frequenting other women, he revealed a desire to write to his old friend, Mme Foucaud. Was Louise's cousin sufficiently reliable to deliver a letter to her? Louise was not to be jealous: "You may read the letter if you want on condition that you do not tear it up." He did not expect Louise to behave like an ordinary woman; she must use her head, not merely her heart, in dealing with him.

This provoked a new salvo of demands that he come to Paris, which he countered with pathetic descriptions of his bereaved mother's suffering and her dependence upon him.[137] His fundamental honesty, however, continued to emerge in his letters. He was able to be evasive while assuring her of his passionate love; but from the beginning of their correspondence, he continued to give her psychological clues about himself that should have warned her to mistrust his avowed passion. He confessed, for example, that, from childhood, he had been a showman, a clown. Because of that quirk, something he saw or heard might leave him cold; yet he could become irritated, wounded, or excited if he began to write about that thing to which he had been indifferent. He made no secret of his cowardice as a child, of his later "excessive continence," of the deliberate education of his nerves. He said forthrightly that there had been a time when he had needed money so urgently that he would have married for it, but that he now hoped never to marry.[138] After saying that he would drop the matter of Mme Foucaud to avoid distressing Louise further, he sent his letter to Mme Foucaud to her the following day, for her edification. It was not to her liking, a bit too affectionate, and the stage was set for a new epistolary wrangle. The only true passion of his past, he insisted, had been for Mme Schlésinger, and he had been quite candid with Louise about that.

Flaubert, in the meantime, needed to go to Paris to see Pradier about the memorial bust of Dr. Flaubert, and in early October he began to promise Louise an imminent visit.[139] When several weeks transpired without his appearance, she deduced that his health was bad and volunteered to go to Croisset to care for him. He found that quite unnecessary. He might be the victim of all manner of accidents and maladies, but he shed them as water off a swan's neck and was born to live as an old man. Moreover, he wanted her to understand that he was capable of hard, sustained work. He could work for two weeks at a stretch without need for exercise or diversion—without ever leaving his room. He would not welcome her at Croisset, finally, because of the "scenes" her presence would provoke.[140] She must not doubt his love for her, but simply understand that he was not like other men—meaning that he should not be judged by ordinary standards. Even if they were not to see each other for the next ten years, he had no doubt that they could again be as passionately united as they had been in Mantes.[141]

These assurances quite failed to improve Louise's temper, and, at that point, she met Maxime Du Camp in Paris and learned of the proposed walking trip. The crescendo in her anger drove Flaubert to exasperation.[142] When he finally reached Paris, about the tenth or eleventh of November,[143] he spent most of his time with Pradier and Du Camp, giving Louise only momentary attention and leaving her outraged.[144] He sought to calm her by explaining that he preferred to be with her when he could devote himself entirely to her, and promised to return quickly for that occasion. It would appear that he honored that promise on 30 November and remained with her until 1 December.[145]

Whatever Louise lacked in insight she made up in persistence. Her solution to the dilemma was a barrage of abusive letters, which caused him to describe their correspondence as epileptic. Once again he tried to convince her not to be mistaken by his youthful appearance, as underneath his skin there was a peculiar old age. Everything about life revolted him, even if he did not know why. If his way of life and personality wounded her so, why did she not leave him? She would be better off if she were to forget him, though he would never be able to forget her. He specifically denied he had been going to prostitutes, having found long since that the pleasures of prostitution are a myth.[146] Even though their affair was in ruins by the end of

December, they saw each other once again in late February of 1847, their sixth meeting. The uncomfortable scene in a Parisian hotel room enabled Flaubert to reach the conclusion that their tempers were incompatible.

Whatever Louise's faults—and they have been entertainingly depicted elsewhere[147]—Flaubert never sought to blame her for his failure in love. He said that the skin on his burned hand was more wrinkled than that of a mummy, and that it was more insensitive to heat and cold than the other one. He thought that his soul had also passed through fire and had emerged with a similar insensitivity. He urged Louise not to upset herself further about his infirmity, since nothing could be done about it.[148]

Meanwhile, the Breton walking trip, a three-month tour, had been scheduled for 1 May. Flaubert went to Paris immediately beforehand and toyed with the idea of seeing Louise, but thought better of it.[149] Despite the collapse of their affair, their correspondence did not entirely cease, though it became infrequent. Flaubert's letters to Ernest Chevalier prove that the walking trip was a joy for Flaubert, and they included nary a word about Louise. It would seem that Flaubert wanted the formality of a mistress, along with the luxury of not seeing her or thinking about her. When a letter from Louise did reach him toward the end of the trip, conveying her continuing irritation, he responded that she had taught him a sad fact of life: that there is as much distress and bitterness in happy love as in rejected love.[150]

There had been some noteworthy coincidences in the unraveling of that "happy love." We may have forgotten, for instance, that Flaubert began work on his martyred Saint Anthony about the time he took Louise as his mistress; and he had virtually completed his notes for The Temptation of Saint Anthony before embarking for Brittany with Maxime, that is to say, shortly after his final meeting with Louise. In the second place, there had occurred in Mantes an incident which had "chilled him to his very core," though he had said nothing of it to Louise at the time. The previous September, when Flaubert had arranged his third meeting with Louise, she had said to him, as they walked under trees in a garden, that she would not trade her happiness for all of Corneille's glory. The remark stupefied him and characterized the gulf between them: the shallow female writer who put happiness above art, in contrast to the male who believed that happiness is an illusion, ruinous to those who seek it, and that nothing but art matters.[151] We ought to be struck by his early awareness of their incompatibility and note that it seized him at a moment of supposed passion and harmony. That he did not immediately break off the unfortunate liaison is a key to his psychology. "You do indeed love art," he wrote Louise in response to her protest, "but it is not your religion."[152] Poor Louise could no more have understood the salvation Flaubert sought than she could have been its agent.

By the time Flaubert returned to Croisset after his walking tour, he had effectively broken with Louise; but he returned to life with mother, and the return coincided with a resumption of nervous troubles. It is unclear whether he again experienced the violent seizures of 1844, or whether he was merely emotionally distressed and irritated by troubles in the family. On one hand, he quite accepted the life of privation he had learned from an early age, a life of suffering from nerves, a life without anyone's company; but he knew that it was not his choice. Nor did he choose the unpleasant responsibilities that intruded upon his solitude at Croisset.[153]

It seems unlikely that the nervous troubles reflected regret for Louise, or they would have appeared during the months of the tour. Indeed, the history of that affair must confirm Du Camp's later assertion that Flaubert fell in love only once in his life, with Mme Schlésinger in Trouville, an implication that he had never really loved Louise Colet.[154] Writing in the early Freudian tradition, Theodor Reik saw that passion for the older, unavailable woman as substitute love for the mother: the older woman, frequently envisioned as an angel—as in Flaubert's youth[155]—who would save him from his sexual dilemma, allegedly the Oedipus complex, or from what was possibly a strong but unconscious homosexual bent. From that context would emerge sadistic tendencies, which were admittedly evident in Flaubert's treatment of Louise, and which some have found in Flaubert's later novels.[156]

The Freudians were on firmer ground in their understanding of the association between masochism in the male and male femininity, which is strikingly characterized by passive sexual behavior. Dreams of being sexually overpowered and impregnated do not mean that all women are masochists, but that the male masochist imagines the female role.[157] Louise Colet's downfall was not due to the fact that she pursued Flaubert relentlessly or was physically unattractive to him. On the contrary, he was sexually attracted, and her aggressiveness was the necessary behavior of the angel coming to his rescue. The trouble was that, once she had cornered him in Paris, she required him to perform as an aggressive male. He had evidently always been sufficiently potent to perform under duress and, in the aftermath, was always disappointed, frustrated, or revolted. He realized that he was not like other men without knowing quite why life had so molded him, but his pathetic condition was beyond Louise's understanding.

The early Freudians were impressed by the insight into masochism that was depicted in Flaubert's work on Saint Anthony. The masochist unconsciously desires to humiliate himself profoundly and to experience pain, from which he derives not merely pleasure but the hope of being exalted. His pride shows through his tortures; the pain he experiences gives proof of his superiority. Flaubert's Saint Anthony treasured his self-castigation and self-privation,[158] as we see in this passage from the final version of the work: "But what works have I not accomplished! Lo! for these thirty years and more I have been dwelling and groaning unceasingly in the desert! Like Eusebius, I have carried thirty-eight pounds of bronze upon my loins; like Macarius, I have exposed my body to the stings of insects; like Pachomius, I have passed fifty-three nights without closing my eyes; and those who are decapitated, tortured with red hot pincers, or burned alive, are perhaps less meritorious than I, seeing that my whole life is but one prolonged martyrdom."[159]

Flaubert's psychology also attracted the attention of physicians not of the Freudian school, who were struck by the apparent abnormality of his love life. According to their formula, Flaubert fell into the category of psychasthenia, a neurosis characterized by morbid anxieties and obsessions. Pierre Janet, one of Charcot's students, was the first to describe accurately the feeling of inadequacy (or *sentiment d'incomplétitude*) that characterized the psychasthenic, the patient who says "I cannot" rather than "I will not." This feeling of inferiority presumably conceals a secret delusion of grandeur and leads psychasthenic individuals into peculiar attitudes and behavior. They have great love affairs, but the object of their affections is apt to be imaginary, or someone who has been converted into an ideal. Like Flaubert, they are unable to adapt to the realities of love. Wilhelm Stekel related psychasthenia to a tendency to asceticism, often concealed with an aesthetic mask, but founded in sexual hypochondriasis or impotence.[160]

The tour through Brittany may have removed Flaubert temporarily from the arena of his torments, but it took him into deeply religious country, into close proximity to foliage and the sand, to the sea and the sky; and he came away more than ever compelled to write of man and God. For a few months he plunged into further reading in the solitude of Croisset and finally began his writing in May of 1848.

As Flaubert prepared to write his first draft of *Saint Anthony*, he was far from carefree despite the cessation of letters from Louise

Colet. He was genuinely concerned for his mother, yet she was demanding and obviously irritated him. Alfred Le Poittevin had died in early April at the age of thirty-two. His terminal suffering had brought Flaubert to his bedside, reuniting them briefly; and it was Flaubert who wrapped Alfred in his shroud. A subsequent note to Du Camp, perhaps one of Flaubert's finest and most moving letters, perfectly mirrored his grief and great regard for Alfred, but also reflected his respect for death as the liberator from life. He had experienced, he wrote, "an inexplicable sense of happiness and freedom" for Alfred.[161]

The erratic behavior of Flaubert's brother-in-law, Ernest Hamard, also became a great concern in 1848. The poor man had never entirely recovered from Caroline's death two years before and became increasingly unbalanced after the February Revolution. In his extreme enthusiasm for the Republic, he threw 30,000 francs, not to speak of family silver and diamonds, into political causes in a period of four months. The Hamard family had endeavored to have him committed to an asylum, but he had regained his sanity upon learning of the attempt to put him away. He next announced his intention to become a comedian and planned an immediate debut at the Comédie-Française; and he made it known that he wanted to take charge of his infant daughter. The Flauberts refused to give her up, leading Hamard to bring suit against Mme Flaubert to regain custody of the child. The court postponed a judgment in order to inquire into Hamard's competence, and the matter festered for many months without resolution. Mme Flaubert, however, had been humiliated in court when the plaintiff's attorney described her as a woman most difficult to live with.[162]

Croisset, in short, was not turning into the peaceful hermitage of Flaubert's expectations, and he was understandably envious when he learned that Du Camp was planning a trip to the Near East.[163] In time, it was agreed that Flaubert should accompany him, for Mme Flaubert apparently recognized that her son's health might profit from the extensive trip, anticipated to last between fifteen and eighteen months. Though Flaubert knew that his mother would be troubled by his tour of potentially dangerous country, he feared that the difficulties at home would be even greater were he not to go; and he was supported by old Dr. Cloquet, who recommended the trip to a warm region.[164] Meanwhile, Flaubert struggled to complete his *Saint Anthony*, and he did so in September of 1849, the month before his anticipated departure. He at once read the manuscript to Maxime Du Camp and Louise Bouilhet, and their adverse criticism made him quite ill.[165] The trip gave the manuscript opportunity to mature on a shelf.

The Great Adventure

As Maxime Du Camp's account of the trip to the Near East did not square in every detail with Flaubert's notes and letters, Du Camp's accuracy has been held in question. (We can postpone the issue of his motives until later on.) His literary memoirs were written and published long after the events he reported, so that we ought not to be surprised that he erred in detail; and as both Bouilhet and Flaubert had already died, errors relating to Flaubert's life were not immediately detected. Benjamin Bart, who recognized the problem long ago, properly recommended caution in the use of Du Camp as a source, and stressed the need for confirming the valuable information he provided.[166] In Du Camp's description of Flaubert's initial seizure in January of 1844, for example, his medical observation has been established as reliable, but he was in error as to time and place.[167]

A similar generalization may be made about the decision to allow Flaubert to accompany Du Camp to the Near East. Both men revealed that Mme Flaubert gave her consent reluctantly and on the grounds of medical necessity; Du Camp alone emphasized his critical intervention in extracting that consent, but his account may have been an exaggeration. Both men related that Mme Flaubert had agreed to spend considerable time with her family in Nogent-sur-Seine during her son's absence; but Du Camp alone portrayed Flaubert's dejection after he had taken his mother to her family. That portrait, too, may have contained exaggeration, though it must be argued that Du Camp's description of Flaubert's behavior during his preparation for departure was absolutely consistent with Flaubert's personality as we already know it—that is to say, with his masochism.

When Mme Flaubert had finally given her consent to the trip to the Orient early in 1849, something Flaubert had desired with painful intensity, there followed no burst of excitement or enthusiasm on his part, but rather a period of depression. And Du Camp came to learn that the pattern was normal for Flaubert. He sought things passionately, to a point of illness, desperately unhappy at denial, cursing destiny. And then, the moment he had acquired the desired thing, he felt deceived and seemingly lost interest. "The dream," Du Camp observed, "satisfied him considerably more than the reality.... His eyes were bigger than his stomach." Things at a distance seemed of enormous dimension to him; familiarity not only diminished whatever it was he had desired, but led to disgust.[168] Louise Colet would have understood the accuracy of that portrait.

The two men were scheduled to leave Paris on 29 October 1849. Several days in advance, Flaubert took his mother to Nogent and then proceeded to Du Camp's apartment in Paris. Du Camp found him stretched out on a black bearskin, utterly undone for having left his mother, nonplussed by the distances and the duration of the trip, certain that he would never see France or Mme Flaubert again. Only the fear of ridicule kept his nose pointed at the Orient. Several days later, his zeal returned, and he became fixed to the notion of discovering the sources of the Nile. His regrets surfaced momentarily as their ship left Marseille, as he watched the coast of Provence fade in the distance.[169] There followed a flood of letters to his mother, that is, to "chère bonne mère, pauvre mère, or pauvre chérie," testimony to the guilt he felt for having found it necessary to leave Croisset. His letters caressed and reassured: all was going well, and Maxime was taking care of him as if he were a child. He wrote to Achille and to Louis Bouilhet, begging them to see his mother frequently, reminding them of her desperate need for regular attention.[170] In the spring of 1850, as the two friends were boating up the Nile into Upper Egypt, he proclaimed his good health and admitted getting fat.[171] Indeed, he was regaining the weight he had lost during his correspondence with Louise Colet.

Poor dear Mother, however, was spared the unseemly news of the tour that began reaching Louis Bouilhet. The travelers were offered an assortment of sexual novelties, and Flaubert seemed compelled to share them in frank detail with Louis, who had been left behind in Rouen, confined to one mistress. In Cairo, they had witnessed dancing by two male performers dressed as women, who were described by Flaubert as delightful in their perversion, in the depravity of their facial expressions, and in the femininity of their movements. Having described the lascivious performance, he remarked that it had been too artful to be exciting; yet he added that he had had to go out two or three times to urinate during the performance, a nervous reaction he attributed to the music. And he got a headache that lasted for the rest of the day.

Bouilhet was also informed of the widespread use of male prostitutes in Egyptian society, along with the admission that, since Flaubert and his companion were traveling for experience and instruction, they felt it their duty to test that "mode d'éjaculation." As all the bathboys were prostitutes, Flaubert arranged to hire a bath for himself alone; but upon arrival he found that his boy had gone for the day.[172] Because Bouilhet was intent upon knowing whether the experiment had ever been completed, Flaubert said that he had returned to the baths, to a husky young boy marked by smallpox, who had worn a large white turban, which Flaubert had found amusing. *"But,* I shall do it again. For an experiment to be well done, it must be repeated."[173]

Such letters were heavily censored in the standard edition of Flaubert's correspondence, either by Flaubert's niece Caroline, or by the editors themselves, with no indication of the omissions. Had Theodor Reik seen the originals, it would have strengthened his opinion that Flaubert's association with Alfred Le Poittevin, with Louis Bouilhet, and later with Ivan Turgenev, indicated a repressed homosexual attachment.[174] Those biographers who did see the original correspondence were compelled to arrive at an interpretation. (Jean Bruneau is now editing new volumes of unabridged letters.) Enid Starkie noted that Flaubert's most pornographic prose was written later in life to Jules Duplan, whom he frequently called "vieux pédéraste"; and that in a letter to Duplan, 27 March 1867, Flaubert described a school for young pederasts. But Starkie, being quite aware of Flaubert's delight in lewd situations and stories, was properly hesitant to reach any definite conclusion about an actual sexual relation. Indeed, was that school imagined or real?[175]

Benjamin Bart deduced that the open homosexuality in the Near East served to bring the sexual ambivalence in both Flaubert and Du Camp "into the forefront of their consciousness." The two joked frequently about homosexuality, even to a point where Flaubert would act the "mincing mistress to Maxime's feigned advances." Bart was quite right in concluding that it had been innocent play, though revealing of their deeper natures. If capable of affairs with women, Flaubert had always preferred men. His real affection went to Le Poittevin, to Du Camp, and to Bouilhet.[176] Yet there remains no evidence that he had been conscious of any sexual attraction to them, nor did he ever reveal a hatred for women. Instead, he wrote his books to vent a hatred of stupidity, and he was obsessed by human failure. He showed a special compassion for women in general, however, and, as Emile Zola knew, women sensed that Flaubert was a feminine type.[177] His sexual abnormality, in other words, was not overt homosexuality, but masochism.

Du Camp tells us of an incident in Egypt which he recognized as an example of Flaubert's morbid obsessions, but which we would recognize as an exercise in sadomasochism. If we eliminate the embroidery born of Du Camp's poetic license and realize that the story was written thirty years after the event, the elements of a precise medical observation remain. They had left the Nile valley on a four-day excursion into the Egyptian desert during hot weather. At the end of the first day the camel bearing their waterskins accidentally fell, and the flasks burst open. They proceeded, however, confident that they could buy water from other caravans (which turned out not to be the case) and aware that they would reach a spring in several days. After some hours without water, Flaubert began reminiscing about lemon ices at Tortoni's until the chatter became unendurable for Du Camp. As it was impossible to stop Flaubert's torturous talk, the two had to separate. Flaubert rode at the head of the party; Du Camp brought up the rear. The incident had been especially memorable as the only inharmonious moment during the entire Near Eastern trip.[178]

Louis Bouilhet, meanwhile, was being regaled by tales of sexual triumphs and temptations, which must have contrasted cruelly with his humdrum opportunities in Rouen. Even if we generously discount for the braggadocio that was customary when the literati recounted their venereal exploits (a sign that they were more like commoners than they liked to believe), one can safely assume that this had been *un tour copulatif*. At Qena, Du Camp and Flaubert walked through the prostitutes' quarter, Flaubert for once resisting the pressing invitations, but freely dispensing alms. He had refrained, he said, "in order to retain the despondency of the scene," adding that "there is nothing finer than these women calling to you. If I had responded, another image would have superseded this one and attenuated its brilliance."

At Isna, however, he overcame his artistic stoicism to visit a celebrated courtesan, Kuchuk Hanem. She received the two travelers at two in the afternoon, perfumed their hands and danced for them briefly, having summoned musicians. They returned for the main performance about six to find an additional four female dancers and singers, all of them supposedly educated, "bluestockings," which confirmed Flaubert's belief that all women of letters, no matter the country, are whores. The entertainment lasted until half past ten, with interludes of lovemaking, in which Flaubert claimed to have had five good orgasms, the third being especially notable. Kuchuk was not eager to have them spend the night, fearing that the presence of Europeans would attract thieves. Nevertheless, Du Camp spent the night alone on a divan, while Flaubert accompanied Kuchuk to her bed. She was exhausted from her dancing and fell asleep. He spent the night awake, watching her sleep, comparing the experience with nights of pleasure in Paris.[179]

Roughly ten weeks later, as our tourists were returning from Upper Egypt, Flaubert revisited Kuchuk Hanem in Qena. He found her changed, apparently recovering from an illness; and her appearance saddened him, perhaps accounting for his remark, "I fired only one shot." In compensation, he found a "belle bougresse" and a "grosse cochonne," or so he told poor Louis Bouilhet.[180]

The Egyptian episode lasted six months. On 17 July 1850, they sailed from Alexandria for Beirut, where they remained a few days longer than planned because of the engaging local French colony.[181] This would seem to have included Camille Rogier, who offered them young girls before and after lunch. Du Camp was able to avail himself of this opportunity but once, as he suffered from a chancre of Egyptian origin; but Flaubert claimed to have had three of the girls before eating and one after dessert, shocking them by washing his genitals in their presence.[182] This all may have been true, but we must never forget Flaubert's love of invention and his delight in outrageous stories.

At the beginning of August, they set out for Jerusalem, and by September they were in Damascus, from where Flaubert recorded a curious remark which suggested a kind of sexual neutrality. He asserted that love is like the need to urinate. "Whether one discharges into a good vase or into a clay pot, it must come out; and chance alone procures the receptacles for us." In the same letter he revealed his sensitivity to Syrian men between eighteen and twenty, calling them handsome and magnificent.[183]

They arrived in Constantinople on 13 November 1850, by which time both men were suffering from venereal infections, the third of the trip for Du Camp. Flaubert thought that his own chancre dated from Beirut, and he was now obliged to dress his injured organ each morning and night. He visited the district of the male bordellos, where the boys were usually long-haired Greeks, but his incapacity made him merely a sightseer.[184] As these unseemly details were omitted in earlier editions of Flaubert's letter of 14 November to Bouilhet, those earlier medical investigators who suspected that Flaubert had contracted a venereal infection in the Near East were handicapped in their attempts to diagnose it. They did know of his two nights with Kuchuk Hanem, in March and early June of 1850; and they knew that toward the end of that year, he had begun to complain of losing his hair. By February of 1851, he acknowledged that he was becoming bald and fretted that it was a sign of premature senility. Du Camp made light of Flaubert's worries, and, in his lucid moments, Flaubert recognized that Du Camp was right: "My reaction is female, unworthy of a man and a Republican—and I know it." Nevertheless, he felt a keen humiliation.[185]

Was this loss of hair a manifestation of secondary syphilis as the early medical scholars proposed?[186] The answer has to be *no*. If the chancre that Flaubert was treating in November was of syphilitic origin, it is unlikely that the secondary stage of syphilis would have begun as early as December. What is more, there is a veiled reference to his hair in a melancholy passage written the previous September, which hints that his baldness had already been perceived.[187] The simple fact is that Flaubert, at twenty-nine, was fast losing the athletic proportions of his youth, well on the way to that bald and rotund figure of familiar portraits; and he feared being taken for a worn-out office clerk.

On the other hand, there can be no question that Flaubert was suffering from a venereal infection. His description of a chancre would suggest either syphilis or chancroid, a painful, ulcerative condition of the genitals that is common in hotter climates. At the time of Flaubert's infection, chancroid was believed to be a form of syphilis, as its causative organism was not discovered until 1889. But a less well-known venereal disease, lymphogranuloma venereum, also more common in warmer climates, not only produces temporary genital sores, but marked gland enlargements in the groin and pelvis of the victim. In recent years, moreover, a variety of venereal diseases have been recognized as caused by bacterial, viral, or protozoal infections and infestations, which are sexually transmitted in most cases. Thus, when someone in the nineteenth century complained of an attack of the pox, we can no longer simply assume that it was syphilis, gonorrhea, or chancroid, the three principal diseases spread by sexual intercourse. Urethritis, for example, has a clinical appearance similar to gonorrhea.[188]

In Flaubert's case, the diagnosis is further complicated by the suspicion that he had had a venereal infection long before he ventured into Egypt. We have already noted Benjamin Bart's remark that the outbreaks on Flaubert's skin, first evident in the summer of 1844, led Flaubert to wonder if he had had a venereal infection. The slowness of his recovery from his nervous ailment, plus the periodic appearance of annoying boils, finally induced Flaubert to consult a Parisian physician in May of 1849. His verdict was "chronic syphilis of long standing," the possible cause of the nervous ailment.[189] That diagnosis seems unfounded, because Flaubert never seems to have suspected syphilis until he experienced symptoms that signaled its second stage; and because only in a most unusual case of syphilis would the secondary symptoms have persisted for five years. We can understand the physician's deduction, of course, given the primitive knowledge of syphilis and Flaubert's sexual experience. What that diagnosis does tell us, however, is that the nervous ailment was not regarded as *le grand mal,* but as some mysterious reaction to a physical cause. As for boils, though they may well be associated with a number of diseases, it is now known that certain constitutional conditions predispose people to crops of boils; and it is reasonable to suppose that Flaubert was vulnerable to periodic eruptions during those many months of depression when he sought to cope with his nervous ailment.

Thus it seems probable that Flaubert was not syphilitic by 1849 and was therefore susceptible to infection. He, himself, believed he had been infected in Beirut, thanks to Camille Rogier's hospitality in late July, 1850. If the infection was syphilis, as both Du Camp and he would have necessarily supposed, the chancre or ulcer ought to have appeared before the end of August and to have healed by the end of November. We already know that he was treating the chancre in mid-November and pronounced himself as nearly healed in mid-March of 1851.[190] Though syphilis does not always develop so precisely, the evident irregularity denies us a convenient certainty. The infection, in fact, may have been contracted later than Flaubert believed, and it may have been another ulcer-producing disease. Only after reaching Naples did he believe himself to have recovered, and he boasted of several sexual contacts; but his admitted abstention later in Rome was a confession that all was not well.[191]

Professor Bart, basing his conclusions on unpublished materials in the Lovenjoul collection and on Flaubert's original travel notes in the Bibliothèque historique de la Ville de Paris, believed that Flaubert had finally been reduced to chastity by the debilitation of the six-month-old infection. He had a low fever, facial neuralgia, a rash on his belly, and pain in one testicle.[192] Such symptoms do, indeed, sound like the characteristics of secondary syphilis;[193] and it may have been complicated by other debilitating infections contracted in countries where Flaubert, as a foreigner, would have had little natural immunity. Had Flaubert ever exhibited clear symptoms of tertiary syphilis in later years, which he did not, we could be more confident of the diagnosis. Du Camp's claim that Flaubert died of an epileptic seizure has been interpreted as a deliberate falsehood to conceal the fact that he died as a result of venereal disease.[194] That remains to be proved. Moreover, the perilous possibilities of later syphilis were unknown when Du Camp wrote his memoirs.

By the time Flaubert and Du Camp reached Italy, they had been absent from France over fifteen months. Flaubert had paid continual attention to his mother, sending her frequent and lengthy letters describing the more seemly details of the tour. The very volume and tone of his letters (and our awareness that the prospect of the long trip had troubled her) make it fair to infer that the letters he received from her en route were calculated to remind him regularly that he had left her behind to suffer alone. About a year after his departure, she evidently resolved to join him, to meet him in Italy for the tag of the trip. She seems to have raised the matter as early as August of 1850, by which time the travelers had reached Jerusalem. Flaubert answered that she could join him either in Naples or Venice, if the matter of providing for Caroline at Croisset permitted. In any case, he left it to his mother to decide.[195] By early October, he had had no word of her decision,[196] but learned in early November that she would join him. He expressed pleasure at her decision, adding that he was concerned about what would happen to little Caroline.[197]

His equivocation persisted. Hearing a week later that his mother proposed to have his Uncle Parain accompany her, Flaubert approved the arrangement; *but*, he disapproved of leaving Caroline behind. Would Mme Flaubert not continually worry about the child? If the child should become ill, "would you not reproach yourself?" Would not Mme Flaubert's absence offer Hamard the excuse to take his child? No, it was unthinkable that the child's welfare should be sacrificed for his own benefit! If Mme Flaubert felt that she could not bring the infant with her to Italy, then he, Flaubert, would cut short his trip. He could no longer bear, he told her, having her pine away at Croisset or spending his time in continual anxiety about her. Perhaps she should obtain a reliable medical opinion as to whether the trip would do Caroline any harm.[198]

The possibility that life with mother was to be resumed immediately put him into a melancholy mood. He wrote to Bouilhet in Rouen, never mentioning his mother, but ending with a sigh: "Why do I have this gloomy desire to go back to Egypt, go back up the Nile, and see Kuchuk-Hanem again? Well, I spent an evening there such as one rarely has in life. I enjoyed it to the full. I wished you had been there."[199]

155

A few days later, still apparently steeped in pessimism, he addressed his mother on the subject of women and marriage. It is a pity we cannot know whether Mme Flaubert made any connection between his views on women, which were wounding to her sex, and his anticipation of their reunion. He did, indeed, express deep sympathy for the plight of women, which was characteristic of him; but he also made no secret of his antipathy. Females, he asserted, are taught to lie when very young, and it is a teaching that goes on all their lives. Everything is done to turn them into cheats, after which they are bitterly criticized for being exactly that. Despite his previous horror of the "moral corset," he found himself becoming a moralist; and one of the chief benefits of his trip had been his discovery of the universality of evil—of the chicanery of people everywhere.[200]

His mother had used the occasion of Ernest Chevalier's marriage to ask Flaubert when he meant to marry. The trip, he responded, had not changed his outlook. On the contrary, the more he had seen of the world, the more he was inclined to withdraw into his shell, and he hoped to remain a bachelor. He pictured himself, at twenty-nine, as beyond the marriageable age and established in his chosen way of life; marriage for him would be an appalling apostasy. Despite Alfred Le Poittevin's death, Flaubert had not forgiven him for marrying or forgotten the irritation that the marriage had caused him. Besides, if he is to write about the realities of life, must he not stand apart from it? "Involved in life, you see it poorly.... Thus, I believe that the artist is a monstrosity, something outside nature." He meant to continue to live as he had lived before the trip, caring nothing for the world or for position in it. He assured his mother that it pleased him to be certain that he would never love anyone as he loved her. "You will never have a rival, never fear."[201]

In mid-January, in Athens, Flaubert learned that his mother was still bent on joining him in Italy, but had determined to leave both Caroline and Parain at home. It was understood that Du Camp would abandon the tour upon her arrival. Flaubert insisted that she reconsider bringing Parain, because he knew that she would not want to stray far from hotels, and he wanted her to have a companion so that he would be free to sight-see.[202] As the weeks went by, as he avowedly counted the days until he would see her toward the end of March, he expressed his fear that she would find Italy dreadfully cold. He advised very warm clothing, furs, even a footmuff. He warned her to expect changes in his appearance: he had taken on weight, and his hair was thinnish. He forecast baldness on top within two years.[203]

They met at long last in Rome, in April of 1851. She found that the Greek god was not only withering into bourgeois rotundity, but that he was far from well. She found him coarsened, and she complained of the roughness of his manners. He was surprised, though often aware of the need to restrain himself; and he soon discovered that she was anxious to return to Croisset. They went northward to Florence and on to Venice, where a decision was made to cut the trip short. By then, Mme Flaubert was suffering from boils, and his debilitating ailment made a return to Croisset advisable. "I am exasperated," he wrote to Du Camp, "in every possible sense of that word."[204]

Mesdames Colet and Bovary

In mid-May, meanwhile, Louise Colet became aware that Flaubert's trip to the Orient was nearing an end. She had been recently widowed, on 21 April, an event that cannot have caused her anything but the most perfunctory grief; and her latest liaison, with the Republican deputy Désiré Bancel, had run its unhappy course. It was time to reengage Gustave's attention. She wrote to him in Italy asking to see him for one last interview, promising to remain calm and gentle during their encounter. Weeks passed with no response. On 15 June, she learned that Flaubert and his mother had been in Paris for three days, and that they had just left for Croisset. She composed a second letter, asserting that she was on the verge of a trip to England, and that she would pause in Rouen for the interview. When she received no response in five days, she determined to force the issue by going to Rouen on 26 June. The day before her departure, she received two letters from Flaubert that upset her extremely, but failed to deflect her from the task at hand. They met briefly at the Hôtel d'Angleterre, as close to England as she got. She asked to be allowed to pay her respects to Mme Flaubert, which Flaubert refused; and she proposed to become his mistress, which he rejected with some firmness. He would come to see her occasionally, but that was all.[205]

Their correspondence resumed in July. She complained of having found him cold in Rouen. He answered that, on the contrary, he had endeavored to be on good behavior, though not to be tender, as that would have been hypocritical. If she could only be less tempestuous, he would enjoy her company; but he was too old for her emotional scenes. In subsequent notes, he mentioned that he had a sore throat and that he had begun work on a new novel [*Madame Bovary*].[206] She chided him for being tied to his mother's apron strings.

Writing to Maxime Du Camp a few months later, he admitted that her reference to his filial bondage was a valid one. In fact Flaubert's letter to Du Camp testified to his awareness that his preference for a secluded, chaste existence was associated with a hatred for life that dated from his youth. Moreover, he endeavored to articulate that outlook during the very early weeks of his work on *Madame Bovary*. His youth had soaked him in an "opiate of boredom" sufficient to last for the remainder of his days, leaving him not only a hatred for life, but a hatred for anything which reminded him that life must be endured. He had dragged his affliction everywhere: to school, to Paris, to Rouen, to the Nile. Why had he not kept mistresses? Why had he advocated chastity? Why had he remained in a provincial backwater? Not because he lacked energy or potency, but because he had not been cut out to be a man about town in Paris. "Few men have had fewer women than I. That is the punishment for devotion to *plastic beauty*."[207] As before, Louise was irritated by his seclusion and demanded explanations. All he would say was that the secret was buried in his past. Alfred had known it, and he was in his grave.[208]

Toward the end of 1851, Flaubert spent six weeks in Paris. There remain a few brief notes he wrote to Louise during his visit, mostly suggesting arrangements for a dinner or a rendezvous. That he seemed prone to postponement was not lost on Louise, and he was quite capable of notifying her that he would come at three-thirty, but leave at five-thirty. Her protests only fed his annoyance.[209] Yet, he continued to write to her in 1852, and always in affectionate terms. But he also wrote to Henriette Collier during those months, and in the same tone of exaggerated affection. He seemed determined to maintain ties with old friends, male or female, and he employed his considerable literary skills to remind them of his long attachment and his great regard. His amorous language proved nothing but a fond memory. It was a suitable style for flattering ladies of all ages from the security of his study, but it could only irritate Louise. He cited his novel to account for his inability to go to Paris as frequently as he would like, encouraging her with a prediction that the book would be completed in twelve or eighteen months. He would then go to Paris more often.[210]

Not only had he vastly underestimated the time *Madame Bovary* would require, but he was far from eager to live in Paris. He admitted it when telling Louise that Louis Bouilhet had decided to move there from Rouen. The city annoyed him, he told her; it was the scene of too much idle chatter. As for Bouilhet's decision, he added,

"I shall be left alone; my old age will begin."[211] In early June, to avoid going to Paris as he had promised Louise, he joined her for several days in Mantes.[212]

After his return from the Orient, Maxime Du Camp had participated in the revival of the *Revue de Paris* and pursued his photography, an art in which he was a pioneer. As Flaubert labored over the tribulations of Emma Bovary, Du Camp was drifting into successful journalism and was distressed to see Flaubert shackle himself to Croisset. He exhorted Flaubert to move to Paris before it was too late, to board the literary bandwagon and make a name for himself. He asserted that "the breath of life" could only be found in Paris, and that there could be no salvation for gentlemen outside the city. "My dear Sir," the novelist replied, "Humanity is everywhere, but there is more nonsense in Paris than elsewhere." To become famous was not his principal concern. He aimed at something better: to please himself. Success ought to be a result, not a goal.[213] Du Camp was hurt, for which Flaubert was sorry, but he bridled at being told how to live his life. "We are no longer following the same course, nor sail in the same boat. . . . I seek not a port, but the high seas. If I should be shipwrecked, I absolve you of mourning."[214] The friendship was never quite the same again.

In the autumn, Flaubert met Louise briefly at Mantes.[215] Some weeks later, she evidently informed him that she was pregnant, then cancelled the diagnosis. For three weeks he suffered a dreadful fear: he could not bear the idea of becoming a father. He must never be guilty of transmitting to anyone the torments and shames of existence. He was within a day of being thirty-one when he wrote her of his dismay, and it is evident, from his letter, that he had also been horrified that a pregnancy would have compelled him to accept a conventional, bourgeois existence.[216] In the aftermath, he confessed to her his adolescent desire to castrate himself. "Last year, when I told you about my idea of entering a convent, that was my old leaven rising again within me." There comes a time, he added, when one needs to make oneself suffer, to abhor one's flesh, to throw mud in one's face, so hideous does it seem. Had he not had a love of form, he "might have become a great mystic." Adding his nervous attacks to the picture, "the involuntary deterioration of ideas and images," made him believe that he knew what it is to die. "I have often felt my soul ooze away. How often I have felt myself close to madness—and you know my authority with the mad and how they like me!"[217]

The monasticism of Croisset, as Flaubert said to Du Camp, enabled him to please himself. His insight into his solitude would emerge again in the final version of *Saint Anthony*. Hilarion, a former disciple of Saint Anthony, says to the hermit: "Hypocrite! Burying thyself in solitude only in order the more fully to abandon thyself to the indulgence of thy envious desires! What if thou dost deprive thyself of meats, of wine, of warmth, of baths, of slaves, of honors? Dost thou not permit thy imagination to offer thee banquets, perfumes, women, and the applause of multitudes? Thy chastity is but a more subtle form of corruption and thy contempt of this world is but the impotence of thy hatred against it! Either this it is that makes such as thyself so lugubrious, or else 'tis doubt."[218]

Flaubert's withdrawal, of course, was incomplete. Having seen Louise in Mantes in early November, 1852, he saw her again in Paris in February; and they were together for five days in Mantes in May.[219] His dental difficulties had recurred before the latter rendezvous, and he warned her that his mouth would hardly be presentable. He was slowly losing his teeth, like his hair, and remarked that one is hardly born before putrefaction sets in. He had been a complete person only between the ages of seventeen and nineteen, "splendid in fact," after which he had experienced a speedy deterioration. Not that he wanted his youth back, as it had been a time of terrible frustration, when he had been consumed by all possible kinds of melancholy and by thoughts of suicide. His nervous illness, he told Louise, had been a good thing in that it had converted all that mental distress into a physical phenomenon, enabling him to cope with his problems with a clearer head. The five days in May that Flaubert granted Louise made for an unusually long sojourn; he presented himself with a mouth infected after the loss of a tooth, and was hardly able to eat after the abscess was lanced.[220]

One cannot read Flaubert's letters to Louise in 1853 without sensing what an agony the composition of *Madame Bovary* had become for him. Moreover, he had at last become aware that its completion would take far longer than originally anticipated. In virtually every letter, he groaned over the difficulties of making sentences, rewriting, and correcting. His passion for craftsmanship, for style, has since become celebrated; and it takes nothing away from his literary grandeur to note that his passion was rooted in masochism, that he was a secularized saint living a martyrdom for art.[221]

During Flaubert's first liaison with Louise, he had never hidden from her his conviction that their affair could not last. During the second liaison, he tortured her persistently and subtly with details about himself and his past—a virtual forecast of her inevitable defeat. He admitted that he had always liked prostitution for its own sake: that the sight of a seductively dressed woman walking in the rain beneath gas lights had always excited him in the way that the sight of a monk had always touched some ascetic, hidden corner of his soul. Both responses represented to him the negation of human relationships.[222] After a severe hailstorm, which had broken windows and ruined crops in Normandy, he informed Louise that he was little touched by collective misfortune, that he rendered unto humanity what it rendered unto him: indifference! He was not his brother's keeper.[223] He even gave her his recollection of his first seizure nearly ten years before, and he endeavored to describe the subsequent nervous attacks.[224]

Yet, he continued to see her every two or three months. In July, he sent his mother off to Trouville, spending several subsequent weeks in Nogent and Paris before joining her again.[225] His letters from Trouville in August expressed the hope that the sojourn might enable him, finally, to put his youth behind him; but his expressions of nostalgia, and his inclination to dote on his disease, were fair warning that he was incapable of shedding his past. He was sad on the eve of his departure from Trouville, fearful that he had not savored its sights and smells to the full; and he managed to return to Croisset through Pont-l'Evêque, scene of his initial seizure.[226]

Louise responded by demanding closer ties with Flaubert, a posture that smacked of marriage, especially when she renewed the request to meet his mother. It came at a moment when Flaubert was crushed by the knowledge that Bouilhet was at last carrying out his promise to move to Paris, making frequent trips there to get settled. Their cherished Sundays together would soon be at an end. Flaubert's tolerance of Louise diminished with his fretful mood. He told her that his mother had become so withdrawn that she was not even seeing her own friends. Louise, hoping that Bouilhet's move to Paris would encourage Flaubert to do likewise, sought Bouilhet's assistance in cornering him. Flaubert, meanwhile, tried to shut off Louise's campaign by assuring her that his mother would be pleased to receive her later in the winter.[227]

As Louise kept up the attack, Flaubert decided to go to Paris with Bouilhet in November, remaining with him from the tenth to the twenty-second. Louise seems to have been in tears most of the time and made her usual difficult scene at the moment of his departure; and he cannot have improved her temper by telling her, in a subsequent letter, how much he was missing Bouilhet. In talking to

Bouilhet about Flaubert, Louise was highly abusive, calling him an egotist and a monster, among other unpleasant things. The conversation was reported to Flaubert, along with Bouilhet's suggestion that Louise remained determined to become Flaubert's wife.[228] His infrequent letters gave her a new cause for complaint; but Flaubert told Bouilhet he had a clear conscience in the affair. He had never made promises that were not kept, or given her any false hopes.[229]

His claim was not entirely true. He had never encouraged Louise to believe that their affair could be anything but transitory, but he had recently promised to present her to his mother. She brought the matter up again in January of 1854, pressing for a visit to Croisset. He again refused, saying that his mother would be cold, hardly proper; nor would she come with him to Paris to pay a call on Louise.[230] In February, he stopped in Paris while on a trip to Nogent on family business.[231] Louise complained that he saw other people—not just her—and that he failed to send her flowers. In response to her charge that he was an egotist with "a sickly personality," his tone was sufficiently sharp to alarm her. She proposed that they halt their quarreling, to which he readily agreed; and her subsequent letters were dedicated to descriptions of her suffering.[232] By summer, when Flaubert planned to go to Paris to look for an apartment, he wrote to Bouilhet, "Not a word of my arrival to anyone, of course," as he hoped to avoid unpleasant encounters. He was well aware of Louise's reputation for vicious retaliation.[233]

It has been difficult to date precisely the events of their final rupture. Some years later, Flaubert regaled his literary friends with the story of his last visit to Louise's apartment at 21, rue de Sèvres. He arrived at nine-fifteen on an evening in October, 1854. She had expected him at nine and attributed his late arrival to a preference for other women. They sat down opposite each other by the fireplace, and he attempted to apologize by saying he had been inadvertently delayed; but she would have none of it and kicked him on the legs from the chair where she sat. He told his friends that he had been seized with a desire to kill her, but was restrained by a sudden vision of a *cour d'assises*. He saw the gendarmes, the judges, the audience, he heard the creaking of his chair in the dock; and he got up and fled from the apartment, never to return.[234] His description of the event had perhaps improved with time, but dramatization is forgivable in a novelist.

The next episode in their break apparently occurred sometime between 15 and 25 November 1854, when Louise attempted to take Croisset by storm.[235] Flaubert later told his literary friends that she arrived at his home to demand an explanation for his behavior in the presence of his mother; and that he had treated her with such harshness that his mother had felt his performance to be an affront to womankind.[236] Louise published her version of the occasion in the first of two novels in which she featured him in order to revile him—in *Une Histoire de soldat,* where she portrayed herself with nearly insufferable self-righteousness, self-esteem, and self-pity. Flaubert appears as Léonce, the callous lover, who sees her occasionally, but leaves promptly for home on schedule. It is made clear in the novel that Louise had found Flaubert's ardor odd, perplexing, and frustrating.

In the novel, she arrived at the country home at night. She could see Léonce's silhouette at the window and knew he was there. A servant opened the door, and she was coldly received. Two hours later, she was shown out into a stormy night by Mme Flaubert, described as a woman hardened and ill-tempered in her widowhood. Louise would have us believe that she left convinced that Flaubert would return to her, and that his failure to do so led her to suffer emotionally to a point of serious illness.[237]

The following spring Flaubert was staying in Paris at the Hôtel du Helder. Coming in late on the night of 5 March 1855, he was told that Louise had come to the hotel to see him. The following morning he sent her what has been called his final love letter: "Madame: I have been informed that you went to the trouble, last evening, of coming here three times. I was not in; and since I greatly fear that further persistence on your side would expose you to affronts from mine, good manners force me to warn you: I shall *never* be in. My salutations." On the margin of the letter, in Louise's hand, are three words: *lâche, couard,* and *canaille.*[238] The end had come at last.

The Goncourts noted that Flaubert later talked of the affair with no apparent bitterness; but he would also later remark that he had endured the two liaisons with Louise—the only liaisons of his life—as a burden.[239] That would seem to be confirmed by Maxime Du Camp, who described Louise's intrusion into Flaubert's life as a persecution and Louise as imperious and insatiable.[240] Certainly Du Camp's assertion that Louise did not mellow with age, but remained a treacherous backbiter, full of bitterness and hate, is borne out by the transparent characterizations in her novels. In *Lui,* the second novel in which Flaubert appears as Léonce, he comes off as a miser, as a man of "no soul," with a narrow mind and spirit.[241] She talked rather too freely of the affair, how she had loved Flaubert with all her heart, while he had loved her only physically; and she could find nothing but "material love" in his books. At some point in the liaison, she gave him a cigar case on which she had had a family stone inlaid, with the inscription *Amor nel cor*. She was infuriated to find the same device in *Madame Bovary*, and it must have awakened the terrible suspicion that there was some of herself in the unfortunate Emma. It is obvious that Flaubert's conduct in the affair was not beyond criticism; but he was at least more discreet than she in its aftermath, and he had the better last word: "I shall say of her what Danton said of Marat: she is unsociable."[242]

In the summer of 1854, when the Flaubert-Colet affair was over, save for the final dramatic episodes, Flaubert seems to have had a brief association with the actress Beatrix Person. It is unclear whether he sought her out to satisfy his physical needs, or whether he was conducting a bogus affair to seal the one with Louise. The cryptic allusions to it in his correspondence suggest that it had been inconsequential as far as he was concerned.[243]

More serious was a gross swelling and inflammation of his tongue, which caused great discomfort. The attack lasted nearly a week and was accompanied by fever. His tongue became sufficiently large to impede eating and talking, and he passed three nights without sleep. The attack occurred at Croisset, and he wrote Bouilhet that he would consult Dr. Philippe Ricord (the specialist in venereal diseases) when next in Paris. In the meantime, he was going to continue taking heavy doses of potassium iodide, a specific for syphilis in the nineteenth century.[244] He also experienced a discoloration of his genitals for about three weeks.[245] Because Flaubert revealed, in addition, that he had become a heavy pipe-smoker (as many as fifteen pipes a day),[246] some have speculated that the swollen tongue, a glossitis, derived from overuse of tobacco. Two other possibilities seem more likely. Evidently Flaubert related the glossitis and the genital discoloration to his venereal infection of 1850, after which, we must presume, he would have received the standard treatment for syphilis: mercury as well as the potassium iodide he indicated. Enlargement of the tongue is one symptom of mercurialism, or mercury poisoning, though there are other standard symptoms—metallic taste and emaciation—which Flaubert did not report.

We have, moreover, evidence of dental trouble and buccal infections in Flaubert as early as 1842, long before the trip to the Near East, which led to periodic loss of teeth. We also know that later in life he suffered from abundant and infected salivation, which required frequent mouth rinses, and which considerably disgusted him. This symptom strongly suggests a medicinal stomatitis, that is, an inflammation of the mouth that can result from the prolonged use of mercury; but there are other forms of stomatitis, such as acute catarrhal stomatitis, which could have been produced by Flaubert's periodic dental infections. The evidence is insufficiently clear as to whether his painful glossitis derived from one or several causes.[247]

There had arrived at Croisset, meanwhile, an English governess, Juliet Herbert by name. Very little is known about her and her association with Flaubert, and his biographers disagree as to whether she became his mistress for a time after the second fiasco with Louise Colet. She remained at Croisset from 1853 until Caroline's marriage in 1864, and there can be no doubt that Flaubert became fond of her. She was certainly the most mysterious of his alleged mistresses; and as there are few references to her in his correspondence (abridged or unabridged), some have concluded that Caroline must have destroyed the evidence of a liaison when she was gathering Flaubert's letters for publication. That seems implausible, since Caroline meant to sell his letters and knew their financial value. She was quite capable of cutting or bowdlerizing letters such as those to Bouilhet or Duplan before publication; but what we know of Caroline's character indicates that she would not have disposed of anything that could be sold.

Enid Starkie, one of the biographers who worked from the original letters at Chantilly, concluded that the assumption of a liaison with Juliet Herbert was unfounded; and the very idea of a middle-aged Victorian spinster running off to Paris for sexual orgies was quite beyond Starkie's toleration.[248] She was probably right. Readers of the Goncourt *Journal* know, to the distress of some of them, that when the literati of the Second Empire began to dine together regularly, it was as much for the exchange of smut as for the exposure of lofty ideas. There was a good deal of boasting about sexual prowess, but Edmond de Goncourt never took Flaubert's boasting or his fascination with the obscene at face value. He called Flaubert a "faux cochon," who tried to be the equal of his friends—who were true *cochons*.[249] Many of his letters to women in his later years were salted with suggestions of passionate attraction, but common sense forces us to recognize them as blarney. That is why Starkie was on the right track when she doubted that Juliet Herbert had been Flaubert's mistress and when she suspected that normal sexual relationships had meant nothing to Flaubert.[250]

The woman in his life at that moment was Emma Bovary, and he would not be finished with her until 1856. Though the setting of the novel was Normandy, and though many researchers have unearthed

Norman contemporaries whom Flaubert used as models for his characters, he despised being associated with realism—because he so despised reality. What is more, when asked who had been the model for Emma, Flaubert's response was: "Madame Bovary? c'est moi," which was neither a facetious nor a disingenuous answer. He no doubt did draw upon an instance of infidelity known in his region; it is incontestable that his research for the novel was wonderfully precise; we know that he turned to Louis Bouilhet especially for accuracy in medical detail. Thus the casual reader is entitled to believe that he is being given a superb and, apparently, impersonal view of the reality of Emma Bovary's world and her desperate boredom with it. But being the limited creature she was, Emma could never have described her anguish with the words that Flaubert used. The events in the story were not from his actual life, but the despair, as described, was his.[251]

In his earlier novels, then unpublished, the first *Sentimental Education* and the *Temptation of Saint Anthony*, the autobiographical elements were not skillfully concealed. One might logically conclude that the gender shift in *Madame Bovary*, that is, the device of concealing his views by having a woman express them, was a measure of his advancing craftsmanship. But the fact is that, in his youth, he wrote a story in which he had a little girl relate some of his own experiences.[252] *Madame Bovary* most surely *did* reflect Flaubert's arrival as writer and artist; it was the work of Flaubert "the master," to borrow Starkie's appropriate phrase. The question that remains is whether, with that novel, Flaubert meant to reveal a maturing insight into himself, and whether his explanation, "Madame Bovary? c'est moi," was a franker statement than his hearers could ever have suspected, much less understood.

It has been remarked several times that Flaubert gave Emma the characteristics of a hysteric. Because he also depicted her panic, when "she felt her soul slipping away quite like the wounded who felt life itself oozing from their bleeding wounds," in terms so identical to the description of his hallucinations given to Hippolyte Taine, the serious possibility is raised that Flaubert suspected that his own nervous attacks had been of a hysterical nature. This is the more remarkable in that, at the time Flaubert was writing his novel, conventional wisdom held that hysteria was exclusively a female disorder, originating in the uterus, and that hysterical attacks were to be seen most frequently in passionate women deprived of sexual intercourse and in young widows. Hippocrates himself had prescribed marriage as the cure; but, in the early nineteenth century, that easy solution was beclouded by the fear that marriage for too ardent women could lead to other maladies resulting from sexual excesses.[253]

It has been further noted that Flaubert, in *Madame Bovary*, related sexual repression to a variety of neuropathic disorders. The reader may be inclined to remember the novel as the story of the heroine who has been made unhappy, and thus emotionally unbalanced, by her marriage. In fact, Flaubert undertook to sketch her entire psychological development, to show in detail the conflict between her ideals and aspirations and the environment she despised. As a child she invented little sins in order to prolong her time in the confessional, and she continued to be seriously unbalanced. Flaubert did not reveal the nature of the invented sins, but psychiatrists tell us that little girls who are mythomaniacs generally invent sexual sins. He added to his description of her childhood the laundress who came monthly to the convent, bringing the sentimental novels that Emma devoured, cultivating those romantic visions of life which put us out of touch with reality and lead inexorably to disaster: *le bovarysme.* After her mother's death, Emma revealed the morbidity that Flaubert had displayed in 1846 after the deaths of his father and sister. Thereafter, she seemed to slip into a dream world quite similar to that of schizoids; and Flaubert portrayed her as cyclothymic—as having alternate periods of depression and elation.[254]

Finally, Flaubert gives us an Emma who has grown up to be sexually inhibited or repressed. He even used the word *refouler,* which became the medical meaning of *to repress* in French, as well as other words that Freud would use fifty years later. We cannot know how familiar Flaubert may have been with the latest theories of neuroses or psychopathologies. While it is true that some of the revolutionary work which began to redefine the nature of hysteria—demonstrating it to be an emotional rather than a physical phenomenon—or to link sexual inhibition with subsequent neuroses, was published shortly *after* the publication of *Madame Bovary,* that does not necessarily prove that Flaubert was unaware of the theories. One of the important pioneers was Dr. Auguste Morel, a specialist in mental disease and chief physician at the Saint-Yon Asylum in Rouen. His ideas had been broached in lectures before scientific societies; and Flaubert, as a member of a distinguished medical family in Rouen, would have had easy access to medical information.

On the other hand, Flaubert the letter writer always seems to have been aware that he had denied himself love: "Why? I do not really know. Was it out of pride, or out of fear? As a youth I loved profoundly and in silence, after which I nearly died of a nervous ailment, brought on by a series of irritations and troubles."[255] He understood, whether from experience or medical treatise, that he was sexually repressed, and that the ultimate penalty had been periodic hysterical crises, hallucinations, and great anguish. He meant to portray Emma not as an adulteress or debauched woman but as a woman whom we today would call sick or neurotic, repressed and schizoid. Indeed, his initial plan had been to portray Emma as a virgin, a pathetic creature buried in the provinces, growing old in her disappointment with life, until she reached the final stages of mysticism and frustrated passion.[256] That abortive conception provides us the most obvious link between the Flaubert in both Saint Anthony and Emma, and confirms his assertion, "Madame Bovary? c'est moi."

Thus, despite the gender shift in *Madame Bovary*, that novel was as subjective as Flaubert's other works. He may have laced his letters with antiromantic pronouncements, dedicating himself to impersonalism and impassivity, and engaging in painstaking research; but he knew how much of the romantic survived in him. It is a pity that so many literary personages in subsequent generations took Flaubert at his word, accepting fully his claims that the story of Emma Bovary had been totally invented, and that he had put "neither his feelings nor his life into it. . . . Art must be elevated above one's personal likings and nervous susceptibilities. It is time to give art, by way of a merciless method, the precision of the physical sciences."[257] He believed, and taught, that the artist should approach the true through a rigorous cultivation of the beautiful, by conquering style and form. Toward that end, he labored with great regularity in his study, never waiting for inspiration. His files were well ordered, and he could not have worked if his books had not been arranged in a particular way. That was the Flaubert who inspired Walter Pater and Henry James later in the century and James Joyce and Ezra Pound after that.

The other Flaubert was quite indifferent to the beauty of things around him—the furnishings of his house, for instance, which were heavy and indelicate.[258] And the real Flaubert not only put his "personal likings and nervous susceptibilities" into his novels and stories, but gave particular expression to his dislikes and his hatreds. Given Flaubert's aesthetic formulas, later writers found it all too easy to ascribe those dislikes and hatreds to a dispassionate view of reality, giving them an authority, a validity, that would have been sharply undermined by a recognition of their subjectivity. As it was, the message conveyed went beyond *bovarysme*. Not only are we compelled to feed on dreams which are quite unrealizable and which bring us to ruin, but it is that very phenomenon which makes human life a horror. Flaubert's view of art as the only escape from the ordinary life he hated amounted to a proof that art is superior to life. His vision would remain unaltered for the remaining twenty-four years of his life.[259]

Boils and Nerves

It would be agreeable to think of Flaubert, after years of unhappiness and labor, as emancipated by the success of *Madame Bovary*, as achieving serenity in particular. The novel did, indeed, bring him fame; but he proved to be incapable of surmounting the evil and perversity he saw about him, perhaps because he never came to terms with the flaws within himself. He was thirty-four when he completed his novel in the spring of 1856, and Maxime Du Camp immediately bought it for publication in serial form in the *Revue de Paris*. The editorial staff found the book too long and detected passages likely to provoke the imperial censors, a serious matter, as the editors had already been warned twice for indiscretions and faced suppression in the event of a third offense. The perfectionist who publishes, however, believes he has achieved perfection without editorial assistance; and this first encounter with editors proved to be painful. The first installment finally appeared on 1 October, and, within a few weeks, the police were taking an alarming interest in his prose.

In retrospect, it seems likely that Flaubert's prose was deemed offensive to religion and morality because the regime was largely interested in the opportunity to strike down a liberal journal. In the trial that resulted it was easy for the defense in court to prove that Flaubert had certainly not held up Emma as a model for young women; but, while he was acquitted, the *Revue de Paris* was suspended and ultimately suppressed.[260] The incident no doubt promoted the sale of the bound volumes when they appeared in 1857, but it only deepened Flaubert's contempt for conventional morality as embodied in the bourgeois.

He had initially meant to rework his *Saint Anthony* after the completion of *Madame Bovary*, but he again set it aside early in 1857 to begin work on *Salammbô*, a novel about Hamilcar's alleged daughter. He told the Goncourts that he had chosen Carthage as the locale for his new novel because, in his view, it had been the most rotten civilization in the history of the world. They found that choice consistent with his obsession with the marquis de Sade and with his delight in stories of human stupidity.[261] Be that as it may, Flaubert threw himself into an orgy of research on the geography, flora, and fauna of North Africa; and he read Polybius in particular for the history of the Punic Wars and of the mercenaries' revolt against Carthage. Polybius had merely mentioned a daughter of Hamilcar. Flaubert gave her life as Salammbô and invented her passions as well.[262] In the spring of 1858, passing again through Marseille, he made a trip to North Africa to savor the atmosphere of the setting. Old memories directed him to the house where he had spent a night with Mme Foucaud eighteen years before, but nothing seemed familiar.[263]

If anything, his habits of work were increasingly intensive, and stories of his solitude began to make the rounds. His passion for perfection had become a veritable disease, exhausting and immobilizing him, as well as accounting for the slowness of his writing. He could no longer really admire writers freer than he in the use of language—Balzac and Mérimée, for examples. It was said that he had given his servant instructions to speak to him only on Sundays, in order to say to him, "It is Sunday, Monsieur." He had developed an aversion to exercise, and his mother had to pester him to set foot in the garden. She told the Goncourt brothers that it was not unusual, when she returned from a trip into town, to find him in the same place, in the same position, as when she had departed. This immobility in his study, this life in a manuscript, disturbed and frightened her.[264]

Maxime Du Camp would say that *Salammbô*, which occupied Flaubert from 1857 into 1862, if less appreciated as a literary work than *Madame Bovary*, revealed more of the author: his personality and temperament, his gifts and defects. He meant that Flaubert had indulged his taste for sadism as in no other work, and to a degree not esteemed by more sensitive readers; and he knew that Flaubert had preferred *Salammbô* to *Madame Bovary* and had been irritated to be identified habitually as the author of the latter book.[265] The reader today may find it hard to believe that the endless violence and gore in *Salammbô* comes from the same man whose taste and craft he has learned to admire in *Madame Bovary*, and the revelation that Flaubert preferred the evidently inferior work is also surprising. After hearing him complete the reading of *Salammbô* aloud, the Goncourts concluded that Flaubert was crude, that exaggeration alone appealed to him, and that he was always on the verge of excess: "In a word, he loves painting on wood, glass beads, and is a kind of Tahitian Homer."[266] While today's reader of *Salammbô* may share the Goncourts' dislike of the novel, he would not likely reach their facile conclusion that Flaubert had been inferior to his books, or accept their suspicion that he had derived his knowledge of sadism from reading Sade. In no other work did Flaubert more clearly reveal his insight into the association of sexual frustration with hysteria, and with the tendency to seek relief in mysticism or religious fanaticism.[267] His understanding, in fact, was so far from crude as to attract the attention of psychologists.

In *Salammbô, le bovarysme* has been shipped to North Africa. During the mercenaries' revolt against Carthage, one of the barbarian commanders, a Libyan named Mâtho, has become infatuated with Salammbô, daughter of Hamilcar. His dream of possessing her was impossible, given their social difference and the fact that she was a virgin priestess dedicated to the cult of Tanit. Flaubert gives us a second impossible dream as a backdrop: the high priest Schahabarim, Salammbô's mentor, has also fallen in love with Salammbô, though the fact that he is a eunuch is a handicap.

The critical moment in the story arrives when the barbarian forces trap and surround a Carthaginian field army. Mâtho, meanwhile, in his search for Salammbô, has violated the temple within Cathage and stolen the veil of Tanit. We are to understand that the field army under Hamilcar, and Carthage itself, will be lost unless the sacrilege can be avenged and the veil recovered. Salammbô, therefore, is induced by the high priest Schahabarim to go to the barbarian camp and seduce Mâtho if necessary to recover the veil. Salammbô experiences a hysterical attack before complying with Schahabarim's instructions. In fact, Mâtho himself experiences what seem to be attacks of hysteria because of his frustration in love. When Salammbô reaches Mâtho's tent, she demands the veil; he violates her sexually as had been anticipated, and then falls asleep. "Inflamed with a murderous desire," she is about to slay him with a dagger, when Mâtho is awakened by shouts. The Carthaginians have set fire to the Libyan camp. In the confusion, Salammbô takes the veil of Tanit and makes for the Carthaginian lines.

Her appearance gives the Carthagianians great hope as they fight their way out of the trap and regain the protection of the city walls. Thereafter, Salammbô prays nightly for Mâtho's death. Yet, at the end of the story, when Mâtho has been captured and mutilated to a point of imminent death, she sees him in his final agony and yearns to feel again the embrace she experienced in his tent. Karl Gumpertz, who knew of Reik's earlier analysis of Flaubert as a masochist, proposed that *Salammbô* was in fact an illustration of female sadomasochism, or what he called the Judith complex. A female who derives an abnormal, sadistic pleasure from destroying the male will exhibit a strong inclination to frigidity. She will offer herself presumably only for external or patriotic reasons.[268] A similar conception of female hysteria had already been proposed in 1891 by the American gynecologist, A.F.A. King, and by the Austrian neurologist, Moritz Benedikt, who described the woman who exposes herself to rape while seemingly rejecting it. Though Benedikt had published on hysteria as early as 1864,[269] it seems most unlikely that Flaubert gained his understanding of female sadomasochism from medical literature.

Louise Colet spoke favorably of *Salammbô* in the hope of a reconciliation with Flaubert. He acknowledged her remarks, but failed to respond to their intent.[270] He had already warned Ernest Feydeau about Louise: "She is a pernicious creature. For a laugh, read her *Une Histoire de soldat*. You will recognize your old friend described in reprehensible hues [as Léonce]."[271] As for his long liaison with Louise, he remembered it as a very long irritation but one that bore no wound.[272] Despite its repute for being the supreme happiness, he had never found anything in love except troubles, storms, and grief. He meant to keep as wide a gulf as possible between himself and womankind.[273]

Wise as that decision may have been, it did not bring Flaubert serenity. When he was working on the proofs of *Salammbô*, he had a bad attack of boils, serious enough to put him in bed; and six months later, when he was in a rage over hostile reviews of *Salammbô*, boils again made their appearance.[274] We find him bedridden again with a "formidable" boil soon after the marriage of his beloved niece, Caroline,[275] an event which reinforced his sense of loneliness. Flaubert's tendency to develop boils at moments of depression or anguish is the factor which cast doubt, earlier, on their importance as a reliable indication that he had suffered from syphilis.

Because her father, Emile Hamard, had drifted into alcoholism and madness, Caroline had been reared by Flaubert and his mother. There were two suitors for her hand: Dr. Franklin Grout, who became a psychiatrist, and Ernest-Octave, a lumber merchant from Neuville near Dieppe, who had no surname, since his grandfather had been illegitimate and his mother had only a given name. Flaubert advised Caroline to marry Ernest-Octave, because he was likely to become rich—and he could not bear the thought of her being poor. That advice, coming from Gustavus Flaubertus, Bourgeoisophobus, should convince us that his diatribes against the bourgeoisie had nothing to do with class or wealth. It was necessary for the court to provide Ernest with a surname, however, and though the court recommended the name Philippe, Caroline seems to have chosen Commanville.[276] The marriage took place on 6 April 1864.

As we shall see, the promise of wealth was an illusion, and Flaubert would pay dearly for his advice. Death would spare him the knowledge of Ernest Commanville's untimely and unseemly end, in the house of a mistress whose existence had been unknown to Caroline. She took refuge afterward with Dr. Grout's sister. Grout, meanwhile, had never married; and, on the eve of his retirement in 1900, Caroline became his wife.[277]

After Caroline left Croisset in the spring of 1864, Flaubert felt abandoned and struggled with depression, claiming that it required an exercise of will to go on living. "How badly ordered the world is," he wrote. "Of what use is ugliness, suffering, sadness? Why do we have aspirations impossible of fulfillment?" In that frame of mind, he set to work on a large novel he knew would require many years, the second version of the *Sentimental Education*. The loss of Caroline brought home the fact that he was aging, and he dared not postpone the tale of his own unfulfilled aspiration. The topic was distasteful, but he had never managed to put it behind him. Working on it guaranteed that he would be drenched in sad memories, that he would see everything "draped in black."[278]

At some point in this period of his life, his spending began to exceed his income, and he admitted to debts in Paris for furnishings, clothing, and writing supplies. A *notaire* was authorized to sell a family farm in Courtavent, but matters proceeded slowly, to Flaubert's annoyance. We are not surprised to read that he again had several bouts with boils.[279] The sale was finally completed after two years of anxiety, and Flaubert learned that his share of the proceeds would be 15,566 francs. He was now able to repay 500 francs he had borrowed from Ernest Commanville; to use 5,000 francs to repay his backlog of debts in Paris; and to entrust the remainder, about 10,000 francs, to Ernest's care.[280]

If anything, his solitude deepened as he labored on *Sentimental Education*. George Sand called him an anchorite, and he replied that the term was closer to the truth than she might realize. For weeks on end he spoke to no one except his mother on Sundays.[281] Following her marriage, Caroline customarily visited Croisset only twice a year, in the spring and the fall. Flaubert made occasional visits to her home, but interruptions of his work bothered him intensely. He would become irritable and anxious, and the visit would be brief.[282] His mother worried about him, especially after she began to suspect that he was not being candid about his finances. But, as Flaubert knew, it was her nature to worry, to torture herself continually. When legitimate reasons for anxiety were lacking, she invented them. She had a gift for intruding herself into situations that would make her unhappy.[283] It was a personality Flaubert had good reason to understand, and he believed that nothing remedial could be done.

Flaubert's insight into his mother's penchant for unhappiness calls to mind his long-standing ambivalence toward her. No one doubts that he was devoted to her; but she was a person who, in making life difficult for herself, made it difficult for others. *How* difficult she was for Flaubert is a matter of some curiosity. Reading his letters before and after his break with Louise Colet, one is struck by references to Mme Flaubert's increased mobility and sociability *after* the break. She received old friends again and traveled more, and Flaubert practically ceased to complain of being tied down by her. Unless he had persistently exaggerated her demands upon him as a way of keeping Louise at bay, it would appear that Mme Flaubert became less demanding once the rival woman disappeared from the scene.

Even so, in *Sentimental Education* he showed great understanding of the demanding mother and her techniques to hold a son at home: "In a gentle voice, broken by sobs, she started talking to [Frédéric] of her loneliness, of her old age, of the sacrifices she had made. Now that she was unhappier than ever, he was deserting her. Then, referring to her approaching death: 'Good heavens, show a little patience! You will soon be free!'"[284]

The story of Frédéric Moreau's unrequited love for Sophie Arnoux in *Sentimental Education* has long been recognized as Flaubert's representation of his own unrequited love for Elisa Schlésinger. But the novel also contained situations and qualities no less autobiographical. Once the novel was published, it was often assumed that Flaubert had meant to shock his readers by apparently suggesting that the happiest moment in a man's life is his first visit to a brothel. Flaubert's point was quite to the contrary: he wanted his readers to understand that a man, in that particular situation, believes that his experience in the brothel has put him on the threshold of the amorous bliss he has anticipated with adulthood; in fact, life will be downhill from then on, and love will bring heartache, not bliss.[285] How right Emile Faguet was to say that Frédéric Moreau, psychologically speaking, was the son of Dr. and Mme Bovary.

One is struck by the lack of energy in Frédéric and others in the novel. Their inability to adapt to, or cope with, their century emerges as a malady, and their consequent anxiety is the most frequent sign of their degeneration.[286] It is evident that Flaubert, like other writers in his circle, was aware of Dr. Joseph Moreau's theories which related vitality—especially intellectual vitality—to neuroses. Indeed, when he was working on *Sentimental Education*, he noted that the sickly Goncourts were in Vichy for a cure, adding, "But then we are all sick! The result of this fine occupation we have."[287] One would wonder if Frédéric Moreau had been consciously named by Flaubert as a tribute to Dr. Moreau's presumed command of psychological truth.

While it may well be that Flaubert's political ideas were fluctuating and far from precise, that he knew more about what he was against than what he was for, he did reveal in *Sentimental Education*, and elsewhere at the time he was writing the novel, a political and social outlook quite consistent with his dismal view of humanity and life. One of the persistent themes in the novel is the picture of the Parisian population as a pack of cheats and sharpers. Flaubert leads us to expect little improvement in the future. He gives us Sénécal—first as radical reformer in 1848, later as brutal employer—as indication that the reformer's concern for humanity is entirely theoretical, and that he is quite indifferent to individuals, a bounder like all the rest.[288] From such an outlook came Flaubert's occasional pronouncements in favor of government by mandarins. "Axiom: Hatred of the bourgeois is the beginning of virtue. I include in this word *bourgeois* the bourgeois in working clothes as well as the bourgeois in frock coats. We, and we alone, meaning the learned, are the People, or to put it better, Humanity's tradition."[289]

In the years immediately following World War II, when French intellectuals were excited about the defeat of fascism and optimistically welcomed wider participation in public affairs, Flaubert was decried for his failure to have been engaged politically in his own time. By the 1960s intellectual fashion had changed. Since life and thought were suddenly perceived as increasingly uniform, engagement was seen as a subtle form of enslavement. Flaubert was then rediscovered as the writer who had sought to think freely (which was to say, differently) and who expressed that difference in hostility to most everything then established: politics, society, the arts, religion.[290] His skepticism and nonconformity—qualities surely associated historically with freedom, but in his case productive of confinement—had been redefined as liberty. He had been a haunted writer, pitifully frustrated, shackled throughout adulthood by the disappointments and disenchantments of his youth. "I have a hatred for life," he had written at the age of thirty, "and for everything that reminds me that life must be borne."[291] He, at least, could have had no illusion of his liberty.

He was grateful, in the summer of 1869, that the enormous task of composing *Sentimental Education* was coming to a close, and he anticipated presenting the work to Louis Bouilhet for his criticism. Bouilhet, however, was ill, far sicker than Flaubert seems to have recognized, and he died on 18 July. "What good is writing now," Flaubert lamented, "since he is no more!"[292] His grief was profound. "In losing my poor Bouilhet," he later wrote, "I lost my midwife, the one who saw through my thought more clearly than I myself."[293] Bouilhet's death, in fact, proved to be only the first in a torrent of calamities for Flaubert. Within a few days of the publication of *Sentimental Education,* it became painfully clear that the book was not attracting critical acclaim. Even many of his friends were either baffled or dismayed by it. In rejecting Flaubert's vision of life, they denied themselves the pleasure of his extraordinary literary talent.[294]

The evident failure drained him of energy and shattered his morale. Early in 1870, he was beset by influenza and by an eczema on his face, and boils soon appeared here and there on his body. The health of his dear friend Jules Duplan gave cause for worry; and Duplan's death on 1 March quite overwhelmed him.[295] Jules de Goncourt was the next to go, on 20 June, and his death sharpened Flaubert's sense of loss and solitude. Moreover, his mother's increasing deafness and infirmity added to his preoccupation with death. He noted that only three of the company that had begun dining together at the Magny Restaurant were still alive: Edmond de Goncourt, Théophile Gautier, and he. "I no longer have anyone, absolutely no one, with whom to talk. I am alone as if deep in the desert."[296] He had, indeed, returned to his work on *Saint Anthony,* and it gave such trouble that he imagined a continual sob in his throat and feared he might be becoming hypochondriacal.[297] He reflected upon the quirks in his own personality. "Psychological problem: Why am I *very cheerful* after a visit from Michel Lévy [publisher of *Sentimental Education*]? My poor Bouilhet often said to me: 'No man is more moral nor loves immorality more than you. A piece of stupidity delights you.' There is much truth in that. Is it an effect of my conceit? or out of a certain perversity?"[298]

Flaubert's morale, in sum, had seriously ebbed even before the outbreak of war between France and Prussia on 19 July 1870, following which his letters reveal a deepening bitterness and anger. He was initially aroused by the "stupidity" of the popular enthusiasm for war.[299] Then, as the military news became ominous, though he had very faulty information, he became genuinely concerned for the outcome. His relatives from Nogent-sur-Seine descended upon Croisset to avoid the advancing Prussians, until he had fourteen people under his roof—yet he complained that he still did not have anyone to talk to. After the overthrow of the Second Empire on 4 September, he avowed he would defend the new Republic, but without enthusiasm or faith in its future. France would become a Poland, he predicted, and ultimately a Spain.[300] Nevertheless, his fighting instincts were aroused, and he took a place in the National Guard of Croisset as a lieutenant, expressing hostility to those who wanted peace at any price.[301]

This show of determination was paper-thin. The war came close to undermining his stability, but he remained sufficiently rational to recognize that he was more depressed and pessimistic about the future than anyone around him. He also knew that his morale had been sapped by the loss of his dearest friends quite before the outbreak of the war, and he claimed that his faith in himself had been greatly eroded, no doubt by the failure of his recent novel.[302] As for the conduct of the war, he was pathetically inconstant. He would succumb to the conviction that all was lost, and then suddenly occupy himself with suggestions for military moves that would retrieve the situation.[303]

But above all, it would appear that his despair and loneliness, his inconsistency and instability, derived from his longtime doubts about mankind and his own country and from his horror of life, which left him with no resilience when those days of reckoning came. He had prided himself on his indifference to politics, to form of government, apparently feeling no loyalty to the regime under which he lived. On the other hand, he had emerged from 1848 with a profound contempt for its intellectual reformers, and he had welcomed the coup d'état of 1851 which had sealed the Second Republic's doom. Despite the prosecution of *Madame Bovary* in 1857, which infuriated him, he accepted the patronage of Princess Mathilde in the 1860s (and it helped bring him the Legion of Honor in 1866). He frequented the princess's salon and received invitations to the Tuileries, which he did not disdain.[304]

Suddenly that world came to an end on 4 September 1870. He said quite frankly that he feared, more than the war itself, the society that might emerge from it, a society both military and republican, "antipathetic to all my instincts." The Muses would find no home in it.[305] Everything he loved was going to be lost: "A mandarin like me will no longer have a place in the world." It made him feel over eighty years of age when he contemplated "the End of the world,"[306] and he could not even think of sitting down to write. He was, he wrote to George Sand, the saddest man in France, dying of grief as he contemplated the coming era, which would be not merely military, but utilitarian, American, and Catholic—for he predicted a religious revival following the defeat. The age of what he called *le pignouffisme*, meaning the age of the common man or the boors, was beginning, a time uninhabitable for mandarins. "I am very sick, in mind and spirit."[307]

But the war did bring him more immediate, if less cosmic, worries. Nearby factories had to be closed down, and the unemployed poor began roaming the countryside in search of food. To give to a few was to risk pillage by the many. Mme Flaubert's decline was evidently hastened by the shock of the invasion; it had reached a point where she could not make up her mind about matters, and he found being caged with her at Croisset nearly insupportable.[308] By December, the region around Rouen had been occupied by the enemy, and the Flauberts were obliged to lodge two soldiers in Rouen and ten more at Croisset, plus six horses. The Prussians behaved well, but the very idea that the enemy would be camped in his house and garden was almost more than Flaubert could bear; and he told Du Camp that, in a frenzy, he had thrown papers, letters, and books into the fireplace before moving into Rouen. In the city, his mother became taciturn. She complained about not having visitors; but when they would call, she would not say a word to them. Caroline had gone to London to escape the war, which Flaubert disapproved, wanting her at home for assistance with his mother.[309]

It would seem that Flaubert did not possess the inner resources to remain firm in the face of adversity. He gave way nearly completely to despair, showing no faith in either his country or its people. The war revealed that he had long been an exile in his own land. He admitted to his niece that he wanted to leave France forever; it was a country henceforth uninhabitable for people of taste. And Maxime Du Camp would later say that Flaubert's desolation, after the invasion of his study, triggered the revival of his nervous attacks.[310] While he would deplore the Commune of 1871 and would have supreme contempt for its radical ideologists, the Prussian invasion affected him more deeply. He also believed that it had aged his mother ten years.[311] For several months after the armistice, he vomited nearly every day, until he feared he had developed cancer of the stomach.[312]

Several weeks after the suppression of the Commune, he made a brief trip to Paris and was overwhelmed and disgusted anew, not so much by the smell of corpses or by the sight of ruined buildings, as by the attitude of the people. "One half of the population wants to strangle the other half," he wrote, "and that other half shares the same interest." After returning home, he wrote that he felt no hatred for the Communards "for the reason that I do not hate mad dogs." But he thought he could never forgive the Germans, and that he could never again tolerate the company of one of their countrymen.[313]

Despite his disgust with Paris, he was obliged to go there repeatedly in the later summer for dental treatment. His dentist, wanting to avoid pulling any more teeth, cauterized and filled several of them; but Flaubert continued to suffer great pain. As his mother could no longer be left alone, Caroline had to come from Dieppe to stay with her in Flaubert's absence.[314]

His political views, if never notably precise, were more expressly antidemocratic after the events of 1870–71; they epitomized the logical flowering of his hatred for mankind, for the people in general. He brooded over what they would read if free and compulsory instruction should become the rule. In his opinion, the popular press was a school for brutality, since it dispensed with thought. The most immediate remedy, he argued, was the abolition of universal suffrage. The masses had to be respected only because they contained "the germs of an incalculable fecundity." Therefore, give them liberty, but not power. That must belong to a natural aristocracy—to those of talent. George Sand, considerably to the left of Flaubert, was put off by his fear of the people. Very well, he responded, let us stop talking about brutalizing the commoners. The problem is to enlighten the enlightened classes, to begin with the head, for that is where the sickness is. "Unlike me, you are full of gentleness. I should like to drown my contemporaries in latrines."[315]

For the few he loved, however, Flaubert never spared himself. In the autumn of 1871, he neglected his *Saint Anthony* to trouble himself with various projects to memorialize Bouilhet: not simply matters involving his grave and monument, but efforts to get a volume of his verse published and his play, *Aïssé*, performed at the Odéon. The people with whom he had to negotiate exasperated and wearied him. Discussing his management of "Bouilhet's corpse," he remarked: "Never have I been so submerged by a disgust for life."[316] The municipal council of Rouen had not found Bouilhet sufficiently distinguished to merit a monument, while the play had a good first night on 6 January, and that was all. The theater was nearly empty the second night—two and a half months of arduous labor had gone for naught.[317]

Before 1870, there had been evidence of financial ease in Flaubert's letters. He had often offered money to friends in need. After that date, we become aware that bills were overdue and unpaid. The cost of his apartment in Paris, which had put him momentarily into debt several years before, continued to be a drain; but it would appear that his mother and he did not easily recover from the high cost of feeding roving bands of unemployed during the war. One large outstanding bill was for wine, most of it drunk by their Prussian guests. He told his niece that he had nearly choked with anger on receiving some assessment papers.[318] Reducing their domestic help permitted their property at Croisset to decline. Returning from Paris in March of 1872, where he had taken his mother because he could not leave her alone, he found the house in a deplorable state. The smell was dreadful, and he was driven into "a temper bordering on madness." His mother was declining fast, which also upset him. He fantasized again of a convent where he could be free.[319]

Mme Flaubert died toward the end of the first week in April. He was crushed, "broken by fatigue and grief," as he put it. Flaubert was then fifty. He had lived near her, and for her, for over twenty-six years—a duty after his father's death, but ultimately a necessity. He might complain about his servitude, but he also found he could not do without it. Her death removed the keystone of his existence, and he wondered how to begin life anew. Since Croisset had been included in Caroline's dowry, the property passed to her rather than to Flaubert, but with the proviso that he should keep his quarters. He was unsure he could bear to live there alone, yet was contemplating giving up his apartment in Paris because his friends were either dead or dying. One month after his mother's death, he managed to eat his dessert without tears, and he was beginning to work again on *Saint Anthony*. By mid-May, he seemed resolved that Croisset would remain his refuge, but his emotional seizures became more frequent.[320]

Flaubert had been free from his nervous attacks from about 1849 until some time in 1870. Beginning in 1870, he was given bromide, a remedy that had become fashionable about 1866. Several forms of the drug were used as medicaments, but as potassium bromide was considered the safest and most efficacious, it seems probable that it was the only one he ingested. Its prescription does not offer us definite proof of the administering physician's diagnosis, for bromide was then given for a wide variety of nervous ailments: as a specific to sedate the nervous system, and as an anticonvulsive in treating *grand mal* and hysteria. Alphonse Daudet would later suppose, when taking the drug himself, that Flaubert's well-known struggle with words and his slowness in composition could be attributed to large doses of bromide which clouded the mind. In fact, Flaubert's difficulty in finding the right word much antedated his use of bromide, and a glance at his original manuscripts is quite sufficient to demonstrate that Flaubert's painful literary pace was due to what one physician called "a tyrannical need for perfection."[321]

The Final Years

Because posterity has known Flaubert from his published books and letters, it remembers his deep pessimism and cynicism, his conviction that most men drift passively and pointlessly through life, and his rejection of life as a horrible business. Both his politics and aesthetics derived from that outlook, so that he seemingly consigned to the rubbish heap all those who failed to rank art above life, or who failed to escape life through a devotion to beauty. After reading Zola's *L'Assommoir* [The Pub], he found the premises underlying it ignoble: "To depict the truth does not appear to me to be the first essential of art. To aim at the beautiful *is* the essential, and to attain it if one can."[322]

Flaubert's contemporaries, on the other hand, could recognize another Flaubert. If they knew his hatred for the world of commerce, for the critic who produces nothing but judges everything, or for the learned gentleman who considers himself an artist thwarted by circumstances, they also knew him as a man who had many good friends, who liked them immensely, and who either overlooked—or was ignorant of—their failings. His love of life's ordinary pleasures, of friends, food, and drink, could conceal his horror of life itself; and he was greatly loved by those around him, unlike Baudelaire, who had been left alone because of his more obvious bitterness. Flaubert might elsewhere reflect his contempt for humanity, but he put himself out for individuals, showing concern for their literary efforts and willingness to give money to those in need. He had a kind heart and a great capacity for compassion that stands in sharp contrast with his passion for sadism.[323] It would appear that he endeavored to cultivate, during the final period of his life, a more charitable outlook; but the biases of a half-century were a formidable barrier, and his time was short, for he would outlive his mother by only eight years.

Moreover, his loss augmented his instability. In Paris on business in June of 1872, be became so overwhelmed with fury against mankind that he canceled a trip to Vendôme, where he had been invited, as a distinguished guest, to attend the unveiling of a monument to Ronsard. He had also been upset by the sight of Gautier, who was obviously dying, and he admitted to having "wept like an idiot" at the Schlésinger boy's wedding.[324] The following month he took his niece to Bagnères-de-Luchon, ostensibly for her health, but also to seek a cure for his nerves and irritability. The sight of the vacationing bourgeois revolted him, and he was quite unconvinced by a physician who attributed his nervous sensibility to overuse of tobacco. He wondered if he was not doomed to the fate of Jules de Goncourt, suggesting that the recently completed *Saint Anthony* might well be subtitled *The Height of Insanity*. But in a lighter moment, he described his malady as "the insupportability of the multitude."[325] In the autumn, he was disappointed to learn that Mme Schlésinger was postponing a visit to Croisset, as he wanted to receive her and "have her sleep in his mother's room."[326]

Théophile Gautier died that autumn. "He died out of disgust for modern life," Flaubert wrote. "The fourth of September [the fall of the Second Empire] killed him. That day, indeed, the most cursed of French history, inaugurated a new order in which people like Théo play no part. . . . He was the last of my close friends. He ends the list. He died of modern swinishness, his own words. . . . He had two hatreds: hate for shopkeepers in his youth, that fertilized his talents; hatred for the hooligans [Communards] in his mature years, this killing him."[327]

George Sand, meanwhile, having recognized Flaubert's lingering grief for his mother, advised him to marry. He found the idea fantastic, while recognizing that she was doing her best to raise his morale. The "feminine being," he responded, had never fitted into his existence; he was not rich enough; he was too old; and he was too decent to want to inflict himself on anyone for life. Besides, he possessed a fundamental ecclesiastical quality that others had not recognized.[328] He meant that his illness was quite incurable.

He did admit to having changed in one respect after 1870: he had become a patriot. Not that he had seen any lessening of the public stupidity, as he put it, but he had come to lament the probable death of his country. The Prussian victory had touched his conscience. It did not make him love his countrymen the more, but he feared that the future would be even more intolerable unless the French virtues, which he had always mocked, were to survive. He still lashed out at the bourgeois, but now he blamed them for having lost their instinct for self-defense, a hint of second thoughts about his own conduct in 1870. He claimed to sense a rising tide of barbarism and hoped to be dead before it swept everything away. "Never have the things of the mind counted for so little, or a hatred of greatness, or disdain for the beautiful, or literature despised, as now. I have tried to live in an ivory tower, but a flood of shit threatens the walls."[329] His newly found patriotism would compel him to attend the funeral of Adolphe Thiers, whom he regarded as a true patriot; and he astonished himself by weeping for the "king of *prud'hommes.*"[330]

Otherwise, his gloom seemed to deepen in 1873. His negotiations with publishers, on behalf of Bouilhet's and his own affairs, were so financially unpromising that he was continually irritated and claimed to be experiencing palpitations of the heart. He concluded that he should withhold *Saint Anthony* until a more profitable moment should arrive.[331] He complained of a persistent grippe and a bad cough, which finally forced him to remain indoors. Though he began to take delight in Laure de Maupassant's young son, Guy, and felt he must encourage his predilection for literature—at the very moment when he, himself, was threatening to renounce publication for good—he also managed to convert that pleasure into pain by dwelling upon the loss of Alfred Le Poittevin, Guy's uncle.[332]

During a momentary respite from anguish in March, he asked himself what manner of disturbance had been unsettling him to the core. "I do not know, except quite surely I have been very sick, hazily."[333] Returning to Croisset from Paris shortly after the first anniversary of his mother's death, he at once visited her room and then spent a lugubrious afternoon. For some weeks he threw himself into a frenzy of work, fourteen or more hours a day, preparing Bouilhet's *The Weaker Sex* for performance, until he exhausted himself and took to sleeping ten hours at night and two more hours in the daytime. The pace forced a vacation upon him during August.[334]

Working on Bouilhet's play gave Flaubert ideas of writing one of his own, *The Candidate*, in which he would indulge his hostility to democracy and the bourgeois. Venting his spleen did not seem to relieve his temper, and he was rather terrified by the prospect of rehearsals and public performance. He admitted to becoming increasingly "irascible, unsociable, and intolerant," signing himself Saint-Polycarpien, but pursued his theatrical project in the hope that it would make money. Hearing its lines in rehearsals made him nauseous, and once again he succumbed to a frightful cold: coughing, dripping, spitting, and running a fever at night. Meanwhile, he had released *Saint Anthony* for publication during Easter week, but

183

had learned that it would be prohibited in Russia as an offense to religion. Far from anticipating these literary events, he confessed his melancholy, saying that he felt empty and abandoned.[335]

The Candidate was first performed on 11 March 1874 at the Vaudeville, and it was a fiasco. Flaubert pretended to be indifferent, but he was as much personally humiliated as he was financially disappointed.[336] To make matters worse, reviewers trampled on *Saint Anthony* in the major journals, for reasons clear to anyone who has tried to read it. But as it was the most personal of his books, he was especially affronted and attributed the negative reviews to personal hatred. Evidently fearing that he had reached the breaking point, he consulted Dr. Alfred Hardy at the Hôpital Saint-Louis in Paris. To one of his correspondents, he wrote that Hardy had called him "a hysterical woman, a phrase I find profound." He reported to another correspondent as well that Hardy had called him "a hysterical old woman," and that he had answered, "Doctor, you are quite right."[337] Hardy seems to have been the first physician to see Flaubert's attacks as hysteria. That Flaubert had found the diagnosis insightful was later taken as evidence that he had never believed himself to be a victim of *grand mal;* and, in making that diagnosis, Hardy was commended for having sensed Flaubert's feminine characteristics.[338]

Flaubert agreed to go to Switzerland for relaxation, "to de-neuropath" himself, as he put it, since he felt deeply weary: not only stupid, exhausted, and isolated, but in the last stages of decline.[339] Before going on vacation, he had to take his ailing maid, Julie, to the Hôtel-Dieu in Rouen. He had not set foot in the place for many years, and the sight of it upset him. He was overcome by a violent stomachache, but he attributed it to more dental trouble, suspecting that he would have to have the last molar on his right side extracted.[340]

Switzerland repelled him immediately. He declined to be moved by the marvels of nature, and he growled at the sight of German and English tourists. The leisure gave him time to brood over his literary failures, success having eluded him for over a decade; and he had the offending tooth removed in Lucerne. Upon his return to Croisset, he claimed that the trip had only bored him. Settling in to work on *Bouvard and Pécuchet,* he moaned of his solitude and missed Bouilhet with every word he wrote. In September, however, he managed to admit that the weeks in Switzerland had benefited him. He was much less flushed and nervous, and could climb the stairs more easily.[341]

In such a moment of improvement, he wrote to Edmond de Goncourt, knowing that Edmond had been dispirited since Jules's death four years before, and urged upon him Voltaire's recommendation about gardening, "the wisest moral lesson in existence." Flaubert confessed that he had tried in vain to turn himself into a neurotic, but had been fundamentally too intelligent to go through with it. As "distractions do not really distract us, any more than stimulants really stimulate us," all that remained was to set to work courageously and not to dwell upon the past.[342] Flaubert, in fact, seems to have been struggling to follow his own advice, working hard to keep his mind off himself;[343] but it was a novelty that could hardly compete with a lifetime of dismal introspection. In the spring of 1875, his morale was as soggy as ever, he was again taking potassium bromide for his nerves, and he had begun to submit to hydrotherapy. Having noted that his "psychic weakening" had a hidden cause, he added that he found himself returning again and again to the memories of his childhood. An "invincible depression" captured him and caused him serious doubts about *Bouvard and Pécuchet*.[344] On passing through Rouen that May, he paused at Achille's house for a drink, and with the visit to his childhood home he was stricken with bitter memories. He had a headache by the time he reached Croisset and did not have the heart to make a tour of all the rooms.[345]

Early in the summer of 1875, he seems finally to have understood that the financial reverses Ernest Commanville had been experiencing since 1873 had reached a point of unmistakable disaster. Because Flaubert had reared Caroline as if she had been his own daughter, and because he had entrusted some of his capital to Ernest for investment, expecting to receive interest periodically, he had an obvious claim on reliable information from the Commanvilles; and they had hidden the truth from him until they were on the brink of ruin. He felt as if his heart were in a vise, as there was a suggestion that Croisset might be sold. Although he thought its loss would be a fatal blow to him, he assured his niece that he was ready to make any necessary sacrifice. He put his remaining farm, in Deauville, up for sale and realized 200,000 francs toward the end of August, which allowed him to help Ernest buy up an outstanding note.[346]

Ernest escaped bankruptcy, but Caroline was the principal beneficiary, as she avoided the sale of the assets—including Croisset— that constituted her dowry. (Under French law, a husband administered a dowry and could benefit from its income, but the spouse retained ownership.) Even though Flaubert lent, rather than gave, the money to Ernest, from whom he expected interest, he was quite rightly anxious about his own financial future. After what he had learned of Ernest's affairs, he knew that a loan to him was a poor risk, and he had nothing more than a mediocre income from his books. He found himself unable to write and suffered fits of weeping. In September, he gave up on *Bouvard and Pécuchet* and tried to begin work on his tale of *Saint Julian the Hospitaler*.[347]

Flaubert's friends, meanwhile, began to come to his rescue. The local public prosecutor, Raoul-Duval, and Senator Agénor Bardoux, who knew firsthand of Ernest's financial tangle, moved to obtain either a state pension or sinecure for Flaubert. He was grateful, but wanted a position that would not require extensive residence in Paris, a difficult stipulation. But he was nearly fifty-four and felt much too old to change his ways. "I am a man of the decadence," he explained, "neither Christian nor stoic, and not made for the struggles for existence."[348] The good-hearted George Sand, having heard that Flaubert might lose Croisset, assured him that she would buy it, if it were not beyond her means, so that he could remain there for the rest of his life. He was extremely touched by her generosity and explained that Ernest would be unable to touch Caroline's dowry. Croisset would be sold only as a last resort, and that seemed unlikely.[349]

Flaubert was the last great friend of George Sand's life. His earlier letters to her had always expressed great regard, but she had known that he liked her as a person, not as an artist. She was essentially indifferent to style and wrote too fluently to impress him.[350] She had long tried to convince him, quite unsuccessfully, to change his literary ways by altering his outlook: to open his heart to his readers and give them inspiration rather than desolation. Professor Bart has cogently suggested that her pleading finally had an effect in 1875, whether or not Flaubert was aware of it. We find him that year referring to her as Mother Sand in his letters (he also called her "mon maître"), and on one occasion he thanked her for a letter which he described as having been "tenderly maternal."[351] This may account, during his deep depression that year, for the character of the *Three Tales*, of which *Saint Julian* was the first he undertook. He may also have been moved by the beauty of his own financial sacrifice for the Commanvilles, a saintly gesture that could have led to a martyrdom of poverty. Whatever the case, the central figures in all the *Three Tales* would see God, a blessing that Flaubert knew would never come to him or to most other people, given the horror of life, but an uplifting possibility for readers that would have pleased Mme Sand had she lived to read the stories. She died at Nohant on 7 June 1876. Flaubert attended the funeral and was greatly distressed.[352]

All three stories revived themes and experiences that had been central to Flaubert's life for many years. His Saint Julian was drawn from what one physician called "the rich mental family of ascetics." He is not the hallucinated person we are given in *Saint Anthony,* but the obsessional neurotic. Flaubert showed a remarkable understanding of the affliction.[353] In his third story, *Herodias,* he returned to the Oriental or exotic setting that had always fascinated him, as in *Salammbô*. But the second tale, *A Simple Heart,* the most touching and effective of the three, was based upon the scenes and memories of his childhood and youth; and he took great pains to see that the Norman descriptions and place names were correct. Félicité, the central figure in the story, was at least in part drawn from old Julie, the faithful servant who had been with the family since Flaubert had been a boy, and who would outlive him. The most striking autobiographical feature of the story, however, is found in the passage where Félicité is struck down by a coachman as she walks along the road to Honfleur. In April of 1876, Flaubert repeated the trip from Pont-l'Evêque to Honfleur, reliving the drama of January 1844, as he prepared his background material for the story.[354]

He completed *A Simple Heart* in August. Despite George Sand's death the previous June, Flaubert's spirits were on the rise that summer as he approached the end of the tale. He seemed to work without his habitual agony, and he took time to swim in the river each evening.[355] He became aware that his health, both physical and mental, was substantially improved, and that he could again work for long hours. It would almost appear that the work on the *Three Tales* had been therapeutic, and that *A Simple Heart* in particular had enabled him to break the chains of his past and to begin anew. It may be, too, that George Sand's death had the same effect. Although he wept at the sight of her coffin and felt as if he were burying his mother a second time, his letters in the aftermath were not repeatedly laced with the lamentations that characterized his correspondence after the death of other close friends. He missed her, of course, but her passing seems to have enabled him to accept his mother's death. To his niece he admitted that he had been profoundly ill after his mother's death without quite understanding the cause; but now the fog was lifting, and he felt rejuvenated.[356]

The improvement lasted about eighteen months. Even when he reported some palpitations of the heart, as he did in the spring of

1877, he attributed them to his intensive work on the last of his *Three Tales,* which was costing him sleep and causing him to drink too much coffee. But he no longer had to take potassium bromide, he was much less preoccupied by the death of old friends, his letters became less acid, and the reader of his correspondence becomes hopeful that Flaubert was at last mellowing. Only toward the end of that year do we get hints that he was reverting to an unwholesome regime, which included no exercise. He complained of hemorrhoids, of severe pains in the back of his head, and of not sleeping well.[357]

In 1878, his old preoccupations regained their ascendancy. A young medical student from Rouen, who had attempted some writing and who revered Flaubert, visited him repeatedly later that year. He was struck by Flaubert's isolation, an existence "Cyclopean" in scope, dominated by notions he had held for many years, seasoned with regrets about the past: regrets for his *father,* for Bouilhet, for Gautier.[358] All that autumn, in fact, he was sunk in depression, overwhelmed with gloominess, brooding about his isolation, and concerned about new Commanville business reverses. No sinecure had yet been arranged for him, but he asserted that he was not so much fearful of future privations as he was frightened that his mind was being sullied by base commercial preoccupation. He was becoming a grocer. It might be necessary to refuse an official function. He reached a point in midwinter of genuine concern about his own emotional state and admitted that he *was* quite concerned that he might have no future.[359]

On 25 January 1879, he slipped on a patch of frost, suffering a severe sprain and cracking a fibula. His local physician, Dr. Charles Fortin, put him to bed and told him he would be confined for six weeks—six weeks of reading and smoking. He assured the Commanvilles that the accident had been minor, especially in comparison to his "real cares and griefs." Fortin was very attentive, and Edmond Laporte came in frequently, often spending the night to relieve Flaubert's loneliness. The letters he wrote during his confinement, however, attest to the hardly unexpected fact that he bore his recuperation with a maximum of complaints and pessimism.[360]

While still abed, he learned that Ivan Turgenev and Juliette Adam had approached Gambetta on his behalf, requesting for him a post at the Bibliothèque Mazarine then held by the dying Silvestre de Sacy. Flaubert agreed to accept a pension if it could be obtained, even though he was reluctant to accept anything that would require living away from Croisset. An article in *Le Figaro,* mentioning his poverty, mortified him as an invasion of his cherished privacy, and he was enraged to learn, thereafter, that another candidate had won the position at the Mazarine. The news left him deeply demoralized.[361] Guy de Maupassant, then an employee of the Ministry of Public Instruction, joined the effort to arrange a pension; and Flaubert, having regretted sanctioning the effort initially, ended by telling Maupassant he would still accept if the terms could remain secret to protect his honor. He had just discovered that Ernest Commanville had sold his sawmill disadvantageously, a forecast of even greater financial restrictions.[362]

Toward the end of April, Flaubert had recovered sufficiently to get about, but the activity caused pain and swelling. One of his last molars also flared up and had to be extracted, after which he reported eye trouble and kidney pain. A large boil appeared to the left of his nose; and Dr. Fortin, no doubt aware of Dr. Hardy's earlier diagnosis, told Flaubert that he was increasingly showing signs of being "une grosse fille hystérique," which Flaubert admitted was only too true.[363] He said, indeed, that nothing seemed to be going right, that he was fed up with life. In his despair, he again gave way to fits of tears.[364]

When Maupassant reported that progress was being made on the pension, Flaubert said that he was grateful, of course, but that he also felt an "invincible repugnance" to accept it. He had nothing left but his pride and begged that it not be taken from him. Secrecy must be maintained; he must not fall again into the hands of journalists.[365] Soon after, he was offered the post of *conservateur adjoint* at the Mazarine: 3,000 francs a year and no duties. He had hoped for 5,000 a year and an apartment, but at least he was not obligated to go into an office to earn the pension. The prospect of "disguised alms" revolted him, but he went to Paris in June, calling on Jules Ferry, the minister of public instruction, to thank him. The pension began on 1 July 1879, and Flaubert found the first trimester payment, 750 francs, waiting for him.[366]

Dr. Fortin, meanwhile, had advised Flaubert to resume his use of potassium bromide, as well as valerian, as a sedative. While in Paris that summer, he spent many hours conducting research at the Bibliothèque Nationale; he complained that the extensive reading made his eyes water. His leg no longer pained him, but his articulation had not returned to normal. He returned to Croisset at the end of August, planning to spend the entire winter at home, correcting proofs for a new edition of *Sentimental Education* and hoping to complete his *Bouvard and Pécuchet.*[367]

His peace was soon disturbed by the appalling news that his dear friend Edmond Laporte, one of the people who, out of regard for Flaubert, had lent Ernest Commanville money, was now at loggerheads with Ernest over finances. Flaubert soon found himself in the crossfire, and Caroline forced him to break with Laporte. Poor Flaubert had been kept in the dark by the Commanvilles and never understood that Ernest had been a dubious businessman and that Laporte had behaved quite properly. Flaubert could ill afford to lose another friend, while Laporte, knowing the truth of the situation, deplored the unnecessary collapse of the friendship. The two were never to be reconciled. Money matters, Flaubert would later say, gave him the same aesthetic sensation that one ought to get if plunged into a latrine.[368]

Thus, instead of the calm that he required to complete his projects, Flaubert labored under the pressure of great unpleasantness; and before the year was out, he complained of great fatigue. His bitter outlook boiled to the surface: "The insupportability of human stupidity has become a *disease* with me, and the word is inadequate. Practically all human beings have the gift to exasperate me, and I breathe freely only in the desert." Many young writers, valuing his opinion, sent him their books, and he groaned over the obligation to comment on them. In February, he was outraged to learn that the young writer he most cherished as a disciple, Guy de Maupassant, was being threatened with legal action for indecencies.[369] Although his weariness with life was hampering his work, he also knew by April that the first volume of *Bouvard and Pécuchet* was virtually completed, and he began making plans for a trip to Paris—all the while regretting the stupidities he would meet there.[370] He was to be spared them.

The Long Medical Debate

Flaubert had scheduled his trip to Paris for 9 May 1880, a Sunday. On Friday evening, the seventh, he dined with his friend and neighbor, Dr. Charles Fortin, after which they recited Corneille. Flaubert slept until after eight o'clock the following morning. It was his custom to take a long, hot bath after rising, and to read the mail and a newspaper after he had dressed. Between ten and ten-thirty that Saturday morning, evidently feeling indisposed, he called Julie through an open window and asked her to summon Dr. Fortin. Julie found that Fortin had just taken a boat for another medical call. When she returned to the house, Flaubert was still on his feet, but somewhat giddy. He was not alarmed, telling her that he was about to have a

190

fainting spell, and he lay down on a divan. But the servants were frightened, and one of them set off to fetch Dr. Tourneux, one of Fortin's best friends, from Rouen. According to Tourneux's later account, the servant reached him about eleven-thirty, and they arrived at Croisset about noon.

Tourneux had been an interne under Flaubert's brother Achille, at the Hôtel-Dieu in Rouen, and he had been a guest at Croisset several years before this emergency summons. He had never treated Flaubert, but knew something of the patient from previous conversations with Fortin; and he most certainly would have discussed the case with Fortin after this particular call. He left no specific notes on the Flaubert case, but was interviewed several decades later by René Dumesnil when Dumesnil was preparing his medical thesis. Fortin, who had kept notes, suffered from mental troubles sometime after Flaubert's death and set fire to his laboratory, destroying his notes and manuscripts.[371] This enhanced the circulation of rumors about Flaubert's illness and death by those who had never treated the man. It was assumed that the physicians had not spoken out in order to conceal some unpleasant or shameful medical fact.

From Fortin's obituary, written by Tourneux in the local medical journal, we can deduce only a bit of information about both physicians' opinion of the case. Both men deeply resented the revelations Maxime Du Camp would publish about Flaubert's illness, because Du Camp had known that Flaubert had endeavored to conceal his seizures. Unveiling them was an unpardonable treason. It becomes obvious that both Fortin and Tourneux believed that Flaubert had been the victim of *grand mal* when young; but that as an adult, except for the brief recurrence of attacks after 1870, he had suffered chiefly from the memory of the seizures, "a perpetual nightmare."[372]

It bears noting that Dr. Fortin's medical credentials were dubious by the standards of his own day. He was an *officier de santé*, a public-health officer legally authorized to practice medicine without having obtained the doctorate. (The French government stopped granting such authorizations in 1872.) Fortin originally practiced medicine in the navy before settling in Canteleu, adjacent to Croisset. We find him treating Flaubert's mother beginning about 1865. He was a simple country doctor with a reputation for good sense, and solid judgment, and for being a reliable friend—qualities that would have pleased Flaubert.[373] But there is no reason to believe that he ever witnessed one of Flaubert's nervous attacks; it is more likely that he made the assumption of *grand mal* on the basis of what Flaubert told

191

him. Since Dr. Tourneux specifically used the term *morbus sacer*, we understand that neither physician had in mind a partial epilepsy or seizures that were epileptiform.

When Dr. Tourneux consented to speak out, he recalled that Flaubert had had "an apoplectic appearance" for some time before his death, and Fortin had believed him to be arteriosclerotic. He noted the earlier nervous attacks, but added correctly that Flaubert had not suffered any for a number of years. When Tourneux reached Croisset on the fatal Saturday, he found Flaubert stretched out on his Turkish divan. His face was flushed—"apoplectic"—and he gave no sign of breathing, though the heart was still faintly beating. There had been no disturbance, as would have been the case in an attack of *grand mal,* or any evidence of dribble or contractures. Flaubert's pipe was near him, still warm and full of tobacco. Within a few minutes, his heart ceased beating. On the basis of Flaubert's appearance, Tourneux attributed death to a ventricular hemorrhage.[374]

Ernest and Caroline Commanville, in Paris, were notified in the early afternoon that Flaubert had been stricken with apoplexy. Caroline immediately sent a message to Maupassant, asking him to join them at the railway station at six o'clock for the trip to Croisset. Upon their arrival, they found Flaubert on his bed, little changed except that his neck was swollen with black blood. Maupassant gave the details to Emile Zola in person and to Ivan Turgenev in a letter written several weeks after the funeral. He cited the sudden death, followed in due course by the appearance of the "black collar," as proof of apoplexy. As the body became rigid in death, the hands had contracted. Maupassant's observations were quite consistent with Dr. Tourneux's later testimony. Maupassant spent three days beside the body and helped Doctors Fortin and Pouchet wrap it in a shroud. "The days that one believes himself to be happy," Maupassant wrote, "do not compensate for such days as those."[375]

Maxime Du Camp, as we already know, had long believed that Flaubert's nervous attacks had been *grand mal;* and when he revealed that fact in his *Souvenirs littéraires,* initially published in the *Revue des deux mondes* the year after Flaubert's death, he provided a consistent, if inaccurate, account of that death.[376] In fairness to Du Camp, it must be added that others had reached the same conclusion after attending the funeral. Edmond de Goncourt, having received word of Flaubert's death on Saturday the eighth, went to Croisset for the funeral several days later with Claudius Popelin. The next morning, Georges Pouchet, who was a naturalist, told Goncourt that Flaubert had not died of a stroke, as the physicians wanted it believed, but during an epileptic seizure. He said that Caroline's request to have one of Flaubert's hands molded had been denied, as the contracture prevented making a cast. Pouchet added that there had been foam at Flaubert's mouth "with all the symptoms" of epilepsy.[377] Such revelations inaugurated an intense controversy about the cause of Flaubert's death *and* the nature of his prior illness. For Dr. Dumesnil, endeavoring to show in his thesis that the reliable medical evidence indicated a stroke or cerebral hemorrhage as the cause of death, was further convinced that Flaubert had never been an epileptic.

At the time of Flaubert's death, however, even those who believed that he had died of a stroke, also assumed that his nervous attacks had been epilepsy—and this was necessarily an assumption, since Flaubert himself never used the word. His reticence was attributed to shame. Not until after the turn of the century did Flaubert's readiness to accept the diagnosis of "hysterical old woman" strike medical scholars as possible evidence that he had never supposed himself to be a victim of *grand mal*. Moreover, the outrage among Flaubert's friends, upon reading Du Camp, stemmed not from his having published a false account of Flaubert's death, but because he publicly revealed the secret that Flaubert had presumably labored to keep hidden. That the revelation should have come from a literary friend was the more intolerable; and they found especially disgusting Du Camp's remark "that Flaubert had been a writer of rare talent, and that, without the nervous illness that seized him in his youth, he would have been a man of genius."[378]

Maupassant attributed Du Camp's action and remarks to jealousy, lamenting that men of letters, more than those in other professions, seemed driven to run each other down. "If you need a friend, do not choose him from the ranks of writers." And what a pity that "a man who could be such a faithful, devoted friend himself" should have been so betrayed![379] Thus did Maupassant sound the note that would be echoed within the literary world until very recent times: criticism of Du Camp for being unable to pardon Flaubert for his literary genius or for ignoring Du Camp's advice to abandon Croisset for Paris and the wordly honors and rewards that could be his. Although Du Camp insisted he had never doubted that Flaubert's literary talent was superior to his own, he was held to have been guilty of a vile attempt to downgrade Flaubert.

Du Camp may well have been hurt when his well-meaning advice was rejected by Flaubert, and they were never again as close as before that unfortunate incident. Yet, they remained on familiar terms to the end, and no one knew Flaubert's quirks of personality better than Du Camp. In recent years some scholars have rediscovered those attractive characteristics in Du Camp that Flaubert had evidently recognized. He aspired to different goals, perhaps, but he wanted them for Flaubert, too, and believed that some of Flaubert's enterprises were misguided.[380] No doubt, Flaubert's life and art would have been different had not illness struck him at an early age. Anyone who had been aware of the agony of that life might legitimately associate Flaubert's painful literary productivity with it, and come to the quite ingenuous, if debatable, conclusion that Flaubert would have been a more productive or distinguished writer had he been more emotionally sound.

The literati, in fact, were quick to charge Du Camp with malice, because they had been jealous of his close association with Flaubert. Indeed, as a close observer of men and events, Du Camp knew too much for the comfort of many; and some on the left had never forgiven him for his powerful attack upon the Communards, whom he called "traitors to their wounded country, arsonists, and murderers."[381] It brought him the election to l'Académie française in 1880, a mark of success many of the literati ostentatiously despised. That election seemed consistent with Du Camp's failure to have shared the literati's conventional hostility to the July Monarchy or the Second Empire. In their minds, he was an established scoundrel long before he "betrayed" his friend.[382]

For a time, the suspicion of suicide confused the issue of Flaubert's death. Georges Charpentier, Flaubert's last publisher, had received a short letter from him about a week before the end.[383] It expressed such profound exasperation, such a sense of weariness, that Charpentier was convinced he had taken his own life. One physician, speculating on that theme, claimed that the black collar around Flaubert's neck indicated that he had strangled himself in the bath. Other letters written by Flaubert during his final week of life, however, were not written by a man who aspired to the grave; and none of Flaubert's reliable biographers has accepted the proposal of suicide.[384]

The serious debate about Flaubert's illness did not open in medical circles until the turn of the century. At that stage of the debate, we must keep in mind that the physicians engaged in it meant *grand mal* when they used the term *epilepsy*. By that date, however, rapid advances had been made in the study of hysteria. It had become apparent that the difficulty of discerning the distinction between epilepsy and hysteria in many patients inevitably called into question previous diagnoses of epilepsy; and the ancient assumption that hysteria was linked to the uterus (*hystera*) had been destroyed by Dr. Jean Charcot and his associates when they found hysteria-like conditions in men, not just in women.[385]

In 1862 Charcot had been assigned as a medical resident to the Salpêtrière, an old hospital primarily used to house between four and five thousand elderly women. It was really a medical poorhouse. The appointment was not brilliant, but Charcot recognized a number of rare neurological diseases among his patients and saw the opportunity for clinical research. Between 1870 and his death in 1893, Charcot was considered to be the leading neurologist in Europe. With his disciple, Dr. Paul Richer, Charcot worked to distinguish between epileptic and hysterical convulsion. The first male patients were admitted for study and treatment in 1884, and Charcot published his *Leçons sur l'hystérie chez l'homme* the following year. The two also published illustrations of convulsive seizures, which demonstrated their belief that men had always been subject to hysteria, and that seizures had taken different forms over the centuries.[386]

The Salpêtrière—originally without laboratories, examining rooms, or teaching facilities—was transformed by Charcot into a modern medical institution. It became his practice to examine patients on Tuesday mornings in the presence of other physicians and medical students, and he gave public lectures on Friday mornings that were attended by a throng of students, physicians, and writers. Whatever may have been the errors of his methods, he was responsible for expanding the psychiatric horizon of such writers as Maupassant, Daudet, Zola, and Proust; and he had seen the "fixed ideas" of the unconscious as the nuclei of certain neuroses, a notion to be developed by Pierre Janet and Sigmund Freud.

As for his methods, it was soon recognized that his patients had not been carefully studied as to background or segregated in the hospital. The result was a kind of mental contagion, especially since Charcot habitually discussed cases and symptoms in the presence of patients. His assistants became aware that patients rehearsed their demonstrations before being brought into the examining room, and they knew that some of his results were suspect. As they were also aware of his despotic temperament, they often showed him only what he wanted to see. Consequently, his description of the three phases of a typical attack of what he called grand hysteria was passé before the end of the century.[387] Charcot had also recognized the class of symptoms that is now called conversion hysteria: the derangements of sensory perceptions such as blindness, the anesthesias, hysterical pains, tics, muscular spasms, and muscular contractures, as well as the "flaccid paralyses"—the inability to use limbs correctly.[388]

A change in the style of hysterical phenomena from the nineteenth to the twentieth centuries complicates immeasurably the historian's task of medical diagnosis. When Charcot was developing his description of the typical attack of grand hysteria, he noted that its first phase was epileptoid. The patient would have a warning of the impending attack, the premonitory aura: it was accompanied by either mental excitement, a feeling of agitation, a cough or tremor, or perhaps a hallucination. There might be a palpitation, a sense of tightness in the head, a feeling of excessive warmth or of an obstruction in the throat. The patient would soon lose consciousness, the breathing would be reduced, there could be a swelling of the neck, foam at the mouth, and a violent oscillation of the arms and legs. It becomes clear why Charcot was at pains to distinguish between true *grand mal* and grand hysteria.

The second stage of grand hysteria, according to Charcot, was some form of clownism, most usually the *arc de cercle*, the body bent into a rigid arc. Once it was recognized that Charcot's hysterics knew what behavior was expected of them, that behavior evoked less sympathy from physicians; and new forms of hysterical behavior would replace the old. The arched back, in fact, is no longer seen; and we must suppose that it may not have been seen before Charcot observed a case of it at the Salpêtrière. In similar fashion, the *obvious* conversion symptoms that were observed in the nineteenth century are only infrequently seen today; thus it appears that the comprehension of hysteria came close to eliminating the earlier phenomena. Potential hysterics today will often find their satisfaction in some of the other psychoneuroses. For reasons as yet inadequately explained, the muscular manifestations of hysteria in the nineteenth century have given way to visceral manifestations in the twentieth: from wild demonstrations to the gastric ulcer.[389]

In some rural areas, however, where the population has been untouched by the Freudian revolution and is relatively unaware that physical symptoms can result from emotional disturbance, or where the familial style of life can result in the early observation of sexual scenes between adults by children, the classic forms of hysteria are still seen. Such people have not learned to seek more socially acceptable or disguised avenues for the discharge of emotional disturbances and offer us examples of the patients studied by Josef Breuer and Sigmund Freud in the 1890s when they first presented evidence that a disturbance of sexuality, rooted in the forgotten past, was critical in the pathogenesis of hysteria. In time, that disturbance was understood to include a child's "love deprivation" with a consequent "love craving" as the basic trait in the hysterical personality.[390] Since we have already noted those characteristics in Flaubert as a child, it is clear why some physicians, by the beginning of the twentieth century, wondered if he had been a hysteric rather than an epileptic.

The medical debate about Flaubert's illness was befogged from the start by his admirers' desire to preserve his memory from any taint of a degrading malady. Even into the early twentieth century, epileptics were believed to be abnormal in personality, to have a permanent mental disturbance which produced egocentricity, eccentricity, supersensitiveness, impulsiveness, and emotional poverty or rigidity—the "epileptic character." In time, the victim was believed to suffer a decline in intellectual power and a drift into moral perversions. Only after 1930 was the stereotype exploded.[391] A recent medical writer has argued that the Flaubertians seized upon hysteria to eliminate epilepsy, and that some of them even related his convulsions to syphilis in the campaign to find something less shameful.[392]

In fact, the medical controversy among physicians themselves revealed prejudices or aversions that, on occasion, undermined the pretension of scientific objectivity. Dr. Michaut, who took great interest in the cases of literary people, complained of the tendency to equate illness with mental decline. In 1898, he argued not only that Flaubert had been an epileptic, but that he might not have written his masterpieces had he not been an epileptic. He supposed that Flaubert's initial attack left an indelible imprint of melancholy on him, which accounted for the tone of the novels; but implicit in his remarks is a hint of the older medical association between illness and genius.[393] He also insisted that epileptics never die of a seizure, but succumb rather frequently to a cerebral congestion. Thus he took the side of Doctors Fortin and Tourneux.[394]

A Dr. Gélineau, who also busied himself with the cases of literary people, cited the evidence of an epileptic seizure given by Dr. Pouchet to Edmond de Goncourt, remarking that Pouchet had been a learned physician and a long-standing friend of Flaubert. He meant that here was a medical friend who had not tried to hide the truth.[395] But Michaut questioned the value of Pouchet's testimony on the grounds that he had been a naturalist and physiologist, not a doctor of medicine. Pouchet, in fact, did have a medical degree, but he had never practiced medicine and was a naturalist by profession. Michaut also doubted the validity of Du Camp's information, pointing out that Du Camp and Flaubert were "ex-friends," and that Du Camp would have regarded the epilepsy as a blemish.[396] This brought Dr. Legrand into the fray, who said that he had been with Du Camp at the moment he received the news of Flaubert's death, and that Du Camp had burst into tears in a fashion unlike that of an "ex-friend."[397] Dr. Le Pileur, although a friend of Legrand and absolutely certain that Legrand had seen and heard Du Camp's sobbing, remarked that his grief did not pardon the bad taste he had shown in revealing something that should have been kept secret.[398]

So far, no physician had denied that Flaubert had been an epileptic; the argument had merely focused upon whether he had died of an apoplectic or an epileptic seizure. Late in 1900, a new commentator, Dr. Binet-Sanglé, began the expansion of the case by publishing a brief review of Flaubert's emotional history. Binet-Sanglé quite accepted the fact of Flaubert's epilepsy, but he was struck by the apparent periods of frigidity and by Flaubert's expressed desire, as a young man, to castrate himself. He recalled that Flaubert's crying spells had been first reported at age forty-nine, and that Dr. Hardy had called him a hysterical woman at age fifty-two. If one added to the picture Flaubert's melancholy, his thoughts of suicide, his hallucinations and love of solitude, a retarded emotional development was suggested.[399] Binet-Sanglé stopped short of calling Flaubert a hysteric; but it does seem likely that a man who had published in the fields of neurology and psychology would have known that Charcot had maintained that both male and female hysterics would show an indifference to sexual intercourse.[400]

Dr. Michaut quite agreed that the attention paid to Flaubert's epilepsy had overshadowed other medical symptoms. In particular, he thought that Flaubert had exhibited remarkable inconsistencies. He was famous for his hatred of trite or conventional expressions, of everything banal or bourgeois, of mediocre literature and bogus artists. Yet, how long he tolerated Louise Colet, who incorporated most of those hateful qualities, and how capable he was of even complimenting her on her properly forgotten novels! Among friends he could behave like a schoolboy (he wore out George Sand with his adolescent antics when he was her houseguest). What could have been more bourgeois than his admission that he had refrained from killing Louise because of a vision of the criminal courtroom? He lived as a hermit, yet was obsessed by prostitution and brothels and admitted a profound interest in the lowest kinds of sexual degradation. Flaubert had said that the mere presence of a bourgeois could disgust him to a point of vomiting; yet, he gave his first great novel a bourgeois setting. Flaubert recognized and explained such inconsistencies on the grounds that the artist is a monstrosity, a quite unnatural being; he depicts wine, love, women, and military glory in order to be neither a drunk, a lover, a husband, nor a footslogger. That confession, Michaut proposed, was the measure of Flaubert's peculiar neurosis.[401]

Flaubert's own physician, Dr. Fortin, felt impelled to break his long silence to lend support to those who advocated an examination of the "psychic physiology" of geniuses in order to understand their work. As we already know, Fortin remained silent on the issue of epilepsy, but he was willing to reveal a mental oddity about Flaubert's literary technique. In order to write, he had had to fall into what Fortin called a second state. The subjects he treated would then come to him as images or pictures. Once he had returned to his conscious state, retouching his work became extremely difficult. Fortin especially remembered Flaubert for a remark made late in life: "We live in a desert, no one understands anyone else; and our minds, darkened by the unknown, leads us blindly down the road of life, which is blocked at both ends by an X."[402]

It is improbable that Fortin understood the working of Flaubert's creative imagination, and the use of terms like *second state* and *conscious state*, not to speak of *the subconscious* used in the article's title, were probably misleading. On the other hand, Fortin, who had had emotional problems himself, was at least aware that Flaubert's habits of work were related to a peculiar mental set, and that he had been a man profoundly conscious of his solitude and had seen no point to life.

Dr. Félix Regnault was the first physician to challenge the diagnosis of epilepsy in Flaubert's case, and he did so in the context of a lecture criticizing the conventional association between genius and epilepsy. Because men of genius seemed subject to nervous ailments such as neurasthenia, hypochondria, hysteria, various neuroses, or even mental derangement, it had become medical gospel in the nineteenth century to attribute such disorders to cerebral hyperfunction, as illnesses striking an overworked organ. Did that mean that nervous troubles were actually a condition of genius, or that one should be a genius if one has a neurosis? The matter was so little understood in 1900, he complained, that to know that a man of genius suffered convulsive attacks was sufficient evidence to declare him an epileptic. He objected in particular to the teaching of the Italian psychiatrist and criminologist, Cesare Lombroso, who, like his master, Auguste Comte, referred most mental facts to biological causes. Lombroso believed that genius was a form of epilepsy, thus a morbid, degenerative condition that could lead to insanity and even to crime.

Admitting that medical science knew more about epilepsy than it did about hysteria, Regnault nevertheless argued that not enough was known to justify the recently published assertions that Flaubert had been an epileptic. He thought that Du Camp's description of the initial seizure in 1844 pointed more to hysteria than to epilepsy, as did the subsequent attacks. The victim of *grand mal* falls suddenly, without choosing the spot, and often does damage to himself. Flaubert had warning of the attack and took pains to lie down on his bed as a precaution. Had he bitten his tongue, foamed at the mouth, or urinated after an attack, it would have been noted by Du Camp. Regnault knew that Flaubert, as a child, had been timorous and given to fits of anger and that he became so deeply absorbed in reading that he would bite at his tongue, twist a lock of his hair, or even fall to the ground. But such falls, if suggestive of *petit mal*, might have been the result of distraction. Flaubert remained a nervous type into adulthood, subject to neuralgias, gastralgias, headaches, depression, visual hallucinations, frights, and obsessions, symptoms related to hysteria.[403]

Dr. Binet-Sanglé now agreed that Flaubert might have been a hysteric, but continued to insist that he had also been an epileptic. Unlike Regnault, he believed that epileptic seizures could be preceded by various auras (or warnings), which could last anywhere from a half-minute to several hours, offering the victim the opportunity "to choose his place." Consequently, Binet-Sanglé proposed that Flaubert be considered an hystero-epileptic, not a simple hysteric.[404] The debate indicates that Dr. Regnault meant *grand mal* alone when he characterized epilepsy, and the distinctions he drew between epilepsy and hysteria—by that reckoning—remain valid today as a rule of thumb. It would appear that Dr. Binet-Sanglé had had experience with seizures which he believed were epileptoid, but which had not strictly conformed to the pattern of classic *grand mal*. We shall see that he was on the threshold of the great complexity that epilepsy has become in our time, the complexity that had made the distinction between epilepsy and hysteria such a diagnostic dilemma.[405]

In the meantime, René Dumesnil had reviewed the medical controversy in preparing his dissertation, *Flaubert et la médecine,* which was accepted by the Paris medical faculty in 1905. His interview with Dr. Tourneux had convinced him that Flaubert had not died during an epileptic attack. Although Du Camp's description of Flaubert's seizures in 1844 was the only complete description of them Dumesnil could find, he found it medically precise and acceptable, rejecting only Du Camp's medical conclusions. In brief, Dumesnil rejected the diagnosis of *grand mal,* arguing for hysteria in an epileptoid form and finding substantial neurotic symptoms. Because physicians had not understood the frequency of hysteria, most seizures had been called epilepsy; but Dumesnil knew from Flaubert's letters that he had anticipated his attacks, that they lasted longer than attacks of *grand mal,* and that he had remained conscious during them. Dumesnil was also struck by the infrequency of the attacks: they had ceased by the time of the trip to the Near East, they reappeared during the war in 1870, only to disappear again during the last few years of his life.

As for the neurotic symptoms, Dumesnil placed little stock in the theory that they had been rooted in Flaubert's childhood. Flaubert's generation had reputedly suffered from a strange malady—either Byronian spleen or Chateaubriandic weariness—so that a suicidal tendency was a fad, not proof of emotional disorder. Flaubert's admitted frigidity in his youth was not to be taken seriously, since the passion he conceived for older women indicates that he had not been insensible. His thought of having himself castrated was labeled a simple caprice, for who among us, Dumesnil asked, has not had "some notion of that sort during his life." The real sources of Flaubert's neurotic tendencies, as Dumesnil would have it, were his inclination, as a youth, to read too late at night and to overwork; and, living in the midst of young people who elevated disgust for life into a principle, he developed a morbid character and became obsessed by a mania for analysis, "a trait common to all intellectual neurotics."[406] It will be perceived that Dr. Dumesnil, if settling for hysteria, could not be counted among the Freudian fanatics.

His thesis was at once reviewed as an important contribution likely to persuade most readers. But the editor of *La Chronique médicale,* while admitting that Flaubert had apparently died of a cerebral apoplexy, did not think that fact should destroy the symptomatology of epilepsy so laboriously assembled by Dr. Binet-Sanglé, which appeared to be unassailable. Dumesnil had speculated that the origin of the fatal cerebral trouble could have been the syphilis acquired in the Near East, but, in the absence of an autopsy, that had to remain hypothetical.[407] Dr. Regnault reminded readers that he, in 1901, had reached the conclusions of Dumesnil's thesis of 1905.[408]

A second medical thesis, submitted to the Paris faculty in 1905, was written with a knowledge of Dumesnil's conclusions by Philibert de Lastic, who brought a greater psychological sophistication to bear on the case. Lastic insisted that Flaubert's profound discouragement and ennui dated from a remarkably early age and was already evident in his letters at age twelve, too early to have been an acquired snobbery. Lastic meant that Flaubert had not acquired a fashionable outlook from schoolmates or from Alfred Le Poittevin, but had found Alfred a congenial companion who shared his morbid disposition. Moreover, Flaubert was aware that such disillusionment bred weakness, even impotence: an inability to adapt to everyday reality, an inability to enjoy the present. It produced a genuine fear of action, which reminds us of Flaubert's sudden reluctance to leave for the Orient with Du Camp after so many months of preparation and anticipation. His work habits, as an adult, revealed the feebleness he felt. He had great difficulty getting his projects started, and he needed complete isolation to get on with his tasks—obviously knowing, and fearing, that the least interruption could distract him. Literature became everything to him, and he would have agreed with Mallarmé that the world had been created for the purpose of producing a good book. Everyday life, indeed, life itself, was inferior to art; and Flaubert the artist believed that he and his kind possessed the answers that could save lesser mortals. This explains his comments when standing before the destroyed Tuileries in 1871: "That would not have happened if they had understood *The Sentimental Education*."[409]

The case next fell into the hands of two American physicians, the first of whom, an oculist, was impatient with the attempts to make Flaubert's nervous ailment fit the classic description for epilepsy, and annoyed at Dumesnil's "French attempt" to provide a new medical classification for Flaubert. We are informed that Flaubert was the victim of unrecognized eyestrain. Whatever may have been his nervous disorder, it was the consequence of overuse or misuse of eyes, eyes that had been ametropic—having imperfect refraction. As evidence, the oculist cited Flaubert's absorption in reading as a child, which had sometimes caused him to fall to the floor, and the coincidence of Flaubert's intensive preparation for his examination in law with the first seizure in 1844.[410] The second American was considerably more insightful, condemning those who had added to the popular notion of the degenerative origin of genius, and recognizing that Flaubert's physicians had not understood the nature of his case. Noting the psychic resemblance of Flaubert and Emma Bovary—both had had convulsive attacks after emotional crises—this physician diagnosed hysteria and denied that Flaubert had suffered from *grand mal*.[411]

In France, meanwhile, medical interest in the case flagged for several decades until Louis Conard began the publication of a substantial edition of Flaubert's letters in 1926. Dr. Regnault, who had classified Flaubert as a hysteric as early as 1901, insisted that the published letters offered none of the evidence necessary to call Flaubert an epileptic, but did provide ample evidence of the emotional state that had been the source of the first attack of hysteria, especially in a letter in the autumn of 1843 expressing the hatred he felt for his native Normandy.[412] A new medical thesis then appeared which made the sound point that physicians have difficulty distinguishing between *grand mal* and hysteria, because they rarely see the attacks and merely hear about them from patients, a point reiterated in our own time. In that respect, the diagnostic dilemma in the case of a patient long since dead is not significantly different from that of a living patient. In Flaubert's case, there remains acceptable testimony that his attacks did not begin in childhood, but at age twenty-two. By 1928, that fact was understood to weigh heavily against the possibility of *grand mal*, which ordinarily first appears in childhood. It is highly improbable that an initial attack of *grand mal* will occur beyond the age of twenty.[413]

As the diagnosis of *grand mal* became increasingly discredited,[414] it became necessary to accept something other than an epileptic convulsion as the cause of Flaubert's death. Maupassant's and Zola's description of the swollen neck and the red throat, which had suggested apoplexy at the time, was again seen as evidence of a stroke or cerebral congestion. Jean-Maurienne suggested that an aneurysm in the aorta had ruptured, forming the "black collar" visible on the surface of the skin—in other words, that a sac on the wall of the artery, caused by some disease or injury, had broken. He was at once accused of a deliberate attempt to sully Flaubert's reputation by mentioning a condition of shameful origin, as aortitis was then thought generally to be caused by syphilis. Jean-Maurienne had not listed syphilis as the cause and pointed to Flaubert's unhygienic regime at Croisset: too much eating and too little exercise for an overworked, anxious, hypertense man who had a tendency to headaches.[415]

If one of Flaubert's venereal infections was syphilis (which seems likely if not proved), he then would have been eligible for a form of cardiovascular syphilis, which strikes about ten percent of untreated cases (and Flaubert's treatment was useless by our standards). Syphilis of either the great vessels or the medium-sized arteries could have contributed to a cerebral hemorrhage (apoplexy) or to a ruptured aortic aneurysm.[416] But let us not forget that Flaubert's correspondence revealed clear signs of hypertension by the time he was fifty, related to overwork, anxiety, and lack of proper exercise.[417] The consequent high blood pressure in the arteries surely made him a candidate for vascular failure, with or without the assistance of tertiary syphilis.

Our literary sleuth, Gérard-Gailly, became convinced that even Flaubert's initial attack at the age of twenty-two had been a minor cerebral congestion and rejected the arguments for both epilepsy and hysteria. After many months of emotional strain as a despondent law student, Flaubert had been subjected to intense cold on a January night. Gérard-Gailly argued that the subsequent neurotic behavior was the effect of Flaubert's discovery that he would henceforth be unqualified to pursue a normal life.[418]

Just when it seemed that epilepsy had been ruled out as Flaubert's malady, a new medical thesis was published in 1932 which readmitted the ailment. During World War I, French doctors had reported observing cases of epilepsy which did not conform to the pattern of classic *grand mal*. Not only did the initial seizure come after childhood, but the victim retained a memory of the aura and often of the seizure itself. Dr. Brault became the first to propose that Flaubert had been an epileptic of this sort—that his epilepsy had not been *grand mal*.[419] The problem, henceforth, would be to distinguish between the symptoms of hysteria and those of the newly recognized epilepsy, as the reader will have immediately sensed that the extreme tensions of wartime could have spawned widespread hysteria whose symptoms were epileptoid.

The use of the electroencephalograph, the device which measures brain waves, dates from the 1940s. It gave medicine notable new insight into epilepsy that was quantitative, but also greatly complicated the study of epilepsy as a medical phenomenon. Use of the electroencephalograph enabled Dr. William Lennox to define epilepsy as "merely a disturbance of the normal rhythm of the electrical potentials of the brain." We are to understand that rhythm is inherent in nature; dysrhythmia, in man, means disease. In particular, when you have paroxysmal dysrhythmia in the brain, you will have epilepsy, a formula of elegant simplicity. On the other hand, the new information about the nature of epilepsy forced the conclusion that there is no such thing as a *typical* epileptic seizure; and, as in the case of hysteria, it seems likely that the seizure phenomena in epilepsy have changed over the centuries. What is more, the equation of epilepsy and dysrhythmia in the brain does not explain the cause of the dysrhythmia,[420] but invites the deduction that epilepsy could be an *effect* of the disease, the symptom of a profound disturbance or injury. Indeed, another authority, Dr. Ursula Slager, calls epilepsy a symptom of neuronal irritation or excitation, which often accompanies other diseases. Its sudden appearance in an adult suggests an underlying abnormal growth of tissue (neoplasm), an abscess, infarct, or other lesion.[421]

Beyond revealing the dysrhythmia in the brain, the use of the electroencephalograph (or EEG) confirmed the growing suspicion that other forms of epilepsy exist. They are the psychomotor epilepsies, a group which includes amnesia, automatisms, illusions, hallucinations, frank psychiatric disturbances with delusions, mania, and depression, as well as bizarre motor activity and altered consciousness. Some psychomotor patterns *may* be associated with convulsions, thus falsely suggesting *grand mal*. What is more, the controversies about the psychomotor epilepsies have intruded upon the fields of psychology, psychiatry, and legal medicine besides adding to the complexities of neurological diagnosis.[422]

Today, psychomotor epilepsy essentially means *temporal-lobe* epilepsy. In most cases, there is only a brief loss of consciousness, and the patient does not fall to the ground in a coma. The attack will last from thirty seconds to two minutes (longer than in *petit mal*); there may be some twisting or writhing in the bodily extremities or trunk; and the clouding of the consciousness is profounder than in *petit mal*. There will be a complete amnesia during the entire attack in most cases, but only partial amnesia for the events of the attack in others. Some authorities argue that the seizures will first develop in childhood or adolescence; others state that the attacks may occur at any age. If the victim is forewarned by an aura, it will be in the form of a complex illusion, hallucinations of sight, taste, or smell, and a feeling of *déjà vu*. The victim may sleep at the end of the seizure.

There seem to be no precipitating factors in most cases. In a few cases attacks have been related to a specific precipitating factor, such as listening to music. Even rarer are seizures precipitated by light, including a flickering light. The role of emotional stimuli is controversial, but it would appear that the coincidence of attacks following acute emotional experience is too infrequent to make it a significant precipitating factor.[423]

The victim of epilepsy may experience two varieties of warning that an attack is approaching: The *prodromes* come hours or even days before a seizure; the *auras* are experienced only seconds or minutes in advance—and are more commonly reported by patients. Prodromes encompass both physical and psychic disturbances, including headaches and vertigo, twitches and jerks, which will come to be recognized by the victim's relatives or friends—more than by the victim himself—as signs of an approaching seizure. Whereas *aura*, the traditional word for warnings, really refers only to that portion of the onset of a seizure of which the victim has any memory. In *petit mal*, as the loss of consciousness is immediate, there can be no aura. In *grand mal*, the aura may last long enough for the patient to witness the beginning of the rigidity; but most patients describe no aura at all, and only a rare patient experiences an aura sufficiently prolonged to enable him to lie down or find privacy.[424]

In ruling out epilepsy in Flaubert's case, Dr. Dumesnil had argued that Flaubert's sensory aura had continued into the seizure, and that he had always had opportunity to choose a place to lie down. That would, indeed, militate against *grand mal*. In 1960, Dr. Gallet criticized the Dumesnil thesis on the grounds that Dumesnil had not distinguished between the prodromes and the aura; in other words, that Flaubert had been warned of impending seizures by their prodromes rather than by the short-lived aura. This accounted not only for Flaubert's ability to seek his bed, but for his unwillingness to go into his garden for weeks at a time. Noting the frequent excuses given by Flaubert for his failure to honor his promises to see Louise Colet, Dr. Gallet deduced that Flaubert had had prodromes of impending seizures, which had forced him to concoct childish excuses.[425]

One can dispute some of Gallet's contentions without denying the possibility that Flaubert had been a victim of temporal-lobe epilepsy. Gallet had, for instance, a conventional notion of the hysterical attack: it must include theatrical attitudes, wild movements, crying, and senseless babble. By that reckoning, Flaubert did not qualify. But that reckoning is far too limited to encompass hysterical behavior, especially in a day when the individual did not know what behavior was anticipated of the hysteric. Gallet thought that Du Camp's failure to mention a biting of the tongue or an evacuation of urine during Flaubert's seizures, part of Dumesnil's case against epilepsy, was no evidence at all, as *no* writer in that day would have stooped to such prosaic details. That is sheer conjecture and not well founded. Gallet may not have known that Du Camp was a physician's son, and that he had devoted himself to a vast recitation of prosaic details as a journalist. What is more, a generation of writers who called themselves realists and naturalists was not noticeably guilty of euphemism.

Finally, Gallet saw in the uniformity of Flaubert's attacks further evidence of organic etiology, meaning epilepsy rather than hysteria. The aura was presumably always the same and was followed by the same brutal beginning of the convulsion. As described by Du Camp, the aura was visual. Flaubert would see a flame in his left eye, then in his right eye. He remained conscious throughout the seizure, even when he could no longer speak. This suggested to Dr. Gallet an epilepsy centered in the left occiput—the left rear of the skull. The cessation of the attacks for a number of years, only to reappear later in Flaubert's life, was troublesome for Gallet. Perhaps the arterial hypertension that would provoke the fatal stroke also accounted for the brief resumption of seizures in 1870; or perhaps the attacks never actually ceased, but were merely concealed by Flaubert's seclusion and the discretion of his friends. Dr. Gallet recognized that the image of the van and its driver, a feature of the initial episode, regularly reappeared with each subsequent attack and was evidence for calling the attacks hysteria. But how do we know, he asked, that a van had been on the road that night in January of 1844? Was it not possibly a hallucination, as in all the subsequent seizures?[426]

Dr. Gallet's rather transparent determination to shape the evidence in Flaubert's case to force a diagnosis of epilepsy serves as a warning of the difficulties and dangers in distinguishing between epilepsy and hysteria. The differentiation sometimes depends not so much upon what the patient exhibits or reports, but upon the surrounding circumstances, which require a knowledge of the patient's family and history. (Unlike Flaubert, of course, the living patient is also subject to psychological and electrical examinations which assist in differentiation.) Without such inquiry, it is difficult to distinguish, for example, between epileptic and hysterical amnesia. The dispute about the migraine, whether it is of organic or emotional origin, reminds the historian that medicine can still recognize the mysterious and the unknown. Some physicians, having noted that both epilepsy and migraine are attack phenomena, whose symptoms are recurrent and often periodic, suspect that migraine is an autonomic epilepsy, a form of diencephalic epilepsy. Others suspect that migraine is a vegetative neurosis, a physiologic vasomotor manifestation of repressed hostility, initially directed specifically toward the family and later to frustrations in general.[427]

The inquirer into the patient's history must be aware that epilepsy is both genetic and acquired. A subject may suffer an injury to the head or a high fever sufficient to cause structural injury to the brain, and epilepsy may ensue. But the seizures rarely begin immediately, appearing weeks, months, or even years after the injury. Where there is no reason to suspect brain damage, but where a blood relative has been subject to seizures, the subject may well have an inherited tendency to epilepsy—and instances of genetic epilepsy are considerably more numerous than acquired epilepsy. We have no evidence of brain damage in Flaubert's case. That both Mme Flaubert and her granddaughter Caroline suffered from migraines, however, offers the possibility that Flaubert inherited a tendency to epilepsy. Others may see those migraines as evidence of a family environment which bred hostilities.[428]

In genetic epilepsy, the fits are the result of cerebral dysfunction, though there is no evidence of anatomical brain damage. Neither the nature of the underlying abnormality nor the nature of what triggers the seizures is known, but the indication is that genetic epilepsy is a metabolic disorder. Its natural history is not stereotyped, although it ordinarily first appears in childhood. The patient like Flaubert, who develops seizures for the first time as an adult, becomes the tough diagnostic problem. Since epileptics may become morose or eccentric in later life, studies on the personalities of epileptics have endeavored to discover whether this is a reflection of their handicap, a true mental disorder, or an aspect of mental deterioration.[429]

We already know that epilepsy was traditionally held to be responsible for mental deterioration, and Flaubert's alleged epilepsy was held accountable by some for his slow literary productivity. His emotional impoverishment also conformed to a traditional notion about the fate of epileptics. A recent study was designed to determine whether people with psychomotor epilepsy (which would have been Flaubert's variety if he was epileptic) are more often psychiatrically disturbed than are people with other chronic illnesses. A group of patients with psychomotor epilepsy was compared with a group with *grand mal*, as well as with a group suffering from a variety of chronic illnesses not involving the brain. The study produced negative results, thus seemingly denying the traditional views. On the other hand, the researchers did conclude that epileptics in general do have serious difficulties in all important relations with other people, including sexual, suggesting that the superstition, fear, and prejudice historically associated with epilepsy affect the epileptic's outlook.[430] Since there must be serious doubt that Flaubert believed himself to have been epileptic, the negative results of the above study tell us that Flaubert's nervous ailment, whatever it was, offered him an equal opportunity for psychiatric disturbance. A person who has suffered a seizure, whatever may be the specific illness, will be exhausted in its aftermath and will be depressed from the realization that he has had an attack.[431]

Doubts about Flaubert as an epileptic do not permit a convenient diagnosis of hysteria. If anything, hysteria is more difficult to establish than epilepsy. Today, we understand hysteria to be a neurosis characterized by mental dissociation, in some severe cases leading to multiple personality and amnesia; but more frequently it produces somatic symptoms such as convulsions, paralysis, or sensory disturbances. The term implies a disablement without any organic cause. Some cases, initially labeled hysteria, may turn out to be other forms of mental illness. Evidence of hypochondriasis, for instance, may be a symptom of hysteria, but it can also be an early signal of schizophrenia.[432]

There are also illnesses of organic origin whose characteristic symptoms closely resemble those of hysteria, making hysteria a risky diagnosis until the absence of an organic base for the illness has been established. Myasthenia gravis, a disease characterized by excessive muscular fatigue and weakness because of the failure of normal neuromuscular transmission, may give the appearance of hysteria; as can cataplexy, the trance brought on by shock or fright, as in an animal feigning death. To make diagnostic matters worse, the signs of hysteria happen to be easily simulated. The Munchausen syndrome refers to that group of patients, for example, who are skilled in deceiving physicians and in defrauding hospitals. And there are instances when real hysteria conceals real organic disease; this often occurs when a patient means to conceal a major illness by exaggerating a minor disability.

It bears repeating, therefore, that to be confident of a diagnosis of hysteria, we must know the patient's history and environment; and we must understand the motivation of the hysteria to be certain that the stimulus is not conscious or a case of malingering. Since Flaubert's attacks were convulsive, it is germane to emphasize that the hysterical convulsion is usually preceded by emotional distress, the victim generally retains a degree of consciousness during the convulsion, it usually occurs in the presence of onlookers, there is no biting of the tongue or micturation, and the patient does not fall in a dangerous place and rarely injures himself.[433]

If Flaubert's hostility to his legal studies were the only evident motivation for his initial seizure in 1844, we might legitimately suspect him of malingering; but his alienation within the family and his despondence over love provided ample emotional distress for the onset of hysteria, just as did his rage in 1870. We cannot know what portion of his seizures were witnessed or how many he actually had—we know simply that some were witnessed and described. Indeed, Flaubert's convulsions resembled true hysteria in every respect but one. Du Camp tells us that Flaubert became pale when experiencing the aura, a suggestion of epilepsy, whereas hysterics usually become flushed. We are coming to understand, however, that just as boundaries are not sharply demarcated in nature, we may be misguided by traditional attempts to seek an exclusive description of Flaubert's nervous malady. Some cases which are hysteriform also reveal cerebral dysrhythmia, suggesting a closer relationship between *some* cases of hysteria and epilepsy than was traditionally suspected.[434]

Since the focus upon hysteria alone can obscure some other form of mental illness, we should recall that some of the followers of Pierre Janet believed that Flaubert's symptoms resembled psychasthenia—a term now outmoded, but invented by Janet to include a group of neuroses which had been classified as neurasthenia in the nineteenth century. Just as Charcot had demonstrated that hysteria is a psychogenic disease, Janet argued for the psychogenic origin of a group of neurotic manifestations previously thought to be of neurological origin. At the same time, he sought to show that, although the symptoms of psychasthenia resemble those of hysteria, there are critical differences. In particular, the hysteric is unaware of his obsessions (or *idées fixes*), which are displayed in a trance, whereas the psychasthenic is painfully aware of his obsessions and impulses, which produce great anxiety. He is usually unable to act on these impulses, however, though he will exhibit neither the paralysis, the amnesia, nor the subconscious movements of the hysteric. The psychasthenic patient may seem to be normal until it becomes a matter of action, whereupon he seems unable to perform and gradually withdraws from society. Psychasthenia, therefore, can lead to asceticism or to depression. In fact, the term psychasthenia describes what we call today reactive depression or obsessive-compulsive neurosis, a condition we continue to distinguish from hysteria.[435]

The characteristics of psychasthenia also seem similar to the schizoid states: a feeling of being cut off, out of touch, strange, or apart, of not being akin to other people; a feeling that things are out of focus or unreal; a feeling that everything is futile or meaningless, that life is pointless. That does, indeed, sound like Flaubert. But he gave evidence of angry frustration, whereas the schizoid gives the impression of detachment, of an absence of feeling.[436] It may be argued, therefore, that Flaubert did exhibit a tendency to obsessive-compulsive neurosis and to a schizoid state; but his seizures and his perennial anger more closely conform to the observation that "the hysterical fit is essentially a rage reaction."[437]

In consequence, we may legitimately refocus upon hysteria and temporal-lobe epilepsy as the likely fundamentals in Flaubert's case. In the course of an operation in 1938 to relieve severe attacks of temporal-lobe epilepsy, Dr. Wilder Penfield discovered that, when he stimulated the temporal lobe of his patient with a low electric current, the patient vividly experienced an event of his early childhood and felt the same terror that had accompanied the original experience. (The patient had been conscious during the operation, but was under local analgesia.) The incident suggested a close association between repressed memories or emotions and the temporal-lobe region of the brain. The discovery helped to clarify the peculiar nature of the hallucinations reported by victims of temporal-lobe epilepsy. While they may experience hallucinations of sound, smell, taste, and sight, they also experience temporal distortions, a sense of familiarity (*déjà vu*) being the most common. A particular memory may be evoked, or memories may seem to be "escaping" from where they are stored in the mind. The patient may feel either that time "stands still," or that time "rushes by."[438] In Flaubert's attempt to define the true hallucination for Hippolyte Taine, he wrote, "You feel that your personality is escaping you... a loosening of what the memory holds."[439]

As Penfield first demonstrated, electrical stimulation of the temporal lobe during an operative exploration will produce the same, and immediate, stimulation of the memory that the patient experiences during an attack of temporal-lobe epilepsy. The phenomenon suggests a form of hallucination that is fundamentally different from the hallucinations of a patient during a toxic delirium or in a psychotic state. During the exploration, the patient will tell the physician what he is experiencing, reporting incidents in earlier life that have faded (or have been suppressed) from the conscious memory. But the ganglionic patterns formed during those experiences have remained intact and are stimulated by the electrode. The patient does not address himself to a person in the past experience, but always to the physician conducting the operation; he thinks that the induced response is a very vivid dream. In the aftermath, there is a complete amnesia about the details of the experience.[440]

We would agree with Benjamin Bart and his medical consultant, Dr. Arthur Ecker, that Flaubert's seizures were a manifestation of temporal-lobe epilepsy;[441] but we would go beyond them to claim that the seizures were related to hysteria. To approach the source of that hysteria, moreover, is to approach the key to Flaubert's pessimism and his dismal view of life. Forty years after the completion of his medical thesis, Dr. Dumesnil believed the key was Flaubert's inability to pursue and maintain a satisfactory love affair. The celebrated response, "Madame Bovary? c'est moi!" (meaning that romantic dreams do not become reality) was one of Flaubert's two critical admissions. The other was his confession to Amélie Bosquet, in 1859, that he had loved fully, deeply, and silently in his youth without any response. From that galling experience, he had learned the wisdom of Voltaire's recommendation to cultivate one's own garden, which Flaubert read as an admonition to wall in one's heart.[442] He had found that he could not have love and hid the truth from all but his closest friends behind a façade of amorous adventures. Time did not wither the passion of his youth, but only exasperated it. The impossible quest, with its demoralizing and heartbreaking implications, haunted his mind ever after; and he remained an emotional adolescent until the end.[443]

Dumesnil's explanation was correct but superficial. Noting that in his liaisons and flirtations Flaubert had always run after older women with children, some Freudians argued that he was in pursuit of his own mother's image. Consequently, his reluctance to have his sexual desires satisfied was to be explained as a horror of incest.[444] That explanation would be more convincing if it could be shown that Flaubert had abstained from sexual relations with such women and had limited himself to impersonal encounters with prostitutes. In fact, his choice of older women with children facilitated the creation of that "façade of amorous adventures." In a day when divorce was impossible, he risked no permanent commitment, and the woman's status offered the most convenient possible explanation for a gallant chastity. Unfortunately for Flaubert, Louise Colet was quite unwilling to settle for mere ceremony, and on rare occasions her insistence drove him into her arms. His passivity throughout the affair, not to speak of the cruelties unconsciously inflicted upon her, betrayed his sadomasochism.

Beginning in the early part of our century, with Theodor Reik's examination of the Flaubert case, his failure in love was ascribed to a strong, but unconscious, homosexual bent. His friends, however, never seem to have used that term, nor is there any reason to believe that they ever suspected homosexuality, even when they became quite aware of his failure with women. After Flaubert's death, Zola asserted that women had never really respected Flaubert as a man; Zola was aware that his liaisons had been burdens and that his close attachments had invariably been with men. Women liked him as a friend, but most of them did not consider him as a possible lover or husband. Among recent writers, the clearest statement of Flaubert's homosexual bent has come from Benjamin Bart: "The difficulty was that, in love, Flaubert really wanted a man."[445] That could have accounted for Flaubert's ultimate suspicion that success with women was a mark of male inferiority, no matter how much envy it might have aroused.

Professor Bart has also described that pathetic moment in the composition of *Madame Bovary* when Flaubert had completed the passage on Rodolphe's seduction of Emma, but was at a loss about how to handle the subsequent honeymoon atmosphere because, given his own response to sexual union, he could not really imagine such happiness.[446] There remains an additional explanation for that emotional poverty, of which Flaubert had an inkling (although he could not have known the descriptive medical term), and which accounts for his sympathy with Dr. Hardy's verdict, "hysterical old woman." When Flaubert was nearly fifty-eight, his friend Mme Brainne called attention to his feminine nature. He quite concurred: "Lesbos is my native land; I have its refinements and its languors."[447]

As with all other diagnoses of Flaubert's condition, any new one involves conjecture. In that spirit, therefore, let us propose that Flaubert's masochism was associated with a strong tendency to transsexuality rather than homosexuality. This is not to say that Flaubert attempted to live the role of the female sex or was driven by the desire to have the body or the appearance of a female; but that, dating from his childhood, he unconsciously preferred the female role, though he was attracted sexually to women rather than to men. His dissatisfaction with the male role in love may have induced him to experiment with male prostitutes in Egypt, but it failed to deflect him from his established heterosexuality.

Some might argue that Flaubert's sexual passivity was nothing more than a classic manifestation of masochism. His case, however, suggests that a tendency to transsexuality may be the foundation of male masochism. Transsexuality may be defined as a gender-identity disorder and as one of the paraphilias. (A paraphilia is a psychosexual condition which requires an unusual or unacceptable stimulus to achieve sexual arousal, such as masochism, necrophilia, pedophilia, or voyeurism.) Like most paraphilias, transsexuality is quite consistent with heterosexuality. Most of the paraphilias, in fact, are distortions of a man's gender identity. They are rarely found in women, an indication that nature seems to have greater difficulty and makes more errors in establishing the gender identity in the male. Compared to the female, the male exhibits a greater psychosexual frailty.[448]

As the causes of transsexuality are imperfectly known, no absolute claim can be made for its appearance in Flaubert. No one yet knows, for example, the influence of food, drugs, or a mother's placental hormones on pregnancy. Consequently, even if much of existing evidence suggests that most of human gender identity is postnatal, important prenatal aspects may yet be discovered. The child learns his own sex role from persons of the same sex and (by complement) from persons of the opposite sex. When a person important in a child's life, especially a parent, gives either negative or equivocal signals, usually transmitted covertly or subtly, the child will become confused as to his proper role. The little boy growing up is supposed to learn that everything pertaining to the female role is negative and is to be avoided. In this brain coding, he learns not merely what *not* to do, but what to expect from the opposite sex.

Given the opportunity, children will play at copulation, simply rehearsing what will be serious later on. Much of that play is segregated by sex, evidently to avoid contamination while the sex roles are being learned. To prevent or to forbid such play may have a disastrous effect upon the child's gender identification. The inability of a boy to rehearse with other boys, in particular, may lead to gender confusion and an ultimate unwillingness or inability to breed as an adult. It must be understood that this early sexual play does not constitute a love affair. Indeed, when one sees evidence that such play has become an intense prepubertal involvement, it should be construed as a warning of adolescent psychosexual malfunction. In sum, the stimulus to which the libido responds—whether behavior will be normal or paraphiliac—is quite determined before puberty. The pubertal hormones will merely regulate the strength of the libidinal response.[449]

Unfortunately, there are many ways in which a child may be subtly robbed of pride of gender and come to loathe the role he has been destined by nature to play. Those who have approached Flaubert's case with the insights of psychoanalysis have related his failures in love to a mother fixation, which had the effect of deflecting attention from his associations with male relatives and friends. We have already noted that Flaubert, as a child, felt unequal to both the senior males in the family, and became an anomaly in the family: a lonely and unhappy child. Dr. Flaubert clearly preferred his elder son, Achille, who resembled him in temperament; and as Achille was nine years older than Gustave, the brothers had little in common.

Within the morbid atmosphere of the Hôtel-Dieu, Flaubert grew into a timid boy, given to fantasy and the theatrical. His closest companion and playmate was not another boy, but his sister. Their intense devotion to each other could be considered charming only by those unaware of the possible psychosexual consequences. Finally, let us not forget Alfred Le Poittevin: five years older than Gustave, neurotic, decadent, alienated, a pathological case, who replaced the Flaubert males as Gustave's ideal, and who would be dead at thirty-two. We may be ignorant of the details of that friendship, but no one has ever presumed it could have been salubrious for a boy already at emotional loose ends.

From the wreckage of that childhood emerged the great novelist who never reached emotional maturity. During his liaison with Louise Colet, we recall, he was mortified to learn that he might become a father. After three weeks of intolerable anxiety, the terrible threat proved to be unfounded, and he was able to express his revulsion: "A son by me! Oh no, no, no! May my own flesh perish, and may I transmit to no one the stupidity and the ignominies of human existence."[450] His horror of life, which drove him to rank art above all else, meant a foreclosure of parentage. Yet, he left heirs, the offspring of his mind, the most immediate of whom was Maupassant. Others are with us today, purveyors of the bleak outlook whose origin they have no reason to know. To the recent query, "If you could ask one question about life, what would the answer be?" Eugène Ionesco responded, "No."[451]

·4·

Guy de Maupassant by an unknown photographer.

Guy de Maupassant

Despite the difference in our ages, I consider him "a friend"; and then he reminds me so much of my poor Alfred!

Flaubert to Laure de Maupassant, 23 February 1873

ON THE LAST DAY OF HIS LIFE, IN 1893, DR. JEAN CHARCOT REMARKED that Guy de Maupassant's literary work had been the work of a sick man. Maupassant had died insane the month before; but Charcot was referring not to Maupassant's later works, but to those of his whole literary career.[1] On the other hand, Robert Pinchon, the municipal librarian of Rouen, who knew Maupassant as a youth and as an adult, remembered his friend as "strong, lighthearted, full of health, and of good mind and temper, whose written work merely revealed that he did not think the way ordinary people do. In that sense he was unusual, out of the ordinary."[2] The public who read and enjoyed Maupassant's stories believed not only that he was getting rich from literary success, but that he must be a strong and happy man, a young bull on the loose. In the preface for the first edition of Maupassant's complete works in 1907, Pol Neveux ruled against the popular view, calling Maupassant a very sick man, whose illness had struck him at the very outset of his literary success. Neveux, in fact, suspected that Maupassant had fought against illness all his previous life and was not misled by Maupassant's rugged physique or reputation for athletic prowess. The apparent illness that cursed his years of fame and fortune had not been a sudden departure from good health; in fact we must look to his earlier years for the genesis of the views of man and the world that made him perhaps the most convinced pessimist in French literature.[3]

Maupassant's biographers have been denied the volume of sources available to biographers of Baudelaire, the Goncourts, and Flaubert. Maupassant was not a prolific letter-writer, nor in his extreme determination to protect the privacy of his life did he keep an extensive diary. Although he knew that his literary work belonged to the world, he meant to leave nothing in the way of personal papers for posterity. Like any other writer, he revealed himself in every story and novel he wrote, but in a form necessarily open to dispute. We are forced not only to read between the lines, but to filter out that which is reliably autobiographical. His passion for privacy, of course, is a

217

critical clue;[4] and we must ascertain whether it grew from a determination to protect his time for literature, or whether he meant to conceal shameful aspects of his life or character.

Moreover, the conspicuous gaps in his biographical record and the testimony that does not ring true suggest that others conspired, for reasons of their own, to obscure the facts of Maupassant's life. It will become obvious that some of his admirers sought to protect his personal reputation, while others meant to evade any association with the more lurid details of his private life—not to speak of their refusal to share responsibility for it. Given Maupassant's eminence, it is astonishing that his place of birth is uncertain. The date, 5 August 1850, is undisputed. Among the various Norman localities claiming the honor, it seems probable that Guy de Maupassant was born either in Fécamp or in the château de Miromesnil nearby. At the time, his parents resided in Fécamp, but it is reliably known that they rented the château as a summer residence in the hope of establishing an aristocratic address for the baby's birth. The deceptions, in other words, began with Guy's first day.

His parents, Gustave de Maupassant and Laure Le Poittevin, were married in 1846, four months after Alfred Le Poittevin had married Louise de Maupassant. Gustave and Laure were both twenty-six. When Laure proved to be frigid, her husband quickly resumed a promiscuous existence, which made the marriage unhappy virtually from the start. Their rift no doubt contributed to the rumor that Flaubert had been Guy's actual father—it circulated for many years and was exploded only in 1947 by René Dumesnil. Flaubert had not even been Guy's godfather, as has been commonly asserted, nor was he an uncle.

When the child was four, the family moved a few kilometers from Fécamp to the château de Grainville-Ymauville, a charming rural setting which must account for the profound sensitivity to nature that Maupassant revealed in his stories. But it can also be deduced from his stories that a difficult and unhappy childhood led him to conclude at an early age that married life is dreadful and unbearable.[5] He was well on the way, in other words, to sharing the Flaubertian view that it is life itself that is unbearable, to becoming the disciple of *Sentimental Education* and its dogma of the eternal misery of everything.

The unhappy childhood was especially portrayed in Maupassant's first novel, *A Life*, in which he used his mother as the model for the heroine, and in *Waiter, A Bock!*, a short story about a brutal father and a mother who withholds money from him out of her awareness that he spends it on other women. In the latter story the child sees the father strike and beat the mother and remembers the incident as having ruined his life: "I had witnessed the other side of things, the bad side; I have not been able to perceive the good side since that day. What things have passed in my mind, what strange phenomena have warped my ideas, I do not know. But I no longer have a taste for anything, a wish for anything, a love for anybody, a desire for anything whatever, no ambition, no hope."[6]

In 1861, when Guy was eleven, the parents agreed to separate. A legal separation was ultimately executed by a *juge de paix*, through which Laure regained control of her dowry. A second son, Hervé, had been born in 1856, and the father pledged to pay his wife 1,600 francs annually for the support of the two boys. Laure settled with her sons in Etretat; Gustave, by profession a stockbroker, moved to Paris. They were never to live together again, although they maintained a correspondence. Maupassant's biographers have been bemused by the fact that Maupassant, too, despite the bad opinion he had formed of his father, remained thereafter on good terms with him. Yet he held his father accountable for Laure's unhappiness, which touched him profoundly.[7]

There remain several possible explanations for the ambiguity. It has been correctly noticed, for example, that Maupassant revealed a keen sensitivity, almost a sense of torment, when it came to uncertainty about the real father in his stories. He must have known of the gossip about Flaubert and his own mother, and he was to father three unacknowledged children of his own.[8] It is reasonable to conjecture, in the first place, that Maupassant believed his mother's conduct had not been beyond reproach and wondered from an early age about the identity of his real father. His father's morals, of course, had been more obviously disreputable and destructive; but perhaps he had not been solely responsible for the marital fiasco that so demoralized the son.[9]

In the second place, the young Maupassant soon experienced the compulsions of sex himself, or so it has been deduced from the obscene poetry he wrote later in life, some of which was published in 1939 by Pierre Borel. At the age of thirteen, a concealed Maupassant watched the family servant and maid copulating in the barn. His own first partner was a fourteen-year-old country girl named Jeanne.[10] His subsequent sexual athleticism must have engendered some sympathy for his father's fate with a frigid wife without ever minimizing his compassion for his mother's suffering. He came to believe that love is a trap for mankind, not simply for women, who were invented by nature to perpetuate the species. But since women are the bait, men become the victims.[11] Such an outlook not only provided an excuse for his father, but also forewarns us that Maupassant's sexual heroics were to be frustrating rather than consoling.

In 1890, when Maupassant may well have believed that he was doomed to an early death, his fiction seems to have become particularly autobiographical. In *The Olive Orchard*, we are again given Maupassant's belief that his father's desertion of his mother was the critical incident in his life. It had led to Laure's exaggerated loneliness and grief, which increased Maupassant's devotion to her. As Professor Niess has noted, the abandonment of the family by a father was a frequent theme in Maupassant's stories, as was the injured son's revenge; but in this particular version of that theme, Maupassant may well have been acknowledging his own moral shortcomings to make amends for the hatred or contempt he had felt in depicting his father's situation. In his novel *Our Heart*, Maupassant seems to say that he had been unable to fall in love with another woman because he had given all his love to his mother after she had been abandoned by his father.[12] In *The Olive Orchard*, Maupassant even registered his suspicion that the abandonment had been triggered by his father's discovery that his wife had been deceiving him.[13]

The simplicity of Maupassant's literary style—the result in fact of rigorous training and arduous practice—not only contributed to his popular success, but raised doubts about the quality of his work. The obvious and consistent black outlook that seemed to inspire his stories appeared simple as well, yet it was the result of factors that were perhaps more complex than even he recognized.[14] The explanations he gave for why he lived and loved as he did were no doubt ingenuous; but his persistent refusal to explain what he was doing in his literary work—or how he was doing it—was another aspect of his insistence on privacy and independence. Some may have seen it as superficiality, as an inability to analyze, whereas it probably reflected a determination not to examine his past too closely, to keep the wellsprings of his pain and aberrations obscure. Once he had become disturbed or horrified by some aspects of his own personality, it became convenient to attribute their cause to the horror of life itself. He protected himself further by refusing all external affiliations. Invited to become a Mason in 1876, he firmly declined, unable to tolerate the idea of subjecting himself to the regulations of any organization. Nor did he want to be tied to any party, whether political or religious, or to any school or association professing a doctrine. He feared even the smallest chain, whether it came from an idea or a woman, saying that "threads have a way of becoming transformed into cables before one knows it."[15]

One can agree with Maupassant that seeing his father abuse his mother was a shocking experience without attributing his later outlook on life to that moment alone. For one thing, the psychological legacy of a Maupassant-Le Poittevin marriage cannot have been a positive one. Gustave de Maupassant—and there is no reason to doubt that he was the real father—is remembered chiefly as an accomplished skirt-chaser who survived on an inherited income, an amiable man, perhaps, but of no great substance. From what we know of Alfred Le Poittevin, it would appear that Maupassant's later preoccupation with sex was a tendency already evident in both sides of his family. Laure de Maupassant, though something of an enigma, is better known to us. Like her brother, she was sophisticated, willful, and nervous, evidently more accomplished and intelligent than the man she married. She had adored her brother and apparently meant for her son Guy to realize the brilliant literary career denied Alfred by his premature death.

Maupassant was eleven when his father left the household. Although his presence might have made no difference, his absence enhanced Laure's ability to absorb the boy's life into her own— sensitive boy absorbed by gifted mother. The likely result is well known: either physical indifference to women or promiscuity. In the event of promiscuity, which also implies a pronounced contempt for women, the mother is always regarded as different from, or above, the rest. As an adult, Maupassant repeatedly told Laure that she was different from the rest, and she enjoyed hearing it.[16]

One would assume that there had been marital discord at home long before Maupassant inadvertently witnessed the assault upon his mother; we are entitled to believe that the alienation Maupassant attributed to that wretched incident had been brewing for months and years. As a pampered or indulged child, he had been allowed to soak himself in Normandy, to roam freely through countryside and village, on beaches and quays. He came to know all manner of people, watched their toil, heard their complaints, learned of their fears, hopes, and obsessions: a childhood that prepared him to be the depictor of Norman life. If, on the one hand, he had become devoted to his mother, he also spent much time alone, becoming too independent of everyone else. We are reminded that the pampered child is often the neglected child.

At thirty-five, Maupassant recalled a childhood incident that reflected his emotional disturbance and the need for an intelligent, firm hand if he were not to become sadly deformed. He remembered that he had loved cats, yet had a desire to strangle them with his little hands. One day in the garden, he saw something gray rolling in the high grass. A cat had been caught in a trap and was being strangled. It rolled and tore up the ground with its claws; its rapid breathing made a frightful noise which Maupassant never forgot. He could have taken a spade to cut the wire, or summoned a servant or told his father; but he watched it die "with a trembling and cruel joy." When it was quite dead, but still warm, he went up to feel it and to pull its tail. As an adult, Maupassant came to associate cats with women: those delicious feline creatures purr as they are caressed and rub against our skin, looking at us with eyes which seem never to see us, revealing the insecurity of their tenderness, "the perfidious selfishness of their pleasure." And so with women: they open their arms and offer their lips, but as the man tastes the joy of their caresses, he realizes that he holds a perfidious cat, with claws and fangs, "an enemy in love who will bite him when tired of his kisses."[17]

Laure was not unaware that Guy was developing abnormally, and the fact probably pleased her. For several years after the move to Etretat, she undertook his education herself, introducing him to Shakespeare, whom they read together. He might fulfill the literary promise of her brother Alfred; and the recent success of her dear friend Flaubert, with *Madame Bovary*, only encouraged Laure to hope that Guy would someday delight her with similar triumphs. At thirteen, she placed him as a boarder at the Seminary of Yvetot. He bore the confinement with great discomfort, was a persistent troublemaker, and after several years succeeded in being expelled. Laure admitted to Flaubert that Guy, at fifteen, was already a serious young man, too mature for his years, showing signs of a nervous debility that would require a rigorous regime to combat. "He will remind you of his Uncle Alfred, whom he resembles in many ways, and I am sure you will love him."[18] The following year, 1867, she placed him as a boarder at the Lycée of Rouen, where he began a literary apprenticeship with Louis Bouilhet. Maupassant obtained the baccalaureate on 27 July 1869. As Bouilhet died that same month, Flaubert assumed the direction of the young apprentice.

Laure's inability, or unwillingness, to see that her late brother was unsuitable as a model for any boy informs us that she was either unbalanced or ill; and her inability to cope with marriage from the start suggests that her troubles commenced long before her husband deserted her at about the age of forty. She would die on 8 December 1903 at the age of eighty-two, outliving her son Hervé by fourteen years, and her son Guy by over ten years. Or, to put it more dramatically, Hervé died at thirty-three, Guy at forty-three, both of them insane and confined to asylums. In her later years, Laure always denied that there had been hereditary nervous disease in the family, and for the apparent reason that it would have been she who transmitted it. She may have been right, although the tendency to nervous disorders in the Le Poittevin family is suspicious, and her insistence that Hervé died of sunstroke sounds like a determination to avoid the truth.[19] We should remember, however, that she *had* seen a nervous debility in Guy when he was fifteen, "un affaiblissement nerveux" as she called it, and probably regarded it as a happy omen of a literary career.

In 1872, when Laure was just past fifty, she confessed to medical symptoms which must have considerably antedated the confession. That is, nothing much had changed in her health: "I am not exactly ill, but feel excessively, dreadfully weak. There are moments when my head seems worn out, when I actually wonder whether I am awake or dreaming. Such a moment is brief, but very distressing, very painful."[20] Later that year, Maupassant took his first position as a library clerk in the Ministry of the Marine and Colonies in Paris. Both mother and son bore the separation poorly, and, in Maupassant's case, the need to convert himself into a desk-bound bureaucrat made the wrench from home more anguishing. In Etretat, Laure was increasingly subject to nervous crises, never precisely defined, but sufficient to add to Maupassant's anxiety.

Guy's letters to his mother no doubt reflected the tedium of his work at the ministry, but one must also be struck by the intense despair and anxiety in them. At twenty-three, as Steegmuller has aptly put it, Maupassant sounded like a child wailing to his mother. After a brief holiday at Etretat in the autumn of 1873, he was sick at heart upon finding himself back in Paris: "I find myself so lost, so alone, and so *demoralized,* that I am obliged to ask you to send me a few pages. I am afraid of the approaching winter, I feel quite alone, and my long evenings of solitude are sometimes dreadful."[21] Time did not accustom him to the Parisian exile or alter his outlook. Two years later, after his annual two-week holiday in Etretat, which he called his only pleasure during the year, his misery convinced him that he had had no holiday at all. He dwelt upon the idea that his mother had been left alone to face the long winter evenings, just as he had faced the same demoralizing solitude; and he would think of her seated in her chair gazing fixedly into the fire. Despite the warmth of a September day, he felt the first chill of winter and dreaded the cold months ahead when the lamps would have to be lighted at three in the afternoon, when the rain would beat against the windows, when there would be month after month of penetrating cold.[22]

In October, he prayed for the coming of January, when the days would again be lengthening. "December is the black month, the sinister month, the midnight of the year." He knew that when January came he would be saved, that he would survive the terror of the winter.[23] Aware of his mother's nervous attacks, he apologized for writing in that vein, knowing she was already too inclined to see everything in black. In fact, the previous year she had taken to her bed shortly after Maupassant had returned to Paris from his holiday.[24] Because he knew they suffered alike, he could hope that the spring could bring her some distraction, just as the greening of the chestnuts and the springtime odors in Paris served to revive him.[25] In the spring of 1878, however, Laure's illness caused him to take leave for ten days, and despite her extreme weakness, he brought her back to Paris for medical consultation.[26]

It would seem that the physicians she had consulted over the years had been baffled by the diversity of her symptoms; several of them concluded that she suffered from a tapeworm.[27] In Paris, Maupassant took her to his own physician, Dr. Carl Potain, a member of the medical-school faculty, but largely occupied with private practice. Because Potain later reported the details of the case to his students, we have a reasonably accurate statement of his views. Laure suffered from migraines, which, as we already know, are variously attributed to diencephalic epilepsy and to a vegetative neurosis, a physiologic vasomotor manifestation of repressed hostility. She also claimed to have visual problems aggravated by extreme sensitivity to light; and she had suffered for some years from heart trouble and periods of exhaustion not preceded by undue exertion. She had used both ether and chloral for the relief of pain, and gave evidence of frequent emotionality. Potain thought she was seriously afflicted by what he called a nervous rheumatism, which supposedly attacked the spinal cord and would lead to paralysis.[28]

In 1927, when Georges Normandy published the horrifying material he had been collecting on Maupassant's death, he claimed to have interviewed Dr. Pierre Aubé of Rouen about Laure's case. (Since Dr. Aubé died in 1903, it bears mentioning that Normandy had been obliged to withhold the publication of his medical notes until a number of them were released by the death of Joseph Primoli.) Aubé was something of a medical curiosity. He had begun his medical studies in 1844 and had completed his thesis in 1851, but upon his marriage in 1859, he gave up his hospital post and devoted himself, as an amateur, to music and to historical and archaeological research. He knew both Bouilhet and Flaubert; and, having a retreat in Etretat, he was also well acquainted with Laure and Guy de Maupassant. Although he never treated Laure as a patient, Aubé was convinced by his observations that she had suffered from Graves' (or Basedow's) disease for much of her adult life.[29]

That disease, now called exophthalmic goiter or hyperthyroidism, is a metabolic disorder, now known principally to afflict women, which generally appears in the third or fourth decade of life. It is one disease of the thyroid gland where the goiter is rarely large or obvious. In hyperthyroidism, the overactivity of the thyroid gland results in the production of an excess of thyroxine, a powerful hormone. The heartbeat may increase in order to carry oxygen to overactive bodily tissues; the blood pressure may rise; the rate of breathing may become faster; there is likely to be a rise in blood sugar; and the muscles will be tense. Victims live in a continuous state of nervous excitability.

These symptoms remarkably resemble the normal diencephalic reactions to fear which occur when the body prepares for flight. Indeed, the protrusion of the eyeballs and the retraction of the eyelids (known as exophthalmus) which are characteristic of hyperthyroidism give the victim the wide-eyed expression that we associate with fear or terror. The reader may know that adrenalin can produce such reactions in a few seconds, but it is useful only for brief emergency or panic reactions. In contrast, thyroxine produces its reaction in twenty-four or more hours and can sustain a frightened animal, for example, over long periods of time when greater exertion is needed for survival, such as during extreme cold or drought. As in all metabolic disorders, a latent or hereditary disposition can be activated by a psychic factor; and in the human species alone, a period of severe emotional stress *always* precedes the onset of hyperthyroidism. Because animals utilize the excess of thyroxine in flight or in the fight for survival, the overactive thyroid does not produce a morbid condition. In man, that increased vivacity is not employed, because the cortex finds nothing to which to respond.[30]

On the basis of what we know of Laure's behavior, it is justifiable to deduce that she was susceptible to hyperthyroidism and to migraines and that the former was evidently triggered toward the end of her third decade by the collapse of her marriage. The evidence also tends to confirm Maupassant's biographers who have suspected a pronounced tendency to nervous disorders in the Le Poittevin family. It does not follow that either Guy or Hervé de Maupassant was liable specifically to hyperthyroidism, and we must look further for the sources of their nervous ailments even when, as in Guy's case, some of the symptoms resemble his mother's. Potain's diagnosis of her malady was considerably off the mark, but what he believed, of course, was likely to have influenced his subsequent diagnosis and treatment of Maupassant's case.

The nature of Laure's maladies enables us to appreciate the pain and anxiety that blanketed the poor woman's existence, forcing us to recognize the burden of fear besetting her as she was driven to separate from her husband and undertake alone the rearing of her two sons. In her anxiety, she sought to cling to Guy, the elder, and she unwittingly convinced him of the horror of marital life, staining him simultaneously with her own psychology of fear and sense of abandonment. Those letters he wrote her during his bureaucratic servitude in Paris always associated his own loneliness and fears with her isolation in Etretat.

In the summer of 1880, Laure was urged for reasons of health to go to Corsica, where she was attended by Dr. J.-B. Folacci. Maupassant, who had taken a leave without pay from the ministry, joined her there. He befriended Folacci's nephew, Léon Gistucci, who became Maupassant's walking companion on tours of the island.[31] Upon his arrival on Corsica, he found his mother somewhat improved, but he was disturbed to find that she wanted to trail him in a carriage when he went for walks, so jealous was she for his time. After a few days, she again became quite ill, but her exasperated son attributed her illness to fatigue born of the excursions. In fact, an intolerance for heat and periodic bouts of profound weakness are normal characteristics of hyperthyroidism. In any case, Maupassant had to devote his time to her care and abandon further trips into the country; and she made matters worse by fretting about his pending return to France. He came to begrudge the money he had spent for the trip, which he could ill afford; this, however, was one of the few times in his life when he would express annoyance over his mother's behavior.[32]

Laure survived for many years after 1880, gaining an increasing reputation for autocratic and irrational conduct, seen by some as signs of madness and as possible proof of hereditary mental illness in the family. In 1892, her estranged husband informed his attorney that Laure had attempted suicide by swallowing two bottles of laudanum, and that she had been abusing Hervé's widow. He asked whether it would be legally possible to remove Hervé's daughter

Simone from that milieu, or whether it would be better to put Laure in a mental home for her own good. (The letter was published by Baron Lumbroso in 1905.) In recent years, a correspondence between Gustave and Laure has been discovered which attests to her fundamental decency, but reinforces our image of her as a lonely and unhappy woman. What is more, her presumed attempt at suicide occurred shortly after her grief over Hervé's death had been reinforced by the cruel necessity to put Guy in an asylum. It is small wonder that she was in a distressed or depressed state, and hardly a proof of madness. Her friend Zélie Sauteiran de Saint-Clément, who published under the name Léon Sarty, did claim that Laure could be "imperially authoritarian," adding that Maupassant in late years found her vehemence oppressive; but she evidently believed that Laure was quite sane.[33]

It requires no great imagination to realize that Maupassant could have been intensely devoted to his mother while on occasion finding her demands a burden; and we already know that he made her an exception to his general contempt for women. In his novel *Mount Oriol*, he seemingly revealed a revulsion for maternity in particular; and one of his biographers has remarked that Maupassant had no interest in, or use for, human beings before the age of sexual maturity. If he had either compassion or fondness for children, he hid it.[34] One can only speculate about the origins of that revulsion: Had his own childhood provoked an ineradicable horror for that period of life? Did he bear within him a tacit resentment for the woman who gave him birth and forced the horror of life upon him?

He evidently could not bear to acknowledge that he had fathered three illegitimate children. Their existence was revealed in an unsigned article in *L'Eclair* on 11 December 1903, several days after Laure's death: one son and two daughters. When Baron Lumbroso published his *Souvenirs sur Maupassant* in 1905—based upon important, if sometimes dubious, sources—he noted the article but added nothing. In 1926, Auguste Nardy pursued the information given in the article and concluded that the three were undoubtedly Maupassant's offspring. The mother, named Litzelmann, was originally from Strasbourg, and lived in the rue des Dames near Maupassant's apartment. The eldest of the children, Lucien, was born in 1883; Lucienne in 1884; and Marguerite in 1887. Their mother died in 1910. Although the children made no attempt to deny Maupassant's paternity, they had scrupulously honored his preference for anonymity and wanted no publicity. The facts of their lives were published the following year.[35]

In one of the alleged (and undated) letters from Maupassant to his mysterious mistress, Gisèle d'Estoc, he claimed that Flaubert was the only person he had ever truly loved, and that he had lived his life according to the eternal truth Flaubert had once spoken to him: "What a dirty invention life was! We are all in a desert. No one understands anyone else. I mean by that, of course, only élitist natures."[36] The sentiment was unquestionably Flaubertian, but Maupassant had been prepared to receive it by the time he became Flaubert's disciple. But what are we to make of that profession of love? That Maupassant had had profound compassion for his mother, had pitied her, had remained loyal to her, but had not "truly loved" her?

The Good Companion

During his bureaucratic years, 1872–80, Maupassant sought to keep his mind off his job and his body out of Paris, to the extent that his employers would tolerate and time would allow. Our sympathy for the plight of the young Norman bull, deprived of his freedom and sentenced to dreary routine among tedious colleagues, should not blind us to the fact that he did little to endear himself to those who employed him. Indeed, from what we know of his routine, it becomes obvious that he practiced his writing at the office whenever supervision was lax; and his official productivity must have been disappointing for a man of his talent and energy. A sentence in *The Father* epitomized Maupassant's memory of his position: "He led the dull, monotonous life of bureaucrats, without hopes and without expectations."[37] Under those circumstances, his literary apprenticeship provided both a merciful narcotic and the only hope that an existence without expectations might eventually be escaped.

He was required to be in the office from nine in the morning until six-thirty in the evening, six days a week. When he transferred to the Ministry of Public Instruction in 1878 as an *attaché de cabinet*, he often had to put in an appearance on Sundays. Otherwise, Sundays were reserved for boating—unless Flaubert happened to be in Paris. Maupassant was a man of extraordinary physical strength, but it has been argued that he began a routine which abused his physique. He rose at dawn in order to scull; then left for work at eight o'clock, because he insisted on living in a suburb on the river rather than near his job; then he would go rowing again in the evening, retiring quite late. Official reviews of his work were generally favorable, but his mind and energies went elsewhere.[38]

A number of his stories give us life on the river as he knew and lived it during those years: a lusty, rowdy existence, which seems on the surface to have been nothing more than the exuberant high jinks of a remarkably healthy and unrestrained pack of youngsters. In Maupassant's case, however, the license of the river life amounted to an exaggeration of his childhood roaming, to an escape from home and office into a world of dirt and depravity. For a man of his birth and sensibility, such an immersion was pathological. It underscored and deepened his alienation while creating the appearance of comradeship. The physical fatigue he experienced from rowing could only have been salutary, but the indulgences associated with it were morally debilitating and no cure for the demoralization about which he complained to his mother.

His story *Mouche, a Boating Man's Reminiscence,* lets us sample the standards of riverine society: it is about five friends who jointly owned a ship's boat, and who rowed as a religion. They shared a dormitory room in a disreputable tavern in Argenteuil and rowed on the Seine between Asnières and Maisons-Laffitte. The simple tale focuses on a tiny female guttersnipe whom the group adopted and called Mouche (Fly). At the beginning she favored one of the men, but in time slept with them all "without making any resistance." Inevitably she became pregnant, a crisis the group met with an agreement to make no attempt to fix the paternity. They would adopt the child as a group. A subsequent accident to Mouche caused a premature stillbirth, and she could only be consoled for her loss by a promise that they would make her another child—as a group.[39]

The sleazy river life included heavy drinking. It appears that Maupassant's use of alcoholic liquor began in childhood, when his initiation came from Norman fishermen as he spent a day among them on the quays. For the rest of his life, brandy would be his remedy for cold, humidity, and fatigue. He described alcoholic states in a number of his stories, reflecting his familiarity with them, sometimes associating the consumption of alcohol with the need to combat irrational fear, as in *On the River,* which he published in 1881. On the other hand, Joseph Primoli specifically told Baron Lumbroso that Maupassant had not been alcoholic, and there have never been claims that he was a drunkard. The most that can be said is that he was, to some degree, alcoholized and particularly susceptible to other toxic remedies for pain and fear, which he would use in the subsequent decade.[40]

Although Maupassant's good companions all attested to his robust appearance and appetites, he revealed his fear of the cold, dark winters in letters to his mother written before he was twenty-five, which suggested anything but vigor and stamina. We cannot attribute that fear simply to his hatred of bureaucratic life or to his desire to return to his mother's pampering. His boating friends thought that he had been abnormally sensitive to cold, presuming that he was predisposed to poor circulation and arthritis. It is remarkable that he should have chosen to spend so much time on the water with his torso often half-nude. His inability to tolerate cold grew worse with the years. During a visit to England in 1886, he cut the trip short after a cold and rainy day, returning to Paris for that reason alone. Heat, on the contrary, did not bother him, and on a warm day, when others suffered, sweat never appeared on his brow.[41]

When he was about twenty-five Maupassant also began to suffer from migraines, another affliction that would never desert him, to which he may have inherited a predisposition from his mother. Migraine is not a very precise term. In Maupassant's case, it seems to have meant a severe, incapacitating headache. There is the possibility that migraine is a form of diencephalic epilepsy, as one physician claimed in Maupassant's case,[42] but his related symptoms would strongly suggest a physiologic vasomotor manifestation of repressed hostility. The vascular headache, moreover, can be associated with poor circulation, so that it is a reasonable deduction, in Maupassant's case, that his susceptibilities to headaches and to cold were related. Although at the age of twenty-six he complained of heart trouble, compounding the similarity of his mother's symptoms with his own, Dr. Potain told him he was smoking excessively and showing the signs of nicotine poisoning.[43] In any case, the alleged heart trouble vanished, and it is unlikely that he was developing hyperthyroidism, a woman's disease. We are left with the signs of a vegetative neurosis whose genesis had been a repressed hostility to his family.

Thus, at the very moment when Maupassant was considered by friends to be strong as a bull and a congenial companion, he was privately anxious about his health and in search of drugs that would relieve his pain. He consulted medical books and pharmacists wherever he happened to be, yet he seems to have made no association between his excessive physical and sexual activity and his tendency to nervous affliction. In fact, it may be that the frantic activity served unconsciously to conceal the disturbing and distressing tensions he felt internally. Although he was preoccupied with sex throughout his life, the grossest of his farces was written in his mid-twenties—notably, *A la feuille de rose, Maison Turque*, the title being an adaptation of the name of a brothel in Flaubert's *Sentimental Education*. Written in collaboration with Robert Pinchon, the farce was performed privately with the assistance of their boating companions and several writers, all the parts being taken by men. It featured the bourgeois couple who take a room in the Maison Turque on the assumption that it is a conventional hotel (inadvertently providing the occasion for the cuckold and the seducer); a lewd ballet with the dancers necessarily equipped with exaggerated female organs; and a conversation between a cesspool cleaner and the establishment's valet, whose task it was to wash contraceptives for reuse. One cannot avoid the suggestion of exhibitionism. Maupassant informed his mother of the great occasion, but fell short of inviting her to attend.[44]

When Baron Lumbroso published his study of Maupassant's illness and death in 1905, he seemed to suggest that the fatal general paralysis may have been the consequence of an early attack of syphilis, though he also cited evidence to the contrary. Since there remained a question whether Maupassant had had syphilis (and because the absolute association between untreated syphilis and general paralysis had not yet been firmly established), Louis Thomas consulted Lumbroso about his evidence. Lumbroso reported interviews with two physicians who had treated Maupassant, both of whom testified that Maupassant had admitted a prior syphilitic infection.[45] Several subsequent researchers were unwilling to accept that testimony as conclusive, and the problem was further muddled by uncertainty about the cause of Maupassant's ultimate madness.[46] As we now know, only about one-third of the untreated cases of syphilis ultimately develop the destructive lesion of late, or tertiary, syphilis, and the signs of emotional illness that Maupassant increasingly revealed could also have led to madness.

In time, new documents came to light which reinforced the case for syphilis, but provided fuel for a debate as to the approximate date of the infection. Maupassant told Gisèle d'Estoc that he had caught syphilis at the age of twenty, meaning about 1870 or 1871, from a ravishing *grenouille* who was a boating companion. He then began to lose his hair and became alarmed. He went to a physician in the rue de Clichy, where he had to wait more than three hours. When it finally came his turn, he fled, unable to overcome the shame of showing himself nude to a man he had never seen—even a doctor.[47]

The age Gisèle cited cannot have been correct. Long after the publication of the Turgenev letters, it was noticed that he had mentioned a visit from Maupassant in early 1877, when Maupassant was losing all the hair on his body and was accordingly quite unattractive at that moment. He attributed the calamity to a previous stomach disorder. A few weeks later, however, he wrote his boating companion, Robert Pinchon, that he was taking mercury and potassium iodide for a venereal infection. He even boasted of having contracted true syphilis, not merely gonorrhea, proud and delighted that he would henceforth be immune to further infection. The letter, incidentally, was written about a month before the first private performance of his obscene play. As the loss of hair is a frequent characteristic of secondary syphilis, we may legitimately date the infection from 1876.[48]

Given Maupassant's promiscuity, the source of the infection has to remain unknown. He did not limit himself to ravishing *grenouilles*, but in that very summer of 1876 regaled the aging Flaubert with the details of a lecherous encounter along the river with a fat woman.[49] Flaubert was amused as usual by anything grotesque, but cautioned Maupassant to moderate his activity in the interest of literature. "Take care! Everything depends upon one's goal. A man who opts to be an artist no longer has the right to live like other men."[50]

One would wonder if Maupassant was struck by the assumption that he was living as he chose, for his inconsistent conduct in intimate matters suggests his confusion about the course of his life. He could be wildly exhibitionist, yet reveal a surprising modesty; he could boast of his syphilis, yet apparently endeavor to conceal it. The syphilitic attack served to focus his attention more sharply upon himself—that is, upon his nervous troubles, upon his unhappiness at work, even upon his mother's ill health; but it failed to deflect him from the excessive sexuality that was apparently beginning to become a compulsion. In the autumn of 1877, he spent his annual vacation in Switzerland, taking the waters at Loèche for his nervous troubles, or so he told Flaubert;[51] but it is evident from later correspondence that Maupassant was still experiencing the lesions of secondary syphilis. Nevertheless, he cuckolded a pharmacist in Switzerland and stopped at a brothel in Vesoul on the return trip to Paris.[52]

His depression deepened the following year. His mother was not doing at all well, and he was intolerably weary of his work at the Ministry of the Marine and Colonies. He claimed to be overwhelmed by a sense of "the uselessness of everything, of the unconscious nastiness of creation, of the emptiness of the future." He was drawing inward upon himself, as others increasingly bored him; but he was also boring himself, because his outlook was making it difficult to write.[53] He even admitted that women were no longer able to distract or divert him. "The love of women is as monotonous as the minds of men."[54] Flaubert replied with advice from his own experience: if you are bored with the "cul des femmes," stop using them. Buckle down to work and stop devoting so much time to whores and boating. Civilized men, he added, do not require as much locomotion as the physicians insist. Flaubert was obviously concerned that his disciple's literary future was endangered by his mode of living. "You are living in a hell of *merde*."[55] It is a pity that Maupassant was quite beyond the help of the master who knew the disciple's anguish.

In the meantime, Maupassant had brought his ailing mother to Paris for the consultation with Dr. Potain, but she was none the better for it. Nor could she have been, as the wrong diagnosis had been made. She still complained of her heart and continued to have spells of weakness and faintness. Potain told Maupassant that there was nothing organically wrong with her heart or her eyes, reiterating his diagnosis of nervous rheumatism and predicting the possibility of spinal-cord disease and paralysis. Potain recommended that she move from Etretat for good, to a warmer climate—a prospect that upset her considerably. Maupassant's own symptoms were unchanged. He was still losing some hair, though he assured Flaubert that the problem was not of syphilitic origin, but a constitutional rheumatism (much like his mother's) which affected the heart and the skin. The prescribed steam baths, mineral waters, tisanes, and other syrups were having no effect, but were eating up the money he meant to save for his annual vacations.[56]

Life went on, nevertheless, and Maupassant managed to complete his superb story, *Boule de Suif*, in 1879, translated variously as *Ball of Fat*, *The Dumpling*, or *Roly-Poly*, but better left in the original. The story was designed to be published the following year in an anthology, the *Médan Evenings*. When Flaubert read the story before publication, he was delighted: "I am anxious to tell you that I consider *Boule de Suif* a masterpiece. Yes! young man! Neither more nor less, it is the work of a master."[57] What is more, it was a blessing that Flaubert lived to read it and to sense that the disciple had arrived— for he would be dead in a few weeks.

In the background, however, a nasty fracas was brewing which threatened the joy of the literary triumph. A poem entitled "At Water's Edge," first published without much notice, excited the outrage of the municipal authorities of Etampes when it was reprinted there under the title "A Girl." Maupassant himself had boasted that the poem, if chaste in language, was completely indecent in images and subject matter. It concerned a very ordinary young couple on the banks of the Seine who die, as Maupassant put it, from sheer copulating.[58] He wondered if he might not be called before a magistrate, but when preparations were actually made to prosecute him for immorality, the matter ceased to be humorous. Although he knew that the ministry where he was employed was indifferent to the legal question, he also knew that his chief had become increasingly hostile to him as a dilatory employee. The notoriety of a prosecution could become the pretext for discharging him. Fortunately for Maupassant, Flaubert intervened and the charges were dropped.

The tension of that affair coincided with an ominous new medical symptom. Early in 1880, Maupassant reported that he had virtually lost the use of his right eye.[59] He consulted an ophthalmologist, a Dr. Abadie, who diagnosed a paralysis in the accommodation of the right eye, asserted that it was incurable, and warned Maupassant that it could lead to blindness. Its cause was presumably a lesion in the nervous system. On the other hand, Dr. Potain, believing that Maupassant was subject to his mother's maladies, insisted that the eye trouble, the loss of hair, and the earlier heart troubles all had the same basic cause—that is, nerves, caused by a slight irritation in the upper part of the spine. Accordingly, Potain said that the eye condition was curable.[60]

Flaubert saw the eye trouble as further proof that his disciple was far from well and related his anxiety to Maupassant, asking him if he would agree to come to Croisset to be examined by Dr. Fortin just to set Flaubert's mind at rest.[61] Maupassant did as he was bidden. Immediately after the examination, Flaubert indicated that he did not know Fortin's opinion of the case, but was aware that Maupassant seemed to be suffering considerably and had gone to bed at nine o'clock in the evening. A few days later, Flaubert seemed to be convinced that no organic disorder had been found and that, although Maupassant was "totally neuropathic," the case was not as serious as originally feared. Potain's earlier diagnosis, in other words, seemed to have been confirmed.[62]

We do not know what Maupassant told Dr. Fortin about the symptoms, or whether he mentioned the prior syphilitic infection. Since later students of Maupassant's case were aware of the general assumption that Maupassant's ultimate madness was caused by general paralysis (or paresis), and also aware that tertiary syphilis was the cause of general paralysis, they ascribed that knowledge to Dr. Fortin (which he could not have had) and presumed that he must have recognized Maupassant's peril. The deduction was then made that Fortin had withheld the dreadful news from Flaubert.[63] In fact, it is not known what Fortin thought of the case, nor is there any reason why he should have misled Flaubert. Surely he knew that Flaubert was unlikely to swoon at the thought of syphilis, and it would have been an unusual country health officer who would have undertaken to contradict the diagnosis of a member of the Paris faculty. Finally, those who supposed that Maupassant's ocular symptoms in 1880 were of syphilitic origin dated the infection as of 1879, three years later than the actual event.[64]

Boule de Suif was published on 15 April 1880, the inauguration of Maupassant's literary career—and the end of Flaubert's. Maupassant's letters to Emile Zola, to Ivan Turgenev, and to Mme Commanville perfectly mirrored the void he felt. What is more, just as he associated his own illnesses with those of his mother, so did he associate his grief for Flaubert with hers. He had been informed, he told Caroline Commanville, that his mother had been stricken by the news of Flaubert's death and had shut herself up for two days in her room, weeping. "Her last old friend is now gone; and henceforth, her life can have no echo of the good memories of her youth. She cannot discuss the old days with anyone. I sense just now, in an acute manner, the uselessness of living, the sterility of every effort, the hideous monotony of both events and things, and the moral isolation in which we all live, but from which I suffered less when I could talk to him."[65]

In those days of desolation, Maupassant reached the decision to accept an offer to write a series of articles for Arthur Meyer of *Le Gaulois*, the immediate proof of the success of *Boule de Suif*; but he took the precaution, on 1 June 1880, of requesting a three-month leave from the ministry "to recover from nervous ills."[66] Although *Le Gaulois* professed to belong to no party, it was royalist under Meyer and certainly authoritarian in spirit; and some of Maupassant's articles were unquestionably anti-democratic and unfriendly to the Third Republic, not a politics of ideology, but the logical response to his hatred for life. The following year, Maupassant also joined the staff of *Le Gil-Blas*, where he wrote under the pseudonym Maufrigneuse. Meanwhile, he continued to apply for extensions of his leave from the ministry until, in 1882, his appointment was canceled.

A study of his articles in both newspapers has shown that they gradually became more anecdotal and slowly evolved into stories. It can be argued, then, that just as Maupassant had practiced his craft behind the backs of his superiors in the ministries, so did his journalism provide the opportunity to improve his skills. His mother, who had eventually followed Potain's advice to seek a warmer climate and had moved to the Riviera, was anxious that the time would soon come when her son would not have to write for money and could turn to "serious work," by which she meant fiction.[67]

The Prolific Writer

In the decade between 1881 and 1890, Maupassant published twenty-seven volumes, a performance that reinforced the impression of the robust bull at work. By 1880, moreover, the evidence of an active syphilitic infection had most likely disappeared. Given the medical knowledge of syphilis in that day, Maupassant was entitled to believe himself cured and ineligible for further infection. In fact, host and parasite had reached an equilibrium. It may be that continuous overwork and overindulgence during the next decade notably increased Maupassant's vulnerability to the tertiary stage of syphilis, but his incredible literary productivity had nothing to do with a preparalytic cerebral stimulation by the *Spirochaeta pallida*, contrary to an outmoded medical notion sometimes cited to account for Maupassant's prolificacy. Of the many fears of which Maupassant would demonstrate his comprehension, a fear of syphilis was not among them. In only one short story did he feature syphilis as a fatal infection, and his motive was not to illustrate the horror of that disease, but to focus on the patriotism of the infected woman who undertook to incapacitate as many of the invading Prussians as possible. Maupassant gives her a pathetic death in a ward for syphilitics from what would apparently have been the effects of secondary syphilis—a moving but unlikely end.[68]

His own syphilis, in other words, did not disturb him during the 1880s; and his intense activity, which probably contributed to his early ruin, was stimulated by psychic factors, those which had spawned his bleak outlook long before he was thirty and which had made him the victim of poor circulation and severe headaches. The syphilis was latent and could lurk in his body indefinitely as a potential threat to his life; but the hatreds and phobias were alive and active, not merely to fuel the morbidity of his stories and novels, but to threaten his health as well. Since he would end in madness, the medical debate about him endeavored not only to locate the moment his madness was evident, but to ascribe it to one of several possible causes.

Aside from Flaubert, who had reason to suspect that all was not well with the youthful Maupassant, his contemporaries were quite convinced of his fundamental soundness. He evinced a simple and affectionate nature, laughed quite easily, was generous and not given to ostentation. He seemed to be orderly, dedicated to hard work, and determined not to let his body deteriorate. Thus, in 1881, when his first volume of stories was published, including *Madame*

Tellier's Establishment, the marvelous tale of the brothel in Fécamp whose habitués were disconcerted to discover it closed "on account of the confirmation," Emile Zola could answer those critics put off by Maupassant's taste for low life by denying that his outlook was perverted. The stories reflected a healthy, free, earthy love, the "fecund good health and braggartish good humor in everything he writes." Zola ranked him as one of the sanest and healthiest temperaments among contemporary writers.[69]

Unfortunately for that opinion, the works published by Maupassant in subsequent years, if properly read, tell us the unhappy truth about his interior state—about his outlook and his obsessions. Long before 1880, Maupassant had expressed his demoralization and alienation. When a French edition of Schopenhauer became available that year, Maupassant was quite prepared for its message—that existence is suffering—and became its avid reader during those very months when he had begun writing for newspapers. In one of his stories, he would make mention of Schopenhauer's death, adding a statement of great respect for the philosopher and the reason for it: "The immortal thoughts of the greatest shatterer of dreams who had ever dwelt on earth."[70] At the beginning of 1886, when Ludovic Halévy spoke out in the Académie française against the inroads of Schopenhauerian pessimism among the young in France, Maupassant replied in an article called "Our Optimists." He proposed a new law outlawing pessimism. Article 2: "It is absolutely forbidden, under penalty of two to twenty years of forced labor, to be or appear to be unhappy." Article 3: "It is forbidden to all French citizens, no matter what class, to die of hunger."[71]

A recent medical thesis reflects admiration for Maupassant's mastery of psychological phenomena, asserting that his descriptions were as precise and accurate as those in medical treatises. It does not follow that he experienced every aberration he described, as we know, for instance, that he attended the fashionable lectures given by Charcot at the Salpêtrière. On the other hand, the frequency of certain themes in his work suggests a personal preoccupation with them: with fears, obsessions, and compulsions in particular. He also wrote convincingly about hallucination and illusions, sexual anomalies and perversions, alcoholism and drug addiction, melancholia and states of confusion, and he employed his morbid perceptions quite rationally or in an orderly fashion. Although he worked with the materials of madness, he was not yet mad himself; he was sufficiently able to dominate his suffering to weave it into art. Many thought his works were simply pornographic, specializing in all the turpitudes and bestialities, books to be read on the sly or concealed in one's library.[72]

No doubt he would have defended himself in court against a charge of outraging public morality, if only as a necessary defense of literary or intellectual freedom. After 1880, however, such a charge was highly unlikely. Prudish restraint was declining in Western Europe generally, especially in France, where the political uncertainties of the previous decade had been resolved by a firm Republican control of all branches of government, and where the clerical forces, in whose name censorship had often been justified, were in retreat. Erotic literature, whether refined or trash, became more readily available, as did an abundant literature on sexual perversions, both medical and pseudomedical. In fact, it was during the later years of the nineteenth century that some sexual perversions were given their current names (sadism, masochism, and fetishism), and their descriptions were often literary before they were medical. Most facets of sexual life can be found in Maupassant's work.[73]

Even if Maupassant was no longer in danger of prosecution for erotic or obscene literature, that is not to say that he would have disagreed privately with the suitability of such a charge. He had rejoiced earlier in the deliberate obscenity of his farces and poems, giving the impression of a complete absence of inhibition. Yet, he also concealed his syphilis from people he respected or whose respect he coveted. In the later years of his life, his literary exhibitionism was matched by a passion for privacy that went considerably beyond the need to preserve his time for work. He had much to conceal, much that tortured and terrified him, and it became raw material for his stories, through which he coped with his miseries in a disciplined manner.

Many forms of fear appeared in Maupassant's work, but they were always morbid fears, never physiological. We understand that fear is a normal instinct which contributes to the preservation of the individual. Morbid, abnormal, or pathological fears are not associated with self-preservation, but, on the contrary, contribute to self-injury or self-destruction. Normal fear is not a phobia, but phobia is a morbid fear. The fears, or phobias, which Maupassant understood so astutely, derived from abnormal circumstances or mysterious influences which he found inexplicable or irrational, but which he never ascribed to the supernatural. Nor were his victims of phobias or obsessions portrayed as having lost their minds. Their ability to reason was unaffected, and they were fully conscious of the inexplicable horror that had entered their lives: lucid, not mad. People with phobias are particularly susceptible to hallucinations, just as there is an association between phobias and obsessions. But their hallucinations must be distinguished from those suffered by the mad. That is, they are autoscopic phenomena.[74]

Two extreme interpretations of Maupassant's treatment of pathological themes can be found in the medical literature on him. Aided by the knowledge that Maupassant would end his days in an asylum, one group looked to his literary works for evidence of the disease that killed him. Assuming that his tales were the product of precise self-observation, these observers not only detected the signs of approaching madness, but some suspected that Maupassant had suffered from moments of temporary madness long before he was shipped into seclusion: that he had experienced a progressive, systematized delirium with all the characteristics of paranoia, which led in the end to general paralysis.[75] It must be emphasized that members of this group studied Maupassant's case before the connection between general paralysis and the tertiary stage of syphilis had been established.

The second extreme position took into account, quite correctly, that the period in which Maupassant wrote his stories of the terrifying irrational was a time when there was considerable research on psychic behavior, and when public attention was much occupied with such mysterious powers as somnambulism, magnetism, and hypnotism. Since Maupassant was far from indifferent to earning money, as it guaranteed him emancipation from the hated ministry, it was argued that he had catered to current public taste and interest by writing of the mysterious and the irrational. On sending his story *The Horla* to the publisher, Maupassant is said to have predicted that the newspapers would soon report him to be insane; but he insisted that he was quite sane and that the story had been deliberately designed to make the reader shudder.[76]

Maupassant was indeed fortunate in the timeliness of his subject matter, but that does not account for his remarkable insight into the realm of phobias, obsessions, and hallucinations. It bears repeating that Maupassant could not have suffered himself from all the psychopathic maladies he so skillfully described. On the other hand, one can detect several thematic phobias and obsessions in Maupassant's literature, which, because of their repetition, may be considered his own. They gave him insight into related phenomena. It can be shown, moreover, that the various themes in Maupassant's dismal stories of human suffering were united by several common threads drawn from his personal experience. While he might say that a particular story had been deliberately designed to make the reader shudder, he also said that his larger purpose was not to amuse or to appeal to our feelings, but to compel us to reflect on the deeper meaning of events and to understand the occult. In particular, he endeavored to transmit his personal view of life and the world.[77]

He had a pronounced gift for describing anxiety states, and we are given to believe that there is always good reason for the anxiety, even if its cause is mysterious or unknown. In *The Orphan*, the central figure is a disfigured spinster of thirty-six, who takes in an orphaned boy in her loneliness and inevitably dotes on him inordinately. He grows into a sullen, money-hungry adolescent, and she comes to fear him—but without knowing why. As her anxiety blossoms, she is afraid to stay on with him in her remote country house. Her ultimate murder clearly justifies her prior fears, but Maupassant disposes of the matter of guilt by providing the boy with a successful alibi. What interested him was the relation of the lonely woman to the indulged boy and the resulting anxiety.[78]

Maupassant's *On the River* was cited earlier for its description of the alcoholized person. A fisherman has dropped anchor on a beautiful evening. When it comes time to leave, he finds himself unable to raise the anchor and is stranded for many hours in the dark until the arrival of another fisherman, who helps him raise it. In the meantime, he has been seized by gusts of fear and dread, for no apparent reason. When the anchor is raised, it brings up the body of an old woman, which has been weighted with a stone.[79]

In his preoccupation with fear, Maupassant sometimes tried to analyze its essence. In *Fear*, he seemed to indicate that we are only afraid of that which is unknown. Once we have an explanation, fear vanishes.[80] His meaning becomes clearer in *The Horrible*, where he sought to illustrate the difference between the terrible and the horrible. The horrible must have an element which does more than scare, move, or upset; it possesses a sense of mystery, a sense of terror of that which is beyond our natural comprehension, and presumably never will be understood. Thus it is the horrible which we will always fear. As an illustration, Maupassant related a tale featuring cannibalism in the Algerian desert, the assumption being that no normal person can understand, or accommodate himself to, such an act.[81]

Several years after the publication of *The Horrible* in 1883 Maupassant was traveling in Italy when he saw a driver fall from a tall vehicle. He took him to a hospital, where the poor man died. Lumbroso relates that Maupassant asked to be given a piece of his flesh after the autopsy was performed. The physician allegedly accommodated him, and Maupassant took the sample to a cook, had it prepared, and ate it. He was then able to say from experience that human flesh is insipid to the palate and has an odor of stale veal.[82] Perhaps the episode should not be repeated, as its authenticity cannot be satisfactorily documented. Still, in view of its antecedent and Maupassant's refined sense of the horrible, can anyone assert with any authority that the incident could not have occurred? That he should even have wanted it to be believed of him is sufficient to generate horror.

He gives us, in *Madame Hermet*, a classic portrayal of the fear of microbes and disease, in this case in a woman who loses her mind because of a pathological fear of smallpox. Her son is dying of the disease and repeatedly requests that she come to him, but she persists in refusing, fearing that her beauty will be marred. After going mad, she is obsessed by blemishes on her face which, of course, are nonexistent: "I dare not let anyone see me now, not even my son, no, not even he! I am ruined, I am disfigured for life." Maupassant's comprehension of this paranoid phenomenon is the more striking in that its context is the abnormal association of a widow and her son: "The child was brought up in the same way as are all children of much-admired women. She loved him, however."[83]

Little Louise Roque is one of the most important of Maupassant's stories for medical evidence. The story begins with the rape and murder of a twelve-year-old girl by a village mayor, a widower of six months, whose prior anxiety was related to the frustration of his sexual needs. The crime, committed in the mayor's wood lot during the summer, was not immediately solved; and Maupassant uses the onset of the autumnal bad weather which forecasts the end of the year to characterize the disquietude and fear that seized the community and to establish the atmosphere for the mayor's festering anxiety in the aftermath of the crime. His words also reflect his own horror of winter and the cold: "He did not yet know why the darkness seemed frightful to him, but he instinctively feared it, felt that it was peopled with terrors. . . . The night, when one feels that mysterious terror is wandering, prowling about, appeared to him to conceal an unknown danger, close and menacing." And what was that threat? A hallucination—a vision of the naked, bleeding corpse. Once those hallucinations began, the mayor's life became intolerable and his suicide was the result.[84]

The fears that swept over the mayor when he was alone provided only one example of Maupassant's comprehension of solitude. In

Mad?, the story seems to focus on a man tortured and horrified by his own mysterious powers, which he attributes to magnetism: the power to attract objects to himself and the power to hypnotize living beings. But, most of all, the terrified man does not want to be left alone.[85] The brave hunter in *The White Wolf* is suddenly chilled in the lonely woods: "Little by little a fear crept over him, a strange fear that he had never before felt, fear of the shadows, of the solitude, of the lonely woods. . . . In this gloomy silence and the chill of the evening there was something strange and frightful."[86] The same anxiety emerges in *Night: A Nightmare.* In the dream, a man begins to walk through Paris in the evening. Gradually the streets become deserted until the frightened walker finds himself entirely alone.[87]

In *He?*, Maupassant gives us a man who does not believe in marriage, but who has decided to enter into it because he has become afraid to be alone, especially at night, afraid of his own "dreadful thoughts"—a mysterious agony. The tone of the story is precisely that of the letters Maupassant wrote to his mother when he had become a civil servant in Paris. In the story, however, whenever the man is overcome by the attack of anxiety, he experiences a hallucination. He sees a man in his chair, but the image vanishes when the chair is approached. Maupassant makes it clear that the man is not afraid of the specter, but of the thoughts and fears which produce the hallucination.[88]

"Our great torment in this existence," Maupassant wrote in *Solitude*, "comes from the fact that we are eternally alone—all our efforts and all our actions are directed toward escaping this solitude." Yet, nothing ever removes the dilemma; we are always alone no matter what we do. "Gustave Flaubert, one of the great unfortunates of this world, because he was one of the great lights, wrote to a friend this despairing phrase: 'We are all in a desert. Nobody understands anybody.' " Women, Maupassant continued, only increase our sense of solitude, as they provide the illusion of *not* being alone. "After each kiss, after each embrace, the isolation is increased. And how frightfully one suffers."[89]

Because Maupassant first described a hallucination in *He?*, which was published in 1884, those who have searched his stories for evidence of his approaching madness usually found it there. As stories of more terrifying hallucinations were to follow, the implication was that madness was pursuing its implacable course.[90] Unlikely as that now appears, it may well be that Maupassant suspected he might be drifting into madness, although he was confident that he was still quite sane. In any case, the hallucinations in his subsequent stories were always associated with extreme anxiety. The principal figure in *The Specter*, after seeing an apparition, says: "Left alone, I experienced for several seconds the horrible agitation of one who awakens after a nightmare."[91]

Contrary to Maupassant's prediction, no one saw *The Horla* as a sign of approaching madness when it was published in 1887. Not only were his friends aware that it was then intellectually fashionable to be concerned about hysteria and other personality disorders, but several of them claimed to have given him the idea for the story in order to exploit the fashion. In short, he wrote the story despite his fear of madness, not as a result of it. Moreover, his finest work, the short novel *Pierre and Jean*, was yet to come, a sign that his brain had not deteriorated.[92] On the other hand, the modern reader will surely conclude, after finishing *The Horla*, that Maupassant had a remarkable understanding of a deeply paranoid personality: "I quickened my pace, uneasy at being alone in this wood, unreasonably, stupidly terrified by the profound solitude. Abruptly I felt that I was being followed, that someone was on my heels, touching me. I swung round. I was alone."

Maupassant invented the word *horla* to describe the phantom who haunted the key figure in the story: "What is the matter with me? It is he, he, the Horla, who is haunting me, filling my head with these absurdities! He is in me; he has become my soul; I will kill him." The story ends with his attempt to kill the horla by locking it in a room and then setting the house on fire. But even after turning his home into a funeral pyre, he fears that the spirit of the horla may not be dead, inevitably convincing himself that "no, no, I know, I know, he is not dead, so, so, I must kill myself, now."[93]

Who Knows?, written in 1890, was one of Maupassant's last stories. Again we have a paranoid personality who is the victim of hallucinations. The subject is deeply solitary and regards his home as a refuge. One night, his house is emptied of its furnishings by unseen beings. The victim's hallucinations are both visual and auditory, and leave him in a highly nervous state. He consults physicians in Paris about his case, and they advise travel. After many months abroad, he returns to France and decides on a tour of Normandy. In an antique store in Rouen, he comes across his missing furniture. As no one is in attendance, he remains in the store even after night falls, finally obtaining a brief glimpse of the grotesque antique dealer. The police of Rouen are then summoned, only to find that both furnishings and dealer have vanished; and he is informed that the furniture is in his home where it belongs. The frightened man then commits himself to an asylum, fearful that the dealer might pursue him to seek vengeance.[94]

The stories cited so far all illustrate Maupassant's preoccupation with abnormal fear and reveal, in particular, his understanding of anxiety, the paranoid personality, and the fear of being alone. A second theme to pervade his work was an obsession with illegitimacy, which was evident, in fact, long before the birth of his first illegitimate child. It seems likely that the stories which he designed to portray the disastrous results of love were also the offspring of his obsession with illegitimacy. In *Bellflower*, the story of the aged seamstress who limps, we learn that, as a young girl, she was about to be seduced in an attic when the seducer's employer seemed on the verge of discovering the pair. To save her seducer's reputation and position, she threw herself from a window and broke her leg in the fall. The accident left her crippled and condemned her to lifelong virginity.[95] The message is repeated more cruelly in a hunting story, *Love—Three Pages from a Sportsman's Book*. After a female duck has been downed by the hunters, the faithful drake wheels around in search of his mate, only to be shot himself.[96]

Simon's Papa was among the stories published in 1881 in Maupassant's first volume. It is a tale of the pathetic child who does not know who his father is and becomes the victim of his schoolmates' cruel taunts.[97] *The Father* is a painful story of a clerk who falls in love with a girl he sees each morning going to work on an omnibus. Eventually, he succeeds in seducing her, and she becomes his mistress. He deserts her three months later when he discovers that she is pregnant. Ten years later, he meets her by chance on a street and recognizes the boy in her company as his son; he is conscience-stricken about what he has done and overwhelmed by a sense of his loss. But by then it is much too late, as she is married to a good man who is aware of the child's history.[98]

As we noted earlier, Maupassant did not always relate the pain of illegitimacy to the sins of the father; sometimes, especially toward the end of his literary career, he dwells on the guilt of the adulterous mother. Such is the theme in the novel *Pierre and Jean* (1888), the case of two brothers who are immediately drawn as opposites in appearance and action. Jean, we learn, is to inherit a fortune from a bachelor family friend, and it gradually dawns on Pierre that their mother's honor will be threatened if the inheritance is accepted. As he comes to suspect that Jean was the product of an adulterous affair, he is aghast at his own suspicions, which are contrary to his deep attachment to his mother. Yet, he cannot account in any other way for the fact that the friend had left his fortune to only one of the brothers when he had known them both well. When the wretched truth finally emerges and the mother has confessed, Maupassant has her say: "How horrible life is! If by any chance we come across any sweetness in it, we sin in letting ourselves be happy, and pay dearly for it afterward." She puts the blame for the affair on her husband—it is all a result of the fact that she had to marry "a well-meaning lout."[99]

The Olive Orchard (1890), one of Maupassant's last stories, centers on the meeting of a father and his criminal son, who have never before seen each other. The child had been born of a love affair, during which the man discovered that his beloved had been deceiving him. In his fury, he threatened to kill her and to destroy the unborn child he assumed was his. But the woman saved herself by assuring him that the child was not his—a desperate falsehood; the man enters the priesthood after the collapse of his love. Years later, when father and son finally meet, in a confrontation between priest and criminal, Maupassant sets the stage for a brawl in which the priest's throat is cut; but we are left unsure whether the death is the result of murder or suicide. Here Maupassant means to focus upon a more critical issue: the unfaithful woman as the cause of trouble between father and son.[100]

Only about fifty pages of Maupassant's final novel, *The Angelus,* were put on paper, but during the summer of 1891 he described the plot in detail to Auguste Dorchain. The setting is Normandy during the Franco-Prussian War, and the agony of the national humiliation lends depth to the fate of a woman who has been left alone in her château in the path of the advancing enemy. Her husband is serving in the retreating French army. She is about to give birth when the Prussians arrive on Christmas Eve to occupy the château; they put her into the stable, where her son is born in the straw. The child is malformed, his legs crippled, supposedly as the result of a blow given the mother by the soldiers. This is a variation of Maupassant's theme in *Waiter, A Bock!*: the blow to the mother injures her child permanently. But in *The Angelus,* the mother's dedicated care of her incurable son makes his soul finer and leaves him able to suffer more keenly. These abnormalities will lead to his frustration in love for the remainder of his life. Maupassant burst into tears after relating the plot to Dorchain.[101] As in *Our Heart,* he had confessed to his inability to fall in love.

Sexual abnormality was the third theme which compelled Maupassant's attention in his writing. One of his early river stories, *Paul's Mistress,* tells of an innocent young man who falls in love with a girl whom he discovers is a lesbian. Unable to prohibit her affairs with other lesbians, and unable to abandon her, he throws himself into the Seine—one of the few suicides in Maupassant's stories.[102] In 1885, he sent a story to *Gil-Blas* entitled *My Twenty-Five Days*, based upon his visit to Châtel-Guyon in Auvergne, where he was joined briefly by his father. Francis Steegmuller has noted that the two mysterious "widows" in the story were actually two tarts, evidently lesbians, who served as companions for Guy and his father. After the latter departed, Guy and the two ladies devoted themselves to nude bathing and "other eccentricities" to the consternation of their hostess. The story leaves no doubt that Maupassant had taken great delight in the "widows."[103]

A Divorce Case touched upon sexual pathology in the male and is particularly arresting because of Maupassant's own love of flowers and perfumes. The husband in this unhappy marriage has been impelled to marry by "the senseless urge that drives us toward the female." He quickly finds after marriage that he cannot bear to touch his wife; he is disgusted by "the embrace of love." Because flowers reproduce themselves without defilement and give off a marvelous fragrance, the husband soon devotes himself to a greenhouse, where he hides his flowers "like women in harems." No one is permitted to enter. In his summation, the wife's attorney informs the court that the case is "less rare in our age of hysteria dementia and corrupted decadence than one might think."[104] Subsequently, one physician insisted that Maupassant's effective description of sexual perversion in the story had to be the work of a man who was sexually unbalanced himself.[105]

The sketch sometimes called *Feminine Men*, but better translated as *The Man-Tart* (*L'Homme-Fille*), is a curious description of men who lack normal male instincts. They are depicted as charming, but as essentially unstable, unreliable, untrustworthy men; and it would seem that Maupassant thought that the phenomenon was more characteristic of the French than of the English or the Germans. Such men, he claimed, have "the loathesome characteristics of women." When such a man falls in love with a real harlot, it will be a vicious and unhappy affair: "He despises and adores her without seeing that she would be justified in despising him."[106]

Maupassant gives us such a man in *Bel-Ami*, the novel published in 1885. His main character is full of sexual vigor and swagger, yet he is skillfully painted as feminine, as somehow lacking in basic male instincts. Maupassant, imitating Flaubert, often said of him "Bel-Ami, c'est moi." We must remember that, as Steegmuller remarked, Maupassant was always very conscious that his own name derived from *mauvais passant,* evil passer-by. Thus he must have meant that Bel-Ami, the blackguard, was a *mauvais passant,* a true reflection of Maupassant's character. That is why Maupassant's choice of the feminine pseudonym, Maufrigneuse, with which he signed his pieces for *Gil-Blas,* a name out of Balzac beginning with Mau, may signify something deeper: that Maupassant had no sense of normal male decency when dealing with women.[107]

Which brings us to *Useless Beauty,* one of those final stories written in 1890 which seem nakedly autobiographical. The central figure is a handsome woman who expresses her hostility to women's sexual and maternal obligations. Her husband, wrongfully suspecting her of infidelity virtually from the outset of the marriage, endeavors to keep her pregnant so that she will remain unsightly or unattractive to other men. Finally, in revolt, she tells him that one of her children is not his, knowing that the uncertainty will gall him.

As for woman's role, Maupassant wrote: "What a hell! All her youth, all her beauty, every hope of success, every poetical ideal of a bright life, sacrificed to that abominable law of reproduction which turns the normal woman into a mere machine for maternity." The enemy, then, is nature, which forever drives us back toward our natural state. God has put nothing on earth that is "clean, pretty, elegant, or accessory to our ideal." Man alone creates grace, beauty, and charm. In short, art, which man creates, is superior to life, which God creates.[108]

The story is so constructed as to make us think that this is but one more chronicle of poor Laure's fate, until it becomes clear that it is Maupassant's, too—that he is his mother's son. The sexual act is base and vile for him, too—unclean, reflecting the protest in some men, as Steegmuller has put it, that the organs of love and joy should lie *inter urinas et faeces.* Thus did an evil God prevent man from ever idealizing his encounter with woman.[109] Sympathy for the alleged plight of women almost concealed Maupassant's own agony, driven, as he was, by the "abominable law of reproduction," to be base and vile. He could not fall in love, not because he had given all his love to his mother, but because his upbringing had left him without the conventional male instincts.

The Writer in Pain

By the time Maupassant became a professional writer in 1880, at the age of thirty, he was already subject to considerable pain and discomfort. It would appear that the primary and secondary manifestations of syphilis were behind him, and that he had entered the latent period of the disease. On the other hand, he had suffered from headaches for at least five years (they antedated the syphilitic infection), headaches which we have related to the circulatory problems that made him inordinately sensitive to the cold; and the first evidence of an ocular ailment dates from early 1880. At a public lecture delivered in 1909 in Lyon, Léon Gistucci, Maupassant's walking companion in Corsica in 1880, emphasized that Maupassant's headaches were severe by that date—a matter for concern.[110]

None of these maladies withered away after 1880. He told his mother that he had gone to Etretat at the beginning of 1881 and visited their former home. The winter cold had caused him considerable suffering, and he had been chilled by the memories the house had awakened. "I am colder from the solitude of life than from the solitude of the house." He expressed "the enormous bewilderment" that afflicts all human beings and complained anew of a great sense of emptiness. We also learn that, in the same month, he was bedridden for a week with terrible pain in his hand and eyes.[111] Six months later, his eyes were continuing to trouble him.[112] In mid-March of 1883, he was finally compelled to consult an ophthalmologist, Dr. Edmund Landolt. By 1885, he complained that his eyes were getting worse and cited overwork as the cause. He went to Sicily that summer under doctor's orders not to read, the ostensible reason why he was accompanied by a traveling companion who was laboriously reading *Germinal* to him.[113] François Tassart, engaged as Maupassant's valet in 1883, first mentioned a severe headache on 24 April 1885, confirming the continuing association of headaches and eye trouble.[114]

Sometime that year, Maupassant evidently consulted Dr. Henry Cazalis (who wrote poetry under the pseudonym Jean Lahor) in search of relief from pain and from a nervous cough that was hurting his stomach and chest. Several of the prescribed remedies, especially the chloral, which upset his stomach and produced intestinal bleeding, were too harsh. He wanted to limit himself to sodium bromide.[115] In 1886, his letters continued to complain of eye trouble, which remained unaffected by the hydrotherapy he began that year. A treatment started with a steam bath and was immediately followed by a shower and a rubdown, and we get a hint from Tassart that Maupassant was by then suffering from an inability to sleep, no doubt a result of his pain and medication.[116]

He had never lost his love of boating and sailing, which continued to be a major diversion despite his periodic pain. In fact Maupassant seemed to be in excellent health when he was not suffering from pain in his eyes and head. The first indication of physical exhaustion after exercise was recorded by Tassart in June of 1887. Maupassant had set out for an afternoon boating party, magnificently attired for rowing and apparently in fine physical shape. When he returned, he was pale, with violet patches on his face, and his body was quite flushed. After a shower, François rubbed him down with cologne and a horsehair glove. Although the friction was continued a long time, the usual stimulation did not occur; when Maupassant tried to describe the boating party, his voice kept failing him, and he had trouble pronouncing words. He did not recover his strength quickly, but was dull and morose for several days thereafter and began to complain of intestinal pain. Although it was summer, he seemed especially bothered by the dampness of the river valley.[117]

In the autumn, he told his mother that he was feeling very well, thanks to a resumption of steam baths and to living in an overheated house; and there can be little doubt that his trip to North Africa later in the autumn was a search for warmth, both warm temperatures and warm waters, in Algeria and Tunisia. He returned from Tunisia to France in early January, 1888, and purchased a yacht in Marseille, which he named the *Bel-Ami*. He set out on a leisurely cruise along the Côte d'Azur. "If one could but live on board that boat, what peace it would be—perhaps!" In the summer and again in the fall, he went for the baths at Aix-les-Bains.[118]

Not only did the treatments fail to cure, but a new phenomenon began to accompany the headaches and eye troubles about 1888. That would seem to be the date of a postcard sent to Dr. Cazalis on which Maupassant told of going to Princess Mathilde's the previous evening, where he had struggled for words, seemingly losing his memory for everything. In 1889 he had several consultations with a Dr. Pierret, who was convinced that the amnesic attacks were related to the headaches and not to any psychic troubles. The loyal François, meanwhile, was beginning to record Maupassant's headaches with greater frequency, admitting that his master was taking ether and antipyrine for his pain, which curtailed his work and produced indigestion. His difficulties led to a restricted diet and an inability to accept dinner invitations.[119]

It fell to him, in his misery, to visit his brother, Hervé, who had been committed to an asylum outside Lyon earlier that year. He was dreadfully shocked to see how fast the disease was progressing (it was evidently general paralysis or paresis), and when it came time to leave, Hervé began to wail in so horrifying a fashion that Maupassant could not hold back his tears, "looking at the man condemned to death, whom Nature is killing, who will never again emerge from his prison, who will never again see his mother. . . . The poor human body, the poor mind, what obscenity, what a horrible creation. If I believed in the God of your religions, what a limitless horror I would have of Him! . . . If my brother dies before my mother, I believe that I shall become mad myself out of thinking about her suffering. Ah! the poor woman, how she has been repeatedly broken, crushed, martyrized, since her marriage!"[120] Although he had never been close to Hervé (the brothers were as different as those in *Pierre and Jean*), the knowledge of his inevitable death must have been heartrending; but may we not fairly see in his words a fear of his own premature death and a prediction that the mother would outlive both sons.? Hervé was the first to go, on 13 November 1889.

There is no reason to believe that in 1889 Maupassant thought that he, himself, was mad, but his fear of madness had to be well rooted by then. The hallucinations he described in stories like *The Horla* were no doubt the products of his creative imagination, but his own experiences of hallucinatory phenomena surely gave medical precision to his art.[121] The date of their onset is unclear, unfortunately, but the descriptions he gave of them to friends have a fundamental consistency that reinforces the claim that they were quite different in nature from those in *The Horla* or in *Who Knows?* On the other hand, the hallucination Maupassant described in *He?*, the very earliest of such stories (1884), bears considerable resemblance to his own experiences, whatever that may mean.

The particular phenomenon he experienced was first called an "autoscopic hallucination" in 1891; later, the "phantom double"; and still later, the "mirror image." The victim of the hallucination always sees an image of himself. Maupassant told Paul Bourget one evening, apparently in 1889, that he had had a clear hallucination that afternoon. He had been at work in his study, which Tassart was under orders not to enter when Maupassant was writing. He thought he heard the door open and turned around to see himself walk into the room. The figure sat down at the desk across from Maupassant, head in hands, and began to dictate the words that Maupassant had just written. When the recitation was finished, the image rose and vanished. He also told Bourget that it was not unusual to find himself sitting in an armchair upon returning home.[122] Maupassant is alleged to have told Gisèle d'Estoc of a hallucination he had experienced after one of her visits to his apartment. He had tried in vain to resume work. Feeling unsettled, he stretched out for a moment on the sofa. When he arose, he looked at himself in the mirror and was shocked to see that the mirror did not reflect his face. He stood still in his fright, finally noticing at the very bottom of the mirror a distant and distorted form as the reflection of himself.[123]

Maupassant also described such hallucinations to José-Maria de Heredia, but he seemed convinced that they were an intellectual rather than a sensory phenomenon. He believed that every writer has two souls. One soul is the natural self which everyone possesses; the second soul notes, explains, and comments on every sensation which the writer's first soul experiences. It would appear that Maupassant believed that his hallucinations were manifestations of that second soul.[124] Some Freudian scholars, notably Otto Rank and Stanley Coleman, claim to have found an association between the phantom double in literature and the Don Juan legend. That is, writers attracted by both the phantom double and the Don Juan theme tend to be psychopathic and narcissistic. They reveal an abnormal eroticism and take an excessive pride in sexual achievement, but either fear the consequences of grandiose eroticism or are fundamentally frustrated in their heroic love.[125] Though such an equation may be tenuous as a general rule, Maupassant was indeed one of its examples, and his erotomania will require special attention.

Maupassant's hallucinations, in short, have been related to both psychic and physical phenomena, and the long medical debate about his case was encumbered from the start by the issue of his syphilis. When Baron Lumbroso first published a description of Maupassant's eye trouble in 1905, it was presumably based upon a letter from Dr. Landolt, the ophthalmologist who had examined Maupassant in 1883. The trouble was described as a distention or dilatation of a pupil. In 1906, Louis Thomas, who was not a physician, asserted that, since pupilar troubles are a factor in the diagnosis of general paralysis (or paresis), the eye trouble was a symptom of the general paralysis that would ultimately destroy Maupassant. Dr. Lagriffe disputed that conclusion in 1908, saying that pupillary inequality can be observed in other diseases besides general paralysis. Since Maupassant had never lost his sight, Lagriffe ruled out glaucoma and proposed that Landolt had observed an iritis of syphilitic origin.[126]

In 1910, Dr. Antoine Lacassagne supported Louis Thomas's view that Landolt's diagnosis meant that Maupassant had been a general paralytic by 1883. Landolt himself was finally driven into print on the matter in 1910. Regretting the need to violate his patient's privacy, Landolt protested against the recent assumptions that Maupassant had been syphilitic. Indeed, Maupassant had repeatedly denied ever having had syphilis, and Landolt had never seen any evidence of iritis. It has been assumed that Landolt was simply endeavoring to protect his patient's reputation by fogging the record, but that does not take into account that Maupassant was quite capable of concealing his prior syphilis. Moreover, fifteen years before, Landolt had told Edmond de Goncourt that there had been nothing structurally wrong with Maupassant's eyes. His eyes were simply not properly coordinated, and the problem was "behind the eyes." He meant a nervous problem, but did not mention syphilis specifically.[127]

The reader needs to be reminded that, although Alfred Fournier had proposed syphilis as the cause of general paralysis in 1894, a positive association between the two had not been established by 1910. Even if Landolt had privately concluded in 1883 that Maupassant's nervous problem would end in general paralysis, he would not have suspected syphilis as the cause. On the other hand, the reason he would have questioned Maupassant about a syphilitic infection is that pain in the eyeballs is an occasional manifestation of secondary syphilis. We cannot know why Maupassant would have denied his prior infection, unless it was an instance of his passion for privacy; or perhaps Landolt and Maupassant concurred that the syphilis was long since cured, could no longer be a factor in the eye trouble, and might better be handled with discretion.

It might be added parenthetically that even after 1913, when the connection between general paralysis and tertiary syphilis had been confirmed, there was still no justification for ascribing Maupassant's eye trouble in 1880 or 1883 to syphilis. While it is true that some paralysis of the ocular muscles often occurs in cerebral syphilis (one form of tertiary syphilis), Maupassant cannot have suffered from its symptoms more than a dozen years before he died. The tertiary stage lasts from a few months to five years before the victim dies.[128] He would have been in the latent stage when his eye trouble became a painful dilemma.

Dr. Pillet, in 1913, was the first physician to get the debate on the right track by relating the eye trouble to the migraines. In reviewing the prior literature on the case, Pillet noted that the paralysis in the accommodation of the left eye had been periodic, like the headaches, and concluded that Maupassant had suffered from severe ophthalmalic migraines,[129] in which visual difficulties typically precede the onset of the attack. In Maupassant's case, the term *ophthalmoplegic migraine* would seem to be more appropriate. In this malady, the headache comes on first, followed by evidence of oculomotor paralysis, usually of the common oculary motor nerve. The loss of certain eye movements can either accompany the headache or come after it. Since the paralysis is transitory and may not even occur with every headache, the victim may very well not associate the two painful phenomena.

In 1927, when Georges Normandy published his account of Maupassant's illness and death, he had the use of Dr. Landolt's notes. Landolt had first examined Maupassant on 19 March 1883. He found the left eye normal but with a slight astigmatism. The right eye was found to be weak: myopia with slight astigmatism. He saw nothing abnormal about the pupils. When Maupassant returned a month later in apparent difficulty, Landolt found the left eye to be irregularly dilated. During the next month, the pupil grew increasingly triangular, inhibiting its proper accommodation. The transitory nature of such attacks persisted into 1887, at which time the abnormal dilation of the left pupil became permanent, and the mobility of both pupils became limited.[130] Such findings may well have indicated that the latency was collapsing and suggest a tenable date for the beginning of tertiary syphilis.

The argument really came full circle in 1929 when Voivenel and Lagriffe asserted that Maupassant's migraines had been of syphilitic origin, and that the eye trouble in early 1880 had been the sign that the infection was not latent. They specifically rejected the migraines as the source of the eye trouble.[131] Ten years later, a medical thesis was presented by Delpierre which also seemed to suggest that Maupassant's syphilis, dating from 1876, had never really become latent in that the violent ophthalmalic migraines are presumably characteristic of syphilitics. Dr. Delpierre added, however, that the general paralysis was not evident until about 1886 and did not affect Maupassant's ability to produce coherent works until 1891.[132]

Professor Charles Ladame, who lectured and wrote about the Maupassant case in 1919 and had considerable influence upon literary historians, became dissatisfied with his initial views as with those published subsequently by others. In particular, he thought that the migraines and eye troubles were not being satisfactorily accounted for, and that the case was not closed. Ladame was a friend of Pierre Borel, whose integrity he respected. After Borel published Gisèle's *Cahier d'amour* (1939) and wrote *Maupassant et l'androgyne* (1944), Ladame concluded that he must review the case. Gisèle had claimed to have talked to Dr. Landolt, who allegedly told her that Maupassant had had eye damage—a lesion—from at least 1880. This suggests the possibility of syphilis in the nervous system or a case of general paralysis. We do not know the date of the alleged interview with Dr. Landolt, a fact important only in that some of Maupassant's physicians, after his death, claimed that they had foreseen the end when they had diagnosed syphilis as the cause of the eye trouble. Accordingly, it would be wiser to accept the Normandy version of Landolt's opinion of the case and to suspect that Landolt may have altered his testimony later. Ladame, however, in agreement with Delpierre in 1939, concluded that Maupassant had been stricken with a syphilitic infection of the nervous system of the visual tract for at least ten years before the infection became diffused into the central nervous system and attacked the brain in 1891.[133] Such views do not mesh with the pathology of syphilis as it is understood today.

What is not understood today is why approximately one-third of the untreated cases of syphilis will ultimately develop the destructive lesions of tertiary syphilis while the remaining two-thirds remain in the latency stage. It *is* known, however, that certain groups within the population are more vulnerable than others—men more than women, for example. It may be that other ailments predispose people to syphilitic disaster; it may be that certain human habits abuse the nervous system inordinately and undermine ultimately that equilibrium achieved by host and parasite, which we call latency. We might wonder whether the ophthalmoplegic migraines left Maupassant particularly susceptible to cerebral syphilis and its ocular paralysis, or whether his use of drugs increased the likelihood of late syphilis. For that matter, did his deep pessimism, his black outlook, contribute to his vulnerability to physical disease?

He seems to have made no particular effort to conceal his use of drugs. In the first comprehensive biography of him, published in 1906, Edouard Maynial suggested that the drugs had been used experimentally out of curiosity, but that opinion has found no support elsewhere. None of the literati of the naturalist generation—Zola, Huysmans, Céard, or Hennique—used or celebrated drugs for intellectual, psychic, or sexual excitation. The general view has been that Maupassant used them only to quiet his pain so that he might continue his writing; and he, himself, said that he had had to use ether almost continually during the writing of *Pierre and Jean*.[134] Several years later, 1890, he was taking antipyrine, a derivative of coal tar, to combat frightful migraines.[135] It may be that he also used hashish and cocaine on occasion, but it would appear that ether was his chief ally. Because all of Maupassant's direct statements about his need for pain-killing drugs referred to his final years—that is, from 1887 on—the first students of Maupassant's illness were unaware that his use of them began much earlier, certainly by 1882. And since he had begun to experience considerable pain even before that date, it may be that his use of drugs began earlier.

In 1882, however, he published a story in *Le Gaulois* called *Dreams,* which, while focusing upon the effects of ether, contrasted its use with that of hashish, opium, and morphine. After inhaling ether, there came "a sort of stupor, a drowsy feeling of comfort, in spite of the pains, which were still present but no longer acute. They were pains such as one could endure with resignation, and no longer that terrible excruciating agony against which the whole tortured body protests." About 1885, he told the mysterious Mme X (who published the revelation in 1912) of hallucinatory experiences which sound remarkably like his description of the effects of ether in the story—in particular, a hypersensitivity to sound that recalls the hypersensitivity to odors suggested in *A Divorce Case.* The perfume of flowers, if not a drug, produces an intoxication that the ether sniffer understands.[136]

These auditory hallucinations, artificially induced, were quite different from Maupassant's visual hallucinations, which seem unrelated to the use of ether. We noted earlier that a number of his short stories, which dealt with various forms of fear, betrayed a remarkable understanding of the paranoid personality. One might infer, therefore, that Maupassant's phantoms were sometimes the product of a pronounced tendency to paranoia. Some of the earliest students of Maupassant's case, indeed, were convinced that his madness had been paranoia rather than general paralysis; and it did not seem to have been recognized, until Dr. Joseph Gabel presented his thesis in 1940, that Maupassant could have been both a general paralytic and a paranoid personality. Gabel had no doubt that Maupassant died of tertiary syphilis, yet he was able to recognize other aspects of the case quite unrelated to the disease. He cited, for instance, Ragusa-Moleti's observation that, during Maupassant's trip to Italy in 1884, he often turned around in the street to see if he was being followed, exactly as such a scene is portrayed in *The Horla.*

Dr. Gabel, in fact, thought that one might also make a case for schizophrenia in Maupassant, which could account for some of his hallucinations, for his sense of being alone, and his indifference to others. Gabel pointed to the story *The Night: A Nightmare* (1888)— about the man who walked through the emptying streets of Paris until he found himself entirely alone—a revelation of a peculiar sense of loss of time that evoked the schizophrenic's conception of the world.[137] We understand today that the schizoid cannot truly fall in love or sustain firm associations with others. Despite his profound need for love and friendship, he has somehow learned, generally at an early age, that love is destructive, that it traps, imprisons, and destroys, and that salvation lies in detachment and loss of feeling. The schizoid's existence, as a result, is infused with a sense of futility and anxiety, which flowers into a disenchantment with life.[138] One cannot quarrel, in short, with Gabel's observation of schizophrenia in Maupassant.

Several conditions have been cited to indicate that Maupassant's poor health showed signs of greater deterioration by 1887 or 1888, among them a change in the nature of his eye ailment and a hint that his pain was becoming more persistent. It has been argued, and denied, that a new tendency to threaten publishers with lawsuits, which emerged in 1888, was further evidence of mental deterioration. The first instance concerned unauthorized cuts in his essay, "On the Novel," published in *Le Figaro* on 7 January 1888, the day before its publication as the preface to *Pierre and Jean*. Steegmuller has insisted that Maupassant's letters indicated that he was not normally hostile to editorial advice, that he could accept recommendations for changes or cuts as long as he was consulted in advance. In this particular instance, not only were the cuts unauthorized, but they happened to distort his meaning. What is more, the essay on his literary doctrine was one of the rare occasions when Maupassant had been induced to expose his ideas. Not only had he reason to be angry at the distortion, but he probably regretted having allowed his privacy to be invaded. The matter was settled out of court—rather quickly according to *Le Figaro*—but Maupassant's letters show that he did not easily forgive the gaffe, pondering legal action for many months thereafter. Never again did he write for *Le Figaro*.[139]

In the spring of 1890, Maupassant consulted his attorney about suing the publisher Charpentier for the unauthorized printing of his portrait in a new edition of an earlier book. His sensitivity about portraits was not new, for, like Flaubert, he held that the reading audience ought to be concerned solely for a writer's work, not for his appearance. About 1885, he had informed a newspaper that he made it a fixed rule never to allow his portrait to be published if he could prevent it. His refusal to permit the use of his portrait as publicity is the more striking in view of his pronounced desire for publicity in the interest of sales, and because he was noted for the pleasure he had taken in showing off his muscles and the clothes of his well-to-do years. Perhaps he feared that his face, alone, might reveal qualities better left concealed, but he intimated that curiosity about his appearance was indiscreet and somewhat profane.

Despite the fact that the threats of legal action were triggered by unauthorized publishing decisions, which writers in general might find to be legitimate grievances, Paul Ignotus has perceived a veiled hostility during a decade of uneasy relations with the publisher Havard, which began in 1880. Maupassant may have been susceptible to editorial recommendations for cuts or alterations, a practical response on the road to swift publication and sales, but the tone of many letters hints at an entrenched dislike of publishers in general. We might suppose that anyone who had learned his craft from Flaubert would have evinced disdain for those who profited from art rather than produced it; but beyond that artistic duty was Maupassant's well-known thirst for the money that preserved him from the society of bureaucrats, and this gave him further reason for resenting a publisher's part in the profits. Ignotus believed that, as Maupassant's illness progressed, his long antagonism to publishers took the form of a persecution complex. If so, it follows that the unauthorized publication of his portrait in 1890 would have especially galled him, given his mania for privacy. We might add that he never agreed to sit for a painted portrait, though a few photographs of him were taken, from which engravings were made.[140]

Although the business of the threatened lawsuits may well be further evidence of Maupassant's decline, it also illustrates the continuity in his personality and outlook. By 1888, he merely gave more obvious evidence—thanks to the revival of the deadly infection—of those quirks of personality that had poisoned his existence for many years. In 1888, after his purchase of the *Bel-Ami*, he prepared and published the best of his travel books, *On the Water*. A reader would think that it was the record of his cruise along the Riviera and his thoughts about life at that moment, but its bleak tone was later seen by his mother and others as a clear signal of the beginning of the end. It has since been demonstrated that *On the Water* was largely made up of articles Maupassant had previously published, some as early as 1881, and that it was not a diary of one particular cruise, but reflected many excursions at sea.[141] Thus, *On the Water* can be considered a document of Maupassant's outlook in 1888 only in that he chose to put such materials together and publish them at that moment.

Though he related different adventures and described going ashore in such places as Cannes and Saint-Raphaël, the overwhelming impression one gleans from the book is of Maupassant's utter hatred for mankind and life. He did, indeed, express pity for the human condition, which only reinforced the darkness pervading those pages. About ordinary people at an inn, he wrote: "I fancy that I behold the deformity of their souls as a monstrous foetus in a jar of alcohol. I attend the slow birth of the commonplaces they continually repeat; I watch the words as they drop from the granary of stupidity into their imbecile mouths." Back at sea on a marvelous summer day, he noted that "I do feel on certain days such a horror of everything that is, that I long for death. The invariable monotony of landscapes, faces, and thoughts becomes an intensely acute suffering. The triteness of the universe astonishes and revolts me, the pettiness of all things fills me with disgust, and I am overwhelmed by the meagerness of human life."[142]

In Agay, he watched a young couple in love. He found them a charming sight in their complete infatuation, but was overwhelmed by sadness. "A felicity I have never known has passed near me, and I surmised that it was the greatest felicity of all." That evening he saw the lovers' profiles through a lighted window at an inn: "My loneliness overpowered me, and in the balmy spring-like night, with the soft sound of the waves on the sand, under the crescent moon shedding its rays over the sea, I felt in my heart such an intense desire to love that I was near crying out in my envious distress." Somewhat later, from the deck of his boat, he turned again to that window and found it closed: "A dull melancholy crushed my heart, and I went below." He spent a restless night and the next day had a sick headache.

"The dreadful pain racks in a way no torture could equal, shatters the head, drives one crazy, bewilders the ideas, and scatters the memory like dust before the wind. A sick headache had laid hold of me, and I was perforce obliged to lie down in my bunk with a bottle of ether under my nostrils." This brought on a numbness, a comfortable state despite the persistence of the pain—but now a bearable pain: a dreamlike state, "but not a dream like that created by hashish, nor the sickly visions produced by opium."[143]

In *On the Water*, Maupassant exposed quite openly the association between his hatred for mankind and life and his rejection of popular government. So antagonistic was he to groups and crowds that he could not go comfortably to a theater or any public entertainment. "I at once experience a curious and unbearable feeling of discomfort, a horrible unnerving sensation, as though I were struggling with all my might against a mysterious and irresistible influence." The crowd, he maintained, cannot reason, but is moved by "irresistible impulses, ferocious wills, stupid enthusiasms that nothing can arrest." The individual who would preserve his integrity must remain apart to avoid contamination.[144]

The diary may have been a patchwork, but it brought together the many threads of Maupassant's tortured existence and was as deliberately autobiographical as any of his last short stories; the reader will recognize, however, that it tells us nothing new. It echoes all the old pains and viewpoints. In 1884, he had written that he was uninterruptedly weary and bored. Everything stupefied him, whether people or events, and he found little of wit, elegance, or intelligence in the world. "When you see close up what universal suffrage produces, you want to mow the people down and to guillotine their elected representatives. But when you see first hand the princes who would then govern us, you become an anarchist."[145] Nor did he misrepresent himself. Those who knew him during the eighties, like Henry Céard, noted his indifference and his belief that life is bad and makes no sense. Jules Lemaître called it pure nihilism. Emile Faguet touched the core of the matter by remarking that Maupassant had never felt the need to detach himself for the reason that he had never become attached to anything. He had found life empty of meaning and men to be animals without hope for improvement. Death—the inevitable ending—was an enormous injustice.[146] At least one physician has speculated that Maupassant's terrible pessimism about life, "a moral sickness," could have been more destructive of his brain than any of the more obvious causes.[147]

The Erotomania

The very earliest examiners of Maupassant's life and death related his mania for privacy to his exaggerated devotion to his mother and to his disdain for most other women, but hastily added that no perversion had been involved. In their view, Maupassant had seen women as defective instruments, but necessary, and had asked nothing more of them than the gratification of his sexual needs.[148] This seemed to account for the impressive number of feminine names linked to his, and for his failure to forge a permanent attachment to any of them. The second round of the inquiry, however, noted the large number of abnormal or unbalanced "heroes" in Maupassant's stories and exposed the fact that he almost always drew his lovers as erotics, and did so with a pathological realism. No longer did his great appetite for copulation seem entirely attributable to his great physical strength; it was also a function of a sex-ridden mind. He had been obsessed with sex as he had been with fear. As evidence came to light that he had early complained of the boredom and monotony of his sexual conquests, it gave credence to the suspicion that Maupassant had sought the companionship of women to combat his solitude, especially to cope with his fear of being alone at night.[149]

While no particular perversion had been defined, the earlier assertions of sexual normality had been undermined.

In 1949, Francis Steegmuller was bemused by Maupassant's adoption of Maufrigneuse as a literary pseudonym. In a day when it was common to take names from Balzac as pseudonyms , why should Maupassant have been the only male journalist to take a name that evoked a woman? Did he mean to identify feminine traits in himself which artists are likely to have and which, in his case, had been acquired from his mother? While Steegmuller did not attempt to resolve the question, he did maintain that Maupassant revealed a remarkable talent for depicting feminine character—so much so that a popular legend developed among his unlettered readers that Maupassant was a pseudonym for a woman.[150]

Steegmuller had been aware, of course, of Maupassant's interest in lesbians, which was revealed in several of his works; and, at twenty-seven, Maupassant had reported an exciting discovery to Flaubert, a boarding house frequented exclusively by lesbians.[151] But at the time Steegmuller was writing his splendid biography of Maupassant, a controversy raged over the authenticity of Gisèle d'Estoc as a source on his private life, and a reputable scholar had good reason to suspect *that* lesbian's testimony on the basis of what was then known. Although Pierre Borel first published Gisèle's *Le Cahier d'amour* in 1939, her existence had been mentioned as early as 1927, when Borel published some of the recollections of Léon Fontaine, one of Maupassant's boating companions. Borel's tendency to literary sensationalism no doubt irritated both Dumesnil and Steegmuller. Some of Borel's revelations, published in bits and pieces over the years, contained contradictions which invited doubts about his facts. At the time he published the diary, Borel believed that the letters Gisèle wrote to Maupassant had been destroyed. He was later permitted to copy letters between them, but was unable to name the collector, or collectors, in whose hands the lurid documents resided.

Despite such contradictions, an impressive number of potential doubters have been converted to believers. We have already noted Professor Ladame's conviction that Borel was a man of integrity, but the character reference was published in a Swiss journal for child psychiatry in 1947, which the literati may be pardoned for having overlooked. Armand Lannoux, editor of *Les Oeuvres libres* and Borel's publisher, felt obliged to verify the authenticity of what Borel presented him. His sleuthing uncovered a genuine Gisèle d'Estoc, a woman in French literary and artistic life, who on occasion had been known as Marie-Elise (or Marie-Paula) Courbe and in later years as Laure Desbarres. Born in Nancy in 1863, she died in Nice at the age of forty-four. A psychological study she wrote of Jeanne d'Arc, the study of a virile genius in female flesh, seemed entirely consistent with Borel's information about her. It seems likely, therefore, that Gisèle d'Estoc was the mysterious *femme en gris* whom the faithful Tassart first mentioned as calling on Maupassant in May of 1887. Both Pierre Cogny and Paul Ignotus have subsequently accepted Borel's documents as genuine, but with the understanding that he may have sometimes been furnished with information that was not entirely accurate.[152]

Thus, it seems probable that Gisèle d'Estoc was writer, painter, sculptor, journalist, and androgyne, just as Borel described her. Even Tassart, who feared that she preyed upon the master's physical strength, admitted that she was a remarkably beautiful woman, always well tailored in pearl or dark gray with simple hats to match. He found her too heavily perfumed, but believed that she came neither from the demimonde nor from the smart set. He thought her manners to be somewhat severe, perhaps the residue of a convent education, a hint that Maupassant had kept his valet in the dark not simply as to who, but as to what, the lady was.[153] Not only did she sometimes dress as a man, but she had developed some notions about the future of sexuality which were not likely to have been acquired in a convent.

She believed that a third sex was evolving of which she was an advance copy. The third sex did not imply neutrality, but rather the active characteristics of both sexes. In her view, men and women are enemies in conventional love affairs. Love is a battleground where true women struggle to absorb the men for their own advantage. They give themselves, in other words, to capture men. As a remedy Gisèle championed a new conception of love based on the absolute equality of man and woman: neither partner gives of himself or herself; there must be no commitment, nothing but pleasure. She had never felt pity for the men or women she had loved, or with whom she had had sexual relations, for she did not love. Nor did she give herself: she was the seducer, mad with sexuality and never satisfied. That, at least, was the theory. In truth, she was a lesbian, and Borel thought that she had, in fact, never been able to give herself to any man but Maupassant.[154]

The letters between them were undated. It would appear from them that Gisèle approached Maupassant to establish the liaison. In response, he represented himself as never having felt love in his entire life, though he had often simulated it. He added, however, that he was sensual. "I rank love among the religions, and religions among the greatest stupidities into which humanity has fallen." Consequently, whenever he saw two lovers, he became annoyed at the stupidity of their error—a sentiment he perhaps expressed to prove the compatibility of their views, but which we know, from *On the Water*, was contrary to reality. She stressed the masculinity of her tastes: "In truth, I am very little female, being androgyne"; and *that* news intrigued him profoundly and led to the liaison.[155] She recorded that he later said to her, "You are truly the woman of my flesh! . . . I have never loved any woman; but you I love desperately, with all the strength of my being." As for Gisèle, she was delighted that she passed in society as a woman, whereas, in fact, she was a woman for Maupassant alone.[156]

Gisèle's diary contained observations about Maupassant's health and outlook which encourage its acceptance as an authentic document and contribute to a rough dating of the liaison. After a night of high passion, for instance, she found Maupassant the next day with no memory of the previous evening. He was pale, complained of a fearful burning at the nape of his neck, and held forth on the stupidity of human existence. On another occasion, he expounded on the emptiness of his life, which so revolted him that he had often contemplated self-destruction.[157] In Tassart's memoirs, there are references to the peculiar lady in gray from May of 1887 to September of 1891, the very period in which Maupassant was evidently losing his battle with tertiary syphilis.[158] The reader will recall that Maupassant had become concerned about his amnesic attacks in 1888 and 1889.

In his erotomania, Maupassant did not limit his sexual attentions to Gisèle d'Estoc during those years of increasing pain. She evidently brought him women she had already seduced, which recalls the fact that he had much earlier revealed a taste for sharing women with others. The rumor that Paul Bourget shared the "delightfully morbid" Marie Kahn with him has never been established as a fact, but the boating companions of his younger days were disposed to a collective lovemaking that Paul Ignotus recognized as suggesting a converted homosexuality. It follows that the attraction to lesbians indicated an excitement in finding a male partner in a woman, which is of course what he had meant in telling Gisèle that she was the woman of his flesh.[159]

This unconscious conversion may also not only account for the well-known instances of Maupassant's sexual exhibitionism, but provide a clue as to how he was able to perform so abnormally. Léon

Hennique once watched Maupassant paint a facsimile of syphilis on his penis, and in the presence of one of his women, express his anxiety about the frightful illness that had reddened his sex organs. When he then took the poor woman by force, she, of course, was terrified in anticipation of the disease that was in store for her. Hennique also told the story of Maupassant's attempt to scandalize the visiting Russian novelist, Peter Boborikine. After dinner, the group went to the Folies-Bergères, where Maupassant picked up a woman. In the presence of his friends, he had intercourse six times with her, after which he went into another room with a second woman for three more encounters.[160] Some may think that such stories are suspect, since they were recorded by Edmond de Goncourt, who by then was immensely jealous of Maupassant's financial success. But they resemble the pornographic pranks of Maupassant's earlier years and are similar in indecency to the request he reputedly made when he was Henry James's dinner guest in London: "There's a woman sitting over there that I'd like to have. Go over and get her for me." The horrified James, of course, did no such thing, and it is hard to know whether Maupassant had been serious, or merely outrageous, in his demand.[161]

Maupassant's sexual reputation was grounded upon what Georges Normandy chose to call in 1927 "an affectation of exceptional virility," of which the demonstration on behalf of Russian literature was merely one of many exhibits. Normandy was unable to explain how Maupassant had accomplished his copulative feats, but clearly suspected that he had acquired a highly abnormal ability to refrain from ejaculation while feigning orgasm.[162] One sometimes hears, as explanation for Maupassant's powers, that he was the victim (or beneficiary) of priapism—a persistent and abnormal erection, the cause of which is still unknown, a painful condition usually quite unrelated to sexual stimulation. That explanation is untenable in Maupassant's case, as priapism results in the destruction of the spongy erectile tissues in the penis, because of the coagulation of blood in the tissue. The chronic impotence which ensues was obviously not characteristic of Maupassant.[163]

Nor did Maupassant's ability resemble several other abnormal patterns of sexual performance that have been observed in various parts of the world. Some men learn to prolong coitus by postponing ejaculation, for an hour or more, in their search for heightened pleasure. There are also medical records of great sexual athleticism, six to ten cohabitations in one night. Such feats, however, are usually carried out by the very young under unusual situations of stimulation, are preceded by a period of abstention, and are of a transitory nature. It is remarkable, however, that such bursts of sexual energy are never associated with neurosis. The performers are not unhappy men.

Since erection is commonly associated only with sexual stimulation, it must be emphasized—to comprehend Maupassant's ability to erect at will—that it does not depend solely on the sex glands and is not simply a sign of puberty. Erections are observed in newborn boys, and in young boys they may last for hours or days (and such cases are not examples of priapism). In the mature male, "the pathologically increased sexual impulse, which *may* assert itself in prolonged erections, is called *satyriasis.*" Most men will lose erection rapidly after the first orgasm and will be quite satisfied. But men like Maupassant, who are able to continue copulation for a half-hour or more after the first erection, will not come to orgasm a second time. The reason is that adequate sexual gratification is unattainable. The apparent sexual prowess is a sham which hides the true sexual condition. Victims of satyriasis suffer from one of the paraphilias, and the abnormality is especially frequent among latent homosexuals. Maupassant's sexuality was that of a sick and frightened man, not the product of healthy lusts or sentimental passion; it was the sexual expression of the boredom, pain, and depression in which his life was so sadly saturated.[164]

Since Maupassant on occasion revealed the characteristics of paranoia—and because some readers will know that Freud believed in an exclusive etiological association between paranoia and homosexuality—we must note that it has since been recognized that paranoids often show no signs of homosexuality, either conscious or unconscious. Consequently, even though Maupassant's promiscuity *and* his indifference to women, like his satyriasis, were probably evidence of latent homosexuality, they do not constitute proof of paranoia. However, it is important to add that Maupassant showed no signs of overt homosexuality, nor did he ever fear that he might become a homosexual, a condition now described by the term *pseudohomosexuality*.

On the other hand, Maupassant was always painfully aware of his inability to fall in love and knew that he had missed, as he put it, the greatest of the felicities. It was an admission of masculine failure. The power motive is the constant factor in paranoid behavior, and its related anxiety is a survival anxiety. Maupassant's was one of those cases in which the sexual organs are used to achieve nonsexual goals, to provide a mask for the failures and fears that were central to his life once he had left his mother's roof. His erotomania was a pathetic attempt to repair his masculine failure, to reassert his masculinity through dramatic sexual conquests of women.[165] In Gisèle d'Estoc, he did, indeed, find his counterpart, the woman of his own flesh. Both were seducers who could not fall in love, both were mad with sexuality, and neither could ever be satisfied. That is what he meant by "the emptiness of his life," expressed so bitterly after a night of reputed high passion.

The Swift Decline

François Tassart, Maupassant's loyal valet since 1883, was aware that Maupassant's health was deteriorating by 1890. Before that date, he set down only occasional references about illness; beginning in 1890, his diary reflected increasing anxiety about his master's state. Tassart was both discreet and honest. There are obvious gaps in his diary where he evidently preferred to ignore the truth, but what he did record has been found to be reliable. Georges Normandy thought highly of Tassart, but necessarily searched elsewhere to fill in the gaps. He got Paul Bourget's testimony from André Maurel, relied upon Pol Neveux (who had been witness to Maupassant's hypersexuality), and had the use of medical notes that became available upon the death of Joseph Primoli. Other sources on Maupassant's last years, as we shall see, provided important material, some of it devoted to preserving Laure de Maupassant's version of events, thus casting doubt on its reliability.

We already know of signs that Maupassant had lost his latency in 1887 or 1888 and was entering the third stage of syphilis. Only in 1890 do we find reports of apparent physical deterioration: he suddenly seemed to be aging, he was thinner, seemingly jaundiced, and given to trembling. He attributed his decay to taking antipyrine to combat the frightful migraines. His insomnia was maddening, and he had begun to complain that noise was preventing him from working and sleeping—the same symptoms experienced by Jules de Goncourt. When he had to go to Rouen that April for the opening of a play, he wrote to his old friend Robert Pinchon to get him a sunny hotel room, one with a good fireplace: "I am sick, stricken with an incurable flu and by frightful neuralgias. I must have tropical heat."[166]

In addition to the old eye trouble and the headaches, he now complained of pains in his joints, and he began to consult a variety of physicians, the most notable medical names in Paris. In May, Drs. Joseph Grancher and Jacques Bouchard were urging him to go to

Plombières and thereafter to a mountain resort noted for its warmth, but he postponed departure in his search for a quieter apartment. In the meantime, he tried a series of steam baths in Paris, but found he could no longer tolerate them. The nutritious, but heavy, diet his physicians had advocated proved to be more than his stomach could tolerate and did nothing to improve his sleep. He began requiring François to stay near him at night, so he could brew him a cup of camomile tea or cup him along the spinal cord if he had difficulty falling asleep or awoke in a nightmare. He finally reached Plombières in August and found it chilly, but he thought that the waters were beneficial. He looked on the cold, or his inability to tolerate cold, as the chief cause of his illness. He must henceforth avoid humid places like Cannes. Since some writers have believed that Maupassant deliberately misrepresented his condition to reassure his mother, we must add that Tassart, too, found him increasingly sensitive to cold later in 1890. And he was reluctant to go out in the evening, as lights bothered his eyes more than ever before.[167]

Early in 1891, he was told by another eminent physician, Dr. Albert-Edmond Robin, to stay home and to rest his eyes for two or three days at a stretch without working. He told his mother that Robin did not think the case was serious. In another note to his friend Dr. Cazalis, however, he admitted that his "attacks of nerves" at night worried him considerably and wondered if the trouble might be traced to his teeth. If anything, the insomnia and headaches got worse in the spring, and he announced his certainty that he had "influenza in the head."[168]

He consulted two additional physicians that spring, Dr. Emile Magitot, a specialist in diseases of the mouth and teeth, and Dr. Jules Déjerine, a specialist in the pathology of the nervous system. He emerged from the consultations with conflicting diagnoses, one threatening and one benign. Which one he believed remains a mystery. Given his general outlook and his knowledge of Hervé's dreadful end over a year before, it is hard to see how he could have failed to seize upon the dire verdict. Yet he ignored the principal recommendations of the physician who gave him fair warning, Dr. Magitot. Maupassant was told with some firmness that he had overworked in literary production too long and that his body had been weakened. If he should continue at the same pace, cerebral activity would soon cease. He was told to take a complete and lengthy rest, outside Paris, but he was advised not to go to Nice, where his mother resided, or to retire to his boat, which was no place for someone as tired in mind and body as he. He was, in sum, to isolate himself in a salubrious region, to do nothing, to think about nothing, and, in particular, to take no medicine except the cold waters of a spa.[169]

Magitot could not have known, of course, that he prescribed for a case of tertiary syphilis, and his prescription could not have stemmed its implacable march. But at least he had recognized his patient's desperate condition and gave him the best possible advice according to the medical knowledge of that day—in fact, it was the only wise advice Maupassant seems to have obtained from the galaxy of Parisian physicians he consulted. Dr. Déjerine, like Potain, Grancher, Bouchard, and Robin before him, gave a consoling opinion, and it was an opinion that carried exceptional weight in that Maupassant had been informed that Déjerine was then regarded as superior to Charcot for nervous maladies. After the examination, Maupassant transmitted the diagnosis to his mother: "You have had all the symptoms of what one calls neurasthenia (Charcot style, what one formerly called hysteria). It is from intellectual overwork: half of all men of letters and at the Bourse are like you. In sum, nerves exhausted by boating, then by your intellectual work, nothing but nerves; but the physical constitution is excellent." Déjerine prescribed a tranquilizing climate, showers, and a long period of rest: "I have no uneasiness about you."[170]

It has been supposed that Maupassant must have altered Déjerine's verdict so as not to worry his mother about his health. On the contrary, he had every reason to prefer that verdict to Magitot's and during the next few months he followed Déjerine's recommendations much more faithfully than he did Magitot's. For the remainder of the spring he went to the Riviera for the warmth. With the approach of hot weather, he moved to Luchon in the Pyrenees to take the waters, but left after several days, finding the sulphurous odors of the baths intolerable. He proceeded to Divonne-les-Bains in the Jura, where, despite a regime of three shower baths a day, he could get no sleep. He wrote to Dr. Cazalis that he had fallen into despair. He could do no work and hated the atmosphere of the spa. Indeed, he remarked that he had had quite enough of life.[171] He insisted upon being given an exceptionally severe hydrotherapeutic treatment known as the Charcot shower, but to his great anger it was refused him. Dr. Cazalis, then residing in Geneva, urged Maupassant to move to Champel near Geneva with the pretext that it would be warmer and drier than Divonne. Maupassant wrote his mother of Dr. Cazalis's recommendation; the letter, posted from Divonne, was apparently the last one Maupassant ever wrote to her.[172] After Maupassant's death, Laure showed Baron Lumbroso two of his last letters.

The one dated 14 March 1891, from Paris, revealed normal handwriting. The other, dated 27 June 1891, from Divonne, showed an evident struggle to organize and write.[173]

In Champel that July, Maupassant's behavior became increasingly disconcerting to those around him. Dr. Cazalis realized the seriousness of his condition and reported his concern to the poet Auguste Dorchain, in whose company Maupassant spent considerable time in Champel. Once again he demanded the coldest, hardest shower, and threatened to leave the spa if denied it. He seemed highly excited, but refused all sedative treatments, seeking only new stimulations. The first signs of delusions of grandeur appeared; he began boasting of his muscular and sexual feats and his financial resources. He also had moments of complete lucidity, such as when he discussed the delights of ether addiction, and when he showed Dorchain a row of perfume bottles from which he drew symphonies of odors. Dorchain also suffered the pain of hearing Maupassant read fifty pages of *The Angelus*, the unfinished manuscript he was convinced would be his masterpiece, which contained the embarrassing autobiographical suggestion of his birth on Christmas Eve in a stable. When he burst into tears at the conclusion of the reading, Dorchain could only join him, recognizing that madness was at hand.[174]

Maupassant returned to Paris for the late summer and early fall, but decided to rent a small house in Cannes to avoid the Parisian winter and to be near his yacht. The house, called the Chalet de l'Isère, was on the *route de Grasse* and was selected because it seemed to be protected from the wind on all four sides. The peace he sought was denied him. His eyes continued to fail, sensitive to all light— even to a candle—and he knew that he would spend a second winter in virtual seclusion. The mistral got on his nerves despite the location of the house, and he complained of being assaulted by mosquitoes. Excursions on the yacht only made him worse, as Dr. Magitot had predicted, upsetting his stomach and chilling him.[175] A note he wrote in late 1891 to Dr. Georges Daremberg, an old friend who was in Cannes for the winter season, was that of a man made quite desperate by illness and pain. He had just discovered, he told Daremberg, that his entire body seemed to be impregnated with salt, a sign that his final agony was beginning.[176] He also wrote to his Parisian attorney, Jacob, and to a local *notaire*, Colle, about a codicil to his will, predicting that he would be dead in two days.[177] To Dr. Cazalis, he wrote that the end was near, explaining that the salt baths he had been giving his nostrils had produced a salty fermentation in his brain. At night, his dissolving brain had been flowing from his nose and mouth in a gummy paste. "IT MEANS IMMINENT DEATH AND I AM MAD. You will never see me again.[178]

Meanwhile, word had been circulating around Paris for some months that Maupassant's delusions of grandeur had become more extreme. In Paris that fall, he told friends that he had been created a count and insisted on being addressed as M. le comte. At Princess Mathilde's house in Saint-Gratien, he told of a visit to Vice-Admiral Duperré's Mediterranean squadron and of salutes fired in his honor and for his pleasure at great expense to the state. Duperré, when later queried about the incident, said that he had never seen Maupassant. In literary circles, it was accepted as fact that Maupassant had lost his mind.[179]

The gossip was probably correct. On the afternoon of 26 December 1891, he set out for a walk on the road toward Grasse. Within ten minutes, he had returned with the explanation that he had seen a phantom that had frightened him. At lunch the following day, he coughed slightly and was then seized with the notion that a bit of the sole he was eating had passed into his lung and might kill him. After lunch, he went sailing on the *Bel-Ami*. One of the sailors told Tassart that Maupassant had experienced some difficulty getting in and out of the boat as if he were losing command of his legs, the first evidence of a loss of muscular coordination.[180]

Maupassant had been given podophyllin, a mild but bitter-tasting laxative, by one of his many physicians; and sometime that same month, one of them concluded that the remedy had been contributing to Maupassant's stomach trouble. When he mentioned that "podophyllin is your enemy," Maupassant understood this to mean that he had an enemy, M. Podophille by name, and he threatened to kill him should he meet him on the road. The physician warned Tassart not to let Maupassant out-of-doors with a loaded weapon, and Tassart thought it was the better part of wisdom to remove the bullets from Maupassant's pistol at once.[181] This seems to be the most reliable explanation of why Maupassant's pistol was empty when he later turned it upon himself.

In fact, the terrible incidents of the next few days have been variously described, and it is impossible to be certain what transpired. On 1 January 1892, it was arranged that Maupassant should take the train to Nice to lunch with his mother and give her a New Year's greeting. According to Tassart, Maupassant had some difficulty shaving himself before departure, but otherwise the day seems to have been passed without incident. Baron Lumbroso derived his account of that day from Dr. Balestre, Laure de Maupassant's personal physician in Nice since the time of Hervé's death in 1889. (He called on her daily until her death in 1903, in what Steegmuller called a health ritual.) Laure's friend Hermine Lecomte de Nouy was later interviewed about Maupassant's behavior that day and gave testimony that differed from Tassart's. Information that came from Laure's associates was probably colored by Laure's desire to avoid any responsibility for the fate of her two sons. She was determined to have it understood, for instance, that the family, who had a remarkable history of sound minds and bodies, had no evidence of a hereditary disposition to illness.

Doubts about the complete reliability of such testimony, however, do not eliminate the possibility that Maupassant did have his odd moments at lunch that day; and it is quite consistent with the nature of his madness that he should have informed the startled luncheon guests that he had been forewarned by a pill he had taken of a coming event which concerned him. He seemed to be feverish and nervous, and, when it came time to leave, is said to have burst into tears as he bid his mother good-bye. Since he was never to see her again, that particular moment was later cited as evidence that he *knew* he would never see her again on the grounds that he had decided to kill himself.[182]

During the evening after his return from Nice, Maupassant suffered a renewal of stomach pain and took to his bed. Sometime after midnight (François put it at 1:45) Maupassant took his pistol from his drawer and tried to fire it several times at his head. He discovered that he was invulnerable to bullets and shouted to François that his blood would not flow if he cut his throat. Before François could intervene, Maupassant grabbed a paper knife and slashed at his throat. Of course, the blood flowed, and he cried out in pain. François called in the two sailors employed to manage the *Bel-Ami,* and a doctor was summoned. From all accounts, we must deduce that the cut was not deep, and that this was not a rationally premeditated suicide attempt, as Mme Lecomte de Nouy asserted. In the first place, Maupassant's stories show that he was not attracted to suicide, and, what is more, the few available details of his suicide attempt are characteristic of someone in an advanced state of the dementia of general paralysis.[183]

Maupassant recovered quickly from his wound, but gave new evidence that he suffered from delusions. He now claimed that war had been declared with Germany, and that François and he must go to the front. We know little about how the decision was made to put

Maupassant in a sanitarium, except that it was made quickly. An attendant from Dr. Blanche's establishment in Passy escorted Maupassant to Paris in a straitjacket (with Tassart still in his service), and they reached the institution on 7 January 1892. The sanitarium, at 17, rue Berton, in the Sixteenth Arrondissement, owed its name to Dr. Esprit Blanche, who had died in 1852. He was succeeded as director by his son, Dr. Emile Blanche, who managed the institution until 1872, when he turned the management over to his colleague and friend, Dr. A. Meuriot, though he continued his medical practice there. As a frequent medical witness in legal cases, including the Troppmann case in 1869, Emile Blanche became a notable figure in Second Empire society.[184]

Upon his internment, Maupassant was examined by Drs. Blanche, Meuriot, and Franklin Grout; and it is not clear whether Meuriot or Grout became the physician primarily responsible for him. The staff had a reputation for strict professional discretion, and the authenticity of press reports on the case, alleged to be taken from the physicians' notebooks, must be doubted. But Dr. Blanche himself, by then seventy-one and a member of Princess Mathilde's circle, may have inadvertently revealed more information than he intended, although he apparently meant to give evasive answers to the questions that were inevitably pressed upon him. For a brief period a few visitors were allowed to call, and Tassart remained with Maupassant for over a year, until 20 April 1893, by which time Maupassant was beyond his help. In fact, Edmond de Goncourt had noted several months before that Dr. Blanche had told Princess Mathilde that Maupassant was reverting to animality.[185]

Baron Lumbroso endeavored to interview reliable witnesses when he was preparing his book on Maupassant's death. Dr. Blanche had died—several months after Maupassant—but he was able to talk to both Drs. Grout and Meuriot. He also interviewed an orderly, Léon Bispalié, who attended Maupassant, as well as one of the sanitarium's inmates, Manuel Hirsch, who was lucid enough to recall Maupassant's behavior. Whether one believes all the stories that emerged or not, they all implied the same paranoiac personality that Maupassant exhibited before internment. Hirsch remembered Maupassant continually pacing the courtyard, crying out about an invisible enemy with whom he wanted to fight and simulating a duel. At night he would seem obsessed by memories of his vast wealth and talked of pederasty; and because he came to believe himself full of precious stones, it became difficult to get him to go to the stool. His suspicion that Tassart was stealing from him may well have been the final blow that induced the grieving servant to abandon the master.[186]

Toward the end he seemed to have had a horror of his friends and never asked to see them. In fact, neither his mother nor father ever made an attempt to visit him. By then, Laure was a virtual recluse in Nice, doting on her health and bemoaning her fate. It may be that she was not told that his case was hopeless; it may be that, after the loss of one son, she could not admit the likely loss of the second. There was a moment in 1892 when she, herself, seemed to be suicidal and when her own internment had to be considered, but she recovered to live on in desolation until 1903.[187]

Death took Maupassant on 6 July 1893 at the age of forty-three, after the terrible, but typical evolution of tertiary syphilis. In his case, it took the form of cerebral neurosyphilis; and from Dr. Blanche's remark to Princess Mathilde that Maupassant became infantile, incontinent, and emaciated toward the end, we may deduce that his symptoms followed the normal course for the disease. No one seems to have thought of notifying Maupassant's father of the death; he read of it in a newspaper. Neither parent came to the burial in the Montparnasse Cemetery on the ninth. "Apart from his glory as a writer," Emile Zola said at the funeral, "[Maupassant] will always remain one of the happiest, and one of the unhappiest, men the world has ever seen: one of those in whom the rest of us see our own humanity aspire, and then see it shattered; the adored, spoiled brother, dying amid our tears."[188] So fortunate in his talents, so unfortunate in his life! We owe it to him to honor the lucidity and energy which he commanded to turn that decade of pain and anxiety into astonishingly fruitful years. Madness came to him, yes, but only at the end of his career, and Carl Jung's cruel verdict that Maupassant's works were the delirium of a general paralytic is quite untenable.[189] But we owe it to ourselves to remember that the dismal portrait of humanity which infused those stories was the vision of a neurotic, immature, pathetic man.

· 5 ·

Alphonse Daudet by Etienne Carjat. Courtesy of the Art Institute of Chicago

Alphonse Daudet

So this redemption by love of which poets sing is a reality!
Daudet, Sapho

READERS WELL AWARE OF BAUDELAIRE, FLAUBERT, THE GONCOURTS, and Maupassant will likely have only the dimmest recollection of Alphonse Daudet and will wonder at his inclusion in such a galaxy. We are driven through his tales, sentence by sentence, in second-year French, an appropriate measure—apparently—of his literary merit. Then we are steered to more nutritious fare as we advance from vocabulary and grammar to literature. The most penetrating of recent studies of Alphonse Daudet opens with the sound observation that Daudet has become a most unfashionable subject in academic circles.[1] He has been tagged as too obvious in his techniques and message to attract a generation which has reserved its laurels for the obscure artist, for the "difficult" writer in particular, who can be deciphered only by the happy, or unhappy, few. It will come as a surprise to learn that Daudet's contemporaries, Edmond de Goncourt and Emile Zola, or their younger contemporary, Marcel Proust, had a high opinion of his literary talent.

To recommend a revival of interest in Daudet is not to argue that he was among the "greats" of the nineteenth century. As Professor Sachs puts it, "Reading Daudet is a frustrating and less than satisfying experience because one is always naggingly conscious of the flaws which diminish even the very greatest of his works. The flaws in Daudet's work are always an integral part of his total conception, for the flaw is in Daudet himself." Yet, his literary achievement, if of the second rank, was far above that of the hack writer; and his novels give us life in France between 1860 and 1890 without the political bias that marred Zola's greater novels about life during the Second Empire.[2]

To recommend Daudet's novels to historians as documents on the later nineteenth century is not to commend them for factual detail. It is debatable, for instance, whether the account of Morny's death, which can be found in both *The Nabob* and Daudet's memoirs, is as reliable factually as the account left by Ludovic Halévy.[3] But Daudet had an extraordinary sensitivity to the world about him. He not only observed its appearance and conduct, but understood the joys and agonies of its inhabitants; he was sympathetic to their plights and concerned about those conditions that threatened their futures. His later works, indeed, seem to preachify. Go to him, therefore, not for actuality, but for a reliable sense of what it meant to be alive in his particular world.

Daudet's own plight today, when he does not meet the standards for successful fiction, is also the unfortunate residue of circumstances having little to do with the issue of his literary talent. The truth about him as man and writer has been deliberately distorted, perhaps beyond repair, and it is probably for this reason that a major biography of him has not been written. Daudet, himself, began the twisting in the semi-autobiographical novel *Le Petit Chose* [Little What's His Name], and in his memoirs. In 1951, Jacques-Henry Bornecque, a professor at Caen, published *Les Années d'apprentissage d'Alphonse Daudet*. He concluded that the distortions made by Daudet, such as his desire to emphasize his youthful poverty as a contrast to his later financial success, were sometimes deliberate, sometimes the product of a selective memory, but on the whole innocuous.

A biography of Daudet, moreover, would have to depend heavily on accounts of his life by his older brother, Ernest, and by his two sons, Léon and Lucien. The family's record in coping with the details of Daudet's life does not inspire confidence, but neither is it grounds for claiming that Daudet was a literary fraud whose history was forever after cleansed by the family in a conspiracy to conceal the terrible truth. It may well be that such postwar critics of Daudet as Luc Badesco were inspired by political, rather than literary, motives and that Alphonse was attacked for having been the father of Léon Daudet, the Catholic royalist and anti-Semite of *L'Action française*. Badesco pointed, for example, to Alphonse's hostility to the Communards of 1871 (revealed in articles he published in *Le Soir* of Versailles that spring) to imply that Daudet had not so much feared the revolutionary chaos in Paris as he had regretted the disappearance of the imperial regime under which he had begun to make his name.[4] French readers were expected to understand that only a foul person could have regretted the Second Empire and that Daudet's heirs were predestined to preach bigotry and authoritarian politics.

Professor Bornecque, who perfectly well knew the difficulties in discovering the truth about Alphonse Daudet, could also distinguish between the polemicist and the true literary critic or historian. He protested Badesco's polemics, but could get Badesco to concede no ground in an exchange of public letters. Daudet remained, for him, that pathetic personality in desperate need to reconstruct his origins and development, whose lies toward that end had never been innocent.[5]

The compulsion to hold Daudet responsible for Léon's politics would seem to imply that sons are necessarily faithful to paternal views and influences. As we shall ultimately see, Alphonse Daudet's political and religious views were ambiguous and virtually undefinable as dogma, although there had been Christian royalism in his family background. Léon's mother, on the other hand, came from a family firmly republican for several generations. The friends of his youth were also mostly republican and, like them, he was actively opposed to General Boulanger during the crisis of 1889. Although Léon had adhered to Edouard Drumont's Anti-Semitic League before that date—that is to say, before he was twenty—anti-Semitism alone cannot account for his anti-Boulangism. For the Boulangist camp was a bizarre collection of both Jews *and* anti-Semites.

While it has been established beyond question that Drumont, as a journalist, was a friend of Alphonse Daudet, and that Daudet aided Drumont in finding a publisher for *La France juive* [Jewish France], concrete evidence of Daudet's alleged anti-Semitism is surprisingly sparse. He never joined the Anti-Semitic League, and he had a falling out with Drumont in 1886, about the time when Léon would have joined the league and the year *La France juive* was published. Like Drumont, Daudet was a patriot concerned for the national regeneration after 1871; but it is hard to imagine the humane and successful novelist as sympathetic to Drumont's particular left-wing anti-Semitism, which contemplated not simply the confiscation of Jewish property and the expulsion of Jews, but their extermination, as a formula for achieving that regeneration. Nor has Professor Sachs found any hint of Daudet's reputed anti-Semitism in his long poem, "The Double Conversion," which concerns a love affair between a Catholic and a Jewess.[6]

Léon, on the other hand, was an active anti-Semite by the time of his civil marriage in 1891 to Jeanne Hugo (granddaughter of Victor Hugo), a marriage that amounted to a reaffirmation of republican principles. It ended in bitterness and divorce in 1895, and probably prepared Léon for his drift into anti-republican politics. Marthe Allard, his first cousin, whom he married in 1903, drew him into Catholic royalism, completing his evolution from anti-Semite to anti-Dreyfusard to Catholic royalist.[7] Although Alphonse did not live to see the completion of that political metamorphosis, we know that he had been distressed by Léon's personal life, and, as we shall see, was far from approving it.

The sins of the sons to fall upon the father also involved attempts by the family to prevent the publication of an unabridged edition of the Goncourt *Journal*. As noted earlier, Alphonse Daudet became Edmond de Goncourt's closest friend in the years after Jules de Goncourt's death. The secret of their fraternal diary was kept until 1883, when Edmond decided to reveal its existence to the Daudets. Since his subsequent attempts to publish the diary provoked serious protest in the literary world, he recognized the necessity of removing the most indiscreet materials before resuming publication. Mme Daudet, however, painfully aware of her husband's sexual habits, was fearful that an unabridged edition of the diary, if published after Edmond's death, would contain intensely embarrassing revelations. Despite his assurances that the diary would prove his affection for the Daudets (which it does), he was never able to set her mind at rest. On the other hand, he dared not show any member of the family the original manuscript, as it contained the record of Alphonse's illnesses and explanations for them.

In April of 1894, the first part of the seventh volume began to appear in *L'Echo de Paris*. It contained a reference to Mme Daudet as "une bohème de l'Eglise." Ernest Daudet, Alphonse's elder brother, took immediate offense and threatened to write a public letter of protest to the newspaper. Alphonse evidently intervened to halt the letter, and Goncourt promised to omit the offensive passage from the book-form edition. Ernest kept the quarrel alive by next objecting to a description of the Daudet brothers' father, Vincent, which Goncourt claimed to have derived from Alphonse. The fact that the portrait differed in detail from that earlier published by Ernest in *Mon frère et moi* probably accounts for Ernest's irritation. Alphonse, who liked Goncourt profoundly, refused to allow such incidents to rupture the friendship; but the stage had been set for later troubles once death had removed the two friends from the scene. Goncourt, who had envisioned dedicating the *Journal* as a tribute to his great literary friendship with Daudet, was considerably upset to find that his pages were wounding the family.[8]

At the time of Edmond's death in 1896, nine expurgated volumes of the diary had been published. His will, which created l'Académie Goncourt, required that body to publish the entire work twenty years after his death. Since that date coincided with the battle of Verdun in 1916, there was a convenient pretext for postponement; but even with the restoration of peace, l'Académie Goncourt temporized, recognizing the probable legal reprisals from those heirs who could imagine themselves injured. An order was obtained from the minister of public instruction forbidding release of the entire manuscript, and it was deposited in the Bibliothèque Nationale.

The Daudet family, meanwhile, permitted the publication of some of Alphonse's notebooks, such as *La Doulou* [The Pain] in 1931, but only after careful editing; thus what we have are extracts. Lucien Daudet, in fact, admitted that the family deliberately destroyed letters from Alphonse's mistress, Marie Rieu, allowing us to wonder what else may have been secretly withheld to protect the memory of their beloved father. The campaign, in short, does not appear to have been a conspiracy to inflate Daudet's literary reputation, as the anti-Daudetists proposed, but a prudish determination to conceal everything sexual in Daudet's life: his long liaison with Marie Rieu before his marriage, his infidelities thereafter, and the syphilis which caused his dreadful suffering in its tertiary stage. After World War II (and with Mme Daudet dead in 1940, Léon in 1942, and Lucien in 1946), l'Académie Goncourt concluded that the time had come to fulfill its legal obligations. Despite the passage of time, Daudet heirs went to court to block publication of the unexpurgated edition but were rebuffed.[9] It would be presumptuous to assert that the court reacted to Léon Daudet's evil reputation as the purveyor of ideas embodied in the fallen Vichy regime, but evidently some of the literati were ready to trace those ideas to Alphonse Daudet in the inevitable postwar search for scapegoats. In any case, the trial focused attention upon the iniquities of the Daudet family, while authorizing publication of the twenty-two volumes of the Goncourt *Journal,* which, after 1958, provided much of the intimate information so long omitted from the heirs' publications.

After so much deliberate obfuscation, Daudet seems destined to remain the elusive character that Professor Sachs found him to be. It does seem possible, however, to explore further the decline in Daudet's literary reputation by relating it to his outlook on life; and we can propose at the outset that lengthy and painful illness contributed substantially to the ambiguity often found in Daudet's mature writings. His books sold well, and he became a wealthy man, a success in his own time like Maupassant. But there the analogy ends. Despite great odds, Daudet attained what Maupassant had decreed to be impossible; but Daudet's very aspirations set him apart from his own time and promoted his relative oblivion, long before any political odiousness was even noticed.

He was born in Nîmes, 13 May 1840, the fifth child of Vincent Daudet and Adeline Reynaud, but the third to survive. Both parents were of bourgeois origin, the father managing a family business which specialized in silk products. From Ernest Daudet we get a description of family life which is nearly idyllic, but which cannot have been the truth. The father's business was declining, especially by 1846, and in ruins by 1848. Vincent was a hot-tempered man, moreover, and devoted to a losing political cause: legitimacy. The results of the revolution of 1848 only increased his irascibility. Alphonse, like his brothers before him, was put out to nurse and spent much of his first six years in the nearby village of Bezouce with the nurse's family. However much he may have exaggerated the unhappiness of his childhood in Le Petit Chose, the emotional deprivation he suffered by being farmed out and his severe near-sightedness and unusually delicate health cannot be disputed. Ernest remembered him as having been given to tantrums. He was to grow into a man with an intense sense of independence and a capacity for concealing his feelings, yet also with a notable tendency to bid for the affection of others. The myopia, Ernest thought, contributed to his tendency to live within himself and forced him to sharpen his powers of observation.[10]

In the spring of 1849, when Alphonse was nine, the family moved to Lyon in an attempt to save one silk factory, which occupied the attention of both parents. In his fictionalized autobiography, Daudet referred to his brother Ernest as "my mother Jacques," an indication that the children were without supervision, and that Ernest had assumed a maternal role. While at Nîmes, the children had been given their primary instruction by the Brothers of the Christian Doctrine. In Lyon, however, they attended a public school, the Collège municipal, where their poverty and cheap clothing set them apart from the other pupils. The humiliation Alphonse felt probably accounts for his later sensitivity to poverty; in fact he attributed his basic pessimism to his seven years in Lyon. He omitted from Le Petit Chose the religious crises which beset him between the ages of ten and twelve, but which were interspersed with periods of remorse. He later called them revolts against belief in "the absurd or the mysterious."[11]

Thereafter, Daudet seems to have divorced himself from organized religion, and, between the ages of thirteen and sixteen, his revolt focused upon conventional existence in general. Although he had distinguished himself in school, especially in composition and translation, he became a notorious class-cutter, devoting himself to what Ernest called a disorderly existence. The delicate and timid child seemed determined to transform himself into a bold, violent type, ready for every available folly. We are told of boating parties on the Saône, of rowing in the rain with a pipe clenched in his teeth and a flask of absinthe or brandy in his pocket, of landings at riverside taverns, of risking collision in the river traffic to the annoyance of the experienced rivermen; he was really too weak for such exploits and would return from them worn out, pale, features drawn, avoiding the family in order to conceal his adventures.

When asked, in later years, about his most enduring amorous memory, he selected—after some thought—an incident during that tumultuous period when he was about fifteen and still a virgin. In the dusk, after a hot, humid day, he was approached in the garden by his mother's maid, who seized the hair at the nape of his neck and said *Viens"* (Come). The sexual sensation which followed was nothing unusual. What he continued to recall with great pleasure was the grabbing of his hair and that one word.[12] He also recalled that, as a schoolboy, he had spent the three days of a holiday in a brothel, having told the family that he had been invited to spend the vacation with a friend in the country. The women had concealed him, fearing a visit from the police. He emerged from the three days with a lasting memory of a woman's silken skin, and with a horror of lentils, the only food he had been given.[13]

Ernest thought it remarkable that Alphonse's sensibility and intellect were not ruined during those rebellious years, since his companions were evidently scum. Alphonse, himself, seemed to account for his survival by suggesting that his outrageous behavior during those years had been calculated, and that he had never lost sight of his real self even when taking a fierce pride in breaking into the broader, and disreputable, world of his adventures. He discovered a gift for observing himself, for judging himself, as if his real self was regularly accompanied by some demanding and fearful supervisor—not a conscience, but a second person, a double, exterior to himself, who observed dispassionately and took notes.[14]

It may be true that Daudet read back into his adolescence a perspicacity that he recognized, in fact, only later in life and cited it primarily to account for the development of his literary technique. His insight suggests, however, that Daudet knew he had never shed his old skin, but recognized both his youthful yearning to be other than he was and his regrets for the inadequacy of his family. While his critics have contended that he successfully remade his image for the consumption of posterity, it would seem fairer to say that he was preoccupied, as an adult, by the frequent necessity to be other than he was, a sobering observation and one root of his pessimism. One should be struck, moreover, by his apparent conviction that his youthful aberrance had been a matter of choice, that it is possible even for children to choose to do right or wrong and to know the difference between them. We shall find him, as an adult with children of his own, concerned with promoting conditions of life which breed happiness and avoid the dissatisfactions with self and family that had been his own fate.

His father never regained his former prosperity, and his business finally collapsed in 1856. His political ambitions had also been frustrated by the coup d'état of 1851, when President Bonaparte checked a possible royalist restoration by assuming dictatorial powers. Vincent Daudet had been led to believe that his royalist loyalties would be rewarded, but the foundation of the Second Empire meant that the brilliant future had been erased. The death in 1855 of his eldest son, Henri, at the age of twenty-three, was a further shock. We know little of Henri beyond Ernest's hint that he had been, like his father, a disillusioned failure. Sometime in 1856 or 1857, Vincent went to Paris to seek employment and tried various occupations to little avail. In short order, the family could no longer pay rent in Lyon and had to disperse. The mother returned to Provence to live with her sister after selling many possessions to pay debts. Ernest, then nineteen, was sent to find work in Paris; while Alphonse was placed as a *pion*, a study assistant or supervisor, in the secondary school in Alès, a town north of his native Nîmes. Although the tale of his mistreatment in Alès, as related in *Le Petit Chose*, was groundless, Alphonse did suffer from the sudden loss of independence, and he knew that the menial position amounted to charity. His employment dated only from 1 May 1857 until 28 October, meaning that he lost the position in the midst of the school year, for reasons unknown. Ernest simply explained that he invited Alphonse to join him in Paris. Having secured a position on the staff of *Le Spectateur* at two hundred francs a month, he could afford once again to mother his younger brother.

The Parisian

Alphonse Daudet reached Paris on 1 November 1857 to share an apartment temporarily with his brother. The two were very different in temperament, and it is difficult to believe that the serious-minded Ernest was not distressed by the bohemian friends Alphonse soon enjoyed. The seventeen-year-old Alphonse is said to have been notably attractive, especially to women, with a pale, somewhat fatigued (even dissipated) look. In January, Ernest's newspaper was suppressed for an imprudent and erroneous article in the aftermath of Orsini's attempt on Napoleon III, and Ernest was forced to seek em-

ployment elsewhere. He was engaged by the vicomte de La Guéron-
nière at the Ministry of the Interior and packed off to Privas to edit
the departmental paper, *L'Echo de l'Ardèche*.

Left alone in Paris, Alphonse seems to have gained a quicker acceptance in literary circles than one might suspect from reading *Le
Petit Chose*. He made friends easily, he took a mistress (Marie Rieu),
and he found a publisher for a volume of poems, all within six
months of his arrival. The poems, *Les Amoureuses* [The Girl-Friends],
were dedicated to Marie. Even though the book failed, Daudet was
favorably noticed on several occasions, beginning in 1860, in *Le
Figaro*. Indeed, he has been censured for having described that period
of his life in such black hues, for having deliberately ignored kind
treatment and success in order to propagate the myth that he had
risen to literary heights despite great handicaps.[16]

The criticism reveals a peculiar insensitivity to Daudet's actual
circumstances during his early Parisian years, which gave him reason for considerable anxiety. We know already that the inadequacy
of his family had long since inclined him to pessimism; that he had
again been left alone, in an alien city far from the sun and warmth of
Provence; that the failure of his poems convinced him that he had not
yet found his literary medium; and that the liaison with Marie Rieu,
though it would last for nearly ten years, was a discomfiture virtually
from the beginning. The principal theme in his first volume of
poems, the "love-sick male who suffers at the hands of a proud or
cruel female," suggests that Daudet, even at eighteen, suspected that
love "is one of the inescapable sorrows of man."[17] No doubt he
formed that outlook before meeting Marie Rieu—and it would remain his property until his death—but that theme, hitched to her
characteristics, would repeatedly appear in his later fiction: the older
woman who has had many lovers and is still involved with several of
them while she is in love with a younger man. We understand from
the start that eventual agony and despair are inherent in the format.[18]

An ingrained suspicion of women can be found in Daudet's works
from beginning to end, a logical concomitant to his sad appraisal of
love. He saw women as instinctively false, bad for all men, especially
those of superior talent. It was a view similar to that of Maupassant
and the Goncourts. They held that woman is the natural enemy of the
man who pursues the aesthetic ideal, an ideal to which woman is
indifferent and which she prevents him from attaining. The possession of talent, therefore, was a mixed blessing. They recognized it for
the gift it is, but held it accountable for their susceptibility to excessive suffering, especially at the hands of women.[19]

It is a further aspect of the ambiguity often found in Daudet that, from an early age, he combined his deep suspicion of women with a pronounced need for them. Edmond de Goncourt had never taken Flaubert's sexual boasting at face value, suspecting correctly that Flaubert was a fake *cochon*, determined to earn the respect of the true and sincere *cochons* who were his friends, among whom he listed Daudet. Even after twenty years in Paris, Daudet struck Goncourt as having retained the tastes and airs of the country gentleman, which Goncourt found peculiarly at odds with what he called Daudet's barroom appetites and his evident attraction to the unwholesome things and places of the city. Daudet admitted deserving his reputation as a seducer of women, noting that he had seduced the mistresses of most of his friends with very little courtship or ceremony. That is, he made it a point to have his women upon his first encounter with them; he deliberately treated them as whores, and always used vile language with them.[20] Thus did Art revenge itself upon womankind.

After the failure of his volume of verse, Daudet found employment as a journalist with *Le Figaro*, whose publisher, Villemessant, was a friend of the duc de Morny, the emperor's half-brother and president of the Corps législatif. Morny, who aspired to create comedy and light opera, liked to staff his office with potential collaborators. In 1860, he hired Daudet as an *attaché de cabinet* at a hundred fifty francs a month, a valuable sinecure in that it enabled him to collaborate on plays with Ernest L'Epine, chief of Morny's office staff. The following year, Ernest Daudet was given one of two positions created to edit the reports of the Corps législatif, the other going to Ludovic Halévy. Neither of the Daudet brothers had been active in politics, and Alphonse, in particular, was indifferent to ideology. He suddenly found himself at the very hub of Parisian political life; and, having little taste for politics, he was affronted by what he inevitably saw. He held the position, nevertheless, until Morny's untimely death in 1865, and during this period three Daudet-L'Epine plays were produced. Recent research, furthermore, has brought to light many unpublished or forgotten pieces by Daudet, that were also written in the early sixties; the sinecure had undoubtedly been a valuable literary apprenticeship, if not a period of literary success.[21]

The years with Morny were the seedbed not only of Daudet's literary flowering, but of the disease that would make an agony of his later years. Between 1861 and 1863, he made three trips to warmer or drier regions—to Algeria, to Corsica, and to Provence—ostensibly because his health had been adversely affected by the Parisian climate. He had, indeed, suffered from a chest ailment in Paris, which his most recent biographer has called an acute tracheitis (an inflammation of the trachea); but the serious ailment, concealed until the recent publication of the unabridged Goncourt *Journal*, was a venereal infection. He was treated by one of Morny's physicians, Dr. Charles-Jacob Marchal de Calvi, and Morny arranged for the leaves of absence during which Daudet recovered. He told Goncourt that he had acquired the pox from a woman of social eminence and, in turn, had infected his own mistress.[22] The particular length of his convalescence points to syphilis, and he was fated to fall victim to one of its tertiary forms.

Between 1866 and 1869, Daudet composed the three works which made his name (*Les Lettres de mon moulin* [Letters from My Mill], *Le Petit Chose*, and *Tartarin de Tarascon*). As Professor Sachs has written, they amounted to a trilogy. They were highly personal, more or less autobiographical, a Parisian's observations of his native region and people styled with wit and affection. In the midst of this productivity, 27 January 1867, he married Julia Allard, whom he had met the previous year, despite his fear, as Ernest put it, that a wife might "quench the pure flame of his spirit and kill his talent." The marriage would appear to be another example of the deep ambiguity within Daudet. His thirst for a literary career seemed compromised, in his own mind, by his desire to recreate the lost family of his childhood. He was aware, moreover, that both of those ideals were threatened by his addiction to sexual temptation. It is true that he had broken with Marie Rieu in 1866 as a necessary prelude to marriage, having taken her into the Meudon woods to break the news, safely out of earshot. As anticipated, she had carried on like a madwoman, rolling at his feet in the mud and snow, to no avail. But he was unable to abandon his taste for many women after marriage and was increasingly attractive to them as he gained in fame and fortune. On one occasion, his wife discovered him nude with another woman, after which she rifled his mail and burned his love letters.[23]

Daudet's preoccupation with his own duality seems to have been expressed in *Tartarin de Tarascon*, whether consciously or otherwise. Not only did he give us a Tartarin-Quixote and a Tartarin-Sancho, but he portrayed Tartarin, the would-be-heroic lion-hunter, as only too easily deflected from his quest by female arms. Tartarin was also a great talker who reflected Daudet's own gifts as a conversationalist. In commenting on the Provençal penchant for laughter, joking, ridicule, and irony, Daudet later wrote that he, too, had not lost the desire to laugh. "Through the mists of Paris, in the spattering of her mud, despite her sadnesses, I have perhaps lost the taste or the faculty for laughter; but to read *Tartarin* is to perceive that there remained in me a fundamental gaiety that could be abruptly rekindled by the fine light down there."[24] Some of the southerners thought that Daudet, in *Tartarin*, had maliciously ridiculed them in his portrayal of Provençal character; but such an interpretation missed both the commentary on his own character and his affectionate nostalgia for that region. Its virtues and its defects were his own.

With the completion of the trilogy in 1869, Daudet entered a peculiar period, a period of apparent depression from which he emerged about 1874. Given his marriage in 1867, the birth of his first son at that year's end, and his literary arrival, the depression might seem to have been unwarranted; and no single reason can account for it. One can only suppose that he suffered in the knowledge that his amorous adventures jeopardized his cherished marriage and wondered at his inability to curtail them. In the second place, disastrous war came to France in 1870, followed by civil war in 1871. At the outbreak of war with Prussia, he had been summering at a family cottage in Champrosay, a village just to the east of Paris along the Seine. According to his own account, he had been scuffling with a friend five days before that event, had slipped on the grass and broken his leg. The injury meant six weeks of immobilization during hot weather as the discomfiting reports from the front filled the newspapers. Along with other vacationing Parisians in the valley, Daudet finally had to return to Paris to escape the approaching enemy. Like all other patriots, he was greatly sobered by the national calamities that followed. It is said that he served in the militia (the National Guard) within Paris during the siege, but reliable details are scarce.

It seems evident, finally, that his dismay over the national fate coincided with serious doubt about his own literary future—a suspicion, in particular, that had mined to exhaustion the autobiographical materials central to his previous works. He seems to have embarked upon an exploration for a new genre as if entering a second apprenticeship. He produced a flood of articles, stories, and vignettes, most of which are now forgotten, based upon his observations of Paris under siege. As he put it, "I was living 'the journal of Robert Helmont' [*Robert Helmont, journal d'un solitaire, 1870–1871*] at the very moment I was writing it."[25]

Such terrible days fixed his attention upon external events and steered him ultimately to experiment with realism, a genre not dependent upon personal memories. In the immediate postwar years, moreover, he was a habitué of Flaubert's Sunday-afternoon gatherings for writers. Often, four of five of them—Flaubert, Zola, Edmond de Goncourt, Turgenev, and Daudet—would dine together, an occasion they named "the hissed authors' dinner." One must suppose that the association also helped to guide Daudet in the direction of the literary objectivity those writers professed to practice. Until he actually reached that point, with the successful novel *Young Fromont and the Elder Risler*, in 1874, Daudet suffered painfully from indecision and doubt. After the failure of his play *The Woman from Arles*, in 1872, he had openly considered the wisdom of abandoning writing as a career. It appears that his wife steadied him to prevent that defection; while Ernest, by then a power at the *Journal officiel* (and soon to be its editor), obtained the position of drama critic for Alphonse, a post he retained for the next sixteen years. Thus did he survive his lengthy crisis to write a series of novels in the realist tradition, to learn anew the connection between family and survival.[26]

La Doulou

His respite from suffering, however, proved to be brief, just long enough to complete two novels, *Jack* (1875) and *The Nabob* (1877). Although the nabob in the story was modeled on François Bravay, a politician from the Gard who had run for a seat in the Corps législatif in 1863, the duc de Morny (barely disguised as the duc de Mora) loomed large on Daudet's vast canvas of Parisian politics during the Second Empire. Bravay's family received the novel as a calculated insult, and Ernest L'Epine broke with Daudet for apparently having sullied the memory of Morny, the statesman who had been their benefactor. On the contrary, a fair reading of *The Nabob* ought to reveal Daudet's immense distaste for politics in general, not just for the Second Empire; and he portrayed Bravay, Morny, and their kind not simply as the beneficiaries of a sordid game, but ultimately as its victims. The political world he had observed firsthand, of course, *was* that of the Second Empire, and *The Nabob* ought to be recommended reading for those scholars who have claimed that Daudet regretted its passing. On the other hand, because he was truly nonpolitical, he was not among those who anticipated a republic of virtue once the Empire vanished.[27]

After the publication of his novel *The Kings in Exile* in 1879, some accused him of writing a defense of monarchy, others of having ridiculed not only monarchy but his own family political traditions, which suggests that no clear political bias was either intended or evident. Two years later, he published *Numa Roumestan*, the story of a southern politician married to a northern woman. The format allowed him to examine the conflicts such regional differences can hatch; but political ideology was so far from Daudet's mind that the reader never learns what the hero's politics were.[28]

During the composition of *The Kings in Exile,* in the autumn of 1878 to be precise, Daudet admitted that he had begun to experience considerable pain in his right arm and called it an articular rheumatism.[29] During that winter, he found it difficult to sustain his established routine of work. He felt sluggish, drowsy, sometimes dozing at his table, and noticed a quaver in his handwriting. A prolonged rest seemed to be in order, and he went to Champrosay for that purpose in the late spring. After a few weeks there, he felt quite recovered, only to awaken one night in June to find his mouth full of warm blood. He believed that he had vomited a large clot. Dr. Carl Potain was summoned at once and became, thereafter, both family physician and family friend. The incident recalled the respiratory ailment Daudet had suffered while in Morny's employ, when there had been some coughing up of blood (hemoptysis), usually caused by bleeding lungs or bronchi. Because Daudet's own description of the incident implied a vomiting of blood (hematemesis), the origin of which would have been in the abdomen, it remains unclear whether the incident in 1879 was of a different nature from those of 1861 or 1863.[30]

It is also unclear what Potain thought of the case. Daudet's friends seem to have believed that the hemmorhage had originated in the lungs, the result of a pulmonary lesion, and understood that Potain suspected pulmonary tuberculosis. Members of the family, however, testified that Potain thought the attack had been the result of five or six years of overwork, that the condition was temporary and required only rest and an appropriate regimen. And it has been noted that Daudet reported to Potain a hypersensitivity of his skin which was not a characteristic of tuberculosis. As Daudet never developed other signs of tuberculosis, the rumor that he was tubercular gradually subsided in the following decade.[31]

We have a hint from Daudet, himself, that he had been frightened by the attack and was far from confident that mere overwork was the culprit. In the autumn of 1879, when Edmond de Goncourt found Daudet looking ill, his gestures rigid and cold, Daudet whispered to him during a reception, "I am done for." Goncourt was disturbed all the more as Daudet's appearance reminded him of Jules when he had begun to be seriously afflicted. Early the following year, Daudet, Zola, Goncourt, and Turgenev dined together before the latter's departure for Russia. Daudet led off the conversation by relating how he had awakened to find the clot of gluey blood in his mouth, adding that he had subsequently experienced three similar incidents when in bed. All those present then recited their own ailments and revealed their fears of impending death. Osbert Sitwell cited that conversation to illustrate his contention that writers, as a group, are inordinately frightened of illness and death because of their unusually subtle and delicate nerves, their unusual sensitivity and susceptibility. He did not mean that writers are invariably morbid and morose, but that they are subject to fits of rebellion against the human lot—a susceptibility that accounts, in part, for the artist's attempt "to gain immortality by other than physical means."[32] His observation, in other words, suggests that a writer's horror of life derives, in part, from an inordinate horror of death. Daudet's later history must raise doubts about the universal application of that view.

Daudet's hemorrhages had been painless, but the "rheumatic pains" about which he had begun to complain in 1878 continued to get worse. Thermal baths at Néris-les-Bains in Auvergne, advised by Dr. Potain, provided no relief and, in time, seemed to make his pain worse. Late in 1881, he told Edmond de Goncourt that he had begun to experience difficulty in urinating. On one occasion the previous June, he had gone the entire day without being able to urinate. Potain, suspecting a stricture, had recommended a particular surgeon, but Daudet had been procrastinating in the matter and had received no treatment. By 1882, rheumatic pains were sufficiently severe to interfere with his sleep; and Charcot, by then a good friend of Daudet but not yet his physician, had concluded that Daudet was threatened with locomotor ataxia (tabes dorsalis), probably within six months, and that Dr. Potain, unable to see what was wrong, was incompetent in the case.[33]

It is not clear exactly when Daudet finally consented to visit Dr. Félix Guyon, the distinguished urologist. It was probably in 1882. Guyon probed the bladder and checked the prostate, finding nothing to interfere with urination—that is, no stones or gravel, no stricture or infection. In retrospect, we understand that the urinary difficulty was the first evidence of ataxia, the incoordination of voluntary bodily actions and movements. In retrospect, Daudet recognized that "the *nothing*" Guyon had found was "the beginning of *everything*: the Invasion." Goncourt recorded the first evidence of peculiar bodily movements in the spring of 1883. Daudet had asked for a rug for his knees. Then, unable to remain seated, he hobbled about the room with short quick steps, complaining that he was experiencing sharp pain in his foot, adding that he might find it necessary to have morphine.[34]

Over a dozen years later, Dr. Augustin Cabanès called on Daudet to inquire about his progress on a highly autobiographical book rumored to be entitled *Mes Douleurs* [My Pains] and said to be an indictment of the field of medicine. Daudet explained that the book had been planned for a good many years, but that he was far from completing it, a number of other projects having taken precedence. Daudet, unfortunately, failed to indicate exactly when he had inaugurated the project, but the evidence points to 1884. He began to take notes on his illness and his pain, but neglected to date the entries in his journal. It would appear that he abandoned the entries at some point for two to three years, then resumed them without explanation for the interruption. When the Daudet family permitted extracts from the notebook to be published in 1931, they provided, despite the regrettable omissions, an obvious and coherent story of the evolution of a case of tabes dorsalis.[35] He had entitled his notes *La Doulou,* not *Mes Douleurs,* the Provençal form apparently striking him as more truly reflective of pain.

André Ebner, who wrote the introduction to *La Doulou,* mentioned the date 1884 as the apparent beginning of the journal. His father, Jules Ebner, served Daudet as secretary from 1870 until Daudet's death in 1897, and was also employed as an editor of the *Journal officiel.* During Daudet's lengthy visits to Champrosay, the son would often accompany him to take dictation. Elsewhere, too, we find evidence that not until 1884 did Daudet regard his suffering as so intense as to confront him with a moral question about it. Returning from Edouard Dentu's funeral, he told Edmond de Goncourt that his suffering was so great that he nearly envied the peace and insensibility of the one to be buried. Perhaps, indeed, his time was short. After looking at himself in a mirror, he noted: "Vaulted from forty-five to sixty-five. Twenty years of life have escaped me. Father's death. The Wake. The shrouding. What I saw [in 1875] returns to me, haunts me."[36]

He recalled the prodromes, the symptoms warning of what was to come: the peculiar pains, really shooting pains, cutting and flooding his body; his burning eyes, a dreadful pain seemingly caused by the reflection of light; a tingling in his feet; an acute sensitivity to noises, the grating of the fireplace scoop and tongs, the irritation caused by ringing bells; hypersensitivity of the skin; the lessening of sleep ("I watch the web of a spider whose work begins at four in the morning"); a feeling of suffocation when stretched out in bed—and of fright.[37]

As the signs of ataxia became evident in 1883, he feared he might require morphine; and he evidently first obtained it from his father-in-law, Jules Allard, who was no physician, but who was being treated for a painful bladder ailment by a homeopath with conventional homeopathic treatment, supplemented with several small injections of morphine every week. Allard urged his son-in-law to seek similar relief and provided the morphine, certainly by 1884. Not only was Dr. Potain unaware of this nonprofessional prescription, but his ignorance may have contributed to his under-estimation of the seriousness of the case. He again, in 1884, just after the publication of *Sapho*, prescribed a season at Néris-les-Bains. While that novel, probably the best known of Daudet's works today, was clearly the story of his liaison with Marie Rieu, it carried hints of the pain Daudet was suffering: "Two hours of waiting [to see Dr. Bouchereau] in those huge salons, high and cold, filled with a silent afflicted crowd; the hell of pain in which they traversed all the zones in succession, passing from room to room to the doctor's office."[38]

As the muscular incoordination grew worse, Daudet was beset by fear and embarrassment. His awkward gait attracted attention that mortified him, and his sense of diminished strength turned to terror when, on the street, he realized the impossibility of running: "On the boulevard Saint-Germain a vehicle bears down on me. A marionette out-of-order.... The street to be crossed, what a terror! More eyes, cannot even hurry the step. Terrors of the octogenarian.... Thoughts of suicide....(Strychnine.) But one has not the right." No more talk of rheumatism; he pronounced the word ataxia for the first time in 1884.[39]

Since tabes dorsalis (locomotor ataxia) was not established to be a form of tertiary syphilis until the twentieth century, Daudet's conviction that his illness was a retribution for his earlier sexual license has sometimes been interpreted as a moral, rather than a medical, opinion. In fact, Daudet began to consult other physicians in 1884, his friend Charcot and Dr. Alfred Fournier in particular. In telling Goncourt that he was paying the penalty for prior venereal infections, Daudet accurately reported Dr. Fournier's opinion of the case. At that particular moment, in the spring of 1884, Daudet had developed a hydrocele (a pear-shaped swelling of the scrotum), which, rightly or not, was also suspected to be a syphilitic outbreak. Consequently, he went to Fournier in secret to prevent Mme Daudet from learning the truth, and submitted to surgery in early June.[40]

Dr. Fournier had first proposed a probable association between syphilis and locomotor ataxia during a series of lectures in 1875 at the Lourcine Hospital, acknowledging that Dr. G.-B.-A. Duchenne of Boulogne had observed, in 1859, that a number of his patients suffering from ataxia had reported prior syphilitic infections. By 1880, Fournier was convinced that locomotor ataxia was of syphilitic origin and began to teach that view at the Saint-Louis Hospital despite its rejection by most physicians. He recognized that the objection to his theory derived from the vast variation in the onset of the tabes. While a substantial number of his cases revealed tabes in the seventh or eighth year after syphilitic infection, he had observed—among eighty-nine cases—a variation of two to twenty-two years. This suggested to him a variety of adjunct conditions which affected the onset of tabes: abuse of alcohol, sexual overindulgence, mental overwork, or a chronic irregularity in one's daily habits; and he believed that ataxia was more likely to strike those predisposed by heredity to nervous disease. What he taught about the etiology of tabes he applied equally to the onset of general paralysis (paresis), calling them both tertiary stages of syphilis.[41]

Daudet's confidential remarks to Edmond de Goncourt indicate that he agreed with Fournier's assessment of his case, conventional medical opinion notwithstanding; and we know today that Fournier's knowledge of clinical syphilis was nearly complete despite the absence of the laboratory tests available only in the twentieth century.[42] Tabes dorsalis can appear as early as five years after the syphilitic infection, but generally appears more than ten years after infection and sometimes more than twenty years later. Tabes is really syphilis of the spinal cord, a degenerative process involving the dorsal roots and posterior columns. Shooting pains in the legs, about which Daudet complained, are an early indication of the disease and are sometimes felt in the back and arms. The pain is sudden, brief, intermittent, the attacks lasting from a few moments to a few days; and the pain is so severe as to make its victims consider suicide. Visual acuity is soon affected, and the patient may complain of double vision (diplopia) as Daudet did in *La Doulou*.

The degenerative process will also involve the joints, especially the knee joints. The loss of balance (ataxia) experienced by the patient will be worsened when he is not aided by vision, at night for example; and the bladder disturbances, which Daudet reported, stem from a loss of sensory nerve supply to the bladder. There will be abdominal crises involving both pain and vomiting with a tendency to constipation. Although the victim will experience muscle cramps with the shooting pains and complain of numbness, tingling, or aching in his legs and feet, he will also sometimes report an absence of feeling in his flanks or on the soles of his feet. Diminished libido and potency appear in time.[43]

We may assume that Daudet's shock at having "vaulted from forty-five to sixty-five" was an exaggeration, but there can be no doubt that his general physical state declined rapidly and that he became overanxious. "Since the beginning of my illness, I can no longer bear to see my wife or children lean out of a window." Even if they approached a railing on a balcony or a bridge, he felt an immediate trembling in his hands and feet. "Anxiety; pallor." His eyesight—never good—worsened, and his sensitivity to light greatly increased.[44]

"Every morning a dreadful contracture in my sides. I read at length, seated on my bed, the only endurable position. Poor old wounded Don Quixote at the foot of a tree, on his rump in his armor, a steel buckle pressing the kidneys cruelly.... Then the chloral [to induce sleep], the *'tin-tin'* of my spoon in the glass, then repose. During the months that this armor has confined me, I have not been able to release myself, to breathe.... What I suffered yesterday evening—in the heel and in the sides! No words to describe it; one can only cry out.... How many times one must die before dying!" The muscular disability which made walking a peril also affected his handwriting and embarrassed him profoundly if he had occasion to put pen to paper in a public place. "Impossible to write at times, especially if I am standing. The other day at the Crédit Lyonnais [the bank], rue Vivienne. Death of Victor Hugo [1885], necessary to sign the [funeral] register. Surrounded, watched—dreadful." Such notes reveal Daudet to have been a first-rate clinician. On the symptoms of tabes, nothing compares to *La Doulou* in subjective literature.[45]

For a brief time after Fournier's diagnosis in 1884, Daudet had hoped that iodine treatments would eventually give him relief; but the following year, after a frank conversation with his good friend Dr. Charcot, all hope for a cure vanished. "Long talk with Charcot. It is quite what I thought. I have it for life. The news did not strike me the way I would have anticipated.... Now that I know it is forever, a not very long forever, *mon Dieu*, all I ask is that I not have to change my cell, that I not have to descend [into that black space] where thought is no more." He knew that he had a disease of the nervous system and was told that it attacked the medulla of the spinal cord in particular.[46]

Thus, 1885 was a watershed in Daudet's life. Although he had been ill before that date, he only then learned that he would be crippled and in pain for life. He became increasingly preoccupied with his illness, discussing it more frequently and in detail with Edmond de Goncourt, but he was also concerned about the effects of his illness upon his work and upon those among whom he lived. He had rejected the temptation of suicide, yet admitted that his suffering had become so frightful that the idea of terminating it lurked in the back of his mind; and he had calculated how many drops of opium would be required to end his life. He insisted on knowing the ghastly details of Jules De Goncourt's last months, suspecting that he would experience the same phenomena.[47] Charcot recommended that Daudet go to Lamalou, the spa in the Cévennes where Dr. Duchenne of Boulogne was in residence. The suggestion that Daudet see the specialist who had made the pioneer study on the origins of tabes was no doubt intended to encourage Daudet and to avoid the impression that there could be little help. Daudet did go to Lamalou in 1885, and thereafter, until 1893, he returned annually despite the inefficacy of hydrotherapy.[48]

The Daudet family also moved from the avenue de l'Observatoire to the rue de Bellechasse in 1885, closer to the heart of the city and only a few doors from Charcot, who lived at the intersection of the boulevard Saint-Germain and the rue Saint-Dominique.[49] We learn, thereafter, of troubles within the family (some of obvious origin, others mysterious) which increasingly compelled Daudet's attention. He had forced Léon into medical school despite Léon's preference for a literary career, and the boy's resentment soon became a disruption at home. It may be that Daudet sought to spare his sons the perils of the literary life, for he would later advise Lucien against it. But Daudet's preoccupation with suffering and illness seems to have led him to override Léon's preference, and he noted in *La Doulou* that he had recommended a study of Pascal's neurosis as Léon's medical thesis topic. In fact, it is clear from *La Doulou* that Daudet meant his ultimate book on illness and pain to be something of a comparative study of how distinguished writers had responded to them, not merely a record of his own suffering.

"Spent the day in Auteuil [with Edmond de Goncourt]. Garden full of roses . . . where I was haunted by the image of poor Jules, dazed under his straw hat, lost in empty space. . . . Jules de Goncourt and Baudelaire. The maladies of literary men. Aphasia. . . . Preoccupied for a month about the end of the world about which I have had a precise vision. I read that Baudelaire, toward the end of his intelligent life, was haunted by this same idea of deliverance. The aphasia came on shortly after. . . . The great Flaubert, how he labored in the quest for words! Was it not the enormous amount of bromide he absorbed which made his dictionary so rebellious? . . . Heinrich Heine concerns me a great deal. Illness which I feel is similar to mine." He also compared himself to Benjamin Constant and Madame de Staël in the use and abuse of drugs. And finally, "Montaigne, old friend: complains especially about physical pains."[50]

One must not assume that Daudet sought to turn poor Léon into a collaborator by forcing a medical education upon him; rather, one should understand that a man in his condition could only wish for the advancement of medicine and envy the career which could abate human suffering. After 1885, moreover, Daudet was distressed to discover that Léon was becoming the victim of Schopenhauerian pessimism, the fashion of his generation. It may be that the issue of his son's medical education was an aspect of Daudet's more positive response to life and incompatible with Léon's outlook. Daudet began to feel a good deal of despair about the young generation, finding it insensitive to traditional values and indifferent to the family in particular. His own family began to suffer considerable internal strain; and, after the birth of their third child in 1886, Daudet and his wife, also a writer who had worked closely with her husband in a common study, began to work in separate rooms as if to lessen conflict.[51] It may be that arguments with Léon sharpened Daudet's resolve to cope, as a writer, with the moral aspects of his own pain, and to combat the younger generation's bleak conclusions about life, a matter to which we must return. He remarked, "Intellectual and moral growth out of pain, but only to a certain point." Evidently he discussed such matters with Edmond de Goncourt, who was convinced that Daudet's intellect improved and became more refined after illness struck him.[52]

On the other hand, Daudet was also worried about his need for various drugs and their negative effects upon him. By the autumn of 1885 he could no longer sleep without the aid of chloral, which suggested addiction, as did his need for morphine. He talked of going to his father-in-law for an injection, of his acute pain as he struggled down the street, of his gradual relief as the morphine took effect; and then of his return home, to its tranquil enclosure, in the drugged state of the *haschisché*. By 1887, it is evident that Léon was also equipped to give his father shots. On one occasion when he had given him two injections, but had refused him a third, Daudet had thrown himself into a carriage to get two more from his father-in-law. An evening at the theater or a party was unthinkable without Léon on hand with a ready needle.[53]

Toward the end of 1887, he tried acetanilide as an alternative drug, but found its side effects distressing. Small doses gave his lips a bluish cast. When he required greater amounts, the drug affected both his circulation and his bodily functions, and his whole face turned blue. He complained that his rectum, instead of emptying, tended to draw in like an octopus. When he took an enema, he feared that the clyster apparatus would be swallowed; and he likened the results of an enema to bird droppings with an occasional licorice stick. Morphine it had to be. The day after his departure for Lamalou in 1889, Mme Daudet called on Edmond de Goncourt to express her dismay over the amount of morphine her husband had come to require. He continually pestered her for shots—every ten minutes as she put it—and she had resolved to give him no more after his return and had so informed him. Léon's position, she explained, was different. He was out of the house much of the time and was available to give Daudet only two or three shots a day.[54]

Meanwhile, Edmond de Goncourt continued to jot down the symptoms of Daudet's illness. The ataxia made walking an effort by 1885. He could no longer descend a staircase without a banister or walk unassisted on polished floors, and he occasionally lost all feeling in the lower part of his body so that his legs got tangled. He began to experience some contracture of his hands during 1886 and compared the phenomenon to the shriveling of dry leaves. By then, bromide, probably prescribed as a sedative, had been added to his list of drugs. It dulled his mental faculties and led him to conclude—erroneously in fact—that Flaubert's struggle for words had been attributable to large doses of the drug. Despite the use of powerful narcotics, he was rarely free of intense pain. Goncourt witnessed a terrible evening when Daudet, smitten with shooting pains in his feet, kept walking from one end of the salon to the other, in continual danger of falling but catching himself on the furniture, while uttering little cries of anguish.[55]

We can understand Daudet's increasing reluctance to attend dinners or other gatherings. He offered as an excuse the notion that he had been giving too much of himself to others who did not give enough of themselves in return; he picked on Emile Zola, in particular, as having been pilfering ideas and phrases from Goncourt and him. In truth, he had become sensitive to the awkwardness of his gait, imagining that he attracted undue attention. Goncourt found him profoundly depressed after a dinner at the Abel Hermants, where he had had a bad time with unfamiliar stairs and polished floors. "Do you know what happened to me?" he blurted out. "I was not even able to sign the register; I could only scribble!" He seemed to be convinced, moreover, that his disease would end in the deterioration of his mind, which he feared more than death, and probably assumed that others anticipated it as well. His ultimate horror, therefore, was that he would come to disgust those whom he liked and loved. His desire not to be seen revived his thoughts of suicide. It is known that in 1886 and 1887 he broke with various friends, including Edouard Drumont. It was at this very time that he was disturbed by family matters, and he appeared to be rejecting friends before they might have cause to reject him.[56]

Daudet's fear of madness was not entirely unfounded. Although tabes dorsalis, as one form of neurosyphilis, does not ordinarily result in madness—and would not in his case—the signs and symptoms of paresis and tabes can coexist: taboparesis.[57] We cannot know whether Fournier or Charcot warned Daudet of that possibility, or whether (as seems more likely) he simply was haunted by the memory of Jules de Goncourt's fate. He recorded a peculiar mental episode that had occurred in his study, calling it an effect of either hypnotism or fatigue, but probably seeing it as a prodrome of impending mental disaster. As he was writing a letter, he was struck by the whiteness of the paper, as if all the light in the room were concentrated in the page, leaving the rest of his table and the room in shadow. A servant entered to put something on the table, and Daudet lifted his head. He immediately lost his bearings, and the spell lasted for two or three minutes. The servant tried to explain to him what he had just done, apparently in response to Daudet's blank expression; but Daudet could not understand the words, nor could he recall them after his recovery. Neither did he recognize his study during the episode, though he knew where he was. To orient himself he wandered about touching books and doors, saying aloud to himself, "It is through that one that you enter." Upon recovery, his first thought was for the whiteness of the page on his table.[58] The incident may well have been provoked by one or more of the drugs he was using.

Daudet was quite aware that his illness was impeding his work, not because of mental disorders, but because of intestinal upsets and terrible pain. Diarrhea followed constipation; he had bouts of intercostal pain (between the ribs); the shooting pains in his feet would lead to a loss of feeling in his legs so that, in bed, he would not know where they were; the pain would sometimes seem to infuse his entire body; and the shots of morphine usually induced vomiting. The ataxia made handwriting difficult, forcing him to dictate frequently; and even his attempts at recreation were undermined by his disease. On a short walk in the park at Champrosay in 1887, he stumbled over the root of a tree, then staggered about wildly attempting to recover his balance. Such an incident both embarrassed and frightened him. If he went for a ride to avoid the distress of walking, he was likely to have to descend more than once to vomit. By 1889, stomach crises were virtually a daily occurrence, often interrupting his meals. Although he believed that it was the morphine that produced vomiting (and sometimes mental sluggishness), it is a symptom that happens to be a classic characteristic of tabes dorsalis.[59]

The failure of all known treatments (including the annual visits to Lamalou) to work any improvement in the case led Dr. Charcot to experiment with a new method of therapy, the Seyre suspension, which reputedly had been used with some success in Russia. It was administered in a hydrotherapy establishment supervised by a Dr. Keller. After all the other patients had departed for the day, the suspension took place. Descriptions of the treatment are imprecise, but it was designed to reverse the crippling effects of the ataxia by stretching the patient's joints. The patient (or victim) was suspended in air for several minutes, and in the final minute held up by his jaws alone. We are not surprised to learn that Daudet experienced severe pain in the nape of his neck upon being lowered to the ground. He claimed to have undergone thirteen treatments, evidently beginning them in the summer of 1888 and concluding them in February of 1889 after some episodes of spitting up blood. Charcot admitted that the suspensions could have produced the bleeding, and the two old friends were somewhat estranged ever after. The brutal treatment, of course, could have had no curative effect, and Daudet had a slow recovery from the ordeal.[60]

One begins to understand why Dr. Cabanès and others supposed that La Doulou, when published, would amount to an attack upon physicians and their practice of medicine. That seems never to have been Daudet's motive. He wanted to produce a study of pain, probably a comparative study of writers' reaction to pain, and, being a novelist, he initially assumed that a novel would be the ultimate format. In the summer of 1888, however, after reading those pages in the Goncourt Journal which detailed the illness and death of Jules de Goncourt, Daudet was so struck by the power of Edmond's prose that he lost confidence in his own ability to match it through a novel and admitted that he would either have to find another genre or abandon the project. Putting the material in the form of confessions was an obvious solution, perhaps suggested by his intention to include Rousseau's illness in the work, but such a format would be impossible for a married man with an unsavory past. He continued to weigh the project, but never seemed to have settled on a form, and the study of pain never materialized.[61]

In 1891, he told Goncourt that he would leave his medical notes to Léon, then a medical student, rather than to Charcot, who had asked for them. "If I were to publish them," he said, "it would be said that I have plagiarized my son!" He had not forgiven Charcot for the harsh suspension treatments and now scored him for never having visited Lamalou, for never having observed the effects of such a place upon the ill. He did not mean to entrust such a personal document to an insensitive physician. Léon subsequently abandoned his preparation for a medical career, which in fact he had never wanted, with the excuse that he was being abused by Charcot and others on the medical faculty. The suspicion remains that Léon devised an escape from a disciplined regime with an explanation that his father was certain to understand and accept. Thus, when a newspaper reporter was sent to interview Daudet following the announcement of Charcot's death in 1893, on the assumption that the two men had been friends, Daudet declined to be interviewed on the grounds of Charcot's bad treatment of Léon.[62] But the truth of the matter remains obscure.

The search for a suitable format had troubled Daudet long before his problem with *La Doulou*. He had won renown with a trilogy of autobiographical novels published between 1866 and 1869, and gained in fame with a group of more objective novels published between 1874 and 1881. Professor Sachs has noted an erosion of Daudet's objectivity after that date, a gradual retreat from realism until 1890, when the break from that genre was complete. In retrospect, it is evident that Daudet moved toward objectivity as he gained in maturity and command of his craft, and that he retreated from objectivity as his illness took hold and as he became preoccupied with the tensions in his family. While we may regret the anxiety Léon caused him—and deplore the consequences of his failure with Léon—concern for his family did prevent Daudet from dwelling uniquely on his own *doulou*.

During the first few years of his illness, Daudet tried to conceal the true horror of his pain from the family, and since what they later wrote of Daudet's illness benefited from hindsight, we cannot know for certain to what degree Daudet succeeded in veiling his pain.

Though he poured out his troubles to Edmond de Goncourt, he believed that, until 1889, the family had been spared them. Mme Daudet, as we have noted, did express alarm at the amount of morphine he was demanding, and Daudet admitted several months later that he had been forced to reduce his daily injections to one, since the drug had been making him "difficult to live with." At the same time, he feared that he could no longer hide his true state from the family without the support of morphine, and he confessed that his strength had been reduced to a point where he had to ask assistance to go up and down stairs. The confession moved him to tears as he added that death was never far from his mind.[63]

From what Daudet said to Goncourt, we may deduce that the cachexia (a general physical wasting) was evident to all by 1890. His dependence upon Ebner was so complete—for assistance in writing, for aid in walking or getting into carriages—that he brooded unnecessarily about the possible loss of him. It seems evident, too, that the dependence upon drugs lessened only briefly. He acquired the means to give himself morphine surreptitiously to avoid his wife's wrath, but did so maladroitly because of his muscular deficiency. The result on one occasion was an infection in his thigh. A dose of chloral no longer provided more than an hour or two of sleep. As he increased his consumption of it, he appeared to be more than ever saturated with drugs, his memory foggy.[64]

Under such circumstances, his obsession with physical paralysis and mental deterioration could only increase. At Lamalou, in the summer of 1890, he became fixed on cases similar to his own in his mania to learn what the future held for him. When Edmond de Goncourt supported him during a walk that autumn in the garden at Champrosay, Goncourt was shocked by the trembling of Daudet's body, by the clicking of teeth at one end of it and the shuffle of feet at the other, accompanied by a mixture of curses about his wretched body and words of reassurance for Edmond's benefit. Meanwhile, Mme Daudet had become ill, apparently as a result of her distress about her husband. He insisted on staying with her at night and tried to avoid getting up so as not to awaken her—a martyrdom considering his chronic inability to retain urine and his habit of getting up seven or eight times every night. He began to take increasing amounts of morphine that autumn, and we learn that during one evening the following June he gave himself five morphine injections, one after the other, which enabled him to become witty and bright for the remainder of the evening.[65]

In the spring of 1892, Daudet thought the moment had come to consult additional physicians. The continual need to urinate had begun to plague him during daylight hours, and he endeavored to combat it by remaining seated whenever possible; and he was troubled by sexual impotence, a normal symptom in tabes dorsalis. For a few days, he submitted to a regimen prescribed by a Hungarian physician named Gruby, who claimed—to the irritation of conventional members of his profession—to cure afflictions with an esoteric diet, and whose particular clientele suggested a special compassion for the well-to-do. Immediately after rising in the morning, Daudet was compelled to eat a soup made from a great number of grains and vegetables. After several days of unpleasant aftereffects, he concluded that death was preferable to the treatment. He then turned to Dr. Albert-Edmond Robin of the Paris faculty, but Robin wanted to talk about literature rather than medicine, and Daudet's confidence was quickly shaken.

His third choice was Dr. Charles-Edouard Brown-Séquard, a physiologist with a medical reputation properly enough acquired but now in some question because he had turned to a controversial method of treatment. He had been born on Mauritius in 1817 of an American father and a French mother, and took his medical training in Paris. He practiced and lectured in both Europe and America until, in 1878, he replaced Claude Bernard at the Collège de France in experimental medicine. The direction of his experiments was made public in a paper he read before the Société de biologie on 1 June 1889 on the rejuvenescence of men after injections of a testicular extract produced from dogs and guinea pigs. A series of eight injections was allegedly required to produce both psychological and physiological rejuvenation. Since his audience thought he looked twenty years younger than his actual seventy-two, it concluded that he had been experimenting on himself with happy results. Daudet began the treatments in the summer of 1892 and found the injections to be extremely painful, producing what he called a contracture of his entire being. He was encouraged to pursue them, having heard from Léon that Emile Zola was also taking the treatment for sexual reasons. For a time, Daudet believed he was walking more freely as a result of the treatment, but he was frightened when a new degree of immobility came over him at night. The injections, in fact, had no erotic results. He finally abandoned them in the spring of 1893 and claimed that his mind seemed to improve at once. There was reason to suspect that the injections had been reducing him to animality.[66]

That is the last we hear of medical innovations in Daudet's case. He may have experienced brief improvement in 1892 as claimed, for remissions—especially from pain—are characteristic of tabes and would have been unrelated to Brown-Séquard's injections. Thereafter, we read of Daudet's continual decline and of the frightful pain as he wasted away, aghast at the longevity of his disease and appalled by the multiplicity of its horrors. He began to experience halts in his breathing during sleep, which Mme Daudet attributed to excessive use of drugs, and which naturally alarmed her. He talked privately of suicide, though he had earlier promised his wife that he would not take his life. She had divined, evidently as early as 1889, that he was suicidal, and had so effectively begged him to live for the children and her that he abandoned the idea of suicide forever after. Even so, he reached a point in 1895 where he feared he could not much longer tolerate the pain and was consuming quantities of drugs to keep from screaming.[67]

The Merchant of Happiness

During the day of 16 December 1897, Daudet worked on the revision of one of his recent novels, *The Little Parish Church*, turning it into a play in collaboration with Léon Hennique. That evening, at dinner with the family, he seemed in good spirits. He was chatting during the soup course when, without any warning, he fell back in his chair. A muffled rattle in his throat was followed by a more obvious one. Dr. Potain was immediately summoned, as well as Dr. Gilles de la Tourette, who lived only a few steps away. Determined attempts were made to revive him by employing several methods of artificial respiration, but to no avail. The fatal attack had occurred about seven-thirty, and death must have been virtually instantaneous, as is frequently the case with tabetics. In the medical press, tabes was given as the cause of death, without any mention of syphilis, for the etiology of tabes was still a matter of controversy. In *L'Aurore* of 18 December 1897, Georges Clemenceau predicted that Daudet's work would survive, because it had been infused with love for everything that lives or wishes to live. But the French State, suspicious that Daudet did not love the Republic, ignored the opportunity for a national funeral, and he was buried privately at Père Lachaise. The fact that the list of Daudet's pallbearers included illustrious men on both sides of the Dreyfus Affair—Emile Zola and Edouard Drumont—was testimony to the fact that the novelist had been above politics.[68]

Those who had known Daudet remembered him for his wit and charm. The general reader, as the years went by, came to think of him as having been the cheerful writer of sunny stories. That his attractive and charming heroes and heroines were often victims of illness and decay seemed to escape notice. Indeed, one student of Daudet, after an impressive survey of his characters' illnesses, some of which we know to have been his own, became convinced that Daudet had not meant to move or touch us with the sadness of human decline, but to horrify us with the ghastly ills to which the flesh is heir: his was a brutal vision of reality, a bitter outlook on life. One can only agree that the cretin in *Numa Roumestan*, the idiot brother in *The Nabob*, and the madman in his terminal seizure in *The Immortal* are not objects of beauty. Madness, hysteria, and nervous ailments were of special interest to Daudet; we know that he attended lectures by Charcot at the Salpêtrière (*The Evangelist* was dedicated to him); and, from *La Doulou*, we know that Daudet was keenly aware, not only of his own suffering, but of the wretched human beings he observed at spas and in doctors' waiting rooms. At least one character dies a violent or natural death in every Daudet novel, and a substantial number of Daudet's heroes regard suicide as the remedy for their miseries. Pain and death are the principal themes of his books. This should not surprise us if we recall his preoccupation with his unfortunate childhood, his resentment of sexual bondage, his lengthy periods of literary demoralization, and the many years of fearful pain.[69]

What is astonishing in Daudet, what sets him apart from the literary pessimists of his era, is that this preoccupation with pain did not exhaust his sensibility. He retained a compassion for the meek, an affection for those condemned to the squalor he had escaped by the pen. More and more, as illness presumably came to absorb him, he wrote on behalf of social causes. No doubt the causes touched him deeply; but no one who reads his works published after 1882 will doubt that Daudet was becoming a moralist, that his objectivity was eroding, to use again Professor Sachs's phrase. His own pain and the troubles within the family offered good grounds for turning inward and pulling down the shades; yet, he somehow managed the strength to look outward as never before, sometimes in polemical or bitter tenor to be sure, but with clear intention to right wrongs and to sweeten human existence.

The Evangelist, published in installments in *Le Figaro*, midwinter 1882–83, and as a book later that spring, was the first striking example of this new genre. It featured Jeanne Autheman, a banker's wife, founder and president of the Evangelical Women. The character of the order was summarized in its prayer book, *Morning Hours*, where we find the motto, "A woman brought the world down, a woman

303

will save it." From the prayer book, we are instructed that laughter and gaiety are the properties of a corrupt heart. A father, a mother, a husband, children, all disappoint our affection; and, in any case, they die. To attach one's heart to them is a bad investment. To love Christ—and to love him alone— is the path to take. Christ does not mislead, Christ does not die; but He is jealous of our affection and requires all of it. Thus, He makes war on idols and expels from our hearts anything able to rival Him.

Daudet was inevitably accused of having attacked religion in general through the book, but this was a charge that quite missed his point. He had been inspired to write the novel after learning about a fanatic female evangelist who had been attracting girls to a lay convent she had established to train missionaries. The girls were encouraged to renounce family ties, to break with their families. Daudet, with his firm dedication to the family as our most vital social unit, was appalled by such counsel. He meant the book to be an attack upon the fanaticism which could sap French society, and it amounted to an expression of sympathy for all parents who had been deprived of their children.[70]

Daudet had the misfortune to alienate some individual or group with almost every one of his novels; *The Evangelist* was no exception, and the hostility hurt him. His recent critics have supposed that his wit and charm were designed to curry favor, to win the love and affection he had missed in childhood and sometimes lost through publication. We know the reason why he doted on the family, but the assertion that he presented a false front in society not only presumes, quite erroneously, that wit can be contrived, but ignores the humanity which pervaded his spirit. Léon, in particular, remarked on the genuine interest his father had taken in every person who crossed his path. He sometimes had quarrels and broke with his old friends, but he revealed no systematic suspicion of humanity and considered disdain of people to be a form of ignorance. His very kindness and sociability enabled him to reach everyone regardless of station, and his insight into others facilitated his work as a novelist. To him, dogmas, formulas, and theories could only be impersonal or inhumane.[71]

We should not fancy him to have been eternally in society as he had an evident need of solitude despite his sociability. Throughout his life, whenever he was especially anxious about his spiritual or physical health, he retreated for days or weeks, once to a lighthouse on the Sanguinara Islands off Corsica. His marriage permitted no such retreats, but the frequent sojourns at Champrosay amounted to a flight from society. While we know that he talked of his troubles to Edmond de Goncourt, his closest friend, he did not make a habit of unburdening himself to others. On the contrary, he was usually in good humor and on good behavior. We read of him going to Goncourt's *grenier* for the regular Sunday afternoons, shining and sparkling, livening up the discussion as soon as he arrived despite his acute pain. He was "the apostle of life," as Gustave Toudouze put it. One day when he found Goncourt suffering from shingles he pretended to believe that his friend was suffering as a way of commiserating with Daudet, not wanting him to suffer alone "like a solitary drunk of suffering." The originality of the literary discussion which ensued delighted the host and raised his spirits. [72]

Daudet's family knew that his outlook on pain was admirable, and this recognition may have been the key to their determination to preserve his memory from critics. They had seen Maupassant in their home in his later days, coming for an evening only if he could be assured that Edmond de Goncourt would not be present, fearful of possible revelations in Edmond's *Journal*, arriving with eyes dilated and a grim demeanor, speaking rarely, chilling the atmosphere of that usually lively house. [73] But they had seen Daudet, surrounded by sick people in a hotel garden in Lamalou, endeavoring to reassure the nervous and the despairing, advising them to avoid egotism as it makes suffering more atrocious and unbearable. At home, he taught that disease and sorrow produce a unique form of maturity, which lends truthfulness to language. The sick live on their capital rather than on its interest. He believed that, except for his illness, he would have been a conventional author, trembling over criticism, duped by praise and empty triumphs, "prey to the sillinesses of the profession." He confessed his weaknesses, but thought, nevertheless, that illness had purified them. "I tell a sick person: 'Give yourself distractions and through your spirit wrestle to the very end; and do not weary and harass the people about you.'" He met poverty early in life, and pain later on, by sharpening his senses, but without bitterness. The longer he lived, the more his own experience convinced him that no one, no matter how destitute or base, is beyond discovering joy and happiness in life. He meant to convince all unfortunates that good can be found in the most unfortunate existence and began to speak of himself as a merchant of happiness. [74]

Thus, not only did his later novels become more didactic, but he reached a moment of wanting to be—through them—the consoler of mankind. Whatever may have been the original motive for starting a notebook on his illness and pain, he ultimately meant to go quite beyond the mere description of his own suffering to study the effects of illness on the morale of other literary figures. A year before his death, he explained the delay in publication by saying that he wanted the book to provoke thought, a desire that required exceptional reflection on his part.[75] "Poor human beings!" he had already noted. "It is unnecessary to tell them everything, to give them my experience." He meant to be more "tender and kind, indulgent," and began to take pride in not imposing the dark injustices of his own suffering on others. Although the book was never written, the fragmentary notes we have reveal a Daudet of great moral strength and energy.[76]

Even as he drifted toward being the merchant of happiness, Daudet persisted in writing didactic novels to expose evil and injustice. After the publication of *Sapho* in 1884, Daudet contemplated writing a book about the Académie française. He had been apprehensive about standing for election to the Académie; and, after investigating the preliminaries necessary for candidacy, he became so appalled that he vowed never to stand. This will account for Edmond de Goncourt's decision to name Daudet as executor of his will with the responsibility to found the rival Académie Goncourt. Mme Daudet seems not to have agreed with her husband's decision, and her negative point of view may well have contributed to the tension in the family that had risen by 1886.

The book on the Académie française, *The Immortal*, finally serialized in *L'Illustration* between May and July of 1888, also revealed Daudet's opposition to some of the intellectual novelties fancied by the postwar generation. The central figure in the novel, a scholar named Astier-Rhéu, who aspires to be one of the forty immortals of the Académie, finally reaches immortality thanks to intrigue and fraud, and to his wife's unfaithfulness; and the poor man ultimately kills himself after recognizing the degree of his debasement. Readers were shocked by the very number of contemptible maneuvers Daudet portrayed as necessary for election to the Académie, and the book necessarily made him enemies.

Daudet meant to associate this official corruption with the latest intellectual fads he had been distressed to find in Léon, ideas which seemed to justify dubious behavior. He provided Astier-Rhéu with a son, Paul Astier, "one of our fine Struggle-for-lifeurs!" the new race of ravenous young ones for whom the Darwinian slogan of "the struggle for life" served as a scientific justification for all sorts of villainies. Daudet even pursued Paul Astier the following year, 1889, in a rather successful play called *The Struggle for Life*, which attacked the popular notion that science holds the answers to all human problems.[77] His recent experience with Charcot's suspension treatments must have reinforced his doubts about science, but we know from Léon that Daudet had always encouraged the sick by raising doubts about the medical profession. He believed that though every medical case is new and unique, it tends to be approached by the physician as a typical case of a particular disease. Thus, he warmed the hearts of many fellow patients at spas by arguing that their cases were not really understood by the attending physicians and were not as serious as diagnosed. His intention was partly charitable, of course; but he had talked over the years with the most eminent physicians of his day—Potain, Charcot, and Brown-Séquard—and knew what contemporary medicine had to say about the human condition. Having suffered himself, and having witnessed much suffering, he knew the profound limitations of science as the key to the human riddle and instantly suspected any formula which purported to explain life.[78]

Léon also remembered coming home from school full of gloom after hearing lectures on Schopenhauer to find his father determined to combat the notion that life was absurd or horrible. He spoke of the glory of life, of the dignity of labor, and of love as the only protection we have against our knowledge of death. Only later did Léon understand his father's argument: that Schopenhauerism deflects people from life and destroys the humanity within them. We get the impression, as did Daudet's children, that Daudet's outlook had been molded in the Catholic tradition despite his adolescent rejection of that faith. He taught them that every crime could be forgiven, that nothing was absolutely irreparable when confronted by sincere repentance; he was never impious in action or speech; and he seemed to find utter materialism or atheism odious. On the other hand, he never returned to the Church and usually sought to avoid discussion about religious matters. He once asked Edmond de Goncourt if Jules, in the throes of illness, had been tormented by thoughts about life beyond the grave, a question perhaps prompted by the knowledge of Jules's fixation on Chateaubriand's *Mémoires d'outre tombe*. But Edmond insisted that Jules never alluded to life after death, and Edmond supposed that he had believed, as Edmond did, in total annihilation. Daudet cut short the discussion by saying that he shared that view. He venerated Montaigne and carried his *Essays* on many of his trips to spas. It seems probable that he shared Montaigne's skepticism.[79]

In 1894, Dr. Antoine Lacassagne of Lyon interviewed a number of writers in an attempt to explain how writers function. Daudet confessed not simply a distaste for abstractions such as infinity, eternity, or perfection, but said that he had never been able to visualize them—or that they had never been able to enter his mind. "I had Numa Roumestan, the man of the Midi, say, 'When I am not talking, I am not thinking.' I thought it was a new idea, but have since found its equivalent in Montaigne. In any case, it is a southern formula." He noted that he had been quite myopic from childhood, but that his hearing had always been excellent, the hearing "of a blind man." Although his visual memory was quite good, his memory of sounds was even better, more evocative of the past. When he had difficulty recovering his impressions of a time long past, he would recall what song he would have been singing at that time. Everything else would then return to his mind.

Can one imagine Baudelaire or Maupassant singing! Daudet, in fact, thought he was one of the few literary men of his era who did not hold music in horror. Gautier had called music the most disagreeable of all the noises, an opinion shared by Leconte de Lisle and Théodore de Banville. The moment anyone would open a piano, Edmond de Goncourt would wrinkle his nose. Zola vaguely remembered playing something in his childhood, but could not recall what it had been. Flaubert had feigned great interest in music, principally to please Turgenev, who, in truth, only liked music when it was performed in the home of his mistress, Mme Viardot. But Daudet liked music in any form, including the sounds of bells and tambourines.[80]

His creative powers declined notably after 1890 because of illness. He could not bear to sit long at a desk, handwriting was often impossible, and he was forced to dictate. Although he ordinarily required assistance for even short walks, he was known—in the presence of a critic or of observers likely to pity him—to have held himself erect with enormous effort and to have walked firmly, unflinchingly, unaided. That pride and courage no doubt account for his resolve to continue writing no matter the odds. He knew that his medication curbed his creative powers; his recent inability to dream seemed to be evidence of reduced imagination. Before he had required drugs in order to sleep, he had dreamed a good deal; and his dreams were peculiar in that, as a measure of his constant preoccupation with stories, they had always borne a title. In 1896, the year before his death, he seemingly reversed his literary decline with two superior works, *The Arlatan Treasure*, and a short story, *The Fedor*

Woman—another example, perhaps, of his tenacity and determination.

Otherwise, his writing after 1890 reflected his anxiety about his family and about the future of families in general. One can argue, in fact, that Daudet's customary indifference to politics was only breached when government took measures injurious to the integrity of families or to the provinces from which he had come. He remained profoundly convinced of the influence the soil and local habits have upon us and believed that it could only be injurious to lose one's roots entirely and to forget one's native village. He sensed that to flee from home country is really to flee from oneself. He was wont to advise young writers, once they had had their taste of Paris, to return to their homes; for it was there, if they had any talent, that they could best write a personal book, one with their own mark upon it. The latent antagonism between Paris and the provinces, which emerged so brutally in the civil strife of 1871, distressed him the more because his particular brand of patriotism required the cultivation of strong regionalism; and he knew that centralizers had won the day in 1871. Yet, we find no evidence thereafter of an active sympathy for the monarchists who came to represent decentralization; he seemingly made no connection between cultural and political centralization.[82]

Nor did he advocate the destruction of the Third Republic. After the territorial losses of 1871, he shared the widespread desire for revenge and tended to revere the military, whose task it would be to recover the lost provinces. He told Léon that "those who have formally made a sacrifice of their life stand on a higher plane than all other people." Yet, he took no open part in the Dreyfus Affair despite Léon's pronounced anti-Dreyfus position. Léon's remarks lead us to conclude that Daudet wanted to believe that Dreyfus was guilty, as he shrank from the idea that the chiefs of the army could be guilty of injustice, but he clearly had his doubts about Dreyfus's guilt. Léon even offered to have Henri Rochefort come to the house to assure Daudet that Dreyfus was unworthy of pity, but Daudet evidently denied himself that honor.

On the other hand, Daudet had never had a high opinion of politicians or any patience with the transactions necessary to make government possible. It is said that he had seen too much of politics in the time of the duc de Morny, but it might be better said that he was ignorant of political life. He was quite properly appalled by the parliamentary scandals of the later nineteenth century. His last novel, *The Breadwinner*, gives a particularly vivid picture of his hatred of corruption and of the intrigues of lobbies. But nowhere does he suggest that human foibles would wither away with a change in regime.[83] His dislike of politics seems to have left him unable to distinguish between compromise and corruption, and to have left him peculiarly vulnerable to polemicists and rabble-rousers like Drumont and Rochefort, from whom he was saved only by a sense of decency. His misfortune was to have a son, Léon, whose sensibilities were less refined and who proceeded to a career of bigotry and reaction that tainted the father's reputation.

This is not to say that Daudet, himself, was entirely blameless for Léon's bent. With his devotion to the family ideal, he had been a vigorous opponent of divorce; and, in his mind, the gentlemen of the Third Republic, who had legalized divorce by the Law of 27 July 1884, had committed a sin against mankind. The divorce bill had originated in the Chamber of Deputies in 1882, but it did not become law until two years later when it passed the Senate with the sponsorship of Alfred Naquet of Vaucluse. Naquet was an oddity in French politics: a physician by training, a professor of chemistry, a Jewish mystic, and a radical always associated with the extreme left. His espousal of the divorce issue proved to be unfortunate in that it coincided with the crash of the General Union Bank, which had been engaged in a struggle against Jewish financial institutions. Although officials of the General Union had stooped to fraud in their campaign, they endeavored to escape condemnation by inciting anti-Semitism. Edouard Drumont's virulent anti-Semitism, something the French had not experienced before 1882, was the immediate result.[84]

We noted earlier that Drumont was a friend of Alphonse Daudet, but that it was Léon alone who threw himself into Drumont's causes. Given Daudet's inaction, we have only Lucien's word that Daudet had a horror of divorce, that he reviled the Jew who sponsored its legality, and that he stigmatized a government which accepted a bill that permitted the death of the family. That is not proof of anti-Semitism, but it is an attitude that may have reinforced the bigotry of his son.

Daudet's views on divorce and its Jewish sponsor can also be found in his dull and didactic novel, *Rose and Ninette*, published in the autumn of 1891 and dedicated to Léon, who had married Jeanne Hugo the previous January. Daudet had had serious doubts about the advisability of the marriage, because the Hugos insisted on a civil wedding, which offended the Catholic members of the Daudet family. There is evidence that Daudet wrote his novel hastily as a warning to Léon that divorce must be no easy solution to a troublesome marriage. In 1894, when he feared that Léon's marriage was collapsing, Daudet undertook a second novel on the subject of marriage and divorce—*The Little Parish Church*. We are given a story of a wife's infidelity; but the threatened marriage ultimately survives as the aggrieved husband learns the wisdom of forgiveness. Happiness, in other words, is not a matter of course. We must know misfortune in order to enjoy its antithesis; we must learn that quarrels and different views are insubstantial compared to what is lost by divorce. With Lucien, Daudet secretly visited Edouard Lockroy, Jeanne Hugo's stepfather, in a further attempt to save Léon's marriage, but his mission failed. In 1897, after the divorce, Léon returned to the family home, and a few months before Daudet's death they were forced to move from the rue de Bellechasse to 41, rue de l'Université to obtain more space.[85]

Most writers of the realist or naturalist era, whether or not they acknowledge membership in such schools, hated the pain and suffering of human existence and expressed their abhorrence of life. Pity for a suffering mankind, which we might expect as a concomitant, can indeed be found in their works; but their private expressions of hatred for people in general belie the claim of humanitarianism and drive us to realize that to disavow life is to hold one's fellow man in contempt. Daudet had every reason to know that pain is part of the human condition, but he never found that fact a mandate to despair. He sought to prevent his children from succumbing to the hopeless pessimism that was the latest wisdom; and, although he could depict human misery and agony in his novels, there is no aesthetic joy in such descriptions. For he was able to combine his hatred of pain and suffering with a compassion for those who suffered.[86]

Whatever we may think of such matters today, Daudet was revered in his own time because of his passion for making the younger generation think well of courage and love. Marcel Proust, a frequent visitor at the Daudet's home as a friend of Lucien, noted that the intensity of Daudet's suffering had not altered the perfection and the beauty of his face, that he had lived with incredible grace in the face of cruel pain. "He celebrated life and used it better than most of us: a man of courage and beauty."[87] We should remember him as a sick man who was also well.

What gave him the strength to aid and counsel others who suffered, perhaps, less than he? His devotion to his family, obviously, was a salvation, requiring his attention to torments other than his own. Sick as he was, he still assumed the responsibility for his kin. If his home was a sanctuary, as it was for Flaubert, the Goncourts, and Maupassant (and as it would have been for Baudelaire, could he have settled with *maman*), it never became—for him—the hospice it was for them. There can be no doubt that his disease brought him frightful misery over many years; it was a horror no one would want to minimize. Yet it was not the earliest source of his pessimism. Can it be that the ravages of his physical illness were less incapacitating, less demoralizing, than the perversions, the paraphilias, which gave birth to pessimism in his fellow writers? And what, finally, of his early immersion in Christianity? For that, also, provides a contrast. Did it leave, despite his later rejection of the faith, a sense of the miraculous in life, a sense of the community and the soil of which he was an ineradicable part, which gave him not simply endurance, but the capacity for compassion and a sense of the worth of others? Though his was a life of art, he never ranked art above life.

Notes

Chapter One

1. Dr. J. Hébert de la Rousselière, "La Douleur, soeur et inspiratrice de Baudelaire," *Mémoires de l'Académie des Sciences, Belles-Lettres et Arts d'Angers* 8 (1964): 12; Marcel-A. Ruff, *Baudelaire*, pp. 2–3; Dr. Augustin Cabanès, *Grands névropathes*, 1:265.

2. Enid Starkie, *Baudelaire*, pp. 28–34; Dr. René Laforgue, *The Defeat of Baudelaire*, pp. 22–24.

3. Baudelaire to Narcisse Ancelle, 10 January 1850, *Correspondance générale* 1:122. (Hereafter cited as *Corr. gén.*)

4. Baudelaire to Mme Aupick, 6 May 1861, *Corr. gén.* 3:279–83.

5. Starkie, *Baudelaire*, p. 40.

6. Laforgue, *Defeat of Baudelaire*, pp. 134–35.

7. Claude Pichois, "La Maladie de Baudelaire," *La Médecine de France* 92 (1958): 39.

8. Baudelaire to Mme Aupick, 16 July 1839, *Corr. gén.* 1:5–6.

9. Baudelaire to M. Aupick, 13 August 1839, *Corr. gén.* 1:8–10.

10. Ruff, *Baudelaire*, p. 10.

11. Michel Butor, *Histoire extraordinaire: Essai sur un rêve de Baudelaire*, p. 211.

12. Martin Turnell, *Baudelaire: A Study of His Poetry*, p. 41.

13. Charles Baudelaire, *Lettres inédites aux siens*, pp. 12–20.

14. Baudelaire to the Aupicks, 25 February 1834, ibid., pp. 83–84.

15. Baudelaire to Colonel Aupick, 17 July 1838, ibid., p. 153.

16. Charles Baudelaire, "The Salon of 1845," *Selected Writings on Art and Artists*, p. 35.

17. Baudelaire to Alphonse Baudelaire, 20 November and 2 December 1839, *Lettres inédites*, pp. 189–91.

18. Starkie, *Baudelaire*, pp. 46–48.

19. Ibid., pp. 52–55; Pichois, "La Maladie de Baudelaire," p. 39.

20. Charles Baudelaire, "Mon coeur mis à nu," *Oeuvres posthumes*, 2:106.

21. Martin M. Abbrecht et al., *Syphilis, a Synopsis*, pp. 7–9.

22. Baudelaire to August Poulet-Malassis, ca. 10 February 1860, *Corr. gén.* 3:22.

23. Philippe Auserve, Baudelaire, *Lettres inédites*, pp. 26–28.

24. Charles Baudelaire to Alphonse Baudelaire, 21 January 1841, ibid., pp. 199–200.

25. Auserve, ibid., pp. 201–4.

26. Turnell, *Baudelaire: A Study of His Poetry*, p. 45; Starkie, *Baudelaire*, p. 61.

27. Baudelaire to Mme Aupick, 6 May 1861, *Corr. gén.* 3:282.

28. Alphonse Baudelaire to Charles Baudelaire, 30 April 1841, *Lettres inédites*, pp. 207–10.

29. Auserve, ibid., pp. 30–34.

30. Jacques Crépet, in Baudelaire, *Corr. gén.* 1:15; Starkie, *Baudelaire*, pp. 71–75; Pichois in Baudelaire, *Correspondance* 1:xxxl. (Hereafter cited as *Corr.*)

31. Starkie, *Baudelaire*, p. 84.

32. François Porché, *La Vie douloureuse de Charles Baudelaire*, pp. 96–100.

33. Baudelaire to Mme Aupick, undated [1844], *Corr. gén.* 1:41–46. See also Jean Ziegler, "La Fortune de Baudelaire," *Corr.* [Pichois] 1:lxiii–xc.

34. Ruff, *Baudelaire*, p. 33; Starkie, *Baudelaire*, pp. 138–40.

35. Turnell, *Baudelaire: A Study of His Poetry*, p. 42.

36. Starkie, *Baudelaire*, pp. 145–46.

37. Porché, *La Vie douloureuse de Charles Baudelaire*, p. 102.

38. Starkie, *Baudelaire*, p. 148.

39. Porché, *La Vie douloureuse de Charles Baudelaire*, pp. 103–5.

40. Crépet, *Corr. gén.* 1:73–74; Ruff, *Baudelaire*, pp. 34–37.

41. Charles Baudelaire to Narcisse Ancelle, 30 June 1845, *Corr. gén.* 1:70–73.

42. Jacques Boulenger, *Les Dandys: Sous Louis-Philippe*, pp. 37–48; César Graña, *Bohemian versus Bourgeois: French Society and the French Man of Letters in the Nineteenth Century*, pp. 148–51.

43. Laforgue, *Defeat of Baudelaire*, p. 52; Baudelaire, "Fusées," *Oeuvres posthumes* 2:68.

44. Antun Polanšćak, "Le Mal de Baudelaire," *Studia romanica et anglica zagrabiensia* 24 (1967): 26–27.

45. Baudelaire, "Mon coeur mis à nu," 2:95.

46. Baudelaire to Mme Aupick, 26 March 1853, *Corr. gén.* 1:195–96.

47. Charles Asselineau, *Charles Baudelaire, sa vie et son oeuvre*, pp. 46–47, 85.

48. Baudelaire, "The Painter of Modern Life," *The Essence of Laughter and Other Essays, Journals, and Letters*, pp. 47–49.

49. Polanšćak, "La Mal de Baudelaire," 27–28; Jean-Paul Sartre, *Baudelaire*, p. 66.

50. Baudelaire, "Painter of Modern Life," pp. 27–28.

51. René Johannet, "Baudelaire asocial," *Ecrits de Paris* 159 (1958): 32–37.

52. Baudelaire, "Mon coeur mis à nu," 2:88; F. W. J. Hemmings, *Culture and Society in France 1814–1898*, pp. 38–40.

53. Baudelaire, "Mon coeur mis à nu," 2:94.

54. Butor, *Histoire extraordinaire*, p. 111.

55. Starkie, *Baudelaire*, pp. 206–7, 215, 223–24, 239–42.

56. Edmond and Jules de Goncourt, *Journal*, 28 November 1863, 6:157.

57. Ibid., 17 July 1893, 19:145.

58. André Anthéaume and G. Dromard, "Le Terrain névropathique: Charles Baudelaire," *Poésie et folie*, pp. 332–33.

59. Jules Levallois, *Milieu de siècle, Mémoires d'un critique*, pp. 94–97.

60. Champfleury, *Souvenirs et portraits de jeunesse*, pp. 134–35.

61. Jules Troubat, *Souvenirs du dernier secrétaire de Sainte-Beuve*, pp. 207–8; Alexandre-Louis Schanne, *Souvenirs de Schaunard*, pp. 234–36.

62. Maxime Du Camp, *Souvenirs littéraires* 2:84–85.

63. Baudelaire, "Mon coeur mis à nu," 2:86–87, 105.

64. Goncourt, *Journal*, October 1857, 2:164.

65. Porché, *La Vie douloureuse de Charles Baudelaire*, p. 212; Ellen Moers, *The Dandy: Brummell to Beerbohm*, p. 272.

66. Pierre Emmanuel, *Baudelaire: The Paradox of Redemptive Satanism*, pp. 116–17, 123–24.

67. Baudelaire, "Mon coeur mis à nu," 2:116.

68. For a chronological table of Baudelaire's writings, see Ruff, *Baudelaire*, pp. 174–92.

69. Butor, *Histoire extraordinaire*, p. 79.

70. Ruff, *Baudelaire*, pp. 76–77.

71. Butor, *Histoire extraordinaire*, pp. 79–82.

72. Starkie, *Baudelaire*, p. 307.

73. Baudelaire to Mme Aupick, undated [1845], *Corr. gén.* 1:75.

74. Cabanès, *Grands névropathes* 1:298. He followed Paul Bourget's definition.

75. Baudelaire to Mme Aupick, 4, 5, 16 December 1847, *Corr. gén.* 1:89–99.

76. Dr. G. A. Ladee, *Hypochondriacal Syndromes*, pp. 8–12.

77. Ibid., pp. 1–3.

78. Starkie, *Baudelaire*, pp. 110–13.

79. Goncourt, *Journal* October 1857, 2:164.

80. Ruff, *Baudelaire*, pp. 80–89; Starkie, *Baudelaire*, p. 308.

81. Starkie, *Baudelaire*, p. 359.

82. Henry James, *French Poets and Novelists*, pp. 62–64.

83. Baudelaire to Mme Aupick, 1 January 1861, *Corr. gén.* 3:221.

84. Baudelaire to Mme Aupick, 10 August 1862, *Corr. gén.* 4:99.

85. Baudelaire, "Le Reniement de Saint Pierre," *Les Fleurs du mal*, p. 328; Hébert de la Rousselière, "La Douleur, soeur et inspiratrice de Baudelaire," pp. 26–27.

86. Baudelaire, "Le Voyage," *Les Fleurs du mal*, p. 357.

87. Nadar [Félix Tournachon], *Baudelaire intime: Le Poète vierge*, p. 127.

88. Butor, *Histoire extraordinaire*, pp. 83–85.

89. Baudelaire, "Mon coeur mis à nu," 2:86–87.

90. Charles D. Hérisson, "Le Voyage de Baudelaire," *Mercure de France* 1148 (April 1959): 653.

91. Pichois, "La Maladie de Baudelaire," pp. 39–40.

92. Ruff, *Baudelaire*, pp. 31–32; Porché, *La Vie douloureuse de Charles Baudelaire*, p. 83; Crépet, *Corr. gén.* 1:31.

93. Baudelaire, "Years in Brussels," *The Essence of Laughter and Other Essays, Journals, and Letters*, p. 203.

94. Butor, *Histoire extraordinaire*, pp. 92–93.

95. Porché, *La Vie douloureuse de Charles Baudelaire*, pp. 83–84.

96. Baudelaire to Mme Aupick, 27 March 1852, *Corr. gén.* 1:161–67.

97. Baudelaire to Mme Aupick, 26 March 1853, *Corr. gén.* 1:189–90.

98. Baudelaire to Marie Daubrun, undated, *Corr. gén.* 1:99–103.

99. Starkie, *Baudelaire*, pp. 242–49, 263–67.

100. Baudelaire to Mme Sabatier, 9 December 1852, *Corr. gén.* 1:180–181.

101. Baudelaire to Mme Sabatier, 9 May 1853, *Corr. gén.* 1:209.

102. Baudelaire to Mme Sabatier, 8 May 1854, *Corr. gén.* 1:275–76.

103. Baudelaire to Mme Sabatier, 18 August 1857, *Corr. gén.* 2:87–89.

104. Baudelaire to Mme Sabatier, 31 August 1857, *Corr. gén.* 2:92.

105. Starkie, *Baudelaire*, pp. 328–36.

106. Baudelaire to Mme Aupick, 4 December 1854, *Corr. gén.* 1:315–16.

107. Baudelaire to Narcisse Ancelle, 8 December 1854, *Corr. gén.* 1:318.

108. Starkie, *Baudelaire*, p. 282.

109. Baudelaire to Mme Aupick, 11 September 1856, *Corr. gén.* 1:397–99.

110. Baudelaire to Mme Aupick, 13 September 1856, *Corr. gén.* 1:400–401.

111. Baudelaire to August Poulet-Malassis, 29 April and 4 May 1859, *Corr. gén.* 2:298, 305.

112. Baudelaire to Mme Aupick, 15 December 1859, *Corr. gén.* 2:383.

113. Porché, *La Vie douloureuse de Charles Baudelaire*, pp. 234–35.

114. Starkie, *Baudelaire*, pp. 392–94.

115. Dr. Photis Scouras, "Baudelaire toxicomane," *Hygiène mentale* 25 (1930): 241.

116. Baudelaire to Ancelle, 10 January 1850, *Corr. gén.* 1:114.

117. Dr. Augustin Cabanès, "Une Consultation médicale de Baudelaire," *La Chronique médicale* 9 (1902): 353. See *Corr. gén.* 3:11.

118. Baudelaire, "The Poem of Hashish," *The Essence of Laughter and Other Essays, Journals, and Letters*, p. 65; Althea Hayter, *Opium and the Romantic Imagination*, pp. 151–52.

119. Baudelaire, "The Poem of Hashish," p. 68.

120. Ibid., pp. 73–91.

121. Ibid., pp. 93–104.

122. Baudelaire to Armand Fraisse, ca. 2 August 1860, *Corr. gén.* 3:167–68.

123. Baudelaire to Mme Aupick, 22 December 1865, *Corr. gén.* 5:187.

124. Baudelaire to Ancelle, 26 December 1865, *Corr. gén.* 5:192.

125. Baudelaire to Mme Aupick, 1 January 1866, *Corr. gén.* 5:197.

126. Baudelaire to Mme Aupick, 17 February 1866, *Corr. gén.* 5:269.

127. Baudelaire to Ancelle, 18 February 1866, *Corr. gén.* 5:272.

128. Cabanès, *Grands névropathes* 1:310; Anthéaume and Dromard, "Le Terrain névropathique: Charles Baudelaire," p. 337.

129. Théophile Gautier, "Charles Baudelaire," Preface to *Les Fleurs du mal*, pp. 57–58.

130. Hayter, *Opium and the Romantic Imagination,* p. 158.

131. Ruff, *Baudelaire,* p. 125.

132. Hayter, *Opium and the Romantic Imagination,* pp. 154–55.

133. Goncourt, *Journal,* 11 July 1889, 16:104.

134. Cecil Gendreau, "Le Génie par la drogue?" *Montréal médical* 9 (October 1957): 9–11.

135. Dr. Paul Michaut, "Un Dernier mot sur la maladie de Baudelaire," *La Chronique médicale* 10 (1903): 27.

136. Anthéaume and Dromard, "Le Terrain névropathique: Charles Baudelaire," p. 338.

137. The five: 10 January 1850; 12 January 1858; 26 December 1865; 1 Janaury 1866; and 17 February 1866.

138. Baudelaire to Poulet-Malassis, 16 February 1859, *Corr. gén.* 2:271.

139. Baudelaire to Poulet-Malassis, 16 February 1860, *Corr. gén.* 3:27.

140. Dr. Roger Dupouy, "Charles Baudelaire, toxicomane et opiomane," *Annales médico-psychologiques* 11 (1910): 360–64.

141. Scouras, "Baudelaire toxicomane," pp. 232–40.

142. Ruff, *Baudelaire,* pp. 126–31.

143. Michaut, "Un Dernier mot sur la maladie de Baudelaire," p. 28.

144. Dr. Raymond Trial, *La Maladie de Baudelaire: Etude médico-psychologique,* p. 39; Dr. Raymond Molinéry, "La Maladie de Baudelaire," *Le Paris médical* 91 annex (13 January 1934): 50.

145. Dr. Louis-Antoine-Justin Caubet, *La Névrose de Baudelaire,* pp. 48–50, Cabanès, *Grands Névropathes* 1:304–5.

146. Baudelaire to Mme Aupick, 4 and 5 December 1847, *Corr. gén.* 1:89–98.

147. Porché, *La Vie douloureuse de Charles Baudelaire,* pp. 89–90.

148. Baudelaire to Mme Aupick, 7 and 12 June 1851, *Corr. gén.* 1:133–36.

149. Baudelaire to Mme Aupick, 13 April 1854, *Corr. gén.* 1:274.

150. Baudelaire to Mme Aupick, 4 December 1854, *Corr. gén.* 1:317.

151. Baudelaire to Mme Aupick, 26 March 1853, *Corr. gén.* 1:195.

152. Baudelaire to Mme Aupick, 20 December 1855, *Corr. gén.* 1:350–54.

153. Crépet, ibid. 1:357.

154. Baudelaire to Mme Aupick, 3 June 1857, *Corr. gén.* 2:54–55.

155. Baudelaire to Mme Aupick, 30 December 1857, *Corr. gén.* 2:109.

156. Baudelaire to Mme Aupick, 25 December 1857, *Corr. gén.* 2:105–6.

157. Baudelaire to Mme Aupick, 30 December 1857, *Corr. gén.* 2:108–9.

158. Baudelaire to Mme Aupick, 11 January 1858, *Corr. gén.* 2:119.

159. Mme Aupick to Alphonse Baudelaire, ca. January 1858, *Le Figaro,* 5 March 1922.

160. Baudelaire to Mme Aupick, 19 February 1858, *Corr. gén.* 2:126–30.

161. Baudelaire to Bernard Jaquotot, 20 February 1858, *Corr. gén.* 2:134–41.

162. Baudelaire to Mme Aupick, 26 February 1858, *Corr. gén.* 2:143.

163. Baudelaire to Mme Aupick, 27 February 1858, *Corr. gén.* 2:148–59.

164. Baudelaire to Mme Aupick, 28 February 1858, *Corr. gén.* 2:160–62.

165. Baudelaire to Poulet-Malassis, 1 May 1859, *Corr. gén.* 2:303.

166. Crépet, ibid., 2:333.

167. Starkie, *Baudelaire,* p. 362.

168. Schanne, *Souvenirs de Schaunard,* pp. 230–32.

169. Baudelaire to Mme Aupick, 15 December 1859, *Corr. gén.* 2:380.

170. Baudelaire to Mme Aupick, 15 January 1860, *Corr. gén.* 3:14–15.

171. Baudelaire to Mme Aupick, 26 March 1860, *Corr. gén.* 3:75–76.

172. Baudelaire to Poulet-Malassis, 12 August 1860, *Corr. gén.* 3:163–65.

173. Baudelaire to Mme Aupick, 4 and 21 August 1860, *Corr. gén.* 3:156–57,

174.

174. Baudelaire to Mme Aupick, 11 October 1860, *Corr. gén.* 3:191–92.

175. Baudelaire to Poulet-Malassis, 14 October 1860, *Corr. gén.* 3:197–98.

176. Baudelaire to Mme Aupick, 1 January 1861, *Corr. gén.* 3:221.

177. Baudelaire to Poulet-Malassis, ca. 20 March 1861, *Corr. gén.* 3:257–58.

178. Baudelaire to Mme Aupick, 1 April 1861, *Corr. gén.* 3:263–69.

179. Baudelaire to Mme Aupick, 6 May 1861, *Corr. gén.* 3:278–86.

180. Baudelaire to Mme Aupick, 8 May 1861, *Corr. gén.* 3:291–92.

181. Baudelaire to Mme Aupick, 25 December 1861, *Corr. gén.* 4:18–19.

182. Baudelaire to Mme Aupick, 29 March and 13 December 1862, *Corr. gén.* 4:78, 133.

183. Baudelaire to Mme Aupick, 25 November and 31 December 1863, *Corr. gén.* 4:206–7, 218.

184. Moers, *The Dandy,* p. 268.

185. Ruff, *Baudelaire,* pp. 56–57, 84.

186. Baudelaire to Alphonse Toussenel, 21 January 1856, *Corr. gén.* 1:369–70.

187. Baudelaire, "The Painter of Modern Life," p. 52–53; Anthéaume and Dromard, "Le Terrain névropathique: Charles Baudelaire," pp. 323–24; and Ruff, *Baudelaire,* pp. 141–42.

188. Baudelaire, "Mon coeur mis à nu," 2:120.

189. Pierre Emmanuel, "Baudelaire, un catholique bien suspect," *Revue générale belge* 3 (March 1967): 15.

190. Baudelaire to Mme Aupick, 10 October 1859, *Corr. gén.* 2:356.

191. Baudelaire to Mme Aupick, 8 October 1860, *Corr. gén.* 3:189–90; Emmanuel, "Baudelaire, un catholique bien suspect," pp. 26, 34–35.

192. Jacques Vier, "Baudelaire, poète chrétien?" *La Pensée catholique* 71 (1961): 67–72.

193. Jean Massin, *Baudelaire devant la douleur,* p. 36.

194. Pierre Emmanuel, *Baudelaire: The Paradox of Redemptive Satanism,* pp. 165–67.

195. Baudelaire to Mme Aupick, 26 March 1853, *Corr. gén.* 1:195.

196. Baudelaire to Mme Aupick, 21 June 1861, *Corr. gén.* 3:318.

197. Baudelaire, *Les Fleurs du mal,* p. 241.

198. Starkie, *Baudelaire,* p. 538.

199. Baudelaire to Charles Asselineau, 13 March 1856, *Corr. gén.* 1:373–77.

200. Baudelaire to Mme Aupick, 15 March 1856, *Corr. gén.* 1:377–78.

201. Butor, *Histoire extraordinaire*, pp. 22, 29, 35–43.

202. Starkie, *Baudelaire*, p. 244.

203. Baudelaire, "Mon coeur mis à nu," 2:121.

204. Sartre, *Baudelaire*, p. 113.

205. See Emmanuel, *Baudelaire, The Paradox of Redemptive Satanism*, p. 36, for a somewhat different interpretation here.

206. Baudelaire, "Fusées," 2:56.

207. Butor, *Histoire extraordinaire*, p. 71.

208. Baudelaire, "Mon coeur mis à nu," 2:115.

209. Cabanès, "De Sadisme chez Baudelaire," *La Chronique médicale* 9 (1902): 725–27; Anthéaume and Dromard, "Le Terrain névropathique: Charles Baudelaire," pp. 335–36.

210. Prosper Mérimée to Mme de La Rochejaquelain, 29 August 1857, *Corr. gén.* 8:365.

211. Trial, *La Maladie de Baudelaire*, pp. 41–48.

212. Sartre, *Baudelaire*, pp. 77–78, 126–27; Georges Blin, *Le Sadisme de Baudelaire*, pp. 15–20.

213. Laforgue, *The Defeat of Baudelaire*, pp. 94–109; Camille Faust, *La Vie amoureuse de Charles Baudelaire*, pp. 43–47; Caubet, *La Névrose de Baudelaire*, pp. 100–109.

214. Faust, *La Vie amoureuse de Charles Baudelaire*, p. 69.

215. Ibid., pp. 64–68, 76, 81; Caubet, *La Névrose de Baudelaire*, pp. 110–20.

216. Laforgue, *The Defeat of Baudelaire*, pp. 64–71.

217. Baudelaire to Abel Villemain, 11 December 1861, *Corr. gén.* 4:6–7.

218. Starkie, *Baudelaire*, pp. 430–31.

219. Baudelaire to Mme Aupick, 25 December 1861, *Corr. gén.* 4:18–23.

220. Baudelaire to Abel Villemain, 10 February 1862, *Corr. gén.* 4:64.

221. Sartre, *Baudelaire*, pp. 86–87.

222. Starkie, *Baudelaire*, p. 471.

223. Ibid., pp. 537–39.

224. Champfleury, *Souvenirs et portraits de jeunesse*, p. 138.

225. Johannet, "Baudelaire asocial," pp. 38–39.

226. Baudelaire, "Fusées," 2:61; Sartre, *Baudelaire*, pp. 66–67.

227. Blin, *Le Sadisme de Baudelaire*, pp. 69–70.

228. Anthéaume and Dromard, "Le Terrain névropathique: Charles Baudelaire," p. 334; Azizi, *La Puissance créatrice de la maladie*, pp. 73–75.

229. Asselineau, *Charles Baudelaire: Sa vie et son oeuvre*, pp. 75–76.

230. Baudelaire, *Paris Spleen*, pp. 13–14.

231. Starkie, *Baudelaire*, pp. 383–85.

232. Caubet, *La Névrose de Baudelaire*, pp. 92–98; and Goncourt, *Journal*, October 1857, 2:164.

233. Otto Rank, "Zu Baudelaires Inzestkomplex," *Zentralblatt für Psychoanalyse und Psychotherapie* 1 (1911): 275.

234. Anthéaume and Dromard, "Le Terrain névropathique: Charles Baudelaire," pp. 320–22; Dr. H. Michel-Béchet, "Le Sens olfactif chez Baudelaire," *Archives médico-chirurgicales de province* 25 (1935): 438–47.

235. Anthéaume and Dromard, "Le Terrain névropathique: Charles Baudelaire," p. 341.

236. See pp. 5–6, above.

237. Pichois, "La Maladie de Baudelaire," p. 37.

238. Baudelaire to Poulet-Malassis, 8 May 1859, *Corr. gén.* 2:307–8.

239. Baudelaire to Poulet-Malassis, 10 February 1860, *Corr. gén.* 3:22; Dr. Augustin Cabanès, "Baudelaire et l'avarie," *La Chronique médicale* 25 (1918): 22.

240. Baudelaire to Mme Aupick, 6 May 1861, *Corr. gén.* 3:282–83; Dr. R. Louge, "La Syphilis de Baudelaire," *La Chronique médicale* 34 (1927): 368; Dr. A. Terson, "La Syphilis de Baudelaire," *La Chronique médicale* 35 (1928): 61.

241. Abbrecht et al., *Syphilis, a Synopsis,* pp. 22–23; Dr. R. S. Morton, *Venereal Diseases,* pp. 73–75; and Drs. Ambrose King and Claude Nicol, *Venereal Diseases,* p. 9.

242. Dr. William L. Fleming, "Syphilis through the Ages," a paper read at Vanderbilt University, School of Medicine, 17–18 May 1963; Abbrecht et al., *Syphilis: A Synopsis,* p. 24; and Drs. Richard S. Weiss and Herbert L. Joseph, *Syphilis,* p. 39.

243. Porché, *La Vie douloureuse de Charles Baudelaire,* pp. 227–28.

244. Abbrecht et al., *Syphilis, a Synopsis,* pp. 7–10.

245. Starkie, *Baudelaire,* pp. 52–56, 91–94, 382; Porché, *La Vie douloureuse de Charles Baudelaire,* p. 185; Trial, *La Maladie de Baudelaire,* pp. 19–20, 56–58; Terson, "La Syphilis de Baudelaire," p. 61.

246. Laforgue, *The Defeat of Baudelaire,* pp. 176–77.

247. Cabanès, *Grands névropathes* 1:320–23; Caubet, *La Névrose de Baudelaire,* pp. 44–48; Ruff, *Baudelaire,* pp. 165–66; Pichois, "La Maladie de Baudelaire," pp. 37–38.

248. Charles Baudelaire to Alphonse Baudelaire, 20 November 1839 and 2 December 1839, *Lettres inédites,* pp. 190–91.

249. Dr. Christian Dedet, *Le Figaro littéraire,* 9 March 1967, p. 14; Morton, *Venereal Diseases,* pp. 56–57.

250. Charles D. Hérisson, "A Propos des lettres inédites aux siens, quelques aspects de la vie de Baudelaire de 1839 à 1842," *Revue des sciences humaines* 34 (January–March 1966): 57–69.

251. Baudelaire to Mme Aupick, 15 Janaury 1860, *Corr. gén.* 3:14–15.

252. Pichois, "La Maladie de Baudelaire," p. 38; Baudelaire, "Fusées," 2:78.

253. Baudelaire to Michel Lévy, 7 July 1863, *Corr. gén.* 4:173.

254. Baudelaire to Maréchal Vaillant, 3 August and 26 August 1863, *Corr. gén.* 4:175–77, 182. The second of the two letters may have been directed to Victor Duruy.

255. Baudelaire to Mme Aupick, 10 August 1863, *Corr. gén.* 4:180.

256. Baudelaire to Mme Aupick, 31 August 1863, *Corr. gén.* 4:185.

257. Baudelaire to Mme Aupick, 28 October 1863, *Corr. gén.,* 4:202.

258. Baudelaire to Mme Aupick, 11 February 1865, *Corr. gén.* 5:35.

259. Baudelaire to Mme Aupick, 6 May 1864, and Baudelaire to Edouard Manet, 26 May 1864, *Corr. gén.* 4:231–37, 250.

260. Baudelaire to Ancelle, 7 May 1864, *Corr. gén.* 4:240.

261. Baudelaire to Mme Aupick, 11 June 1864, *Corr. gén.* 4:258–61.

262. Baudelaire to Ancelle, 14 July 1864, *Corr. gén.* 4:278.

263. Baudelaire to Mme Aupick, 31 July 1864 and 14 August 1864, *Corr. gén.* 4:285–86, 293.

264. Baudelaire to Mme Aupick, 22 August 1864, *Corr. gén.* 4:295.

265. Baudelaire to Ancelle, 13 and 23 October 1864, *Corr. gén.* 4:309–10, 320.

266. Baudelaire to Mme Aupick, 3 November 1864, *Corr. gén.* 4:327.

267. Baudelaire to Mme Aupick, 1 January 1865, *Corr. gén.* 5:1–2.

268. Baudelaire to Ancelle, 8 February 1865, *Corr. gén.* 5:29.

269. Baudelaire to Mme Aupick, 15 February 1865, *Corr. gén.* 5:46.

270. Baudelaire to Mme Aupick, 9 March 1865, *Corr. gén.* 5:61.

271. Baudelaire to Mme Aupick, 30 May, 3 June 1865, *Corr. gén.* 5:91, 93, 98, 104–6.

272. Crépet, ibid., 5:120, 122, 126.

273. Baudelaire to Ancelle, 30 November 1865, *Corr. gén.* 5:179–80.

274. Baudelaire to Ancelle, 21 December, and to Mme Aupick, 22 December 1865, *Corr. gén.* 5:180–81, 186–87.

275. Baudelaire to Ancelle, 26 December 1865, *Corr. gén.* 5:192.

276. Baudelaire to Mme Aupick, 1 January 1866, *Corr. gén.* 5:197.

277. Baudelaire to Sainte-Beuve, 15 January 1866, *Corr. gén.* 5:214–15.

278. Jacques Crépet, ibid., 5:215.

279. Baudelaire to Ancelle, 18 and 22 January 1866, *Corr. gén.* 5:219, 229.

280. Baudelaire to Asselineau, 5 February 1866, *Corr. gén.* 5:242–43.

281. Baudelaire to Mme Aupick, 6 February 1866, *Corr. gén.* 5:244–45.

282. Baudelaire to Mme Aupick, 12 February 1866, *Corr. gén.* 5:254–57.

283. Baudelaire to Mme Aupick, 17 February 1866, *Corr. gén.* 5:269.

284. Baudelaire to Ancelle, 18 February 1866, *Corr. gén.* 5:272.

285. Baudelaire to Mme Aupick, 21 February 1866, *Corr. gén.* 5:296.

286. Drs. Wilfred Barton and Wallace Yater, *Symptom Diagnosis*, p. 833.

287. Dr. Photis Scouras, "La Maladie et la mort de Baudelaire," *Aesculape* 20 (1930): 32–33; Ruff, *Baudelaire*, p. 169.

288. Crépet, *Corr. gén.* 5:308.

289. Baudelaire to Mme Aupick, 20 and 30 March 1866, *Corr. gén.* 5:309, 316; Dr. Cabanès, "La Maladie et la mort de Baudelaire," *La Chronique médicale* 14 (1907): 771.

290. Jacques Crépet, "Derniers jours de Charles Baudelaire," *La Nouvelle revue française* 39 (1 November 1932): 642; Cabanès, "La Maladie et la mort de Baudelaire," p. 771; and *Grands névropathes* 1:311–13.

291. Poulet-Malassis to Jules Troubat, 9 April 1866, reproduced in *Corr. gén.* 5:317.

292. Anthéaume and Dromard, "Le Terrain névropathique: Charles Baudelaire," p. 340.

293. Mme Aupick to Poulet-Malassis, 10 April 1866, in Jacques Crépet, "Derniers jours de Charles Baudelaire," pp. 645–46.

294. Thomas Alajouanine, "Aphasia and Artistic Realization," *Brain, Journal of Neurology* 71 (September 1948): 230–31.

295. Mme Aupick to Poulet-Malassis, 11 July 1866, in Jacques Crépet, "Derniers jours de Charles Baudelaire," pp. 647–48, 654–55; Cabanès, "La Maladie et la mort de Baudelaire," p. 772.

296. Dr. Charles Lasègue to Mme Aupick, 22 June 1866, in Jacques Crépet, "Derniers jours de Charles Baudelaire," p. 671.

297. Cabanès, *Grands névropathes* 1:318–20; Crépet, "Derniers jours de Charles Baudelaire," p. 656; Auguste Auzas, *Mercure de France*, 16 September 1912.

298. Porché, *La Vie Douloureuse de Charles Baudelaire*, pp. 296–302; Starkie, *Baudelaire*, pp. 524–26.

299. Cabanès, "Le Monument de Baudelaire," *La Chronique médicale* 9 (1902): 714, 735.

300. Dr. Michaut, "Comment est mort Baudelaire," ibid. 9 (1902): 186–89. See below, chap. 2, pp. 101–9.

301. Abbrecht et al., *Syphilis, a Synopsis*, p. 9.

302. E. de Rougemont, "La Maladie de Baudelaire, d'après son écriture," *La Chronique médicale* 29 (1922): 310.

303. Trial, *La Maladie de Baudelaire*, pp. 61–62, 72; Scouras, "La Maladie et la mort de Baudelaire," *Aesculape* 20 (1930): 29–34; Anon., "The Last Illness of Baudelaire," *Urologic and Cutaneous Review* 38 (1934): 150–51; Cabanès, "Baudelaire 'dans le domaine,'" *La Chronique médicale* 24 (1917): 265; Caubet, *La Névrose de Baudelaire*, p. 139.

304. Dr. G. Bonvicini, "Die Aphasie des Dichters Baudelaire. Ein Beitrag zur Beziehung der zerebralen Sprachstörungen zur Süchtigkeit," *Wiener medizinische Wochenschrift* 82 (1932): 347–49.

Chapter Two

1. André Billy, *The Goncourt Brothers*, pp. 13, 19–20, 29; Alidor Delzant, *Les Goncourt*, pp. 14–16; Henry Céard, ed., *Lettres de Jules de Goncourt*, p. i.

2. Edmond and Jules de Goncourt, *Journal: Mémoires de la vie littéraire*, 30 October and 9 November 1857, 2:172, 174. (Hereafter cited as *Journal*.)

3. Billy, *The Goncourt Brothers*, pp. 17–24, 30; Delzant, *Les Goncourt*, pp. 20–22.

4. *Journal*, 15 March 1864, 1:189.

5. Delzant, *Les Goncourt*, p. 26.

6. Théophile Gautier, *Journal officiel de l'empire français*, 25 June 1870. For a study of the collaborative novels, see Robert Ricatte, *La Création romanesque chez les Goncourt, 1851–1870*.

7. Emile Zola, *Les Romanciers naturalistes*, p. 192.

8. *Journal,* 27 December 1876, 11:118–19.

9. Billy, *The Goncourt Brothers,* pp. 225–27.

10. *Journal,* 15 November 1859, 3:166–67.

11. *Journal,* 20 December 1866, 7:228.

12. Marcel Thiébaut, "Les Goncourt et leur journal," *Revue de Paris* 67 (February 1960): 142, 156.

13. *Journal,* 12 July 1883, 13:45.

14. André Billy, "Le Vrai journal des Goncourt," *Les Annales: Revue mensuelle de lettres françaises* 65 (1958): 24–32.

15. Maurice Garçon, *Histoire de la justice sous la IIIe république* 3:242–46.

16. Dr. Pierre Cogny, Preface to *Correspondance inédite, 1876–1896, d'Edmond de Goncourt et Henry Céard,* pp. 8–9.

17. Billy, *The Goncourt Brothers,* pp. 191–93.

18. Gautier, *Journal officiel de l'empire français,* 25 June 1870.

19. Cabanès, *Grands névropathes* 2:342–51.

20. *Journal,* 29 August 1865, 7:114–15.

21. *Journal,* 31 August 1865, 7:116.

22. *Journal,* 19 June 1870, 8:246; Billy, *The Goncourt Brothers,* p. 33.

23. Lewis Galantière, *The Goncourt Journals 1851–1870,* p. ix.

24. Jules de Goncourt to Louis Passy, 18 July 1848, *Lettres de Jules de Goncourt,* p. 16. (Hereafter cited as *Lettres.*)

25. Jules de Goncourt to Louis Passy, 30 May 1849, *Lettres,* pp. 11–12.

26. Jules de Goncourt to Louis Passy, 9 July 1859, *Lettres,* pp. 20–21.

27. *Journal,* 2 December 1851, 1:41–44.

28. *Journal,* 7 January 1857, 2:70.

29. *Journal,* 7 April 1869, 8:192–93.

30. *Journal,* 3 September 1855, 1:211.

31. *Journal,* ca. 7 May 1856, 1:235.

32. *Journal,* 23 May 1864, 6:207.

33. *Journal,* 13 July 1862, 5:137.

34. *Journal,* 11 May 1859, 3:120–21.

35. *Journal,* 20 May 1862, 5:114.

36. *Journal,* 13 May and 5 June 1862, 5:113, 120.

37. *Journal,* 7 December 1859, 3:174; and 20 May 1862, 5:13–14.

38. *Journal,* 1 July 1856, 2:12–13.

39. *Journal,* 8 June 1862, 5:121–22.

40. *Journal,* 10 July 1865, 7:97.

41. *Journal,* 11 March 1862, 5:70.

42. *Journal,* 21 August 1862, 5:158.

43. *Journal,* 13 October 1855, 1:222.

44. *Journal,* 16 August 1862, 5:147–49; Billy, "Le Vrai Journal des Goncourt," p. 24.

45. Céard, in *Lettres,* pp. 200–201; Billy, *The Goncourt Brothers,* pp. 87–88, 102–5; Ludovic Halévy, *Notes et souvenirs 1871–1872,* pp. 271–74.

46. André Maurois, *Lélia: The Life of George Sand,* p. 405.

47. *Journal*, 5 May 1857, 2:107–8.

48. *Journal*, 22 May 1862, 5:117.

49. Billy, *The Goncourt Brothers*, pp. 175–81.

50. Jules de Goncourt to Louis Passy, 29 September 1849, *Lettres*, p. 24.

51. *Journal*, 16 November 1856, 2:55.

52. *Journal*, 18 December 1860, 4:129.

53. *Journal*, 17 October 1861, 5:11.

54. *Journal*, 19 January 1862, 5:42.

55. See chaps. 30–31.

56. *Journal*, 1 January 1862, 5:39.

57. Céard, in *Lettres*, p. 267.

58. Billy, *The Goncourt Brothers*, p. 189.

59. Barzun, *The Use and Abuse of Art*, p. 43.

60. *Journal*, 13 December 1861, 5:34.

61. *Journal*, 4 July 1857, 2:135.

62. *Journal*, 30 March 1862, 5:86.

63. *Journal*, 10 October 1861, 5:9–10.

64. *Journal*, 27 April 1862, 5:105.

65. *Journal*, 25 May 1862, 5:118.

66. *Journal*, March 1865, 7:63.

67. *Journal*, 25 August 1869, 8:219.

68. Alidor Delzant, *Paul de Saint-Victor*, pp. 131–32; *La Liberté*, 27 June 1870.

69. *Journal*, 19 February 1862, 5:57.

70. *Journal*, 16 November 1864, 7:26.

71. *Journal*, 23 March 1862, 5:79.

72. Barzun, *The Use and Abuse of Art*, pp. 49, 56–58.

73. *Journal*, 23 May 1864, 6:206.

74. *Journal*, 28 July 1862, 5:141.

75. François Fosca, *Edmond et Jules de Goncourt*, pp. 141–44.

76. *Journal*, 12 November 1861, 5:23.

77. *Journal*, 15 July 1856, 2:17.

78. *Journal*, 21 May 1857, 2:114.

79. *Journal*, 18 December 1860, 4:129.

80. *Journal*, February 1854, 1:127.

81. Delzant, *Les Goncourt*, pp. 141–42; Billy, *The Goncourt Brothers*, p. 180; Billy, "Le Vrai journal des Goncourt," p. 24.

82. *Journal*, 21 August 1862, 5:157.

83. *Journal*, January 1855, 1:162; Billy, "Le Vrai journal des Goncourt," p. 25.

84. Edmond de Goncourt, "Comment est mort Jules de Goncourt: Lettre d'Edmond de Goncourt à Emile Zola," *La Chronique médicale* 3 (1896): 473.

85. *Journal*, 21 July 1889, 16:111–14.

86. *Journal*, January 1855, 1:159–60.

87. *Journal*, 21 December 1856, 2:63–64.

88. *Journal,* 20–26 August 1857, 2:154–56.

89. *Journal,* 20 February 1858, 2:200.

90. *Journal,* 23 April 1858, 2:223–24.

91. *Journal,* 23 June 1858, 3:7.

92. *Journal,* 22 May 1860, 4:22.

93. *Journal,* 15 July 1860, 4:47.

94. Thiébaut, "Les Goncourt et leur journal," p. 144.

95. *Journal,* 23 May and 2 August 1864, 6:206, 228.

96. *Journal,* 11 April 1866, 7:177; Dr. Pierre Vallery-Radot, "Les Médicins vus par les Goncourt," *Histoire de la médecine* 1 (1951): 13.

97. Dr. William L. Fleming, "Syphilis through the Ages," pp. 596, 599.

98. *Journal,* 16 February 1857, 2:79.

99. *Journal,* 30 March 1860, 3:244.

100. *Journal,* August 1854, 1:145.

101. *Journal,* late 1854, 1:156.

102. *Journal,* late 1854, 1:156–57.

103. *Journal,* November 1855, 1:230.

104. *Journal,* May 1856, 1:239–40.

105. *Journal,* 15 February 1862, 5:52–54.

106. *Journal,* 8 April 1862, 5:93–94.

107. Jules de Goncourt to Paul de Saint-Victor, 12 July 1862, *Lettres,* p. 185.

108. *Journal,* July 1858, 3:11.

109. *Journal,* 3 January 1864, 6:167.

110. Billy, *The Goncourt Brothers,* p. 191.

111. Dr. Augustin Cabanès, "La Documentation médicale dans le roman des Goncourt: Conversation avec M. Edmond de Goncourt," *La Chronique médicale* 3 (1896): 458.

112. Dr. Joseph Moreau de Tours, *Les Facultés morales considérées sous le point de vue médical de leur influence sur les maladies nerveuses, les affections organiques,* pp. 1–5.

113. Ibid., pp. 12–18.

114. Ibid., pp. 22–26.

115. Dr. Henri Fauvel, "Les Maladies de coeur dans les romans des Goncourt," *La Chronique médicale* 15 (1908): 123.

116. Dr. Joseph Moreau de Tours, *Mémoire sur les causes prédisposants héréditaires de l'idiotie et de l'imbécilité,* pp. 4–5, 9–10, 22–28.

117. Dr. Joseph Moreau de Tours, *La Psychologie morbide dans ses rapports avec la philosophie de l'histoire, ou de l'influence des névropathies sur la dynamisme intellectuel,* pp. 21–26, 33–36, 53–63.

118. Ibid., pp. 67–74.

119. Ibid., pp. 106, 110–16, 129–30.

120. Ibid., pp. 132–35.

121. *Journal,* 13 January and 28 April 1864, 6:171, 199.

122. *Journal,* 2 September 1866, 7:199.

123. Moreau, *La Psychologie morbide,* pp. 201–5.

124. Cabanès, *Grands névropathes* 2:354–60; Jacques Lethève, "Le Thème de la décadence dans les lettres française à la fin du xixe siècle," *Revue d'histoire littéraire de la France* 63 (January–March 1963): 49.

125. Moreau, *La Psychologie morbide*, pp. 138–41, 250–51; Theodore Zeldin, "Biographie et psychologie sous le second empire," *Revue d'histoire moderne et contemporaine* 21 (January–March 1974): 72.

126. Jules de Goncourt to Louis Passy, 30 October 1850, *Lettres*, pp. 41–42.

127. Jules de Goncourt to Louis Passy, 13 June 1851, *Lettres*, pp. 43–44; Eileen Souffrin, "Banville et les Goncourt," *Revue d'histoire littéraire de la France* 49 (January–March 1949): 46–47.

128. *Journal*, 25 March 1857, 2:88.

129. *Journal*, September 1858, 3:50–51; and 12 July 1860, 4:44.

130. *Journal*, 6 April 1857, 2:91.

131. *Journal*, 8 June 1857, 2:124.

132. *Journal*, 9 June and 12 June, 1857, 2:127.

133. *Journal*, 26 April and 27 April 1859, 3:112–13.

134. *Journal*, 12–26 August 1859, 3:141.

135. *Journal*, 30 August 1866, 7:196.

136. *Journal*, 17 and 25 June 1863, 6:77, 88; 15 January 1865, 7:42.

137. See the bibliography of Edmond and Jules de Goncourt in André Billy, *Vie des frères Goncourt* 3:145–57.

138. Jules de Goncourt to Gustave Flaubert, 29 September 1865, *Lettres*, pp. 232–33.

139. Jules de Goncourt to Maurice Tourneux, 18 April 1866, *Lettres*, p. 248.

140. Jules de Goncourt to Philippe Burty, 1 August 1867, *Lettres*, pp. 264–65.

141. *Journal*, 22 and 25 February 1867, 7:241.

142. Jules de Goncourt to Philippe Burty, May 1868, *Lettres*, p. 278.

143. Jules de Goncourt to Gustave Flaubert, May 1868, *Lettres*, pp. 279–80.

144. Jules de Goncourt to Philippe Burty, 2 July 1868, *Lettres*, p. 283.

145. Jules de Goncourt to C.-A. Sainte-Beuve, 2 July 1868, *Lettres*, p. 284.

146. Dr. Pierre Vallery-Radot, "La Fin dramatique de Jules de Goncourt à 39 ans, racontée par son frère," *La Médecine de France* 144 (1963): 11.

147. Jules de Goncourt to Madame Armand Lefebvre, 15 September 1868; to Gustave Flaubert, 23 October 1868; and to Edouard Lefebvre de Béhaine, 17 November 1868, *Lettres*, pp. 290–95.

148. Jules de Goncourt to Gustave Flaubert, 10 February 1869, *Lettres*, pp. 304–5.

149. Jules de Goncourt to Gustave Flaubert, 9 March 1869, *Lettres*, p. 307.

150. *Journal*, 18 April 1868, 8:196.

151. *Journal*, 5 May 1868, 8:201.

152. *Journal*, 22 May 1868, 8:204.

153. *Journal*, 10 June 1869, 8:207.

154. Jules de Goncourt to Philippe Burty, 9 June 1869; to Princess Mathilde, June 1869; and to Philippe Burty, 23 June 1869, *Lettres*, pp. 318–19, 322.

155. *Journal*, 7 July 1869, 8:211.

156. *Journal*, 1 August 1869, 8:124.

157. *Journal*, 17 July 1869, 8:213.

158. Robert Ricatte in *Journal*, 8:214, 222.

159. *Journal*, 6 and 19 September 1869, 8:221–22.

160. Jules de Goncourt to Princess Mathilde, 7 October 1869, *Lettres*, p. 325.

161. *Journal*, 18 October 1869, 8:224.

162. *Journal*, 1 November 1869, 8:225.

163. Vallery-Radot, "La Fin dramatique de Jules de Goncourt à 39 ans, racontée par son frère," p. 12.

164. Dr. Alfred Béni-Barde, *Manuel médical d'hydrothérapie*, pp. 159–66.

165. Ibid., pp. 1, 91, 106.

166. *Journal*, 19 January 1870, 8:230.

167. *Journal*, 1, 5, and 10 January 1870, 8:227–29.

168. *Journal*, February 1870, 8:231–32; Fosca, *Edmond et Jules de Goncourt*, p. 280.

169. *Journal*, late February 1870, 8:232.

170. *Journal*, March 1870, 8:232.

171. *Journal*, April 1870, 8:233–34.

172. *Journal*, 16 April 1870, 8:235–36.

173. *Journal*, 2 May 1870, 8:237.

174. *Journal*, 9 May 1870, 8:238–39.

175. *Journal*, late May and 5 June 1870, 8:240.

176. *Journal*, 11 June 1870, 8:241–42.

177. *Journal*, night of 18–19 June and 19 June 1870, 8:242–46.

178. Cabanès, *Grands névropathes*, 2:361.

179. *Journal*, 20 June 1870, 8:248.

180. *Journal*, 23 June 1870, 9:12.

181. *Journal*, 22 June 1870, 9:10.

182. *Journal officiel de l'empire français*, 25 June 1870.

183. Céard, in *Lettres*, pp. xxii–xxviii; Dr. Augustin Cabanès, "Comment est mort Jules de Goncourt: Lettre d'Edmond de Goncourt à Emile Zola," *La Chronique médicale* 3 (1896): 471–73; Delzant, *Les Goncourt*, pp. 187–89.

184. Billy, *The Goncourt Brothers*, pp. 203–4.

185. Henri, marquis de Ségur; Paul Bourget; and Jules Lemaître, in "Quelques opinions sur les Goncourt," *La Chronique médicale* 28 (1921): 245–46.

186. Dr. Gélineau, "Une Victime de la neurasthénie: Jules de Goncourt," *La Chronique médicale* 8 (1901): 625–31.

187. Dr. G. Scherb, "Quelle était la maladie de Jules de Goncourt?" *La Chronique médicale* 8 (1901): 759–62.

188. Dr. Jules Falret, *Recherches sur la folie paralytique et les diverses paralysies générales*, pp. 8–14, 31, 50, 77–78, 92.

189. Dr. Alfred-Jean Fournier, *Syphilis et paralysie générale*, pp. 2–3, 9–10.

190. Dr. Pierre-Yves Even, *Etude médicale sur Edmond et Jules de Goncourt et leurs premiers romans*, pp. 74–79.

191. Dr. Paul Duplessis de Pouzilhac, *Les Goncourt et la médecine*, pp. 17, 73–74.

192. *Journal*, 15 February 1862, 5:54.

193. Morton, *Venereal Diseases*, p. 82.

194. Ibid., p. 83; King and Nicol, *Venereal Diseases*, pp. 61–62; Weiss and Joseph, *Syphilis*, pp. 129–30.

Chapter Three

1. Claude Berton, "Flaubert, le théâtre et le bovarysme," *Hippocrate* 4 (1936): 555.

2. See Germaine-Marie Mason, *Les Ecrits de jeunesse de Flaubert*, for a short study of the relation between Flaubert's early writings and his works of maturity.

3. Gustave Flaubert to George Sand, 23–24 February 1869, *Correspondance* 6:12. (Hereafter cited as *Corr.*)

4. Flaubert to Ernest Chevalier, 24 June 1837, *Corr.* 1:26–27; Louis Bertrand, "Les Origines morbides de la sensibilité de Flaubert," *Aesculape* 13 (1923): 266.

5. Dr. Pierre Gallet, *Quel diagnostic aurions-nous fait si nous avions soigné Flaubert?* p. 43; Dr. René Dumesnil, *Flaubert, son hérédité, son milieu, sa méthode*, pp. 1–9.

6. Benjamin F. Bart, *Flaubert*, pp. 6–13; Dumesnil, *Flaubert, son hérédité, son milieu, sa méthode*, pp. 22–31, 43–46.

7. Flaubert to Louise Colet, 8 October 1846, *Corr.* 1:362.

8. Flaubert to Louise Colet, 21 October 1846, *Corr.* 1:383.

9. Albert Mignot, *Ernest Chevalier et Gustave Flaubert*, pp. 1–6, 126–33.

10. Bart, *Flaubert*, pp. 13–19; Paul Ignotus, *The Paradox of Maupassant*, pp. 26–30.

11. Flaubert, *Le Moine des Chartreux, ou l'anneau du prieur*, in *Oeuvres de jeunesse inédites* 1:27–30.

12. Flaubert, *Mémoires d'un fou*, in *Oeuvres de jeunesse* 1:493–94.

13. Ibid. 1:495.

14. Theodor Reik, "Zwei Träume Flauberts," *Zentralblatt für Psychoanalyse und Psychotherapie* 2 (1912): 223–24; and "Flauberts Jugendregungen," *Halbmonatsschrift für soziale Hygiene und praktische Medizin* 2 (1911): 77.

15. Frederick A. Busi, "Sartre on Flaubert," *Research Studies, Washington State University* 41 (1973): 13–14.

16. Flaubert, *Intimate Notebook 1840–1841*, p. 18.

17. See Marie J. Diamond, *Flaubert, the Problem of Aesthetic Discontinuity*, for a different view.

18. Flaubert to Caroline Commanville, 12 June 1874 and 10 May 1875, *Corr.* 7:147, 241.

19. Flaubert to Louise Colet, 8 August 1846, *Corr.* 1:226.

20. Flaubert, *Mémoires d'un fou* 1:504–12.

21. Ibid. 1:524–25.

22. Flaubert to Ernest Chevalier, 11 October 1838, *Corr.* 1:31; Bart, *Flaubert,* pp. 41, 44.

23. Flaubert, *Mémoires d'un fou* 1:485–90.

24. Flaubert to Ernest Chevalier, 24 June 1837, *Corr.* 1:25.

25. Flaubert to Ernest Chevalier, 22 September 1837, *Corr.* 1:28.

26. Flaubert to Ernest Chevalier, 18 March and 15 April 1839, *Corr.* 1:45, 57.

27. Flaubert to Ernest Chevalier, 15 July 1839, *Corr.* 1:52.

28. Emile Gérard-Gailly, *Flaubert et les fantômes de Trouville,* pp. 46–55; René Dumesnil, *Le Grand Amour de Flaubert,* pp. 67–68, 78–80; Bart, *Flaubert,* pp. 23–27; Francis Steegmuller, *The Selected Letters of Gustave Flaubert,* pp. 26–27; Florica Dulmet, "Elisa ou la passion de Gustave Flaubert," *Revue de Paris* 76, no. 6 (1969): 57–63.

29. Flaubert to Ernest Chevalier, 22 June 1840, *Corr.* 1:70–71.

30. Flaubert, *Intimate Notebook 1840–1841,* pp. 21–22.

31. Ibid., p. 23.

32. Ibid., p. 26; note by Francis Steegmuller, p. 51.

33. Flaubert to his sister Caroline, 29 September 1840, *Corr.* 1:71–72.

34. Dumesnil, *Flaubert, son hérédité, son milieu, sa méthode,* p. 13.

35. Goncourt, *Journal,* 20 February 1860, 3:227.

36. Bart, *Flaubert,* p. 56.

37. Flaubert, *Novembre,* in *Oeuvres de jeunesse* 2:192–208, 235; Bart, *Flaubert,* pp. 70–79.

38. Goncourt, *Journal,* 2 November 1863, 6:145.

39. Flaubert to Ernest Chevalier, 14 January 1841, *Corr.* 1:77–78.

40. Flaubert to Ernest Chevalier, 29 March 1841, *Corr.* 1:79.

41. Flaubert, *Intimate Notebook 1840–1841,* pp. 35–37.

42. Ibid., pp. 39–40, 45.

43. Flaubert to Ernest Chevalier, 31 December 1841, *Corr.* 1:89.

44. Flaubert to Louis Bouilhet, 26 December 1852, *Corr.* 3:75.

45. Flaubert to Ernest Chevalier, 23 February and 15 March 1842, *Corr.* 1:96–97, 100.

46. Flaubert to his sister Caroline, 16 April 1842, *Correspondance Supplément (1830–63):* 8. (Hereafter cited as *Corr. Supp.*)

47. Flaubert to Louise Colet, 27 December 1852, *Corr.* 3:77.

48. Caroline Commanville, "Souvenirs intimes," in Flaubert, *Corr.* 1:xx; Bart, *Flaubert,* pp. 66–67.

49. Alfred Le Poittevin to Flaubert, 11 September 1842, Bibliothèque Nationale, Nouvelle Acquisitions Françaises, #23825, fol. 84.

50. Flaubert to his father, November 1842, *Corr. Supp.* (1830–63): 15.

51. Flaubert to his sister Caroline, 1 April 1843, *Corr. Supp.* (1830–63): 20.

52. Flaubert to his sister Caroline, 27 July 1843, *Corr. Supp.* (1830–63): 33–34.

53. Flaubert to Ernest Chevalier, 11 March 1843, *Corr.* 1:131; and Flaubert to his sister Caroline, 27 July 1843, *Corr. Supp.* (1830–63): 33.

54. Bart, *Flaubert,* pp. 82–83.

55. Du Camp, *Souvenirs littéraires* 1:219–23.

56. Flaubert to his sister Caroline, 23 May 1843, *Corr. Supp.* (1830–63): 24.

57. Flaubert to Louise Colet, 11–12 December 1847 and 27 December 1852, *Corr.* 2:73, 3:77; Goncourt, *Journal*, 2 November 1863, 6:145.

58. Goncourt, *Journal*, 18 January 1864, 6:172.

59. *Journal*, 9 May 1865, 7:82.

60. Flaubert to Louise Colet, 1 June 1853, *Corr.* 3:216; and Reik, "Flauberts Jugendregungen," p. 80.

61. Alfred Le Poittevin to Flaubert, 26 November 1843, Bibliothèque Nationale, Nouvelles Acquisitions Françaises, #23825, fol. 84.

62. Flaubert to his sister Caroline, 20 December 1843, *Corr. Supp.* (1830–63): 39.

63. Bart, *Flaubert*, pp. 87–88.

64. Du Camp, *Souvenirs littéraires* 1:240–41.

65. René Dumesnil, Jean Pommier, and Claude Digeon in *Corr. Supp.* (1830–63): 38; Jean Bruneau, in Flaubert, *Corr.* 1:943.

66. Gérard-Gailly, *Flaubert et les fantômes de Trouville*, pp. 102–8.

67. Gallet, *Quel diagnostic aurions-nous fait si nous avions soigné Flaubert?* pp. 15–20.

68. Flaubert to Louise Colet, 2 September 1853, *Corr.* 3:331.

69. Flaubert to Ernest Chevalier, ca. 1 February 1844, *Corr.* 1:147–48.

70. Flaubert to Louise Colet, 2 September 1853, *Corr.* 3:331.

71. Du Camp, *Souvenirs littéraires* 1:245–49; "La Maladie de Flaubert," *La Chronique médicale* 3 (1896):584–87.

72. Goncourt, *Journal*, 1 November 1860, 4:109–10.

73. *Journal*, 3 December 1862, 5:216.

74. Du Camp, "La Maladie de Flaubert," p. 587.

75. Du Camp, *Souvenirs littéraires* 1:241.

76. Flaubert to Louise Colet, December 1846, *Corr.* 1:432.

77. Flaubert to George Sand, 29 April 1871, *Corr.* 6:229.

78. Gérard-Gailly, *Flaubert et les fantômes de Trouville*, p. 109.

79. Gallet, *Quel diagnostic aurions-nous fait si nous avions soigné Flaubert?* pp. 32–34.

80. Flaubert to Louise Colet, 27 August 1846, *Corr.* 1:277–78; Dr. George M. Gould, "A Biographic Clinic on Gustave Flaubert," *Medical Record* 69 (1906):570.

81. Bart, *Flaubert*, pp. 97–98; Enid Starkie, *Flaubert the Master*, p. 279.

82. Du Camp, *Souvenirs littéraires* 1:242–25.

83. Flaubert to Ernest Chevalier, 7 June 1844, *Corr.* 1:150.

84. Flaubert to Louise Colet, 7–8 July 1853, *Corr.* 3:270.

85. Flaubert to Hippolyte Taine, ca. December 1866, *Corr.* 5:350.

86. Flaubert to Hippolyte Taine, 1 December 1866, *Corr. Supp.* (1864–71): 94–95.

87. Bart, *Flaubert*, p. 103.

88. Flaubert to Ernest Chevalier, 11 November 1844, *Corr.* 1:157.

89. Flaubert to Emmanuel Vasse, January 1845, *Corr.* 1:158–59.

90. Flaubert, *First Sentimental Education,* pp. 19–37, 72, 108, 127, 130, 142–43.

91. Ibid., pp. 94–95.

92. Flaubert to Louise Colet, 16 January 1852, *Corr.* 2:343–4.

93. Diamond, *Flaubert, the Problem of Aesthetic Discontinuity,* p. 7.

94. Flaubert, *Intimate Notebook 1840–1841,* pp. 43–44.

95. Flaubert, *First Sentimental Education,* pp. 147, 154–55.

96. Ibid., p. 181.

97. Ibid., pp. 205–6, 212–13.

98. Ibid., pp. 281–82.

99. Ibid., pp. 222–34.

100. Goncourt, *Journal,* 6 May 1866, 7:181.

101. Du Camp, *Souvenirs littéraires* 1:300–302.

102. Flaubert to Alfred Le Poittevin, 2 April 1845, *Corr.* 1:163.

103. Flaubert to Alfred Le Poittevin, 15 April 1845, *Corr.* 1:164.

104. Flaubert, *Notes de voyages* 1:15.

105. See Bart, *Flaubert,* pp. 671–75, for his insightful association of the monkey dream and Flaubert's later story of Saint Julian.

106. Flaubert to Alfred Le Poittevin, 13 May 1845, *Corr.* 1:172–73; Bertrand, "Les Origines morbides de la sensibilité de Flaubert," p. 267.

107. Bart, *Flaubert,* p. 31.

108. Dr. Edouard Allain, *Le Mal de Flaubert,* pp. 22–25.

109. Flaubert to Alfred Le Poittevin, 1 May and 26 May 1845, *Corr.* 1:170, 178–79.

110. Flaubert to Ernest Chevalier, 15 June 1845, *Corr.* 1:80.

111. Flaubert to Ernest Chevalier, 13 August 1845, *Corr.* 1:187–88.

112. Flaubert to Ernest Chevalier, late January 1846, *Corr. Supp.* (1830–63): 54.

113. Jules Levallois, "La Véritable Madame Bovary," *La Chronique médicale* 3 (1896): 589.

114. Flaubert to Maxime Du Camp, 7 April 1846, *Corr.* 1:201.

115. Flaubert to Maxime Du Camp, April 1846, *Corr.* 1:204–6.

116. Mignot, *Ernest Chevalier et Gustave Flaubert,* p. 17.

117. Flaubert to Alfred Le Poittevin, 31 May 1846, *Corr. Supp.* (1830–63): 59.

118. Flaubert to Ernest Chevalier, 4 June 1846, *Corr.* 1:206–8.

119. Joseph F. Jackson, *Louise Colet et ses amis littéraires,* pp. 118–25; Francis Steegmuller, *Flaubert and Madame Bovary,* pp. 108–14, and *The Selected Letters of Gustave Flaubert,* p. 22.

120. Flaubert to Louise Colet, 17 October 1846, *Corr.* 1:378.

121. Flaubert to Louise Colet, 4 and 6 August 1846, *Corr.* 1:211–17.

122. Flaubert to Louise Colet, 8 August 1846, *Corr.* 1:221–27.

123. Flaubert to Louise Colet, 9 August 1846, *Corr.* 1:229.

124. Flaubert to Louise Colet, 9 August 1846, *Corr.* 1:229–31.

125. Flaubert to Louise Colet, 9 August 1846, *Corr.* 1:234–37.
126. Flaubert to Ernest Chevalier, 12 August 1846, *Corr.* 1:245–46.
127. Flaubert to Louise Colet, 12, 15, and 16 August 1846, *Corr.* 1:249–58.
128. Flaubert to Louise Colet, 21–22 August 1846, *Corr.* 1:261–62.
129. Flaubert to Louise Colet, 23 August 1846, *Corr.* 1:264–65.
130. Flaubert to Louise Colet, 26 August 1846, *Corr.* 1:271–72.
131. Flaubert to Louise Colet, 27 and 30 August, 2 September 1846, *Corr.* 1:277–78, 280–81, 286–88.
132. Flaubert to Louise Colet, 5 September 1846, *Corr.* 1:293.
133. Flaubert to Louise Colet, 10 September 1846, *Corr.* 1:298–99.
134. Flaubert to Louise Colet, 13 September 1846, *Corr.* 1:305.
135. Flaubert to Maxime Du Camp, ca. 20 September 1846, *Corr. Supp.* (1830–63): 61–62.
136. Flaubert to Louise Colet, 24 September 1846, *Corr.* 1:336.
137. Flaubert to Louise Colet, 27, 28, and 30 September 1846, *Corr.* 1:340, 342–47.
138. Flaubert to Louise Colet, 8 and 21 October 1846, *Corr.* 1:362, 383.
139. Flaubert to Louise Colet, 3, 4, 7, and 8 October 1846, *Corr.* 1:350–54, 358–63.
140. Flaubert to Louise Colet, 17 October 1846, *Corr.* 1:378–79.
141. Flaubert to Louise Colet, 21 October 1846, *Corr.* 1:381–84.
142. Flaubert to Louise Colet, 24 October 1846, *Corr.* 1:390.
143. Flaubert to Gertrude Collier, early November, *Corr.* 1:391–93.
144. Flaubert to Louise Colet, 13 November 1846, *Corr.* 1:394.
145. Flaubert to Louise Colet, 13 November and 2 December 1846, *Corr.* 1:401, 409.
146. Flaubert to Louise Colet, 20 and end December 1846, *Corr.* 1:428–32.
147. Steegmuller, *Flaubert and Madame Bovary*, pp. 108–16.
148. Flaubert to Louise Colet, 20 March 1847, *Corr.* 2:12.
149. Flaubert to Ernest Chevalier, 23 February and 28 April 1847, and to Louise Colet, 30 April 1847, *Corr.* 2:10, 16–17, 19.
150. Flaubert to Louise Colet, ca. July 1847, *Corr.* 2:44.
151. Flaubert to Louise Colet, late 1847, *Corr.* 2:64–65.
152. Flaubert to Louise Colet, late 1847, *Corr.* 2:68.
153. Flaubert to Louise Colet, September, 11–12 December, and late December 1847, *Corr.* 2:46, 73, 75.
154. Du Camp, *Souvenirs littéraires* 2:466–67.
155. Flaubert, *Intimate Notebook 1840–1841*, p. 24.
156. Reik, "Der liebende Flaubert," *Halbmonatsschrift für soziale Hygiene und praktische Medizin* 2 (1911): 101–10; E. Podolsky, "The Epileptic Brain and Its Inflence on History," *Medicine Illustrated* 9 (1955): 393.
157. Theodor Reik, *Masochism in Modern Man*, p. 197.
158. Ibid., pp. 358–59.
159. Flaubert, *The Temptation of Saint Anthony*, p. 18.
160. Dr. J.-F.-R. Brault, *Considérations médicales sur la sensibilité de Flaubert,*

pp. 51–52; Dr. Wilhelm Stekel, *Impotence in the Male* 1:154.

161. Flaubert to Maxime Du Camp, 7 April 1848, *Corr.* 2:81–82.

162. Flaubert to Ernest Chevalier, 4 July and 3 October 1848, *Corr. Supp.* (1830–63): 68–71.

163. Flaubert to Maxime Du Camp, May 1848, *Corr.* 2:85.

164. Flaubert to Ernest Chevalier, 6 May 1849, and to his uncle Parain, May 1849, *Corr.* 2:86, 88.

165. Goncourt, *Journal,* 21 May 1862, 5:115.

166. Bart, "Is Maxime Du Camp a Reliable Witness?" *Modern Language Review* 48 (1953): 17–18, 22–25.

167. Gallet, *Quel diagnostic aurions-nous fait si nous avions soigné Flaubert?* pp. 15–17.

168. Du Camp, *Souvenirs littéraires* 1:406–10.

169. Ibid., 1:438–41.

170. *Corr.* 2:94–141.

171. Flaubert to his mother, 3 March 1850, *Corr.* 2:165.

172. Flaubert to Louis Bouilhet, 15 January 1850, *Corr.* [Bruneau] 1:570–74.

173. Flaubert to Louis Bouilhet, 2 June 1850, *Corr.* [Bruneau] 1:638.

174. Theodor Reik, *Flaubert und seine Versuchung des heiligen Antonius: Ein Beitrag zur Künstlerpsychologie,* p. 139.

175. Starkie, *Flaubert the Master,* p. 4.

176. Bart, *Flaubert,* pp. 225–26.

177. Zola, *Les Romanciers naturalistes,* p. 116.

178. Du Camp, *Souvenirs littéraires* 1:490–94.

179. Flaubert to Louis Bouilhet, 13 March 1850, *Corr.* [Bruneau] 1:602–7. The censored version is in *Corr.* 2:174–76.

180. Flaubert to Louis Bouilhet, 2 June 1850, *Corr.* [Bruneau] 1:635.

181. Flaubert to his mother, 10 August 1850, *Corr.* 2:225.

182. Flaubert to Louis Bouilhet, 20 August 1850, *Corr.* [Bruneau] 1:668.

183. Flaubert to Louis Bouilhet, 4 September 1850, *Corr.* [Bruneau] 1:680—84.

184. Flaubert to Louis Bouilhet, 14 November 1850, *Corr.* [Bruneau] 1:706–7.

185. Flaubert to Louis Bouilhet, 19 December 1850, and 10 February 1851, *Corr.* 2:281, 294–95.

186. Dr. Félix Regnault, "Le Mal de Flaubert," *Revue moderne de médecine et de chirurgie* 27 (1927): 345–46; Allain, *Le Mal de Flaubert,* pp. 36–38; and Dr. Léon Bondoux, *Le Réalisme littéraire de Flaubert est l'application de la méthode des sciences biologiques,* p. 11.

187. Flaubert to Louis Bouilhet, 4 September 1850, *Corr.* 2:237.

188. Morton, *Venereal Diseases,* pp. 16–17, 29.

189. Bart, *Flaubert,* pp. 171, 218–21.

190. Flaubert to Camille Rogier, 11 March 1851, *Corr.* [Bruneau] 1:760.

191. Flaubert to Louis Bouilhet, 9 April 1851, *Corr.* [Bruneau] 1:773, 780.

192. Bart, *Flaubert,* p. 221.

193. Morton, *Venereal Diseases*, pp. 72–73.

194. Jean Pommier, "Les Maladies de Gustave Flaubert," *Le Progrès médical* 75 (1947): 415–16.

195. Flaubert to his mother, 25 August 1850, *Corr.* [Bruneau] 1:671.

196. Flaubert to his mother, 7 October 1850, *Corr.* [Bruneau] 1:692.

197. Flaubert to his mother, 7 November 1850, *Corr. Supp.* (1830–63): 109.

198. Flaubert to his mother, 14 November 1850, *Corr. Supp.* (1830–63): 113–15.

199. Flaubert to Louis Bouilhet, 14 November 1850, *Corr.* 2:257.

200. Flaubert to his mother, 24 November 1850, *Corr.* 2:257–58.

201. Flaubert to his mother, 15 December 1850, *Corr.* 2:267–69.

202. Flaubert to his mother, 18 January 1851, *Corr. Supp.* (1830–63): 120–21.

203. Flaubert to his mother, 9 February 1851, *Corr.* 2:287–88.

204. Flaubert to Louis Bouilhet, 4 May 1851; to Maxime Du Camp, 30 May 1851; Du Camp to Flaubert, 25 May 1851, *Corr.* [Bruneau] 1:779, 783, 805–6.

205. Louise Colet to Flaubert, 14 May and 18 June 1851; Louise Colet's memoranda, 16, 23, and 27 June 1851, *Corr.* [Bruneau] 1:781–82, 784, 810–15; Jackson, *Louise Colet et ses amis littéraires*, pp. 161–63; Marie-Claire Bancquart, in Louis Bouilhet, *Lettres à Louise Colet*, p. 13.

206. Flaubert to Louise Colet, 26 July 1851, *Corr.* 2:313–16.

207. Flaubert to Maxime Du Camp, 21 October 1851, *Corr.* 2:321–23.

208. Flaubert to Louise Colet, November 1851, *Corr.* 2:327–28.

209. Flaubert to Louise Colet, 17 and 31 December 1851, and Flaubert to Ernest Chevalier, 17 January 1852, *Corr.* 2:333, 335, 386.

210. Flaubert to Louise Colet, 24 April 1852, *Corr.* 2:402.

211. Flaubert to Louise Colet, 8–9 May 1852, *Corr.* 2:411.

212. Flaubert to Louise Colet, undated, *Corr.* 2:429.

213. Flaubert to Maxime Du Camp, 26 June 1852, *Corr.* 2:442–44.

214. Flaubert to Maxime Du Camp, July 1852, *Corr.* 2:451–54.

215. Flaubert to Louise Colet, 2 and 7 November 1852, *Corr.* 3:46–47.

216. Flaubert to Louise Colet, 11 December 1852, *Corr.* 3:62–63.

217. Flaubert to Louise Colet, 27 December 1852, *Corr.* 3:76–77.

218. Flaubert, *The Temptation of Saint Anthony*, p. 45.

219. Flaubert to Louise Colet, 17 February and 7 May 1853, *Corr.* 3:96–97, 193.

220. Flaubert to Louise Colet, 31 March and 30 April–1 May 1853, *Corr.* 3:145–46, 185.

221. Flaubert to Louise Colet, 10 April 1853, *Corr.* 3:162.

222. Flaubert to Louise Colet, 1 June 1853, *Corr.* 3:216.

223. Flaubert to Louise Colet, 12 July 1853, *Corr.* 3:274–75.

224. Flaubert to Louise Colet, 7–8 July and 2 September 1853, *Corr.* 3:270, 331.

225. Flaubert to Louise Colet, 22 July 1853, *Corr.* 3:285.

226. Flaubert to Louise Colet, 2 September 1853, *Corr.* 3:329–31.

227. Flaubert to Louise Colet, 7, 12, 17–18, 23, 25 October 1853, *Corr.* 3:363–76.

228. Flaubert to Louise Colet, 28–29 October, 3, 6, 22, 29 November 1853, *Corr.* 3:377–89; Jackson, *Louise Colet et ses amis littéraires,* pp. 203–18.

229. Flaubert to Louis Bouilhet, late December 1853, and to Louise Colet, January 1854, *Corr.* 3:412, 420.

230. Flaubert to Louise Colet, 13 January 1854, *Corr.* 4:6–7.

231. Flaubert to Jules Duplan, 24 February 1854, *Corr. Supp.* (1830–63): 175.

232. Flaubert to Louise Colet, 24 February, 2–3 March, 12–13 April 1854, *Corr.* 4:28–31, 56.

233. Flaubert to Louis Bouilhet, summer of 1854, *Corr.* 4:181–82.

234. Troubat, *Notes et pensées,* pp. 128–29; Goncourt, *Journal,* 21 February 1862, 5:59; Bancquart, in Bouilhet, *Lettres à Louise Colet,* pp. 21, 30–31.

235. Maurice Levaillant and Marc Varenne, "La Dernière lettre d'amour de Flaubert à Louise Colet," *Revue des deux mondes* (1 July 1954): 144.

236. Goncourt, *Journal,* 21 February 1862, 5:58.

237. Louise Colet, *Une Histoire de soldat,* pp. 126–32.

238. Levaillant and Varenne, "La Dernière lettre d'amour de Flaubert à Louise Colet," pp. 139, 144–45; Steegmuller, *Flaubert and Madame Bovary,* pp. 6–7.

239. Zola, *Les Romanciers naturalistes,* pp. 151–52.

240. Du Camp, *Souvenirs littéraires* 2:364–65.

241. Louise Colet, *Lui, roman contemporain,* p. 29.

242. Troubat, *Notes et pensées,* pp. 127–28.

243. Flaubert to Louis Bouilhet, 5 and 7 August 1854, *Corr.* 4:64 and *Corr. Supp.* (1830–63): 184; Bart, *Flaubert,* p. 265.

244. Flaubert to Louis Bouilhet, 5 and 7 August 1854, *Corr.* 4:64 and *Corr. Supp.* (1830–63): 182–83; Morton, *Venereal Diseases,* p. 28.

245. Bart, *Flaubert,* p. 249.

246. Flaubert to Louis Bouilhet, 18 August 1854, *Corr.* 4:68.

247. Dr. Henri Fauvel, "Souvenirs sur Gustave Flaubert," *La Chronique médicale* 15 (1908): 489; Dr. Paul Noury, "Glanes sur les maladies et la mort de Gustave Flaubert," *ibid.* 36 (1929): 63.

248. Starkie, *Flaubert the Master,* pp. 51–54; Bart, *Flaubert,* p. 391.

249. Goncourt, *Journal,* 5 May 1876, 11:92.

250. Starkie, *Flaubert the Master,* pp. 346–54.

251. Erich Auerbach, *Mimesis: The Representation of Reality in Western Literature,* pp. 482–84; Françoise Moser, "Flaubert et ses légendes," *La Médecine de France* 179 (1967): 10–11.

252. Reik, "Flauberts Jugendregungen," p. 75.

253. Dr. Joseph Moreau de Tours, *Les Facultés morales considérées sous le point de vue médical de leur influence sur les maladies nerveuses, les affections organiques,* pp. 101–6; Flaubert to Hippolyte Taine, 1 December 1866, *Corr. Supp.* (1864–71): 94–95; Dr. Philibert de Lastic, *La Pathologie mentale dans les oeuvres de Gustave Flaubert,* p. 91; Pommier, "Les Maladies de Gustave Flaubert," *Le Progrès médical* 75 (1947): 411–12.

254. Dr. Ralph Reed, "Madame Bovary," and "The Death of Madame Bovary," *Lancet-Clinic* 105 (1911): 456–57, 483; Dr. Paul Cololian, "Gustave

Flaubert et la psychanalyse," *Hippocrate* 5 (1937): 488–89.

255. Flaubert to Mlle Leroyer de Chantepie, 30 March 1857, *Corr.* 4:168–69.

256. Cololian, "Gustave Flaubert et la psychanalyse," pp. 489–95; Zeldin, "Biographie et psychologie sous le second empire," *Revue d'histoire moderne et contemporaine* 21 (1974): 69–70.

257. Flaubert to Mlle Leroyer de Chantepie, 18 March 1857, *Corr.* 4:164–65.

258. Commanville, "Souvenirs sur Gustave Flaubert," in Flaubert, *Corr.* 1:xix–xx.

259. Auerbach, *Mimesis*, pp. 487–88; Bart, *Flaubert*, pp. 328, 337–38; Victor Brombert, *The Novels of Flaubert: A Study of Themes and Techniques*, pp. 4–7, 283, 288.

260. The story of the trial is well told in Bart, *Flaubert*, pp. 354–62.

261. Goncourt, *Journal*, November 1858, 3:72–73.

262. Ben Ray Redman in *Salammbô*, p. xxii.

263. Flaubert to Louis Bouilhet, April or May 1858, *Corr.* 4:256.

264. Zola, *Les Romanciers naturalistes*, pp. 175–76; Goncourt, *Journal*, 3 November 1861, 5:17, 1 November 1863, 6:143.

265. Du Camp, *Souvenirs littéraires* 2:209, 368.

266. Goncourt, *Journal*, 21 May 1862, 5:115.

267. Bart, *Flaubert*, pp. 408–9, 419, 424–26; Brombert, *The Novels of Flaubert*, pp. 115–16.

268. Flaubert, *Salammbô*, pp. 198, 216–26, 259, 337; Dr. Karl Gumpertz, "Der Judith-Komplex: Versuch einer Analyse von Hebbels *Judith* und Flauberts *Salammbô*," *Zeitschrift für Sexualwissenschaft* 14 (1927): 293, 299–300.

269. Henri F. Ellenberger, *The Discovery of the Unconscious: The History and Evolution of Dynamic Psychiatry*, pp. 144, 301.

270. Dumesnil, *Flaubert, son hérédité, son milieu, sa méthode*, p. 330; Bart, *Flaubert*, p. 434.

271. Flaubert to Ernest Feydeau, 21 August 1859, *Corr.* 4:325–26.

272. Flaubert to Amélie Bosquet, end of 1859, *Corr.* 4:351.

273. Flaubert to Mlle Leroyer de Chantepie, 18 December 1859, *Corr.* 4:356.

274. Flaubert to Amélie Bosquet, 21 October 1862, and to Théophile Gautier, April 1863, *Corr.* 5:51, 91.

275. Flaubert to Mme Roger des Genettes, 4 May 1864, *Corr. Supp.* (1864–71): 9.

276. Emile Gérard-Gailly, *Le Grand Amour de Flaubert*, pp. 292–96.

277. Steegmuller in Flaubert, *Intimate Notebook 1840–1841*, pp. 4–5.

278. Flaubert to Mme Roger des Genettes, October 1864, to Princess Mathilde, May 1865, and to Mlle Leroyer de Chantepie, 11 May 1865, *Corr.* 5:159–60, 172–73, 175.

279. Flaubert to Frédéric Fovard, March 1865, to Jules Duplan, 22 November 1866, *Corr. Supp.* (1864–71): 23–24, 83; and to Caroline Commanville, 16 March and 10 April 1866, *Corr.* 5:206, 209.

280. Flaubert to Ernest Commanville, April and May 1867, *Corr. Supp.* (1864–71): 104, 112–13.

281. Flaubert to George Sand, 12–13 January 1867, *Corr.* 5:267.

282. Caroline Commanville, "Souvenirs sur Gustave Flaubert," *Corr.* 1:xxxiv–vi.

283. Flaubert to Caroline Commanville, 28 February 1867, *Corr.* 5:280–81.

284. Flaubert, *Sentimental Education*, p. 100.

285. Robert Baldick, ibid., p. 12.

286. Lastic, *La Pathologie mentale dans les oeuvres de Gustave Flaubert*, pp. 63–65, 69.

287. Flaubert to Princess Mathilde, June 1867, *Corr.* 5:313.

288. Flaubert, *Sentimental Education*, p. 200.

289. Flaubert to George Sand, May 1867, *Corr.* 5:300.

290. Christophe Calmy, "Flaubert et le nihilisme de gauche," *Esprit* 2 (February 1963): 251–59.

291. Flaubert to Maxime Du Camp, 21 October 1851, *Corr.* 2:321.

292. Flaubert to Jules Duplan, 22 July 1869, *Corr.* 6:39.

293. Flaubert to Maxime Du Camp, 23 July 1869, and to George Sand, 12 January 1870, *Corr.* 6:40–44, 102.

294. Bart, *Flaubert*, pp. 537–40.

295. Flaubert to Philippe Leparfait, 17 February 1870; to George Sand, 21 and 22 February, 22 March 1870; and to Dr. Dumont, 6 March 1870, *Corr. Supp.* (1864–71): 220, 222–25, 229.

296. Flaubert to Ivan Turgenev, 30 April 1870, *Corr. Supp.* (1864–71): 231; to Edmond de Goncourt, 26 June 1870; to George Sand, 26 June 1870; to Caroline Commanville, 28–29 June and 1–2 July 1870; and to Mlle Leroyer de Chantepie, 8 July 1870, *Corr.* 6:119–25, 132.

297. Flaubert to Maxime Du Camp, 9 June 1870, *Corr. Supp.* (1864–71): 234–35.

298. Flaubert to George Sand, April or May 1870, *Corr.* 6:113.

299. Flaubert to George Sand, 17 August 1870, *Corr.* 6:142.

300. Flaubert to Caroline Commanville, 31 August 1870, and to George Sand, 10 September 1870, *Corr.* 6:145, 148.

301. Flaubert to Caroline Commanville, 15 September 1870, *Corr.* 6:150.

302. Flaubert to Caroline Commanville, 24 October 1870, *Corr.* 6:173–75.

303. Flaubert to Princess Mathilde, 23 October 1870, *Corr.* 6:171–72.

304. Anne Roche, "L'Opposition au second empire dans quelques-unes de ses expressions et représentations littéraires," *Revue d'histoire moderne et contemporaine* 21 (January–March 1974): 42.

305. Flaubert to Caroline Commanville, 22 September 1870, *Corr.* 6:154.

306. Flaubert to Princess Mathilde, 13 and 23 October 1870, *Corr.* 6:166, 171.

307. Flaubert to Caroline Commanville, 28 October 1870, 10 November 1870, and to George Sand, 30 October 1870, *Corr.* 6:178, 183–86.

308. Flaubert to Caroline Commanville, 29 October 1870, *Corr.* 6:182.

309. Flaubert to Caroline Commanville, 18 and 24 December 1870, *Corr.* 6:187–88, 193; Du Camp, *Souvenirs littéraires* 2:511; Commanville, "Souvenirs sur Gustave Flaubert," in *Corr.* 1:xxxiv–vi.

310. Flaubert to Caroline Commanville, 19 December 1870, *Corr.* 6:192; and Du Camp, *Souvenirs littéraires* 2:512.

311. Flaubert to George Sand, 29 April 1871, *Corr.* 6:226.

312. Flaubert to Dr. Jules Cloquet, May 1871, *Corr.* 6:239.

313. Flaubert to George Sand, 11 June 1871, and to Ernest Feydeau, 29 June 1871, *Corr.* 6:248–49, 259.

314. Flaubert to Caroline Commanville, August 1871, and to Mme Maurice Schlésinger, 6 September 1871, *Corr.* 6:268, 270, 272–73, 277.

315. Flaubert to George Sand, 8 September, 4 or 5 October, and 14 November 1871, *Corr.* 6:282, 287, 307.

316. Flaubert to Mme Régnier, 30 November 1871, and to Mme Roger des Genettes, December 1871, *Corr.* 6:312–13, 327.

317. Flaubert to George Sand, 21 January 1872, *Corr.* 6:342–44.

318. Flaubert to Caroline Commanville, 17 September and 12 November 1871, *Corr.* 6:285, 305.

319. Flaubert to Caroline Commanville, 26 and 28 March 1872, *Corr.* 6:359–61.

320. Flaubert to Laure de Maupassant, 7 April 1872, to George Sand, 16 April 1872, to Caroline Commanville, 5 May 1872, and to Princess Mathilde, 5 June 1872, *Corr.* 6:367–68, 373–74, 377–78, 383–84; Du Camp, *Souvenirs littéraires* 2:535–39.

321. Goncourt, *Journal,* 31 May 1886, 14:130; Regnault, "Le Mal de Flaubert," *Revue moderne de médecine et de chirurgie* 35 (1927): 346; Bondoux, *Le Réalisme littéraire de Flaubert est l'application de la méthode des sciences biologiques,* pp. 38–39.

322. Flaubert to Princess Mathilde, 4 October 1876, *Corr.* 7:351; and Bart, *Flaubert,* p. 488.

323. Commanville, "Souvenirs sur Gustave Flaubert," in *Corr.* 1:xl; Starkie, *Flaubert the Master,* pp. 343–47.

324. Flaubert to Caroline Commanville, 23 June 1872, *Corr.* 6:390–91.

325. Flaubert to George Sand, 12 July 1872, to Princess Mathilde, 16 July 1872, and to Caroline Commanville, 22 August 1872, *Corr.* 6:394, 396, 404.

326. Flaubert to Madame Schlésinger, 5 October 1872, *Corr.* 6:427.

327. Flaubert to Princess Mathilde and to George Sand, 28 October 1872, *Corr.* 6:435, 439.

328. Flaubert to George Sand, 28 October 1872, and to Princess Mathilde, November 1872, *Corr.* 6:441–42, 451.

329. Flaubert to Ivan Turgenev, 13 November 1872, *Corr. Supp.* (1872–77): 61–62.

330. Flaubert to Princess Mathilde, September 1877, *Corr.* 8:78.

331. Flaubert to Philippe Leparfait, January 1873, *Corr.* 7:3–5.

332. Flaubert to George Sand, 3 February 1873, and to Laure de Maupassant, 23 February 1873, *Corr.* 7:7–9.

333. Flaubert to George Sand, 11 March 1873, *Corr.* 7:10.

334. Flaubert to Caroline Commanville, 18 and 24 May 1873, to Princess

Mathilde, 3 June 1873, to Ernest Feydeau, 3 July 1873, and to George Sand, 5 September 1873, *Corr.* 7:12, 16, 19–20, 25, 35, 53.

335. Flaubert to Caroline Commanville, 2 December 1873 and February 1874, to Mme Roger des Genettes, December 1873 and 18 February 1874, and to George Sand, 28 February 1874, *Corr.* 7:95–96, 110, 119–22.

336. Flaubert to George Sand, 12 March 1874, *Corr.* 7:125–26.

337. Flaubert to George Sand, 1 May 1874, and to Mme Roger des Genettes, 1 May 1874, *Corr.* 7:133–34, 137.

338. Reik, "Der liebende Flaubert," p. 107; Dumesnil, *Flaubert, son hérédité, son milieu, sa méthode,* pp. 333, 336; Noury, "Glanes sur les maladies et la mort de Gustave Flaubert," p. 62.

339. Flaubert to George Sand, 26 May 1874, *Corr.* 7:139, 141.

340. Flaubert to Caroline Commanville, 12 June 1874, *Corr.* 7:147.

341. Flaubert to Ivan Turgenev, 2 July 1874, to Caroline Commanville, August 1874 and 7 September 1874, *Corr.* 7:158–61, 188, 195; and to Caroline Commanville, 1 July 1874, *Corr. Supp.* (1872–77): 132–33.

342. Flaubert to Edmond de Goncourt, 22 September 1874, *Corr.* 7:202–3.

343. Flaubert to George Sand, December 1874, *Corr.* 7:229.

344. Flaubert to Caroline Commanville, 24 or 25 March 1875, and to George Sand 27 March and 10 May 1875, *Corr.* 7:233–35, 239; and to Mme Brainne, 25 February 1875, and to Mme Roger des Genettes, 12 March and June 1875, *Corr. Supp.* (1872–77): 167–68, 171, 179–80.

345. Flaubert to Caroline Commanville, 10 May 1875, *Corr.* 7:241–42.

346. Flaubert to Caroline Commanville, 8, 9, 14, 15, 17 July 1875, *Corr.* 7:243, 245–51; to Mme Brainne, 18 and 27 July 1875, and Edmond Laporte, 3 September 1875, *Corr. Supp.* (1872–77): 185, 187, 199–200; Bart, *Flaubert,* pp. 646–54.

347. Flaubert to Princess Mathilde, 3 September 1875, and to Caroline Commanville, 21 September and 7 October 1875, *Corr.* 7:256–70; and Commanville, "Souvenirs sur Gustave Flaubert," *Corr.* 1:xxxvi–vii.

348. Flaubert to Caroline Commanville, 24 September 1875, and to Mme Brainne, 2 October 1875, *Corr. Supp.* (1872–77): 205, 210.

349. Flaubert to George Sand, 11 October 1875, *Corr. Supp.* (1872–77): 219–20.

350. Maurois, *Lélia, the Life of George Sand,* pp. 454–55.

351. Flaubert to George Sand, December 1875, *Corr.* 7:280–81.

352. Flaubert to Mme Roger des Genettes, 19 June 1876, *Corr.* 7:307; Bart, *Flaubert,* pp. 700, 704.

353. Lastic, *La Pathologie mentale dans les oeuvres de Gustave Flaubert,* pp. 23–24, 36–37.

354. Gérard-Gailly, *Flaubert et les fantômes de Trouville,* p. 109.

355. Flaubert to Ivan Turgenev, 25 June 1876, to Caroline Commanville, 26 June 1876, *Corr.* 7:312, 315; and to Mme Brainne, 28 July 1876, *Corr. Supp.* (1872–77): 269.

356. Flaubert to Maurice Sand, 25 June 1876 and 29 August 1877, *Corr.*

7:309, 8:65; and to Caroline Commanville, 10 August 1876, *Corr.* 7:338–39.

357. Flaubert to Mme Roger des Genettes, 2 April 1877, *Corr.* 8:26, to Ivan Turgenev, 8 December 1877, and to Caroline Commanville, 13 December 1877, *Corr. Supp.* (1877–80): 52–54.

358. Dr. Henri Fauvel, "Souvenirs sur Gustave Flaubert," *La Chronique médicale* 15 (1908): 455–56.

359. Flaubert to Edmond Laporte, November 1878, and to Mme Brainne, 10–11 December 1878, *Corr. Supp.* (1877–80): 134–36; to Caroline Commanville, 28 November 1878, 14–15 and 21 January 1879, to Princess Mathilde, December 1878, and to Alphonse Daudet, 3 January 1879, *Corr.* 8:165, 170, 179, 183, 190–91.

360. Flaubert to Caroline Commanville, 27 January 1879, February 1879, *Corr.* 8:192–93, 204.

361. Flaubert to Caroline Commanville, 22 February 1879, *Corr.* 8:215–19; to Ivan Turgenev, 5, 10, 14 February 1879, and to Caroline Commanville, 22 February 1879, *Corr. Supp.* (1877–80): 158, 161, 167, 175, 186.

362. Flaubert to Guy de Maupassant, 9 March 1879, *Corr. Supp.* (1877–80): 188–89, to Maupassant, 12 March 1879, to Caroline Commanville, 14 March 1879, *Corr.* 8:232–33.

363. Flaubert to Mme Brainne, 25 April 1879, *Corr. Supp.* (1877–80): 209–10.

364. Flaubert to Caroline Commanville, 6 May 1879, to Edmond Laporte, 8 May 1879, *Corr. Supp.* (1877–80): 218, 222.

365. Flaubert to Guy de Maupassant, 7 May 1879, *Corr. Supp.* (1877–80): 220–21.

366. Flaubert to Edmond Laporte, 10 and 29 May 1879, to Caroline Commanville, May 1879, *Corr. Supp.* (1877–80): 222, 238, 240; and to Emile Zola, 2 June 1879, to Caroline Commanville, 12 June 1879, *Corr.* 8:266–67, 270.

367. Flaubert to Mme Roger des Genettes, 13 June and 14 August 1879, *Corr.* 8:271–72, *Corr. Supp.* (1877–80): 258.

368. Flaubert to Edmond Laporte, 28 September 1879, to Caroline Commanville, 1 April 1880, *Corr. Supp.* (1877–80): 266–67, 325; and Bart, *Flaubert,* pp. 736–37.

369. Flaubert to Caroline Commanville, 31 December 1879, to Mme Charpentier, 13 January 1880, to Mme Roger des Genettes, 25 January and 22 February 1880, *Corr.* 8:340, 348, 357, 402.

370. Flaubert to Caroline Commanville, 14 March and 22 April 1880, *Corr.* 9:6, 26.

371. Dr. Charles Fortin, "Le Subconscient chez Flaubert," *La Chronique médicale* 8 (1901): 31.

372. Dr. J. Tourneux, "Nécrologie—Charles Fortin," *La Revue médicale de Normandie,* 4 (10 January 1903): 26–28.

373. Dr. Augustin Cabanès, "Le Médecin de Flaubert," *La Chronique médicale* 10 (1903): 72–73.

374. Dumesnil, *Flaubert, son hérédité, son milieu, sa méthode,* pp. 106–11.

375. Dumesnil, *Chroniques, études, correspondance de Guy de Maupassant,* pp. 289–90; Zola, *Les Romanciers naturalistes,* pp. 140–41.

376. Du Camp, *Souvenirs littéraires* 2:397.

377. Goncourt, *Journal*, 8 and 11 May 1880, 12:73–74.

378. Du Camp, *Souvenirs littéraires*, 1:253.

379. Dumesnil, *Chroniques, études, correspondance de Guy de Maupassant*, pp. 61–64.

380. Starkie, *Flaubert the Master*, p. 354; Bruneau, in Flaubert, *Correspondance*, 1:xxix.

381. Du Camp, *Les Convulsions de Paris*, 4:331.

382. Dr. Galérant, "L'Epilepsie de Flaubert," *Les Revues médicales normandes* 5 (1963): 642–46.

383. Flaubert to Georges Charpentier, 26 February 1880, *Corr.* 8:403–4.

384. Gallet, *Quel diagnostic aurions-nous fait si nous avions soigné Flaubert?* p. 12; Starkie, *Flaubert the Master*, pp. 301–2.

385. Alan R. G. Owen, *Hysteria, Hypnosis and Healing: The Work of J.-M Charcot*, p. 45.

386. Dr. Jean-Martin Charcot and Dr. Paul Richer, *Les Démoniaques dans l'art*, pp. 91–106.

387. Ellenberger, *The Discovery of the Unconscious*, pp. 89–102; Owen, *Hysteria, Hypnosis and Healing*, pp. 63–64.

388. Owen, *Hysteria, Hypnosis and Healing*, pp. 66–67.

389. Ilza Veith, *Hysteria: The History of a Disease*, pp. 272–74; Dr. William G. Lennox, *Epilepsy and Related Disorders*, 1:489–90.

390. Dr. David Wilfred Abse, *Hysteria and Related Mental Disorders: An Approach to Psychological Medicine*, pp. 6, 234–41.

391. Dr. John Guerrant et al., *Personality in Epilepsy*, pp. 3–11.

392. Galérant, "L'Epilepsie de Flaubert," pp. 645–46.

393. Dr. Paul Michaut, "Le Docteur Flaubert," *La Chronique médicale* 5 (1898): 684.

394. Dr. Paul Michaut, "De quoi est mort Flaubert?" ibid. 7 (1900): 607.

395. Dr. Gélineau, "L'Epilepsie de Flaubert et les épileptiques célèbres," ibid. 7 (1900): 670–72.

396. Dr. Paul Michaut, "La Mort de Flaubert," ibid. 7 (1900): 703–4.

397. Dr. Maximin Legrand [Letter concerning Flaubert], ibid. 7 (1900): 736.

398. Dr. L. Le Pileur, "Gustave Flaubert, Maxime Du Camp, et Wellington," ibid. 7 (1900): 770–71.

399. Dr. Charles Binet-Sanglé, "L'Epilepsie chez Gustave Flaubert," ibid. 7 (1900): 641–47.

400. Owen, *Hysteria, Hypnosis and Healing*, pp. 80–81.

401. Dr. Paul Michaut, "Un Livre à écrire sur Gustave Flaubert," *La Chronique médicale*, 7 (1900): 771–72.

402. Fortin, "Le Subconscient chez Flaubert," ibid. 8 (1901): 28.

403. Dr. Félix Regnault, "L'Epilepsie chez les hommes de génie," ibid. 8 (1901): 31–32; "Observations d'épilepsie sur les hommes de génie et notamment sur Gustave Flaubert ont été jusqu'à présent mal prises," *Revue de l'hypnotisme et de la psychologie physiologique* 15 (1901): 270–73.

404. Binet-Sanglé, "L'Epilepsie de Gustave Flaubert," p. 62.

405. Lennox, *Epilepsy and Related Disorders*, 1:489–90.

406. Dumesnil, *Flaubert, son hérédité, son milieu, sa méthode*, pp. 86–106.

407. Dr. Augustin Cabanès, "La Névrose de Flaubert: Flaubert et la médecine," *La Chronique médicale* 12 (1905): 209–10.

408. Dr. Félix Regnault, "La Maladie de Flaubert," ibid. 12 (1905): 350.

409. Lastic, *La Pathologie mentale dans les oeuvres de Gustave Flaubert*, pp. 100–108.

410. Dr. George M. Gould, "A Biographic Clinic on Gustave Flaubert," pp. 569–71.

411. Dr. Pearce Bailey, "Flaubert's Epilepsy," *Proceedings, Charaka Club* 3 (1910): 7–13.

412. Regnault, "Le Mal de Flaubert," pp. 343–45; Flaubert to Ernest Chevalier, 2 September 1843, *Corr.* 1:146.

413. Allain, *Le Mal de Flaubert*, pp. 26–32; Drs. Walter Bryan Matthews and Henry Miller, *Diseases of the Nervous System*, pp. 289–91.

414. Dr. Giovanni Judica, "Gli attaques de nerfs di Gustave Flaubert: Isterismo o epilessia?" *Medicina Italiana* 14 (1933): 565–66; Dr. Francisco Garrido Quintana, "Es caso Flaubert," *La Medicina Ibera* 30 (1936): 135–36.

415. Dr. Paul Noury, "Glanes sur les maladies et la mort de Gustave Flaubert," *La Chronique médicale* 36 (1929): 64; Jean-Maurienne, "La Maladie et la mort de Flaubert," ibid. 37 (1930): 282–85.

416. King and Nicol, *Venereal Diseases*, pp. 43–44.

417. Dr. Pierre Vallery-Radot, "Un Ecrivain surmené: Quatre ans (1873–76) de la vie de Gustave Flaubert d'après sa correspondance," *La Presse médicale* 65 (1957): 173.

418. Gérard-Gailly, *Flaubert et les fantômes de Trouville*, pp. 109–10.

419. Brault, *Considérations médicales sur la sensibilité de Flaubert*, pp. 13–14.

420. Lennox, *Epilepsy and Related Disorders*, 1:33, 61–62.

421. Slager, *Basic Neuropathology*, p. 172.

422. Lennox, *Epilepsy and Related Disorders*, 1:227.

423. Dr. Roy Grinker, Dr. Paul C. Bucy, and Dr. Adolph L. Sahs, *Neurology*, p. 1029; Slager, *Basic Neuropathology*, p. 172; Dr. Hiram H. Merritt, *A Textbook of Neurology*, pp. 725–27.

424. Lennox, *Epilepsy and Related Disorders* 1:174–76.

425. Gallet, *Quel diagnostic aurions-nous fait si nous avions soigné Flaubert?* pp. 38–40.

426. Ibid., pp. 41–50.

427. Lennox, *Epilepsy and Related Disorders*, 1:234, 250–51, 438–40, 461.

428. Ibid., 2:575, 578–79, 611, 909; Bart, *Flaubert*, p. 93.

429. Drs. Matthews and Miller, *Diseases of the Nervous System*, pp. 285, 287, 289–92; Merrit, *A Textbook of Neurology*, pp. 728–29.

430. Dr. Guerrant et al., *Personality in Epilepsy*, pp. 27, 93, 99.

431. Lennox, *Epilepsy and Related Disorders* 1: 187–88.

432. Abse, *Hysteria and Related Mental Disorders*, p. 8.

433. Matthews and Miller, *Diseases of the Nervous System*, pp. 339–42;

Grinker, Bucy, and Sahs, *Neurology*, p. 1037; Abse, *Hysteria and Related Mental Disorders*, p. 64.

434. Abse, ibid., p. 100.

435. Dr. Pierre Janet, *Les Névroses*, pp. 346–48, 352–57, 367; Ellenberger, *The Discovery of the Unconscious*, p. 375; Dr. Laurence I. O'Kelly and Dr. Frederick A. Muckler, *Introduction to Psychopathology*, p. 202.

436. H. Guntrip, "A Study of Fairbairn's Theory of Schizoid Reactions," in Charles Reed, Irving Alexander, and Sylvan Tompkins, eds., *Psychopathology, A Source Book*, pp. 344–45, 349–51, 362–65.

437. Abse, *Hysteria and Related Mental Disorders*, p. 32.

438. Holzman, *Psychoanalysis and Psychopathology*, p. 94; Dr. Denis Williams, *Modern Trends in Neurology*, pp. 343–44.

439. Flaubert to Hippolyte Taine, ca. December 1866, *Corr.* 5:350, and 1 December 1866, *Corr. Supp.* (1864–71): 94–95.

440. Drs. Wilder Penfield and Lamar Roberts, *Speech and Brain-Mechanisms*, pp. 50–51.

441. Bart, *Flaubert*, pp. 91–96.

442. Flaubert to Amélie Bosquet, November or December 1859, *Corr.* 4:351–53.

443. Dumesnil, *Le Grand Amour de Flaubert*, pp. 9–17.

444. Ignotus, *The Paradox of Maupassant*, pp. 36–38; Steegmuller, *The Selected Letters of Gustave Flaubert*, p. 13.

445. Bart, *Flaubert*, pp. 148, 257, 385–86.

446. Ibid., p. 291.

447. Flaubert to Mme Brainne, 10–11 December 1879, *Corr. Supp.* (1877–80): 287.

448. Drs. John Money and Anke A. Ehrhardt, *Man & Woman, Boy & Girl*, pp. 147–48.

449. Ibid., pp. 18–22, 164, 183.

450. Flaubert to Louise Colet, 11 December 1852, *Corr.* 3:62–63; Pommier, "Les Maladies de Gustave Flaubert," *Le Progrès médical* 75 (1947): 416.

451. *Esquire* 82 (December 1974): 95.

Chapter Four

1. Owen, *Hysteria, Hypnosis and Healing*, p. 216.

2. Dr. Paul Michaut, "La Maladie de Maupassant," *La Chronique médicale* 5 (1898): 733.

3. Pol Neveux, "Etude," in Maupassant, *Oeuvres complètes* 1:xxv–vi, liv.

4. Dr. Charles Ladame, *Guy de Maupassant: Etude de psychologie pathologique*, pp. 8, 23.

5. Ignotus, *The Paradox of Maupassant*, pp. 20–21, 47–57; Dumesnil, *Guy de Maupassant*, pp. 79–82.

6. Maupassant, *The Complete Short Stories of Guy de Maupassant*, pp. 1170–74. (Hereafter cited as *CSS*.)

7. Dumesnil, *Guy de Maupassant*, pp. 72–74; Francis Steegmuller, *Maupassant: A Lion in the Path*, pp. 11–12.

8. Ignotus, *The Paradox of Maupassant*, pp. 206–7.

9. Dr. Lucien Lagriffe, "Guy de Maupassant: Etude de psychologie pathologique," *Annales médico-psychologiques* 8 (1908): 206.

10. Ignotus, *The Paradox of Maupassant*, p. 69; Borel, "Le Cahier d'amour," *Les Oeuvres Libres* 216 (1939): 79–80.

11. Neveux, "Etude," pp. liv–v.

12. Robert J. Niess, "Autobiographical Symbolism in Maupassant's Last Works," *Symposium* 14 (1960): 215–19.

13. Maupassant, *CSS*, p. 468.

14. Ignotus, *The Paradox of Maupassant*, pp. 15–16.

15. Maupassant to Catulle Mendes, 1876, in Dr. René Dumesnil, *Chroniques, études, correspondance de Guy de Maupassant* p. 220. (Hereafter cited as *Corr.*)

16. Steegmuller, *Maupassant: A Lion in the Path*, pp. 29–30.

17. Maupassant, "On Cats," *CSS*, pp. 659–62.

18. Laure de Maupassant to Gustave Flaubert, 16 March 1866, *Corr.*, p. 430.

19. Dr. André Lombard, "Guy de Maupassant: Sa vie, son oeuvre, sa maladie, sa mort," *La Chronique médicale* 15 (1908): 36.

20. Laure de Maupassant to Gustave Flaubert, 29 January 1872, *Corr.*, p. 431.

21. Maupassant to Laure de Maupassant, 24 September 1873, *Corr.*, p. 201; Steegmuller, *Maupassant: A Lion in the Path*, pp. 75–79.

22. Maupassant to Laure de Maupassant, 3 September 1875, *Corr.*, p. 209.

23. Maupassant to Laure de Maupassant, 6 October 1875, *Corr.*, p. 213.

24. Maupassant to Louis Le Poittevin, 23 September 1874, *Corr.*, p. 202.

25. Maupassant to Laure de Maupassant, 21 March 1878, *Corr.*, p. 235.

26. Maupassant to Robert Pinchon, 23 April 1878, *Corr.*, p. 238.

27. Louis Thomas, *La Maladie et la mort de Maupassant*, pp. 19–20.

28. Dr. Albert Le Sage, "Guy de Maupassant: étude médico-littéraire," *L'Union médicale de Canada* 46 (1917): 322–23; Maupassant to Flaubert, 21 August, 11 September, and 16 December 1878, *Corr.*, pp. 243, 247, 256.

29. Georges Normandy, *La Fin de Guy de Maupassant*, p. 33; Dr. P. Derocque, "Nécrologie—Le Dr. Aube," *La Revue médicale de Normandie* 4 (1903): 323–24; Françoise Moser, "Maupassant devant sa maladie," *La Médecine de France* 189 (1968): 17.

30. Dr. A.T.W. Simeons, *Man's Presumptuous Brain: An Evolutionary Interpretation of Psychosomatic Disease*, pp. 175–79.

31. Normandy, *La Fin de Guy de Maupassant*, pp. 36, 44, 73–74, 88–89.

32. Maupassant to Léon Hennique, 29 September 1880, *Corr.*, p. 291.

33. Thomas, *La Maladie et la mort de Maupassant*, pp. 21–24; Jacques-Henry Bornecque, "Dans l'intimité des Maupassant: Laure de Maupassant (d'après des lettres et documents inédits)," *La Revue d'histoire littéraire de la France* 64 (1964): 623–25, 631.

34. Ignotus, *The Paradox of Maupassant*, pp. 191–93.

35. Albert Lumbroso, *Souvenirs sur Maupassant: Sa dernière maladie, sa mort*, p. 122; Léon Deffoux, "Les Enfants de Guy de Maupassant," *Mercure de France* (1 January 1927): 249–50.

36. Pierre Borel, "Guy de Maupassant et Gisèle d'Estoc," *Les Oeuvres Libres* N.S. 195 (1962): 152–53.

37. Maupassant, *CSS*, p. 272.

38. Lagriffe, "Guy de Maupassant: Etude de psychologie pathologiques," p. 208; Thomas, *La Maladie et la mort de Maupassant*, p. 32.

39. Maupassant, *CSS*, pp. 31–37.

40. Lagriffe, "Guy de Maupassant: Etude de psychologie pathologiques," pp. 209–11; Maupassant, *CSS*, pp. 169–72.

41. Dr. Maurice Pillet, "Le Mal de Maupassant," *Aesculape* 3 (1913): 169–70.

42. Ibid., pp. 167–68.

43. Maupassant to Robert Pinchon, 11 March 1876, *Corr.*, p. 214.

44. Dr. Zacharie Lacassagne, *La Folie de Maupassant*, pp. 21–29, 33; Drs. Paul Voivenel and Louis Lagriffe, *Sous le signe de la P.G.: La folie de Guy de Maupassant*, pp. 19–20; Steegmuller, *Maupassant: A Lion in the Path*, p. 59; Ignotus, *The Paradox of Maupassant*, pp. 102–3.

45. Thomas, *La Maladie et la mort de Maupassant*, pp. 38–42.

46. Lombard, "Guy de Maupassant: sa vie, son oeuvre, sa maladie, sa mort," p 37; Dr. Guillaume Delpierre, *Etude psycho-pathologique sur Guy de Maupassant*, p. 24.

47. Borel, "Le Cahier d'amour," pp. 89–90.

48. Dr. Eifer, "La Maladie de Guy de Maupassant date de 1877," *La Revue moderne de médecine et de chirurgie* 22 (1922): 245; André Vial, "Le Mal de Maupassant," *Mercure de France* (1 April 1948): 758–59; Le Sage, "Guy de Maupassant: Etude médico-littéraire," pp. 324–26; Dr. Joseph Gabel, *Génie et folie chez Guy de Maupassant*, p. 10.

49. Flaubert to Emile Zola, 23 July 1876, *Corr.* 7:327.

50. Flaubert to Guy de Maupassant, 23 July 1876, *Corr.* 7:327–28.

51. Flaubert to Turgenev, 6 September 1877, *Corr. Supp.* (1877–80): 26.

52. Flaubert to Edmond Laporte, 6 September 1877, *Corr. Supp.* (1877–80): 27.

53. Maupassant to Flaubert, 5 July 1878, *Corr.*, pp. 240–41.

54. Flaubert to Turgenev, 9 July 1878, *Corr. Supp.* (1877–80): 90; Maupassant to Flaubert, 3 August 1878, *Corr.*, p. 242.

55. Flaubert to Maupassant, 15 August 1878, *Corr.*, 8:135–36.

56. Maupassant to Flaubert, 21 August and 16 December 1878; Maupassant to Laure de Maupassant, 11 September 1878, *Corr.*, pp. 243–44, 247, 256; Moser, "Maupassant devant sa maladie," p. 17.

57. Flaubert to Maupassant, 1 February 1880, *Corr.*, 8:364.

58. Steegmuller, *Maupassant: A Lion in the Path*, pp. 123–24.

59. Maupassant to Flaubert, February 1880, *Corr.*, p. 281.

60. Maupassant to Flaubert, early March 1880, *Corr.*, pp. 282–83.

61. Flaubert to Maupassant, 24 March 1880, *Corr.*, 9:14.

62. Flaubert to Caroline Commanville, 27 March 1880, *Corr.*, 9:17; Flaubert to Turgenev, 7 April 1880, *Corr. Supp.* (1877–80): 327.

63. Lagriffe, "Guy de Maupassant: Etude de psychologie pathologique," pp. 213–14; Thomas, *La Maladie et la mort de Maupassant*, p. 47; Voivenel and Lagriffe, *Sous le signe de la P.G.: La Folie de Guy de Maupassant*, p. 82; Dr. Lombard, "Guy de Maupassant: Sa vie, son oeuvre, sa maladie, sa mort," p. 37.

64. Dr. Antoine Lacassagne, "A propos de Maupassant," *Archives d'anthropologie criminelle de médecine légale et de psychologie normale et pathologique* 25 (1910): 107–8.

65. Maupassant to Caroline Commanville, 24 May 1880, *Corr.*, p. 288.

66. Dr. Pierre Vallery-Radot, "La Maladie de Maupassant d'après sa correspondance," *La Presse médicale* 64 (1956): 1521.

67. Steegmuller, *Maupassant: A Lion in the Path*, pp. 137–46.

68. Maupassant, "Bed No. 29," *CSS*, pp. 570–77; Morton, *Venereal Diseases*, p. 74; Steegmuller, *Maupassant: A Lion in the Path*, pp. 224–25; Delpierre, *Etude psycho-pathologique sur Guy de Maupassant*, pp. 23–24.

69. Ladame, *Guy de Maupassant: Etude de psychologie pathologique*, pp. 14–18; Steegmuller, *Maupassant: A Lion in the Path*, pp. 153–55; Maupassant, *CSS*, pp. 43–58.

70. Maupassant, "Beside a Dead Man," *CSS*, p. 922.

71. André Vial, *Guy de Maupassant et l'art du roman*, p. 160.

72. Dr. Francine Morin-Gauthier, *La Psychiatrie dans l'oeuvre littéraire de Guy de Maupassant*, p. 80; Dr. Félix Regnault, "La Maladie de Guy de Maupassant," *La Revue moderne de médecine et de chirurgie* 24 (1924): 137; Ladame, *Guy de Maupassant: Etude de psychologie pathologique*, pp. 24–25, 33, 38–47.

73. Ellenberger, *The Discovery of the Unconscious*, pp. 282–83, 502.

74. Dr. N. Bajenow, "Guy de Maupassant et Dostoiewsky: Etude de psychopathologie comparée," *Archives d'anthropologie criminelle de médecine légale et de psychologie normale et pathologique* 19 (1904): 4–6; Dr. Robert Hollier, *La Peur et les états qui s'y rattachent dans l'oeuvre de Maupassant*, pp. 10–12, 21, 32–33; Dr. Lucien Lagriffe, "La Peur dans l'oeuvre de Maupassant," *Archives d'anthropologie criminelle de médecine légale et de psychologie normale et pathologique* 28 (1913): 193–94.

75. Dr. Zacharie Lacassagne, *La Folie de Maupassant*, pp. 36–49; Drs. A. Rémond and P. Voivenel, "La Folie de Maupassant," *Le Progrès médical* 24 (1908): 270–71; Lagriffe, "Guy de Maupassant: Etude de psychologie pathologique," pp. 217–19, 227.

76. Ladame, *Guy de Maupassant: Etude de psychologie pathologique*, pp. 9–13.

77. Maupassant, "On the Novel," Preface to *Pierre and Jean*, pp. xlvii–viii.

78. Maupassant, *CSS*, pp. 597–601.

79. Maupassant, *CSS*, pp. 169–72.

80. Maupassant, *CSS*, pp. 299–303.

81. Maupassant, *CSS*, pp. 1066–69.

82. Pillet, "Le Mal de Maupassant," p. 173; Lumbroso, *Souvenirs sur Maupassant: Sa dernière maladie, sa mort*, p. 408.

83. Maupassant, *CSS*, pp. 95–100; Hollier, *La Peur et les états qui s'y rattachent dans l'oeuvre de Maupassant*, pp. 56, 64.

84. Maupassant, *CSS*, pp. 1280–1302.

85. Maupassant, *CSS*, pp. 260–63.

86. Maupassant, *CSS*, pp. 855–58.

87. Maupassant, *CSS*, pp. 795–98.

88. Maupassant, *CSS*, pp. 968–72.

89. Maupassant, *CSS*, pp. 805–8.

90. Lagriffe, "La Peur dans l'oeuvre de Maupassant," p. 194.

91. Maupassant, *CSS*, pp. 812–15.

92. Dumesnil, *Chroniques, études, correspondance de Guy de Maupassant*, pp. ix–xi; Steegmuller, *Maupassant: A Lion in the Path*, p. 260.

93. Maupassant, *The Horla, CSS*, pp. 1313–28; Lagriffe, "Guy de Maupassant: Etude de psychologie pathologique," p. 183.

94. Maupassant, *CSS*, pp. 1268–76; Dr. Lagriffe, "Guy de Maupassant: Etude de psychologie pathologique," pp. 187–90.

95. Maupassant, *CSS*, pp. 310–13; Vial, *Guy de Maupassant et l'art du roman*, p. 183.

96. Maupassant, *CSS*, pp. 165–68.

97. *CSS*, pp. 313–19.

98. *CSS*, pp. 269–74.

99. Maupassant, *Pierre and Jean*, pp. 64–66, 99, 194–95.

100. Maupassant, *CSS*, pp. 466–82.

101. Steegmuller, *Maupassant: A Lion in the Path*, pp. 322–23.

102. Maupassant, *CSS*, pp. 1054–65.

103. Steegmuller, *Maupassant: A Lion in the Path*, p. 232; Maupassant, *CSS*, pp. 1244–48.

104. Maupassant, *CSS*, pp. 518–22.

105. Le Sage, "Guy de Maupassant: Etude médico-littéraire," p. 330.

106. Maupassant, *CSS*, pp. 713–15.

107. Steegmuller, *Maupassant: A Lion in the Path*, pp. 217–19.

108. Maupassant, *CSS*, pp. 1328–39.

109. Niess, "Autobiographical Symbolism in Maupassant's Last Works," p. 214.

110. Voivenel and Lagriffe, *Sous le signe de la P.G.: La folie de Guy de Maupassant*, p. 143.

111. Maupassant to Laure de Maupassant and to Caroline Commanville, January 1881, *Corr.*, pp. 292–93.

112. Maupassant to Robert Pinchon, 7 August 1881, *Corr.*, p. 295.

113. Maupassant to Victor Havard, 21 February 1885, and to Emile Zola, May or June 1885, *Corr.*, pp. 327, 329.

114. François Tassart, *Recollections of Guy de Maupassant*, p. 50.

115. Pierre Borel, "Maupassant, lettres à son médecin," *Les Oeuvres libres* N.S. 165 (1960): 4.

116. Maupassant to Georges Decaux, 2 June 1886; to Victor Havard, 15 September 1886; and to Mme Lecomte du Nouy, November 1886, *Corr.*, pp. 338–41; Tassart, *Recollections of Guy de Maupassant*, p. 65.

117. Tassart, *Recollections of Guy de Maupassant*, pp. 91–92.

118. Maupassant to Laure de Maupassant, September 1887, *Corr.*, p. 347; Maupassant, *Pierre and Jean* (1888), p. 42; Tassart, *Recollections of Guy de Maupassant*, pp. 109–10, 114, 118, 123, 133, 157–58.

119. Borel, "Maupassant, lettres à son médecin," p. 5; Pillet "Le Mal de Maupassant," p. 217; Tassart, *Recollections of Guy de Maupassant*, pp. 156, 170, 178–79; Maupassant to Dr. Georges Daremberg, November 1889, *Corr.*, p. 374.

120. Maupassant to Countess Potocka, 1889, *Corr.*, pp. 366–67.

121. Bajenow, "Guy de Maupassant et Dostoiewsky: Etude de psychopathologie comparée," pp. 7–8; Hollier, *La Peur et les états qui s'y rattachent dans l'oeuvre de Maupassant*, pp. 67–69.

122. Dr. Paul Sollier, *Les Phénomènes d'autoscopie*, pp. 10–11; Stanley M. Coleman, "The Phantom Double: Its Psychological Significance," *British Journal of Medical Psychology* 14 (1934): 260.

123. Borel, "Le Cahier d'amour," pp. 94–95.

124. Dr. Pillet, "Le Mal de Maupassant," p. 173.

125. Coleman, "The Phantom Double: Its Psychological Significance," *British Journal of Medical Psychology* 14 (1934): 260–62, 272–73.

126. Lumbroso, *Souvenirs sur Maupassant: Sa dernière maladie, sa mort*, p. 581; Thomas, *La Maladie et la mort de Maupassant*, p. 48; Lagriffe, "Guy de Maupassant: Etude de psychologie pathologique," pp. 214–15, 357.

127. Dr. Edmund Landolt, "A propos de Maupassant," *Archivio di antropologia criminale, psichiatria, medicina legale e scienze affini* 25 (1910): 389; Moser, "Maupassant devant sa maladie," *La Médecine de France* 189 (1968): 19.

128. King and Nicol, *Venereal Diseases*, p. 162.

129. Pillet, "Le Mal de Maupassant," p. 170.

130. Normandy, *La Fin de Guy de Maupassant*, pp. 76–77; Gabel, *Génie et folie chez Guy de Maupassant*, p. 19.

131. Voivenel and Lagriffe, *Sous le signe de la P.G.: La folie de Guy de Maupassant*, pp. 82–84.

132. Delpierre, *Etude psycho-pathologique sur Guy de Maupassant*, pp. 25–26, 87–88; Dr. Thomas L. Stedman, "The 'Paresia' of Guy de Maupassant," *Medical Record* 92 (1917): 289–90.

133. Charles Ladame, "La Vraie maladie de Guy de Maupassant: Un point de vue nouveau," *Zeitschrift für Kinderpsychiatrie* 14 (1947): 64–68; Borel, "Le Cahier d'amour," pp. 96–97.

134. Lagriffe, "Guy de Maupassant: Etude de psychologie pathologique," pp. 353–55.

135. Pillet, "Le Mal de Maupassant," p. 181; Maurice Talmeyer, *La Liberté,* 25 March 1911.

136. Thomas, *La Maladie et la mort de Maupassant,* p. 35; Maupassant, *CSS,* pp. 567–69; Gabel, *Génie et folie chez Guy de Maupassant,* p. 11; Dr. Pierre Cogny, "Guy de Maupassant et la drogue," *Cahiers de la Tour Saint-Jacques* 1 (1960): 86–91.

137. Gabel, *Génie et folie chez Guy de Maupassant,* pp. 12–13, 20–22.

138. Dr. H. Guntrip, "A Study of Fairbairn's Theory of Schizoid Reactions," Charles Reed, Irving Alexander, and Sylvan Tomkins, eds., *Psychopathology: A Source Book,* pp. 366–68.

139. Pillet, "Le Mal de Maupassant," p. 217; Steegmuller, *Maupassant: A Lion in the Path,* pp. 267–69; Dumesnil, *Chroniques, études, correspondance de Guy de Maupassant,* pp. 353–54, 360.

140. Maupassant to Jacob, 30 May 1890, *Corr.,* p. 381; Ignotus, *The Paradox of Maupassant,* pp. 158–60; Octave Uzanne, "The Portraits of Guy de Maupassant," in Maupassant, *Pierre and Jean,* pp. 229–34.

141. Steegmuller, *Maupassant: A Lion in the Path,* p. 409.

142. Maupassant, *Sur l'eau, La Vie errante, A Family Affair, and Other Stories,* pp. 24–25, 41.

143. Ibid., pp. 44–46, 51, 66–67.

144. Ibid., pp. 70–74.

145. Maupassant to Countess Potocka, 13 March 1884, *Corr.,* p. 307.

146. Bajenow, "Guy de Maupassant et Dostoiewsky: Etude de psychopathologie comparée," pp. 10–13.

147. Pillet, "Le Mal de Maupassant," p. 221.

148. Lumbroso, *Souvenirs sur Maupassant: Sa dernière maladie, sa mort,* p. 322; Lagriffe, "Guy de Maupassant: Etude de psychologie pathologique," p. 367.

149. Pillet, "Le Mal de Maupassant," p. 140–41; Le Sage, "Guy de Maupassant: Etude médico-littéraire," pp. 330, 339–40; Voivenel and Lagriffe, *Sous le signe de la P.G.: La folie de Guy de Maupassant,* p. 100; Coleman, "The Phantom Double: Its Psychological Significance," p. 259.

150. Steegmuller, *Maupassant: A Lion in the Path,* pp. 219–20.

151. Flaubert to Edmond Laporte, 11 April 1877, *Corr. Supp.* (1872–77): 337.

152. Ladame, "La Vraie maladie de Guy de Maupassant: Un point de vue nouveau," p. 64; Dr. Pierre Cogny, Introduction to the 1962 Didier edition of Maupassant's *Notre Coeur;* Ignotus, *The Paradox of Maupassant,* pp. 272–79; Moser, "Maupassant devant sa maladie," p. 20; Tassart, *Recollections of Guy de Maupassant,* p. 79.

153. Borel, "Le Cahier d'amour," p. 71; Tassart, *Recollections of Guy de Maupassant,* p. 245.

154. Borel, "Une Amoureuse inconnue de Maupassant," *Les Oeuvres Libres* N.S. 151 (1958): 128–29, 134–35, 140.

155. Borel, "Guy de Maupassant et Gisèle d'Estoc," pp. 144–45, 147, 150–51.

156. Borel, "Le Cahier d'amour," pp. 73, 76.

157. Ibid., p. 84.

158. Tassart, *Recollections of Guy de Maupassant*, pp. 79, 245, 276, 279, 302.

159. Ignotus, *The Paradox of Maupassant*, pp. 204–5, 229.

160. Goncourt, *Journal*, 1 February 1891 and 9 April 1893, 17:189, 19:94.

161. Steegmuller, *Maupassant: A Lion in the Path*, p. 242.

162. Normandy, *La Fin de Guy de Maupassant*, pp. 70, 86.

163. Money and Ehrhardt, *Man & Woman, Boy & Girl: The Differentiation and Dimorphism of Gender Identity from Conception to Maturity*, p. 290.

164. Stekel, *Impotence in the Male*, 1:39–40, 62–63, 69; Coleman, "The Phantom Double: Its Psychological Significance," pp. 256–57.

165. Dr. Lionel Ovesey, "Pseudohomosexuality, the Paranoid Mechanism, and Paranoia: An Adaptational Revision of a Classical Freudian Theory," in Reed, Alexander, and Tomkins, eds., *Psychopathology: A Source Book*, pp. 388, 402.

166. Dumesnil, *Chroniques, études, correspondance de Guy de Maupassant*, pp. 374–75, 378; Pillet, "Le Mal de Maupassant," p. 181; Tassart, *Recollections of Guy de Maupassant*, pp. 238–39; Voivenel and Lagriffe, *Sous le signe de la P.G.: La folie de Guy de Maupassant*, pp. 112–13.

167. Maupassant to Laure de Maupassant, 20 May and August 1890, *Corr.*, pp. 379–80, 388–89; Tassart, *Recollections of Guy de Maupassant*, pp. 243–45, 277.

168. Maupassant to Louise Le Poittevin, 7 January 1891, and to Laure de Maupassant, 22 February 1891, *Corr.*, pp. 392–93; Borel, "Maupassant, lettres à son médecin," p. 9.

169. Lagriffe, "Guy de Maupassant: Etude de psychologie pathologique," pp. 228–29.

170. Maupassant to Laure de Maupassant, 14 March 1891, *Corr.*, pp. 395–96.

171. Maupassant to Dr. Henry Cazalis, June 1891, *Corr.* , p. 405; Tassart, *Recollections of Guy de Maupassant*, pp. 291–94.

172. Maupassant to Laure de Maupassant, 27 June 1891, *Corr.*, pp. 406–7; Lombard, "Guy de Maupassant: Sa vie, son oeuvre, sa maladie, sa mort," p. 38.

173. Lumbroso, *Souvenirs sur Maupassant: Sa dernière maladie, sa mort*, pp. 40–46.

174. Ibid., pp. 55–56; Lombard, "Guy de Maupassant: Sa vie, son oeuvre, sa maladie, sa mort," p. 38.

175. Maupassant to Dr. Cazalis, Autumn 1891, *Corr.*, p. 411.

176. Maupassant to Dr. Georges Daremberg, December 1891, *Corr.*, pp. 417–18; Vallery-Radot, "La Maladie de Maupassant d'après sa correspondance," p. 1522.

177. Maupassant to the Maître Jacob, December 1891, *Corr.*, p. 419.

178. Maupassant to Dr. Cazalis, December 1891, *Corr.*, p. 419.

179. Goncourt, *Journal*, 9 December 1891, 18:105; Pillet, "Le Mal de Maupassant," p. 181.

180. Tassart, *Recollections of Guy de Maupassant*, pp. 308–9.

181. Normandy, *La Fin de Guy de Maupassant*, pp. 145–46.

182. Tassart, *Recollections of Guy de Maupassant*, pp. 311–12; Steegmuller, *Maupassant: A Lion in the Path*, p. 311; Lumbroso, *Souvenirs sur Maupassant: Sa dernière maladie, sa mort*, p. 76; Hermine Lecomte de Nouy, "Les Tentatives de suicide de Maupassant," *La Chronique médicale* 15 (1908): 39–40; Thomas, *La Maladie et la mort de Maupassant*, pp. 86–87; Pillet, "Le Mal de Maupassant," pp. 183–84.

183. Normandy, *La Fin de Guy de Maupassant*, pp. 147–49; Dr. Renato Bettica-Giovannini, "La Pazzia di Maupassant," *Rassegna di Studia Psichiatrica* 34 (1950): 245, 248.

184. Dr. Jacques Le Breton, *La Maison de santé du Docteur Blanche, ses médecins, ses malades*, pp. 14, 44–50, 54; and Dr. Cabanès, "Guy de Maupassant chez le Docteur Blanche," *La Chronique médicale* 4 (1897): 682.

185. Dr. Le Breton, *La Maison de santé du Docteur Blanche, ses médecins, ses malades*, pp. 78–79, 85; Normandy, *La Fin de Guy de Maupassant*, pp. 160–61; Goncourt, *Journal*, 30 January 1893, 19:69; Steegmuller, *Maupassant: A Lion in the Path*, p. 343.

186. Lumbroso, *Souvenirs sur Maupassant: Sa dernière maladie, sa mort*, pp. 91–97; Lagriffe, "Guy de Maupassant: Etude de psychologie pathologique," pp. 237–38; Tassart, *Recollections of Guy de Maupassant*, pp. 316–22; Guérinot, "Un Geste meurtrier de Maupassant," *La Chronique médicale* 33 (1926): 214.

187. Steegmuller, *Maupassant: A Lion in the Path*, pp. 342–43.

188. Lumbroso, *Souvenirs sur Maupassant: Sa dernière maladie, sa mort*, pp. 98–99; Regnault, "La Maladie de Guy de Maupassant," pp. 133–37; Gabel, *Génie et folie chez Guy de Maupassant*, pp. 25, 35; Dr. Le Breton, "La Fin de Maupassant," *Archives médico-chirurgicales de Normandie* 53 (1962): 59–61; Weiss and Joseph, *Syphilis*, pp. 129–30; Steegmuller, *Maupassant: A Lion in the Path*, p. 345.

189. Dumesnil, *Guy de Maupassant*, p. 234; Dr. Francisco Garrido Quintana, "La Paralisis general progresiva y dos locos geniales," *Medicina Argentina* 13 (1934): 506, 509–10.

Chapter Five

1. Murray Sachs, *The Career of Alphonse Daudet: A Critical Study*, p. vii.

2. Ibid., pp. 181–83.

3. Maurice Parturier, *Morny et son temps*, p. 269; Ludovic Halévy, *Carnets* 1:57.

4. Luc Badesco, "Les Débuts parisiens d'Alphonse Daudet, légende et vérité," *Revue d'histoire littéraire de la France* 63 (1963): 600–602.

5. Jacques-Henry Bornecque and Luc Badesco, "Autour d'Alphonse Daudet, controverse," ibid. 64 (1964): 478.

6. Frederick A. Busi, "The Legacy of Edouard Drumont as an Ecrivain de Combat," *Nineteenth-Century French Studies* 4 (1976): 386–87; Sachs, *The Career of Alphonse Daudet*, p. 35.

7. Eugen Weber, *L'Action Française*, pp. 62–63.

8. Goncourt, *Journal,* 3, 6, 28, 29 May, 27 July 1894, 20:53, 55–56, 65–66, 107; 4 and 16 June 1896, 22:35, 43; Billy, "Le Vrai Journal des Goncourt," pp. 33–34.

9. Ibid., pp. 34–35; Sachs, *The Career of Alphonse Daudet,* pp. 5–11; Lucien Daudet, *Vie d'Alphonse Daudet,* p. 41.

10. Ernest Daudet, *My Brother and I: Recollections of Infancy and Youth,* pp. 291–92, 309, 311, 316–17; Sachs, *The Career of Alphonse Daudet,* pp. 12–16.

11. Alphonse Daudet, *Quarante ans de Paris, 1857–1897,* pp. 177–78, 181–84; Ernest Daudet, *My Brother and I,* pp. 327–29, 333–36; Sachs, *The Career of Alphonse Daudet,* pp. 16–18, 53, 57.

12. Alphonse Daudet, *Quarante ans de Paris, 1857–1897,* pp. 184–85; Ernest Daudet, *My Brother and I,* pp. 346–50; Goncourt, *Journal,* 28 January 1878, 11:177.

13. Goncourt, *Journal,* 14 April 1895, 21:37.

14. Alphonse Daudet, *Quarante ans de Paris, 1857–1897,* pp. 185–86.

15. Ibid., p. 187; Ernest Daudet, *My Brother and I,* pp. 356, 382–405; Sachs, *The Career of Alphonse Daudet,* pp. 19–22.

16. Ernest Daudet, *My Brother and I,* pp. 409–10, 416–17; Badesco, "Les Débuts parisiens d'Alphonse Daudet, légende et vérité," pp. 583–88.

17. Sachs, *The Career of Alphonse Daudet,* pp. 24–31.

18. Alphonse V. Roche, *Alphonse Daudet,* p. 103.

19. Charles Mantoux, *Alphonse Daudet et la souffrance humaine,* p. 249.

20. Goncourt, *Journal,* 5 May 1876, 11:91–92; 15 February 1879, 12:14; 30 July 1892, 18:223, 225.

21. Ernest Daudet, *My Brother and I,* p. 419; Sachs, *The Career of Alphonse Daudet,* pp. 32–33, 48–49; Parturier, *Morny et son temps,* pp. 208–9.

22. Goncourt, *Journal,* 31 January 1876, 11:70; Lucien Daudet, *Vie d'Alphonse Daudet,* pp. 43–44; Roche, *Alphonse Daudet,* p. 33.

23. Sachs, *The Career of Alphonse Daudet,* pp. 58–65; Alphonse Daudet, *Quarante ans de Paris, 1857–1897,* pp. 190–91, 197–98; Ernest Daudet, *My Brother and I,* pp. 447–48; Roche, *Alphonse Daudet,* pp. 69–70; Goncourt, *Journal,* 28 March and 11 December 1880, 12:69, 93.

24. Alphonse Daudet, *Quarante ans de Paris, 1857–1897,* pp. 204–5; Sachs, *The Career of Alphonse Daudet,* pp. 66–68.

25. Alphonse Daudet, *Quarante ans de Paris, 1857–1897,* pp. 222–28.

26. Ibid., pp. 220–21; Sachs, *The Career of Alphonse Daudet,* pp. 73–78; Roche, *Alphonse Daudet,* pp. 41–42.

27. Ernest Daudet, *My Brother and I,* pp. 424–26, 436–39.

28. Sachs, *The Career of Alphonse Daudet,* pp. 115–21.

29. Goncourt, *Journal,* 21 October 1878, 11:221.

30. Ibid., 22 June 1879, 12:32; Alphonse Daudet, *Quarante ans de Paris, 1857–1897,* pp. 250–51.

31. Lucien Daudet, *Vie d'Alphonse Daudet,* pp. 139–40; Dr. Mary Trivas, *Auto-observation d'un tabétique de qualité,* pp. 15–16; Dr. Mario Bertolotti, "La vita tribolata e la morte di Alphonse Daudet," *Minerva Medica* 45 (1954):

144–45; Dr. Marcel Mouquin, "La Maladie d'Alphonse Daudet," *Histoire de la médecine* 5 (1955): 41–42.

32. Goncourt, *Journal,* 20 November 1879 and 1 February 1880, 12:55–62; Osbert Sitwell, *The Man Who Lost Himself,* pp. 4–6.

33. Goncourt, *Journal,* 27 November 1881, 2 February and 14 May 1882, 12:138, 148, 152, 173; Trivas, *Auto-observation d'un tabétique de qualité,* p. 16.

34. Goncourt, *Journal,* 12 April 1883, 13:26; Mouquin, "La Maladie d'Alphonse Daudet," p. 43; Daudet, *La Doulou,* p. 27.

35. Dr. Augustin Cabanès, "La Documentation médicale dans le roman: Conversation avec M. Alphonse Daudet," *La Chronique médicale* 3 (1896): 100; Dr. Maxime Laignel-Lavastine and Dr. Mary Trivas, "Quelques remarques sur l'auto-observation d'un tabétique de qualité," *Le Bulletin de la Société française de l'histoire médicale* 27 (1933): 310–11; and Robert Laulan, "Alphonse Daudet, maladie incurable et lucide," *La Médecine de France* 178 (1967): 31–36.

36. André Ebner, Preface to *La Doulou,* p. 16; Daudet, *La Doulou,* pp. 25, 27; Léon Daudet, *Alphonse Daudet,* pp. 191–92; Lucien Daudet, *Vie d'Alphonse Daudet,* p. 82; Goncourt, *Journal,* 16 April 1884, 13:107.

37. Daudet, *La Doulou,* p. 28; Trivas, *Auto-observation d'un tabétique de qualité,* pp. 17, 19.

38. Lucien Daudet, *Vie d'Alphonse Daudet,* p. 176; Alphonse Daudet, *Sapho,* p. 69.

39. Alphonse Daudet, *La Doulou,* p. 31; Goncourt, *Journal,* 19 June 1884, 13:134.

40. Goncourt, *Journal,* 23, 28, 30 April, and 4, 7 June 1884, 13:111, 114–15, 128–29.

41. Fournier, *De l'Ataxie locomotrice d'origine syphilitique (tabès spécifique),* pp. 1–8, 19–26.

42. Fleming, "Syphilis through the Ages," p. 599.

43. Weiss and Joseph, *Syphilis,* pp. 127–28; Owen, *Hysteria, Hypnosis, and Healing,* p. 40; Abbrecht et al., *Syphilis, a Synopsis,* p. 77; King and Nicol, *Venereal Diseases,* pp. 67–68.

44. Daudet, *La Doulou,* pp. 32–33; Mouquin, "La Maladie d'Alphonse Daudet," pp. 44–47.

45. Daudet, *La Doulou,* pp. 33–35; Goncourt, *Journal,* 23 May 1885, 14:7; Laignel-Lavastine and Trivas, "Quelques remarques sur l'auto-observation d'un tabétiques de qualité," pp. 312–13.

46. Daudet, *La Doulou,* p. 41; Goncourt, *Journal,* 12 July 1884, 1 April 1885, 13:137, 218; Lucien Daudet, *Vie d'Alphonse Daudet,* p. 182.

47. Goncourt, *Journal,* 10 August 1885, 14:30.

48. Mouquin, "La Maladie d'Alphonse Daudet," p. 51.

49. Owen, *Hysteria, Hypnosis and Healing,* p. 229.

50. Daudet, *La Doulou,* pp. 50–53, 56.

51. Sachs, *The Career of Alphonse Daudet,* pp. 140–41, 144.

52. Daudet, *La Doulou,* p. 56; Cabanès, "La Documentation médicale dans

le roman des Goncourt: Conversation avec M. Edmond de Goncourt," p. 460.

53. Daudet, *La Doulou*, pp. 45–46; Goncourt, *Journal*, 10 September 1885; 20 May 1886; 15 February, 10 March, 24 March 1887, 14:33, 127, 198, 206, 210.

54. Goncourt, *Journal*, 6 October 1887, 15:38; and 19 May 1889, 16:77.

55. Ibid., 20 December 1885, 31 May and 25 September 1886, 14:69, 129–30, 149; Daudet, *La Doulou*, p. 54.

56. Goncourt, *Journal*, 17 June, 18 September 1886, 14:133, 146, and 22 September, 26 November 1888, 15:158, 187.

57. Abbrecht et al., *Syphilis, a Synopsis*, p. 79.

58. Daudet, *La Doulou*, pp. 43–44.

59. Goncourt, *Journal*, 2 August, 25 September, 4 October 1887, 10 and 13 June 1888, 15:19, 35, 38, 126–27; 16 and 19 July, 3, 6, and 7 August 1889, 16:107, 110, 118, 120–23.

60. Ibid., 27 January, 24 and 25 February, 3 March 1889, 16:12, 29–31; Daudet, *La Doulou*, p. 47; Laignel-Lavastine and Trivas, "Quelques remarques sur l'auto-observation d'un tabétique de qualité," p. 314; Mouquin, "La Maladie d'Alphonse Daudet," p. 53; Roche, *Alphonse Daudet*, p. 91.

61. Goncourt, *Journal*, 12 July and 14 September 1888, 15:137, 154; and 5 May, 13 and 16 June 1889, 16:71, 89–91.

62. Ibid., 26 July 1891, 18:64; 17 August 1893, 19:161; Eugen Weber, *L'Action Française*, p. 62; Edward R. Tannenbaum, *The Action Française*, p. 54.

63. Goncourt, *Journal*, 10 and 17 October 1889, 16:152, 157.

64. Ibid., 12 and 16 December 1889, 16:185–86, 189; 4, 25, and 26 May 1890, 17:43, 56–58; Mouquin, "La Maladie d'Alphonse Daudet," p. 55.

65. Goncourt, *Journal*, 14 July, 28 September, 30 September, 12 October 1890, 17:79, 112–14, 118; 4 June 1891, 18:36.

66. Ibid., 13 and 31 July, 10 August 1892, 18:215, 225–26, 228; 16 April 1893, 19:97; Lucien Daudet, *Vie d'Alphonse Daudet*, p. 240; Ellenberger, *The Discovery of the Unconscious*, p. 759.

67. Goncourt, *Journal*, 10, 11, 12 July, 12 August, 1 December 1893, 19:141–42, 158, 195; 28 April, 26 August, 1 September 1895, 21:44, 102, 106; 30 April 1896, 22:12.

68. Dr. Augustin Cabanès, "La Dernière Maladie et la mort d'Alphonse Daudet," *La Chronique médicale* 5 (1898): 1–7; Léon Daudet, *Alphonse Daudet*, pp. 14–15; Trivas, *Auto-observation d'un tabétique de qualité*, p. 42; Roche, *Alphonse Daudet*, pp. 137–38.

69. Mantoux, *Alphonse Daudet et la souffrance humaine*, pp. 7–9, 26–27, 36, 39–49, 57, 66–75.

70. Daudet, *L'Evangéliste*, pp. 59, 63–64; Roche, *Alphonse Daudet*, pp. 72–73.

71. Léon Daudet, *Alphonse Daudet*, pp. 22–28.

72. Ibid., pp. 64–66; Dr. Augustin Cabanès, "Alphonse Daudet, médecin consultant," *La Chronique médicale* 33 (1926): 140; Roche, *Alphonse Daudet*, p. 115.

73. Léon Daudet, *Devant la douleur: Souvenirs des milieux littéraires artistiques et médicaux, de 1880 à 1905*, p. 123.

74. Léon Daudet, *Alphonse Daudet*, pp. 90–101; and Lucien Daudet, *Vie d'Alphonse Daudet*, pp. 180, 248.

75. Cabanès, "La Documentation médicale dans le roman: Conversation avec M. Alphonse Daudet," pp. 103–4.

76. Daudet, *La Doulou*, p. 60; Sachs, *The Career of Alphonse Daudet*, p. 152; Trivas, *Auto-observation d'un tabétique de qualité*, p. 8.

77. Daudet, *L'Immortel*, p. 367; Roche, *Alphonse Daudet*, pp. 88–92.

78. Léon Daudet, *Alphonse Daudet*, pp. 96–99.

79. Ibid., pp. 1–3, 9–11, 173–74, 183; Goncourt, *Journal*, 17 July 1891, 18:60–61; Roche, *Alphonse Daudet*, pp. 158–63.

80. Dr. Antoine Lacassagne, "La Psycho-physiologie d'Alphonse Daudet, par lui-même," *La Chronique médicale* 5 (1898): 8–9; Daudet, *Quarante ans de Paris, 1857–1897*, pp. 160–61.

81. Dr. Monin, "La Maladie d'Alphonse Daudet," *La Chronique médicale* 33 (1926): 112; Sachs, *The Career of Alphonse Daudet*, pp. 153, 155, 158–59, 164, 170–71.

82. Léon Daudet, *Alphonse Daudet*, pp. 102–7, 110–11.

83. Ibid., pp. 50–53; Roche, *Alphonse Daudet*, pp. 134–35.

84. Jacques Chastenet, *La République des républicains, 1879–1893*, pp. 126, 181, 212, 321.

85. Lucien Daudet, *Vie d'Alphonse Daudet*, pp. 253–55; Mantoux, *Alphonse Daudet et la souffrance humain*, pp. 185–86; Sachs, *The Career of Alphonse Daudet*, pp. 157–61; Roche, *Alphonse Daudet*, pp. 100, 102, 110, 134.

86. Mantoux, *Alphonse Daudet et la souffrance humain*, pp. 252–71.

87. Marcel Proust, "Sur M. Alphonse Daudet," *La Presse*, 11 August 1897.

Bibliography

Abbrecht, Martin M., et al. *Syphilis, a Synopsis*. Washington: U.S. Department of Health, Education, and Welfare, 1967.

Abse, Dr. David Wilfred. *Hysteria and Related Mental Disorders: An Approach to Psychological Medicine*. Bristol: Wright, 1966.

Alajouanine, Thomas. "Aphasia and Artistic Realization." *Brain, Journal of Neurology* 71 (September 1948): 229–41.

Alexander, Dr. Franz G., and Dr. Sheldon T. Selesnick. *The History of Psychiatry*. New York: Harper & Row, 1966.

Allain, Dr. Edouard. *Le Mal de Flaubert*. Paris: M. Lac, 1928.

Anthéaume, Dr. André, and Dr. G. Dromard. "Le Terrain névropathique: Charles Baudelaire," *Poésie et folie*. Paris: O. Doin, 1908.

Asselineau, Charles. *Charles Baudelaire: Sa vie et son oeuvre*. Paris: A. Lemerre, 1869.

Aubé, Dr. Pierre. "Gustave Flaubert anatomiste?" *La Chronique médicale* 8 (1901): 600–601.

Auerbach, Erich. *Mimesis: The Representation of Reality in Western Literature*. Princeton: Princeton University Press, 1953. Originally published in Berne, 1946.

Auserve, Philippe, ed. Charles Baudelaire, *Lettres inédites aux siens*. Paris: B. Grasset, 1966.

Azizi, Dr. Pirouz. *La Puissance créatrice de la maladie*. Paris: L. Rodstein, 1935.

Badesco, Luc. "Les Débuts parisiens d'Alphonse Daudet, légende et vérité." *Revue d'histoire littéraire de la France* 63 (1963): 581–618.

Bailey, Dr. Pearce. "Flaubert's Epilepsy." *Proceedings, Charaka Club* (New York) 3 (1910): 5–13.

Bajenow, Dr. N. "Guy de Maupassant et Dostoiewsky, étude de psychopathologie comparée." *Archives d'anthropologie criminelle de médecine légale et de psychologie normale et pathologique* 19 (1904): 1–39.

Bancquart, Marie-Claire, ed. Louis Bouilhet, *Lettres à Louise Colet*. Paris: Librairie Nizet, 1968.

Bandy, W. T., and Claude Pichois. "Du Nouveau sur la jeunesse de Baudelaire." *Revue d'histoire littéraire de la France* 65 (1965): 70–77.

Bart, Benjamin F. "Is Maxime Du Camp a Reliable Witness?" *Modern Language Review* 48 (1953): 17–25.

———. *Flaubert*. Syracuse: Syracuse University Press, 1967.

Barzun, Jacques. *The Use and Abuse of Art*. Princeton: Princeton University Press, 1974.

Baudelaire, Charles. *Correspondance générale.* Edited by Jacques Crépet. 6 vols. Paris: Louis Conard, 1947–53.

———. *Correspondance.* Edited by Claude Pichois, with the collaboration of Jean Ziegler. 2 vols. Paris: Gallimard, 1973. Includes the letters published by Auserve in 1966 and Ziegler's study of Baudelaire's finances.

———. *The Essence of Laughter and Other Essays, Journals, and Letters.* Edited by Peter Quennell. New York: Meridian Books, 1956.

———. *Les Fleurs du mal.* Paris: Calmann Lévy, 1894. Includes Théophile Gautier's long preface written in 1868.

———. *Intimate Journals.* Hollywood: Marcel Rodd, 1947.

———. *Lettres inédites aux siens.* Edited by Philippe Auserve. Paris: B. Grasset, 1966.

———. *Oeuvres complètes.* 6 vols. Paris: Editions de la Nouvelle Revue Française, 1923.

———. *Oeuvres posthumes.* 3 vols. Edited by Jacques Crépet and Claude Pichois. Paris: Louis Conard, 1952.

———. *Paris Spleen.* New York: New Directions, 1970.

———. *Selected Writings on Art and Artists.* Edited by P. E. Charvet. Harmondsworth: Penguin Books, 1972.

Béni-Barde, Dr. Joseph-Marie-Alfred. *Manuel médical d'hydrothérapie.* Paris: G. Masson, 1878.

Berner, Dr. Paul, Dr. René Dumesnil, and Dr. Maljean. "Comment sont morts le père et la soeur de Gustave Flaubert." *La Chronique médicale* 29 (1922): 244–46.

Bertolotti, Dr. Mario. "La Vita tribolata e le morte di Alphonse Daudet." *Minerva Medica* (Turin) 45 (1954): 743–48.

Berton, Claude. "Flaubert, le théâtre et le bovarysme." *Hippocrate* 4 (1936): 552–56.

Bertrand, Louis. "Les Origines morbides de la sensibilité de Flaubert." *Aesculape* 13 (1923): 265–70; 14 (1924): 18–23.

Bett, Walter R. C. *The Infirmities of Genius.* London: C. Johnson, 1952.

Bettica-Giovannini, Dr. Renato. "Visita medica à Charles Baudelaire." *Gazzetta degli Ospedali e delle Cliniche* 59 (1938): 822–23.

———. "La Pazzia di Maupassant." *Rassegna di Studia Psichiatrica* 34 (1950): 241–49.

Billy, André. *Sainte-Beuve: Sa vie et son temps.* 2 vols. Paris: Flammarion, 1952.

———. "Le Vrai journal des Goncourt." *Les Annales: Revue mensuelle de lettres françaises* 65, 91 (1958): 23–36.

———. *The Goncourt Brothers.* New York: Horizon Press, 1960. Originally published in 1956.

Binet, Dr. Léon, and Dr. Pierre Vallery-Radot. *Médecine et littérature: Prestige de la médecine.* Paris: Expansion Scientifique Française, 1965.

Binet-Sanglé, Dr. Charles. "L'Epilepsie chez Gustave Flaubert." *La Chronique médicale* 7 (1900): 641–50.

————. "L'Epilepsie de Gustave Flaubert," *La Chronique médicale* 8 (1901): 62–63.

Blin, Georges. *Le Sadisme de Baudelaire*. Paris: J. Corti, 1948.

Bondoux, Dr. Léon. *La Réalisme littéraire de Flaubert est l'application de la méthode des sciences biologiques*. Paris: M. Lac, 1928.

Bonnet-Roy, Dr. F. "Les Goncourt et la médecine." *Le Monde*, 22 June 1946.

Bonvicini, Dr. G. "Die Aphasie des Dichters Baudelaire: Ein Beitrag zur Beziehung der zerebralen Sprachstörungen zur Süchtigkeit." *Wiener medizinische Wochenschrift* 82 (1932): 347–50.

Borel, Pierre. *Le Destin tragique de Guy de Maupassant*. Paris: Editions de France, 1927.

————. "Lettre de Maupassant à Flaubert." *Aesculape* 18 (1928): 280–81.

————. "Le Cahier d'amour." *Les Oeuvres libres* 216 (1939): 71–100. Supposedly written by Mlle X and discovered by Borel.

————. *Maupassant et l'androgyne*. Paris: Editions du Livre Moderne, 1944.

————. *Le Vrai Maupassant*. Geneva: Cailler, 1951.

————. "Une Amoureuse inconnue de Maupassant." *Les Oeuvres libres* N. S. 151 (1958): 121–44.

————. "Maupassant, lettres à son médecin." *Les Oeuvres libres* N.S. 165 (1960): 3–14.

————. "Guy de Maupassant et Gisèle d'Estoc." *Les Oeuvres libres* N.S. 195 (1962): 137–80.

Bornecque, Jacques-Henry. *Les Années d'apprentissage d'Alphonse Daudet*. Paris: Librairie Nizet, 1951.

————, and Luc Badesco. "Autour d'Alphonse Daudet, controverse." *Revue d'histoire littéraire de la France* 64 (1964): 473–78.

————. "Dans l'intimité des Maupassant: Laure de Maupassant (d'après des lettres et documents inédits)." *Revue d'histoire littéraire de la France* 64 (1964): 623–32.

Bouilhet, Louis. *Lettres à Louise Colet*. Paris: Librairie Nizet, 1968.

Boulenger, Jacques. *Les Dandys: Sous Louis-Philippe*. Paris: Calmann Lévy, 1932.

Bourget, Paul. *Essais de psychologie contemporaine*. 2 vols. Paris: Plon-Nourrit, 1899. Originally published in 1883 and 1885.

Brain, Dr. Walter Russell. *Speech Disorders: Aphasia, Apraxia, and Agnosia*. London: Butterworths, 1965. Originally published in 1961.

Brault, Dr. Jacques-Félix-René. *Considérations médicales sur la sensibilité de Flaubert*. Bordeaux: Imprimerie-Librairie de l'Université, 1932.

Brombert, Victor. *The Novels of Flaubert: A Study of Themes and Techniques*. Princeton: Princeton University Press, 1966.

Bruneau, Jean. *Les Débuts littéraires de Gustave Flaubert, 1831–1845*. Paris: Armand Colin, 1962.

Brunon, Dr. Raoul. "A Propos de Madame Bovary." *La Presse médicale* 15 annex (1907): 713–15.

Bryant, John E. *Genius and Epilepsy*. Concord: Ye Old Depot Press, 1953.

Busi, Frederick A. "Sartre on Flaubert." *Research Studies, Washington State University* 41 (1973): 9–17.

———. "The Legacy of Edouard Drumont as an Ecrivain de Combat." *Nineteenth-Century French Studies* 4 (1976): 385–93.

Butor, Michel. *Histoire extraordinaire: Essai sur un rêve de Baudelaire.* Paris: Gallimard, 1961.

Cabanès, Dr. Augustin. "La Documentation médicale dans le roman: Conversation avec M. Alphonse Daudet." *La Chronique médicale* 3 (1896): 100–105.

———. "La Documentation médicale dans le roman des Goncourt: Conversation avec M. Edmond de Goncourt." *La Chronique médicale* 3 (1896): 450–60.

———. "Flaubert a-t-il ou non suivi des cours de médecine?" *La Chronique médicale* 3 (1896): 593–94.

———. "Guy de Maupassant chez le Docteur Blanche." *La Chronique médicale* 4 (1897): 682–86.

———. "La Dernière maladie et la mort d'Alphonse Daudet," *La Chronique médicale* 5 (1898): 1–7.

———. "La Documentation médicale dans l'oeuvre d'Alphonse Daudet." *La Chronique médicale* 5 (1898): 9–14.

———. "Le Dernier livre d'Alphonse Daudet." *La Chronique médicale* 5 (1898): 55–56.

———. "Auto-hallucination: Guy de Maupassant." *La Chronique médicale* 8 (1901): 605.

———. "Une Consultation médicale de Baudelaire: Le Monument de Baudelaire." *La Chronique médicale* 9 (1902): 353.

———. "De Sadisme chez Baudelaire." *La Chronique médicale* 9 (1902): 725–35.

———. "Le Médecin de Flaubert." *La Chronique médicale* 10 (1903): 72–73.

———. "La Névrose de Flaubert: Flaubert et la médecine." *La Chronique médicale* 12 (1905): 209–13.

———. "La Maladie et la mort de Baudelaire." *La Chronique médicale* 14 (1907): 770–72.

———. "Baudelaire 'dans le domaine.'" *La Chronique médicale* 24 (1917): 264–66.

———. "Baudelaire et l'avarie." *La Chronique médicale* 25 (1918): 22.

———. "Baudelaire, opiomane." *La Chronique médicale* 27 (1920): 112.

———. "Alphonse Daudet, médecin consultant." *La Chronique médicale* 33 (1926): 142.

———. *Grands névropathes.* 2 vols. Paris: A. Michel, 1930–31.

Calmy, Christophe. "Flaubert et le nihilisme de gauche." *Esprit* 2 (1963): 251–60.

Carassus, Emilien. *Le Mythe du dandy.* Paris: A. Colin, 1971.

Carrère, Jean. *Degeneration in the Great French Masters.* Freeport: Books for Libraries Press, 1967. Originally published in 1922 as *Le Mauvais Maîtres.*

Carter, A. E. *The Idea of Decadence in French Literature 1830–1900*. Toronto: University of Toronto Press, 1958.

Caubet, Dr. Louis-Antoine-Justin. *La Névrose de Baudelaire*. Bordeaux: Y. Cadoret, 1930.

Céard, Henry, ed. *Lettres de Jules de Goncourt*. Paris: G. Charpentier, 1885.

———. *Correspondance inédite, 1876–1896, d'Edmond de Goncourt et Henry Céard*. Paris: A. C. Nizet, 1965. Preface by Pierre Cogny.

Champfleury [Jules-Français-Félix Husson]. *Souvenirs et portraits de jeunesse*. Paris: E. Dentu, 1872.

Charcot, Dr. Jean-Martin. *Lectures on the Diseases of the Nervous System*. Philadelphia: H. C. Lea, 1879.

———, and Dr. Paul Richer. *Les Démoniaques dans l'art*. Paris: A. Delahaye & E. Lecrosnier, 1887.

Chastenet, Jacques. *La République des républicains 1879–1893*. Paris: Hachette, 1954.

Cogny, Dr. Pierre. "Guy de Maupassant et la drogue." *Cahiers de la Tour Saint-Jacques* 1 (1960): 86–91.

———. Introduction to Maupassant, *Notre Coeur*. Paris: Librairie Didier, 1962.

Coleman, Stanley M. "The Phantom Double: Its Psychological Significance (with special reference to de Maupassant and Dostoevski)." *British Journal of Medical Psychology* 14 (1934): 254–73.

Colet, Louise. *Une Histoire de soldat*. Paris: A. Cadot, 1856.

———. *Lui, roman contemporain*. Paris: Librairie Nouvelle, 1860.

Cololian, Dr. Paul. "Gustave Flaubert et la psychanalyse." *Hippocrate* 5 (1937): 488–95.

Commanville, Caroline. "Souvenirs intimes." In Flaubert, *Correspondance*, 1:ix–xlv. Also published as *Souvenirs sur Gustave Flaubert*. Paris: A. Ferroud, 1895.

Crépet, Jacques. "Derniers jours de Charles Baudelaire." *La Nouvelle Revue française* 39 (1 November 1932): 641–71.

Daudet, Alphonse. *Oeuvres complètes illustrées*. 20 vols. Paris: Librairie de France, 1929–31. Incomplete, but the best available "complete" edition.

———. *La Doulou: La Vie: Extraits des carnets inédits de l'auteur*. Paris: Fasquelle, 1931. The most complete edition of the notebooks, with a preface by André Ebner.

———. *L'Evangéliste*. Paris: E. Flammarion, 1892.

———. *L'Immortel*. Paris: Alphonse Lemerre, 1888.

———. *Quarante ans de Paris, 1857–1897*. Geneva: La Palatine, 1945. Includes both *Trente ans de Paris* and *Souvenirs d'un homme de lettres*, both originally published in 1888.

———. *Sapho*. New York: Modern Library, 1947.

———. "A la Salpêtrière." *La Chronique médicale* 5 (1898): 15–18.

Daudet, Ernest. *My Brother and I: Recollections of Infancy and Youth*. Boston: Little, Brown, 1898. Originally published in 1882.

Daudet, Léon. *Alphonse Daudet.* Boston: Little, Brown, 1898.

———. *Devant la douleur: Souvenirs des milieux littéraires, artistiques et médicaux, de 1880 à 1905.* Paris: Nouvelle Librairie Nationale, 1915.

Daudet, Lucien. *Vie d'Alphonse Daudet.* Paris: Gallimard, 1941.

Dedet, Dr. Christian. *Le Figaro littéraire,* 9 March 1967.

Deffoux, Léon. "Les Enfants de Guy de Maupassant." *Mercure de France* (1 January 1927): 249–51.

Déjerine, Dr. Jules. *The Psychoneuroses and Their Treatment by Psychotherapy.* London and Philadelphia: J. B. Lippincott, 1915.

Delpierre, Dr. Guillaume. *Etude psycho-pathologique sur Guy de Maupassant.* Montrouge: V. Hello, 1939.

Delzant, Alidor. *Les Goncourt.* Paris: G. Charpentier, 1889.

Derocque, Dr. P. "Nécrologie—Le Dr. Aubé." *La Revue médicale de Normandie* 4 (1903): 323–24.

Diamond, Marie J. *Flaubert, The Problem of Aesthetic Discontinuity.* Port Washington, N.Y.: Kennikat Press, 1975.

Dictionnaire de médecine. Paris: Flammarion Médecine-Sciences, 1975.

Dictionnaire français de médecine et de biologie. 4 vols. Edited by Alexandre Manuila et al. Paris: Masson, 1970–75.

Du Camp, Maxime. *Souvenirs littéraires.* 2 vols. Paris: Hachette, 1882–83. Originally published in 1881.

———. "La Maladie de Flaubert." *La Chronique médicale* 3 (1896): 584–87.

Dulmet, Florica. "Elisa ou la passion de Gustave Flaubert." *Revue de Paris* 76, #6 (1969): 57–63.

Dumesnil, Dr. René. *Flaubert et la médecine.* Paris: Société française d'Imprimerie, 1905. Republished in 1906 as *Flaubert, son hérédité, son milieu, sa méthode;* and reprinted in Geneva: Slatkine, 1969.

———. *Le Grand Amour de Flaubert.* Geneva: Editions du Milieux du Monde, 1945.

———. *Chronique, études, correspondance de Guy de Maupassant.* Paris: Librairie Gründ, 1938.

———. *Guy de Maupassant.* Paris: J. Tallandier, 1947.

Duplessis de Pouzilhac, Dr. Paul. *Les Goncourt et la médecine.* Montpellier: Firmin, Montane & Sicardi, 1910.

Dupouy, Dr. Roger. "Charles Baudelaire, toxicomane et opiomane." *Annales médico-psychologiques* 11 (1910): 353–64.

———. "Le Poète de l'opium: Charles Baudelaire." *Aesculape* 2 (1912): 97–99.

Dupuy, Aimé. "En Marge des voyages de Montaigne, Chateaubriand, et de Maupassant, ou quand les domestiques deviennent 'secrétaires'." *La Presse médicale* 65 (1957): 213–14, 261–62.

Earnest, Ernest. *The Single Vision: The Alienation of American Intellectuals, 1910–1930.* New York: New York University Press, 1970.

Ebner, André. Preface to *La Doulou* by Alphonse Daudet. Paris: Fasquelle, 1931.

Egbert, Donald D. "The Idea of 'Avant-garde' in Art and Politics." *American Historical Review* 73 (1967): 339–66.

Eifer, Dr. "La Maladie de Guy de Maupassant date de 1877." *La Revue moderne de médecine et de chirurgie* 22 (1922): 245.

Ellenberger, Henri F. *The Discovery of the Unconscious: The History and Evolution of Dynamic Psychiatry*. New York: Basic Books, 1970.

Emmanuel, Pierre. "Baudelaire, un catholique bien suspect." *Revue générale belge* 3 (March 1967): 15–39.

———. *Baudelaire: The Paradox of Redemptive Satanism*. University, Ala.: University of Alabama Press, 1970. Originally published in 1967.

Esquirol, Dr. Jean-Etienne-Dominique. *Des Maladies mentales considerées sous le rapport médical, hygiénique et médicolégal*. 2 vols. Paris: J.-B. Baillière, 1838.

Even, Dr. Pierre-Yves. *Etude médicale sur Edmond et Jules de Goncourt et leurs premiers romans*. Paris: Bibliothèque Coopérative, 1908.

Falret, Dr. Jules. *Recherches sur la folie paralytique et les diverses paralysies générales*. Paris: Rignoux, 1853.

Faust, Camille [Mauclair]. *La Vie amoureuse de Charles Baudelaire*. Paris: E. Flammarion, 1927.

Fauvel, Dr. Henri. "Les Maladies de coeur dans les romans des Goncourt." *La Chronique médicale* 15 (1908): 123.

———. "Souvenirs sur Gustave Flaubert." *La Chronique médicale* 15 (1908): 449–57, 481–91.

Flaubert, Gustave. *Correspondance*. 13 vols. Editor of first nine volumes unknown. Four supplementary volumes edited by René Dumesnil, Jean Pommier, and Claude Digeon. Paris: Louis Conard, 1926–54.

———. *Correspondance*. Edited by Jean Bruneau. Paris: Gallimard, 1973. Only Vol. 1 [1830–51] has appeared.

———. *Oeuvres de jeunesse inédites*. 3 vols. Paris: Louis Conard, 1910.

———. *Intimate Notebook 1840–1841*. Edited by Francis Steegmuller. London: W. H. Allen, 1967.

———. *Madame Bovary*. Edited by Paul de Man. New York: W. W. Norton, 1965.

———. *Notes de voyages*. 2 vols. Paris: Louis Conard, 1910.

———. *November*. New York: Serendipity Press, 1967.

———. *The First Sentimental Education*. Edited by Gerhard Gerhardi. Berkeley and Los Angeles: University of California Press, 1972.

———. *Sentimental Education*. Edited by Robert Baldick. Harmondsworth: Penguin Books, 1964.

———. *Salammbô*. New York: French and European Publications, 1961.

———. *Temptation of Saint Anthony*. New York: Grosset & Dunlap, 1932.

———. *Three Tales*. Harmondsworth: Penguin Books, 1961.

Fleming, Dr. William L. "Syphilis through the Ages." Paper read at Vanderbilt University School of Medicine, 17–18 May 1963.

Fortin, Dr. Charles. "Le Subconscient chez Flaubert." *La Chronique médicale* 8 (1901): 28–31.

Fosca, François [Georges de Traz]. *Edmond et Jules de Goncourt*. Paris: Albin Michel, 1941.

Fournier, Dr. Alfred-Jean. *De L'Ataxie locomotrice d'origine syphilitique (tabès spécifique)*. Paris: G. Masson, 1882.

———. *L'Hérédité syphilitique*. Paris: G. Masson, 1891.

———. *Syphilis et paralysie générale*. Paper read at l'Académie de médecine, 30 October 1894. Paris: Barnagaud, n.d.

Gabel, Dr. Joseph. *Génie et folie chez Guy de Maupassant*. Paris: Jouve, 1940.

Galantière, Lewis, ed. *The Goncourt Journals 1851–1870*. New York: Doubleday, 1958.

Galérant, Dr. "L'Epilepsie de Flaubert." *Les Revues médicales normandes* 5 (1963): 642–50.

Gallet, Dr. Pierre. *Quel diagnostic aurions-nous fait si nous avions soigné Flaubert?* Paris: R. Foulon, 1960.

Garçon, Maurice. *Histoire de la justice sous la IIIe République*. 3 vols. Paris: Arthème Fayard, 1957.

Garrido Quintana, Dr. Francisco. "Es caso Flaubert." *La Medicina Ibera* 30 (1 August 1936): 131–36.

———. "La Paralisis general progresiva y dos locos geniales." *Medicina Argentina* 13 (1934): 505–10.

Gautier, Théophile. "Charles Baudelaire." Preface to *Les Fleurs du mal*. Paris: Calmann Lévy, 1894.

Gélineau, Dr. "L'Epilepsie de Flaubert et les épileptiques célèbres." *La Chronique médicale* 7 (1900): 670–72.

———. "Une Victime de la neurasthénie: Jules de Goncourt." *La Chronique médicale* 8 (1901): 625–31.

———. "Quelle était la maladie de Jules de Goncourt?" *La Chronique médicale* 8 (1901): 762–66.

Gendreau, Cecil. "Le Génie par la drogue?" *Montréal médical* 9 (1 October 1957): 9–11.

Gérard-Gailly, Emile. *Flaubert et les fantômes de Trouville*. Paris: La Renaissance du Livre, 1930.

———. *Le Grand amour de Flaubert*. Paris: Aubier, 1944. Adds several chapters to the previous title.

Gistucci, Léon. "Le Pessimisme de Maupassant." *La Chronique médicale* 16 (1909): 465–66.

Goncourt, Edmond de. "Comment est mort Jules de Goncourt: Lettre d'Edmond de Goncourt à Emile Zola." *La Chronique médicale* 3 (1896): 471–74.

———. "La Dernière maladie de Jules de Goncourt." *La Chronique médicale* 3 (1896): 464–71. Extracts from the *Journal*.

Goncourt, Jules de. *Lettres*. Edited by Henry Céard. Paris: G. Charpentier, 1885.

Goncourt, Edmond and Jules de. *Journal: Mémoires de la vie littéraire*. Edited by Robert Ricatte. 22 vols. Monaco: Les Editions de l'Imprimerie nationale de Monaco, 1956–58.

———. "Une Visite à la Charité." *La Chronique médicale* 3 (1896): 460–64. An extract from the *Journal*.

Bibliography

Gould, Dr. George M. "A Biographic Clinic on Gustave Flaubert." *Medical Record* 69 (1906): 569–78.

Graña, César. *Bohemian versus Bourgeois: French Society and the French Man of Letters in the Nineteenth Century*. New York and London: Basic Books, 1964.

Grinker, Dr. Roy R., Dr. Paul C. Bucy, and Dr. Adolph L. Sahs. *Neurology*. Springfield: Charles C. Thomas, 1960.

Guérinot, Dr. A. "Un Geste meurtrier de Maupassant." *La Chronique médicale* 33 (1926): 214.

Guerrant, Dr. John et al. *Personality in Epilepsy*. Springfield, Ill.: Charles C. Thomas, 1962.

Guillain, Dr. Georges. *J.-M. Charcot, 1825–1893: His Life—His Work*. New York: Paul Hoeber, 1959. Originally published in 1955.

Gumpertz, Dr. Karl. "Der Judith-Komplex: Versuch einer Analyse von Hebbels *Judith* und Flauberts *Salammbô*." *Zeitschrift für Sexualwissenschaft* (Leipzig) 14 (1927): 289–301.

Guntrip, H. "A Study of Fairbairn's Theory of Schizoid Reactions." Charles Reed, Irving Alexander, and Silvan Tomkins, eds. *Psychology: A Source Book*. Cambridge: Harvard University Press, 1963. Originally published in 1952.

Halévy, Ludovic. *Notes et souvenirs 1871–1872*. Paris: Calmann Lévy, 1889.

Hamburger, Michael. "Puerile Utopia and Brutal Mirage: Notes on Baudelaire and the History of a Dilemma." *International Literary Annual* (London) 1 (1958): 135–52.

Hayter, Alethea. *Opium and the Romantic Imagination*. Berkeley and Los Angeles: University of California Press, 1970.

Hébert de la Rousselière, Dr. J. "La Douleur, soeur et inspiratrice de Baudelaire." *Mémoires de l'Académie des Sciences, Belles-Lettres et Arts d'Angers* 8 (1964): 10–32.

Hélot, Dr. R. "Gustave Flaubert—chirurgien (autobiographie)." *La Revue médicale de Normandie* 4 (1904): 501–3.

Hemmings, F. W. J. *Culture and Society in France 1814–1898*. London: Batsford, 1971

Hérisson, Charles D. "Le Voyage de Baudelaire: Le séjour au Cap de Bonne Espérance en 1841." *Mercure de France* 1148 (January–March 1959): 637–73.

———. "A Propos des lettres inédits aux siens: Quelques aspects de la vie de Baudelaire de 1839 à 1842." *Revue des sciences humaines* (Lille) 34 (1969): 57–71.

Hoffmann, Dr. Gérard. *Le Cas de Maupassant: Etude médico-littéraire*. Paris: Jouve, 1940.

Hollier, Dr. Robert. *La Peur et les états qui s'y rattachent dans l'oeuvre de Maupassant*. Lyon: Imprimeries Réunies, 1912.

Holzman, Dr. Philip S. *Psychoanalysis and Psychopathology*. New York: McGraw-Hill, 1970.

Ignotus, Paul. *The Paradox of Maupassant*. New York: Funk & Wagnalls, 1968. Originally published in 1966.

Ionesco, Eugène. "No." *Esquire* 82 (December 1974): 95–96, 250–58.

Jackson, Joseph F. *Louise Colet et ses amis littéraires*. New Haven: Yale University Press, 1937.

Jacquemet, Dr. Robert-Didier-Henri-Bernard. *De L'état mental de Baudelaire*. Bordeaux: Saugnac & Drouillard, 1922.

James, Henry. *French Poets and Novelists*. New York: Grosset & Dunlap, 1964. First published in 1878.

————. *Parisian Sketches: Letters to the New York Tribune, 1875–1876*. Edited by Leon Edel and Ilse Dusoir Lind. New York: New York University Press, 1957.

Janet, Dr. Pierre-Marie-Félix. *The Major Symptoms of Hysteria*. New York: Macmillan, 1907. Lectures given at Harvard.

————. *Les Névroses*. Paris: E. Flammarion, 1909.

————. *L'Etat mental des hystériques*. Paris: F. Alcan, 1911.

Jean-Maurienne. "La Maladie et la mort de Flaubert." *La Chronique médicale* 37 (1930): 281–85. Originally published in 1928.

Johannet, René. "Baudelaire asocial." *Ecrits de Paris* 159 (1958): 32–39.

Jubleau, Gustave. "Gustave Flaubert et le bromure." *La Chronique médicale* 33 (1926): 55.

Judica, Dr. Giovanni. "Gli attaques de nerfs di Gustave Flaubert: Isterismo o epilessia?" *Medicina Italiana* 14 (1933): 564–67.

Keiser, Dr. Lester. *The Traumatic Neurosis*. Philadelphia: Lippincott, 1968.

Kempf, Roger. "L'Irrédentisme dandy." *Stanford French Review* 1 (1977): 39–52.

King, Dr. Ambrose, and Claude Nicol. *Venereal Diseases*. London: Cassell, 1964.

Kluge, Dr. O. "Ueber den Muskelsinn und ueber seine Darstellung bei Maupassant." *Allgemeine Zeitschrift für Psychiatrie und ihr Grenzgebiete* 60 (1903): 414–42.

Kunel, Maurice. "Quand Baudelaire visitait nos églises (1864–1867)." *Le Thyrse, Revue de littérature et d'art* 69 #5 (1967): 19–23.

Lacassagne, Dr. Antoine. "La Psycho-physiologie d'Alphonse Daudet, par lui-même." *La Chronique médicale* 5 (1898): 8–9.

————. "A Propos de Maupassant." *Archives d'anthropologie criminelle de médecine légale et de psychologie normale et pathologique* 25 (1910): 104–11.

Lacassagne, Dr. Zacharie. *La Folie de Maupassant*. Toulouse: Gimet-Pisseau, 1907.

Lacretelle, Jacques de. "Les Amours de Baudelaire." *Revue de Paris* 71 #4 (1964): 6–11.

Ladame, Dr. Charles. *Guy de Maupassant: Etude de psychologie pathologique*. Lausanne: Edition de la "Revue Romande," 1919.

————. "La Vraie maladie de Guy de Maupassant: Un Point de vue nouveau." *Zeitschrift für Kinderpsychiatrie* 14 (1947): 64–68.

Ladee, Dr. G. A. *Hypochondriacal Syndromes*. Amsterdam, London, and New York: Elsevier, 1966.

Laforgue, Dr. René. *The Defeat of Baudelaire: A Psycho-analytical Study of the Neurosis of Charles Baudelaire.* London: Hogarth Press, 1932. Originally published in 1931.

Lagriffe, Dr. Lucien. "Guy de Maupassant: Etude de psychologie pathologique." *Annales médico-psychologiques* 8 (1908): 203–38, 353–72; 9 (1909): 177–93.

———. "La Peur dans l'oeuvre de Maupassant." *Archives d'anthropologie criminelle et médecine légale et de psychologie normale et pathologique* 28 (1913): 188–99.

Laignel-Lavastine, Dr. Maxime and Dr. Mary Trivas. "Quelques remarques sur l'auto-observation d'un tabétique de qualité." *Le Bulletin de la Société française de l'histoire médicale* 27 (1933): 310–16.

Landolt, Dr. Edmund. "A Propos de Maupassant." *Archivio di antropologia criminale, psichiatria, medicina legale e scienze affini* 25 (1910): 389.

Lange, Dr. Wilhelm. "Die Psychose Maupassants: Ein kritischer Versuch." *Zentralblatt für Nervenheilkunde und Psychiatrie* 32 (1909): 739–54.

"The Last Illness of Baudelaire." *Urologic and Cutaneous Review* 38 (1934): 150–51.

Lastic, Dr. Philibert de. *La Pathologie mentale dans les oeuvres de Gustave Flaubert.* Paris: J.-B. Baillière, 1906.

Laulan, Robert. "Alphonse Daudet, malade incurable et lucide." *La Médecine de France* 178 (1967): 13–16, 48.

Le Breton, Dr. Jacques. *La Maison de santé du Docteur Blanche, ses médecins, ses malades.* Paris: Marcel Vigné, 1937.

———. "La Fin de Maupassant." *Archives médico-chirurgicales de Normandie* 53 (1962): 59–65.

Lecomte de Nouy, Hermine. "Les Tentatives de suicide de Maupassant." *La Chronique médicale* 15 (1908): 39–40.

Legrand, Dr. Maximin. [Letter concerning Flaubert]. *La Chronique médicale* 7 (1900): 736.

Lemaître, Jules. *Literary Impressions.* Port Washington: Kennikat Press, 1971. Originally published in 1921.

Lennox, Dr. William G. *Epilepsy and Related Disorders.* 2 vols. Boston: Little, Brown, 1960.

Le Pileur, Dr. L. "Gustave Flaubert, Maxime Du Camp, et Wellington." *La Chronique médicale* 7 (1900): 770–71.

Le Sage, Dr. Albert. "Guy de Maupassant: Etude médico-littéraire." *La Union médicale du Canada* 46 (1917): 319–40.

Lethève, Jacques. "Le Thème de la décadence dans les lettres françaises à la fin du xixe siècle." *Revue d'histoire littéraire de la France* 63 (1963): 46–61.

Levaillant, Maurice, and Marc Varenne. "La Dernière Lettre d'amour de Flaubert à Louise Colet." *Revue des deux mondes* (1 July 1954): 139–45.

Levallois, Jules. "La Véritable Madame Bovary." *La Chronique médicale* 3 (1896): 587–89. Taken from his *Mémoires d'un critique.* Paris: Librairie Illustrée, 1896.

Lombard, Dr. André. "Guy de Maupassant: Sa vie, son oeuvre, sa maladie, sa mort." *La Chronique médicale* 15 (1908): 33–39.

Louge, Dr. R. "La Syphilis de Baudelaire." *La Chronique médicale* 34 (1927): 368.

Lumbroso, Albert, Baron. *Souvenirs sur Maupassant: Sa dernière maladie, sa mort.* Rome: Bocca, 1905

"Maladie et mort de Flaubert." *Chercheurs et curieux* 9 (1959): 842–46.

"La Maladie et la Mort de Flaubert." *Les Amis de Flaubert* (Yvetot) 15 (1959): 56.

Mantoux, Charles. *Alphonse Daudet et la souffrance humaine.* Marseille: Ricord, 1941.

Mason, Germaine-Marie. *Les Ecrits de jeunesse de Flaubert.* Paris: Nizet, 1961.

Massin, Jean. *Baudelaire devant la douleur.* Paris: Sequana, 1944.

Matthews, Dr. Walter Bryan, and Dr. Henry Miller. *Diseases of the Nervous System.* Oxford: Blackwell Scientific Publications, 1972.

Maupassant, Guy de. *Chronique, études, correspondance de Guy de Maupassant.* Edited by René Dumesnil with the collaboration of Jean Loize. Paris: Librairie Gründ, 1938.

———. *The Complete Short Stories of Guy de Maupassant.* Edited by Artine Artinian. Garden City: Hanover House, 1955.

———. *Oeuvres complètes.* Paris: Louis Conard, 1908.

———. *Pierre and Jean.* New York: P. F. Collier, 1902.

———. *Sur l'eau, La Vie errante, A Family Affair, and Other Stories.* New York: P. F. Collier & Son, 1910.

Maurois, André. *Lélia: The Life of George Sand.* New York: Harper & Bros., 1953.

Maury, Paul. "Flaubert et la médecine." *Le Progrès médical* 28 (1912): 480–82.

Mérimée, Prosper. *Correspondance générale.* 17 vols. Toulouse: Edouard Privat, 1943–72.

Merritt, Dr. Hiram Houston. *A Textbook of Neurology.* Philadelphia: Lea & Febiger, 1963.

M. G. "Flaubert et Jules Cloquet." *Le Progrès médical* 90 (1962): 479–80.

Michaut, Dr. Paul. "La Maladie de Maupassant." *La Chronique médicale* 5 (1898): 731–34.

———. "Le Docteur Flaubert." *La Chronique médicale* 5 (1898): 682–84.

———. "De Quoi est mort Flaubert?" *La Chronique médicale* 7 (1900): 607.

———. "La Mort de Flaubert." *La Chronique médicale* 7 (1900): 703–4.

———. "Un Livre à écrire sur Gustave Flaubert." *La Chronique médicale* 7 (1900): 771–76.

———. "Gustave Flaubert anatomiste." *La Chronique médicale* 8 (1901): 487.

———. "Comment est mort Baudelaire." *La Chronique médicale* 9 (1902): 186–90.

———. "Un Dernier mot sur la maladie de Baudelaire." *La Chronique médicale* 10 (1903): 27–28.

———. "La Pleurésie phthisiogène: Les Goncourt et le professeur Landouzy." *La Chronique médicale* 10 (1903): 801–4.

Michel-Béchet, H. "Le Sens olfactif chez Baudelaire." *Archives médico-chirurgicales de province* 25 (1935): 437–47.

Michelet, Jules. *The People.* Edited by John P. McKay. Urbana: University of Illinois Press, 1973.

Mignot, Albert. *Ernest Chevalier et Gustave Flaubert.* Paris: E. Dentu, 1888.

Mignot, Dr. Roger. *Contribution à l'étude des troubles pupillaires dans quelques maladies mentales.* Medical thesis, Paris, 1900.

Moers, Ellen. *The Dandy: Brummell to Beerbohm.* London: Secker & Warburg, 1960.

Molinéry, Dr. Raymond. "La Maladie de Baudelaire." *Le Paris médical* 91 annex (1934): 49.

Money, Dr. John, and Dr. Anke A. Ehrhardt. *Man & Woman, Boy & Girl: The Differentiation and Dimorphism of Gender Identity from Conception to Maturity.* Baltimore: Johns Hopkins University Press, 1972.

Monin, Dr. "Gustave Flaubert et le bromure." *La Chronique médicale* 32 (1925): 213.

———. "La Maladie d'Alphonse Daudet." *La Chronique médicale* 33 (1926): 112.

Moreau de Tours, Dr. Jacques-Joseph. *Les Facultés morales considerées sous le point de vue médical de leur influence sur les maladies nerveuses, les affections organiques.* Paris: J. Rouvier & E. Le Bouvier, 1836.

———. *Mémoire sur les causes prédisposants héréditaires de l'idiotie et de l'imbécilité.* Paris: F. Malteste, 1853.

———. *La Psychologie morbide dans ses rapports avec la philosophie de l'histoire, ou de l'influence des névropathies sur le dynamisme intellectuel.* Paris. Victor Masson, 1859.

Morel, Dr. Bénédict-Auguste. *Traité des dégénérescences physiques, intellectuelles et morales de l'espèce humaine.* Paris: J. B. Baillière, 1857.

Morin-Gauthier, Dr. Francine. *La Psychiatrie dans l'oeuvre littéraire de Guy de Maupassant.* Paris: Jouve, 1944.

Morton, Dr. R. S. *Venereal Diseases.* Harmondsworth: Penguin Books, 1966.

Moser, Françoise. "Flaubert et ses légendes." *La Médecine de France* 179 (1967): 10–14.

———. "Maupassant devant sa maladie." *La Médecine de France* 189 (1968): 15–22.

Mouquin, Dr. Marcel. "La Maladie d'Alphonse Daudet." *Histoire de la médecine* 5 #2 (1955): 41–55.

Nadar [Félix Tournachon]. *Baudelaire intime: Le Poète vierge.* Paris: A. Blaizot, 1911.

Nagera, Humberto, et al. *Basic Psychoanalytic Concepts on the Libido Theory.* New York: Basic Books, 1969.

Neveux, Pol. Preface to *Oeuvres complètes* by Guy de Maupassant. Paris: Louis Conard, 1908. Neveux's study was written in 1907.

Niess, Robert J. "Autobiographical Symbolism in Maupassant's Last Works." *Symposium* 14 (1960): 213–20.

Nordau, Max. *Degeneration.* Introduction by George Mosse. New York:

Howard Fertig, 1968. Originally published in 1892.

Normandy, Georges. *La Fin de Guy de Maupassant.* Paris: Albin Michel, 1927.

———. "La Migraine de Maupassant." *Aesculape* 16 (1926): 160–63.

Noury, Dr. Paul. "Glanes sur les maladies et la mort de Gustave Flaubert." *La Chronique médicale* 36 (1929): 61–64.

O'Kelly, Dr. Lawrence I., and Dr. Frederick A. Muckler. *Introduction to Psychopathology.* Englewood Cliffs: Prentice-Hall, 1955.

Ovesey, Dr. Lionel. "Pseudohomosexuality, the Paranoid Mechanism, and Paranoia: An Adaptational Revision of a Classical Freudian Theory." Charles Reed, Irving Alexander, and Sylvan Tomkins, eds. *Psychopathology: A Source Book.* Cambridge: Harvard University Press, 1963. Originally published in 1955.

Owen, Alan Robert George. *Hysteria, Hypnosis and Healing: The Work of J.-M. Charcot.* New York: Garret Publications, 1971.

"The Paresis of Guy de Maupassant." *Journal of the American Medical Association* 69 (1917): 1555–56.

P. D. "Une Consultation médicale de Guy de Maupassant." *Revue médicale de Normandie* 4 (1903): 517–19.

Parturier, Maurice. *Morny et son temps.* Paris: Hachette, 1969.

Penfield, Dr. Wilder, and Dr. Lamar Roberts. *Speech and Brain-Mechanisms.* Princeton: Princeton University Press, 1959.

Peralta, Dr. F. "Des célèbres 'comedores de haxix.'" *Actas Ciba* (Buenos Aires) 1942: 1–2, 22–25.

Peyrade, Jean. "Les Premières années parisiennes d'Alphonse Daudet." *Revue des deux mondes* 15 (1966): 377–86.

Pezzi, Dr. Giuseppe. "Patologia e psicologia di Charles Baudelaire." *Riforma medica* 71 (1957): 449–51.

Pichois, Claude. "La Maladie de Baudelaire." *La Médecine de France* 92 (1958): 37–42.

Pillet, Dr. Maurice. "Le Mal de Maupassant." *Aesculape* 3 (1913): 138–43, 167–73, 180–84, 217–21.

Podolsky, E. "The Epileptic Brain and Its Influence on History." *Medicine Illustrated* 9 (1955): 391–93.

Polanšcak, Antun. "Le Mal de Baudelaire." *Studia romanica et anglica zagrabiensia* 24 (1967): 23–32.

Pommier, Jean. "Flaubert et la naissance de l'acteur." *Journal de psychologie normale et pathologique* 40 (1947): 185–94.

———. "Les Maladies de Gustave Flaubert." *Le Progrès médical* 75 (1947): 408–16.

———. "Sensations et images chez Flaubert." *Journal de psychologie normale et pathologique* 42 (1949): 274–94.

Porché, François. *La Vie douloureuse de Charles Baudelaire.* Paris: Plon, 1926.

Profizi, Jacques. *Charles Baudelaire: Étude psychanalytique d'après "Les Fleurs du mal."* Paris: Editions de l'Athanor, 1974.

Proust, Marcel. "Sur M. Alphonse Daudet." *La Presse,* 11 August 1897.

"Quelques opinions sur les Goncourt." *La Chronique médicale* 28 (1921): 245–46.

Rank, Otto. "Zu Baudelaires Inzestkomplex." *Zentralblatt für Psychoanalyse und Psychotherapie* 1 (1911): 275.

Reed, Dr. Ralph. "Gustave Flaubert; Madame Bovary; The Death of Madame Bovary." *Lancet-Clinic* (Cincinnati) 105 (1911): 431–32, 456–57, 482–83.

Regnault, Dr. Félix. "L'Epilepsie chez les hommes de génie." *La Chronique médicale* 8 (1901): 31–32.

———. "Observations d'épilepsie sur les hommes de génie et notamment sur Gustave Flaubert ont été jusqu'à présent mal prises." *Revue de l'hypnotisme et de la psychologie physiologique* 15 (1901): 270–74.

———. "La Maladie de Flaubert." *La Chronique médicale* 12 (1905): 350.

———. "La Maladie de Guy de Maupassant." *La Revue moderne de médecine et de chirurgie* 24 (1924): 133–38.

———. "Le Mal de Flaubert." *Revue moderne de médecine et de chirurgie* 27 (1927): 342–47.

Reik, Theodor. "Flauberts Jugendregungen: Der Liebende Flaubert." *Halbmonatsschrift für soziale Hygiene und praktische Medizin* 2 (1911): 75–84, 101–14.

———. *Flaubert und seine Versuchung des heiligen Antonius: Ein Beitrag zur Künstlerpsychologie.* Minden: Bruns, 1912.

———. "Zwei Träume Flauberts." *Zentralblatt für Psychoanalyse und Psychotherapie* 2 (1912): 222–24.

———. "Aus dem Leben Guy de Maupassants." *Imago: Zeitschrift für Anwendung der Psychoanalyse auf die Geisteswissenschaften* 2 (1913): 519–21.

———. *Masochism in Modern Man.* New York: Grove Press, 1941.

———. *The Secret Self: Psychoanalytic Experiences in Life and Literature.* New York: Farrar, Straus & Young, 1952.

Rémond, Dr. A., and Dr. P. Voivenel. "La Folie de Maupassant." *Le Progrès médical* 24 (1908): 270–71.

———, and ———. "La Responsabilité médicale vue par Maupassant." *Le Progrès médical* 85 (1957): 298.

Ricatte, Robert. *La Création romanesque chez les Goncourt, 1851–1870.* Paris: Armand Colin, 1953.

Richer, Dr. Paul. *L'Art et la médecine.* Paris: Goultier, Magnier, 1902.

Ricord, Dr. Philippe. *Illustrations of Syphilitic Disease.* Philadelphia: A. Hart, 1851.

Roche, Alphonse V. *Alphonse Daudet.* Boston: Twayne Publishers, 1976.

Roche, Anne. "L'Opposition au second empire dans quelques-unes des ses expressions et représentations littéraires." *Revue d'histoire moderne et contemporaine* 21 (January–March 1974): 33–45.

Romains, Jules. *Souvenirs et confidences d'un écrivain.* Paris: Fayard, 1958.

Rougemont, E. de. "La Maladie de Baudelaire, d'après son écriture." *La Chronique médicale* 29 (1922): 310.

Ruff, Marcel-A. *Baudelaire.* New York: New York University Press, 1966.

Originally published in 1958.

Sachs, Murray. *The Career of Alphonse Daudet: A Critical Study*. Cambridge: Harvard University Press, 1965.

———. "Visit to the World of Alphonse Daudet." *French Review* 33 (1960): 501–2.

Sartre, Jean-Paul. *Baudelaire*. Norfolk: New Directions, 1967.

Schanne, Alexandre-Louis. *Souvenirs de Schaunard*. Paris: G. Charpentier, 1886.

Schenk, H. G. *The Mind of the European Romantics: An Essay in Cultural History*. New York: Anchor Books, 1969. Originally published in 1966.

Scherb, Dr. G. "Quelle était la maladie de Jules de Goncourt?" *La Chronique médicale* 8 (1901): 759–62.

Scouras, Dr. Photis. *Essai médico-psychologique sur Charles Baudelaire*. Lyon: Bosc frères & Riou, 1929.

———. "La Maladie et la mort de Baudelaire." *Aesculape* 20 (1930): 29–35.

———. "Baudelaire toxicomane." *Hygiène mentale* 25 (1930): 230–41.

Ségalen, V. "Gustave Flaubert et le bovarysme." *La Chronique médicale* 15 (1908): 491.

"The Sex Life of Great Writers." *American Journal of Urology and Sexology* 16 (1920): 69–70.

Silvera, Alain. *Daniel Halévy and His Times*. Ithaca: Cornell University Press, 1966.

Simeons, Dr. A. T. W. *Man's Presumptuous Brain: An Evolutionary Interpretation of Psychosomatic Disease*. New York: E. P. Dutton, 1962.

Sitwell, Osbert. *The Man Who Lost Himself*. London: Duckworth, 1929.

Slager, Dr. Ursula T. *Basic Neuropathology*. Baltimore: Williams & Wilkins, 1970.

Sollier, Dr. Paul. *Les Phénomènes d'autoscopie*. Paris: Alcan, 1903.

Souffrin, Eileen. "Banville et les Goncourt." *Revue d'histoire littéraire de la France* 49 (January–March 1949): 37–58.

Starkie, Enid. *Baudelaire*. New York: New Directions, 1958. Originally published in 1933.

———. *Flaubert the Master: A Critical and Biographical Study (1856–1880)*. New York: Atheneum, 1971.

Stedman, Dr. Thomas L. "The 'Paresia' of Guy de Maupassant." *Medical Record* 92 (1917): 289–90.

Steegmuller, Francis. *Flaubert and Madame Bovary*. London: Hamish Hamilton, 1958. Originally published in 1939.

———. *Maupassant: A Lion in the Path*. New York: Grosset & Dunlap, 1949.

———. *The Selected Letters of Gustave Flaubert*. London: Hamish Hamilton, 1954.

Stekel, Dr. Wilhelm. *Impotence in the Male*. 2 vols. New York: Grove Press, 1965. Originally published in 1927.

Streketski, Dr. C. "Une lettre—missive du Gustave Flaubert." *Art et médecine* 8 (1931): 22–23.

Tannenbaum, Edward R. *The Action Française*. New York: John Wiley & Sons, 1962.

Tassart, François. *Recollections of Guy de Maupassant*. New York: John Lane, 1912. First published in 1911.

Terrier, Dr. Jean. "La Génie et la maladie chez Guy de Maupassant." Medical thesis, Paris, 1927.

Terson, Dr. A. "La Syphilis de Baudelaire." *La Chronique médicale* 35 (1928): 61.

Thiébaut, Marcel. "Les Goncourt et leur journal." *Revue de Paris* 68 (1960): 141–59.

Thomas, Louis. *La Maladie et la mort de Maupassant*. Paris: A. Messein, 1912. Originally published in 1906.

Tourneux, Dr. J. "Nécrologie—Charles Fortin." *La Revue médicale de Normandie* 4 (10 January 1903): 26–28.

Trial, Dr. Raymond. *La Maladie de Baudelaire: Etude médico-psychologique*. Paris: Jouve, 1926.

Trilling, Lionel. "A Note on Art and Neurosis." *Partisan Review* 12 (Winter 1945): 41–48.

Trivas, Dr. Mary. *Auto-observation d'un tabétique de qualité*. Paris: Editions Véga, 1932.

———. "El Doloroso calvario de Alphonse Daudet." *Revista de Psiquiatría y Criminología* 1 (1936): 215–17.

Troubat, Jules-Auguste. *Notes et pensées*. Paris: L. Sauvaitre, 1888.

———. *Souvenirs du dernier secrétaire de Sainte-Beuve*. Paris: Calmann Lévy, 1890.

Turnell, Martin. *Baudelaire: A Study of His Poetry*. London: Hamish Hamilton, 1953.

Uzanne, Octave. "The Portraits of Guy de Maupassant." Introduction to *Pierre and Jean*. New York: P. F. Collier, 1902.

Vallery-Radot, Dr. Pierre. "Baudelaire: médecine et médecins." *La Presse médicale* 64 (1956): 517–18.

———. "La Fin dramatique de Jules de Goncourt à 39 ans, racontée par son frère." *La Médecine de France* 144 (1963): 11–16.

———. "Lettres inédites de Maupassant." *Le Fureteur: Littéraire, historique, médical, scientifique* 7–8 (1965): 195–99.

———. "Les Médecins vus par les Goncourt." *Histoire de la médecine* 1 (1951): 11–19.

———. "La Maladie de Maupassant d'après sa correspondance." *La Presse médicale* 64 (1956): 1521–22.

———. "Un Névropathe de génie: Le mal de Baudelaire par lui-même d'après sa correspondance avec sa mère." *La Presse médicale* 64 (1956): 919–20.

———. "Un Ecrivain surmené: Quatre ans (1873–6) de la vie de Gustave Flaubert d'après sa correspondance." *La Presse médicale* 65 (1957): 173–74.

Veith, Ilza. *Hysteria: The History of a Disease*. Chicago: University of Chicago

Press, 1970. Originally published in 1965.

Vial, André. "Le Mal de Maupassant." *Mercure de France* (1 April 1948): 758–59.

———. *Guy de Maupassant et l'art du roman.* Paris: Librairie Nizet, 1954.

Vier, Jacques. "Baudelaire, poète chrétien?" *La Pensée catholique* 71 (1961): 67–72.

Voivenel, Dr. Paul, and Dr. Louis Lagriffe. *Sous le signe de la P. G.: La Folie de Guy de Maupassant.* Paris: La Renaissance du Livre, 1929.

———. "A Propos de la paralysie générale de Guy de Maupassant." *La Chronique médicale* 36 (1929): 141–44.

Vulpian, Dr. Alfred. *Maladies du système nerveux: Leçons professées à la faculté de médecine.* 2 vols. Paris: O. Doin, 1879–86.

Wallis, Hugh Roland Eyre. *Masked Epilepsy.* Edinburgh: E. & S. Livingstone, 1956.

Weber, Eugen. *L'Action française.* Paris: Stock, 1962.

Weiss, Dr. Richard S., and Dr. Herbert L. Joseph. *Syphilis.* New York: Nelson, 1951.

Williams, Denis, ed. *Modern Trends in Neurology.* New York: Paul B. Hoeber, 1957.

Zeldin, Theodore. "Biographie et psychologie sous le second empire." *Revue d'histoire moderne et contemporaine* 21 (January–March 1974): 58–74.

Zola, Emile. *Les Romanciers naturalistes.* Paris: F. Bernouard, 1927–29. Originally published in 1881.

Index

Abadie, Dr., 234
Académie française, 44, 67, 306
Académie Goncourt, 67–68, 278–79, 306
Adam, Juliette, 188
Allard, Jules, 291, 295–96
Ancelle, Narcisse, 8, 28–31, 53–58
Aphasia, 56–58
Asselineau, Charles, 11, 13, 38, 58–59
Aubé, Dr. Pierre, 224–25
Aubryet, Xavier, 82
Aupick, Caroline, 1–10, 16, 20–22, 27–37, 46, 53–58. *See also* Baudelaire, Caroline Archenbaut-Defayis
Aupick, Jacques, 1, 6, 10, 11, 16, 27, 29

Babou, Hippolyte, 17
Badesco, Luc, 276
Bailey, Dr. Pearce, 202–3
Balestre, Dr., 269
Banville, Thédore de, 42, 43, 59
Barbey d'Aurevilly, Jules, 35
Bart, Benjamin F., 150, 153–54, 212, 213
Baudelaire, Alphonse, 1–7
Baudelaire, Caroline Archenbaut-Defayis, 1
Baudelaire, *Charles*-Pierre, 294; family life, 1–10; art critic, 4; syphilis, 5, 47–51, 59–60; *le mal*, 7, 17–19, 29, 33, 36–37, 47; *conseil judiciaire*, 8, 16, 28, 30, 45; his *spleen*, 8, 17, 29, 33; suicide attempt, 9; as dandy, 10–19; political views, 12–13; use of drugs, 19–27, 54–57; misogyny, 15, 19–27; life with mother, 27–37; masochism, 37–47; olfactory temperament, 47;

gonorrhea, 50–51; in Belgium, 25, 44–45, 51–58; final illness, 53–60; aphasia, 56, 60; death, 58–60
Baudelaire, Félicité Ducessois, 3
Baudelaire, Joseph-*François*, 1
Béhaine, Edouard Lefebvre de, 78, 103
Benedikt, Dr. Moritz, 172
Béni-Barde, Dr. Alfred, 100, 103–4, 105
Bernard, Claude, 71, 301
Berthelot, Marcelin, 71
Billy, André, 78, 83, 90
Binet-Sanglé, Dr. Charles, 198, 200, 201
Blanche, Dr. Emile, 271
Blanche, Dr. Esprit, 271
Boborikine, Peter, 263
Boils, 154
Bonaparte, Louis-Napoleon, 73, 282
Bonaparte, Mathilde, 75, 80, 99, 100, 177, 271
Borel, Pierre, 219, 253, 260–61
Bornecque, Jacques-Henry, 276
Bouchard, Dr. Jacques, 265, 267
Bouilhet, Louis: replaces Alfred Le Poittevin, 137, 147, 166–76; Flaubert's letters from Near East, 149–55; moves to Paris, 158, 161–62; death, 176
Bourget, Paul, 250, 262, 265
Bovarysme, 111, 169, 171
Brault, Dr. J.-F.-R., 204
Breuer, Dr. Josef, 197
Broussais, Dr. Victor, 125
Brown-Séquard, Dr. Charles-Edouard, 301
Bruneau, Jean, 150
Butor, Michel, 20, 40

Cabanès, Dr. Augustin, 58, 201, 290

Café du Helder, 76
Café Riche, 76
Carrère, Jean, xi
Caubet, Dr. Louis-Antoine-Justin, 51
Cazalis, Dr. Henry, 248, 266, 267, 268
Céard, Henry, 254, 259
Champfleury, Jules-François-Félix Husson, called, 14, 45
Charcot, Dr. Jean, 195–96, 198, 217, 289, 291, 294, 298–99, 303
Charpentier, Georges, 194
Chevalier, Ernest, 113–14, 118, 140, 156
Clemenceau, Georges, 302
Cloquet, Dr. Jules-Germain, 119–20, 147
Cogny, Dr. Pierre, 261
Coleman, Stanley M., 251
Colet, Louise: mentioned, 125, 129, 131, 149, 198; as Flaubert's mistress, 137–46; attempts to revive liaison, 157–65, 172; claims to be pregnant, 159, 215; desires marriage, 161–62; final break with Flaubert, 162–63
Collier family, 121, 124
Commanville, Désirée-*Caroline* Hamard: birth, 136; suit over her custody, 147; marriage to Ernest Commanville, 172–73; marriage to Franklin Grout, 173; and Flaubert's death, 192–93; her migraines, 208; censoring of Flaubert's letters, 165
Commanville, *Ernest*-Octave: marries Flaubert's niece, 172–73; financial reverses, 185–86, 190; quarrels with Edmond Laporte, 189–90
Comte, Auguste, 200
Conard, Louis, 203
Courbet, Gustave, 31
Courmont, Nephtalie Le Bas de, 64
Crépet, Eugène, 46
Crépet, Jacques, 4

Dandyism, 10–19
Daremberg, Dr. Georges, 268

Daubrun, Marie, 21
Daudet, Adeline Reynaud, 279, 282
Daudet, Alphonse: his significance, 275–76; issue of the Goncourt *Journal*, 67, 278–79; his financial success, 279; unhappy childhood, 280–82; religious training, 280; adolescent bohemian, 281, 282; in Paris (1857), 282; and Marie Rieu, 283; his pessimism, 281; suspicion of women, 283; sexual depravity, 284, 285; literary apprenticeship, 284; venereal infection, 285; syphilis, 285, 291; his marriage (1867), 285; promiscuity, 285; ambiguity, 285–86; period of depression, 286–87; beginning of physical pain (1878), 287; urinary problems (1881), 289; Charcot suspects locomotor ataxia (1882), 289, 293; begins notes about pains (*ca.* 1884), 290; use of drugs, 291, 295–96, 300, 302; muscular incoordination, 291, 296, 298; understands no possibility of cure (1885), 293; family troubles, 294–96; fear of becoming disgusting, 296–97; fear of ultimate madness, 297; treatment by Charcot, 298–99; cachexia, 300; death, of, 302; the merchant of happiness, 302–11; the Académie française, 306; the Académie Goncourt, 306; doubts about medical profession, 307; religious views, 307, 312; cultural decentralization, 309; Dreyfus Affair, 309; devotion to family ideal, 303–4, 309–12
Daudet, Ernest, 276, 278, 280, 282, 284, 287
Daudet family, 276–82, 304–5
Daudet, Julia Allard, 66, 278, 279; marriage to Alphonse, 285; domestic troubles, 294–96, 300; concern for husband, 296, 300, 302
Daudet, Léon, 276–77, 279, 294–95, 299, 304, 306–7, 309, 310–11
Daudet, Lucien, 276, 279, 311
Daudet, Marthe Allard, 277
Daudet, Vincent, 278, 279–80, 282

Dedet, Dr. Christian, 51
Déjerine, Dr. Jules, 266–67
Delpierre, Dr. Guillaume, 253, 254
Denis, Pélagie, 104
De Quincey, Thomas, 24, 26
Deschamps, Emile, 42
Dorchain, Auguste, 245, 268
Doré, Gustave, 76
Drumont, Edouard, 277, 297, 302, 310
Du Camp, Maxime: and Baudelaire, 14–15; reveals Flaubert's illness, 124, 126–27, 191, 192–94; house-guest at Croisset (1846), 124–25, 133; trip to Near East (1849–51), 147–57; his accuracy, 148; venereal infections, 152; exhorts Flaubert to move to Paris, 159; publishes *Madame Bovary*, 169; opinion of *Salammbô*, 170; election to Académie française (1880), 194; reaction to Flaubert's death, 198
Ducessois, Marie-Anne, 4
Duchenne, Dr. G.-B.-A., 292, 294
Dumesnil, Dr. René, 191, 193, 201–2, 206, 212, 218
Duplan, Jules, 176
Duplessis de Pouzilhac, Dr. Paul, 107
Duval, Dr. Emile, 58
Duval, Jeanne, 7–10, 16, 19–22, 28, 41, 43–44, 59

Ebner, André, 290, 300
Ebner, Jules, 290
Ecker, Dr. Arthur, 212
Edmond, Charles [Charles-Edmond Chojecki, called], 76
Ehrlich, Dr. Paul, 50
Eliot, T. S., 35
Emmanuel, Pierre, 37
Epilepsy: *grand mal*, 126–28, 191–94, 197–204; Jacksonian, 126; psychomotor, 204–5; temporal lobe, 205–8, 210–12
Estoc, Gisèle, d', 228, 253, 260–62, 265
Even, Dr. Pierre-Yves, 107

Faguet, Emile, 174, 259

Flaubert, Dr. Achille, Flaubert's brother, 112, 136, 149, 185, 191, 215; and Flaubert's seizure, 124–25, 128
Flaubert, Dr. Achille-Cléophas, Flaubert's father, 111–13, 215; treats nervous seizure, 125, 127–28; no sympathy for literary career, 133; death (1846), 136
Flaubert, Anne-Justine-Caroline Fleuriot, Flaubert's mother, 112–13; becomes responsible for Caroline Hamard, 136; the de-manding mother, 141–42, 157–58, 174; the custody suit, 147; con-sents to Near East trip, 148; joins Flaubert in Italy (1851), 155–57; death of, 180; her migraines, 208
Flaubert, Caroline, Flaubert's sister, 112; marriage to Emile Hamard, 134; premature death (1846), 136
Flaubert, Gustave: 73, 76, 98, 287; youthful despair, 111–15; child-hood dreams, 115; alienation, 116–18; reads Marquis de Sade, 118, 120; trip to South (1840), 119–20; youthful depression, 120–21; hostility to democracy, 121, 175–76, 179; law student, 121–24; and Harriet Collier, 121, 123, 158; beginning of dental trouble, 122; first seizure (1844), 124–25; hallucinations, 125, 129; seclusion, 128–37; suspects his femininity, 131; confesses deci-sion to be a writer, 133; the legend of St. Anthony, 134–35; trip to Italy (1845), 134; monkey dream, 134–35; dependence upon friends, 137; first liaison with Louise Colet, 137–46; his perver-sity, 122–23, 138–46, 160–61; de-voted to his mother, 141; walking trip in Brittany (1847), 142, 144; his masochism, 145–46, 150–51, 170–72, 212; trip to Near East (1849–51), 147–57; sexual novelties in Near East, 149–52; suspected homosexuality, 150, 213; visits to Kuchuk Hanem, 151–52; venereal

infection, 152, 203–4; views on
women, 123, 130; resumption of
relations with Louise Colet,
157–65; articulates hatred for life,
158, 175–76, 202, 228; irritated by
Du Camp, 159; agony of literary
composition, 160, 170, 173–74,
181, 194; final break with Louise
Colet, 162–63; mercurialism, 164;
glossitis, 164; reputed affair with
Juliet Herbert, 165; his alleged
objectivity, 166–69; prosecuted for
Madame Bovary, 169, 177; trip to
North Africa (1858), 170; marriage
of his niece, 172–73; excessive
spending, 173; response to
Franco-Prussian War, 176–79,
182–83; devotion to friends, 179,
181; reaction to mother's death,
180; revival of nervous attacks
(1870), 180; post-1870 patriotism,
182–83; literary failures, 176,
183–84; trip to Switzerland (1874),
184; threat of financial ruin,
185–86, 188, 190; influence of
George Sand, 186–87; attempt to
secure a sinecure, 186, 188–89;
deepening depression (1878),
188–90; cracked fibula (1879), 188;
death, 190–92; medical debate
over, 190–215; case diagnosed,
213–15
Folacci, Dr. J.-B., 226
Fontaine, Léon, 260
Fortin, Dr. Charles, Flaubert's
physician, 188–89, 190–92, 197,
199, 234
Foucaud de Lenglade, Eulalie, 120,
134, 139, 142
Fournier, Dr. Alfred, 49, 107, 252,
291, 292
France, Anatole, 78–79
Franck, Adolphe, 80
Freud, Dr. Sigmund, 195, 197

Gabel, Dr. Joseph, 255–56
Gallet, Dr. Pierre, 127, 206–7
Gautier, Théophile: mentioned, 25,
44, 76, 104; death, 182
Gélineau, Dr., 105–6, 197

General paralysis (paresis), 106–7
Gérard-Gailly, Emile, 118, 204
Gistucci, Léon, 226, 248
Goncourt, Annette-Cécile Guérin,
63–64
Goncourt brothers: trip to Italy
(1849), 65; their fraternity, 65–70;
the *Journal*, 65–68, 70, 75; their
élitism, 71–74, 76–79; hatred of
nature, 74; social life, 76, 82;
anti-Semitism, 79, 82; misogyny,
81–90; obsession with illness,
90–95; depression, 94–97; literary
productivity, 97; move to Auteuil,
98–99; opinion of Flaubert, 73,
126, 170
Goncourt, Edmond de: family life,
63; publication of *Journal*, 67–68,
278–79; Legion of Honor, 78; and
the death of Jules, 101–5, 298;
continues *Journal* alone, 101; and
Flaubert's death, 192; hostility to
Maupassant, 263; friend of
Alphonse Daudet, 275, 284, 287,
288, 290, 294, 295, 296–97, 300, 305
Goncourt, Jules de: family life, 63;
hatred of democracy, 70–71,
72–73; bigotry, 79–80; misogyny,
81–90; venereal disease, 85–86,
105, 108–9; his dreams, 86–90;
masochism, 87–90; depression,
95–97; beginning of fatal
symptoms, 97; death, 101–4, 108–9
Goncourt, Marc-Pierre Huot de, 63
Gould, Dr. George M., 202
Grancher, Dr. Joseph, 265, 267
Grout, Dr. Franklin, 173, 271
Gruby, Dr., 301
Gumpertz, Dr. Karl, 171–72
Guyon, Dr. Félix, 289

Halévy, Ludovic, 237, 275, 284
Hamard, Emile: marriage to
Caroline Flaubert, 134; erratic be-
havior, 147
Hardy, Dr. Alfred, 184, 198
Hennique, Léon, 254, 262–63, 302
Herbert, Juliet, 165
Heredia, Jose-Maria de, 251
Hertford, Richard Seymour-

Conway, marquess of, 89
Holmes, Oliver Wendell, 86
Houssaye, Arsène, 76
Hugo, Jeanne, 277, 310
Hydrotherapy, 100–101
Hyperthyroidism, 225–26
Hypochondriasis, 17, 33, 209
Hysteria, 166, 184, 189, 193, 194–213

Ignotus, Paul, 257, 261, 262
Ionesco, Eugène, 215

Jackson, Dr. Hughlings, 57
James, Henry, 18, 168, 263
Janet, Pierre, 146, 195, 210
Jaquotot, Bernard, 30–31
Jean-Maurienne, 203
Joyce, James, 168
Jung, Carl, 272

Kahn, Marie, 262
King, Dr. A. F. A., 172
Kuchuk Hanem, Egyptian courtesan, 151–52

Lacassagne, Dr. Antoine, 251
Ladame, Charles, 253–54, 260
Laforgue, Dr. René, 2, 38, 44, 50–51
Lagriffe, Dr. Louis, 251, 253
Landolt, Dr. Edmund, 248, 251–52, 253, 254
Lannoux, Armand, 260
Laporte, Edmond, 188, 190
Lasègue, Dr. Charles, 55, 58
Lastic, Dr. Philibert de, 202
La Tourette, Dr. Gilles de, 302
Lecomte de Nouy, Hermine, 270
Legrand, Dr. Maximin, 198
Lemaître, Jules, 259
Lennox, Dr. William, 204
Lepelletier, Marie, 83–84, 104
Le Pileur, Dr. L., 198
L'Epine, Ernest, 284, 287
Le Poittevin, Alfred, 114–15, 122, 147, 156, 215
Le Poittevin family, 114, 223
Le Poittevin, Louise de Maupassant, 114
Lévy, Michel, 52, 176
Librairie France, 78

Librairie Nouvelle, 76
Litzelmann family, 227
Lockroy, Edouard, 311
Lombroso, Dr. Cesare, 200
Lumbroso, Albert, 227, 229, 231, 251, 267, 269

Magitot, Dr. Emile, 266–67
Magny Restaurant, 76, 123, 165, 176
Malingre, Rosalie [Rose], 64, 83
Marchal de Calvi, Dr. Charles-Jacob, 285
Marcq, Dr. Léon, 54
Maupassant family, 217–19, 226–27
Maupassant, Gustave de, Maupassant's father, 218; marital separation, 219; lack of substance, 221; concern for Laure's mental state, 226–27; and Maupassant's death, 272
Maupassant, Guy de: becomes Flaubert's disciple, 183, 190, 232–33; helps secure Flaubert's sinecure, 189; and Flaubert's death, 192, 193; sense of privacy, 217–18, 220, 256–57; birth, 218; unhappy childhood, 218–19; early disenchantment with love and marriage, 219–21; literary style, 220; contempt for women, 221, 227; unconventional adolescent, 222–23; literary apprenticeship, 222; career as bureaucrat, 223, 228; demoralization, 223, 226; fear of cold and winter, 223–24, 229, 248; trip to Corsica (1880), 226; revulsion for maternity, 227; no compassion for children, 227; his illegitimate children, 227; and Gisèle d'Estoc, 228, 231; inability to love, 228, 245, 257–59; his boating, 228–30, 248–49; use of alcohol, 229; migraines, 230; nervous affliction, 230; excessive sexuality, 230; date of syphilitic infection, 231–32; deepening depression (1878), 232–33; beginning of literary success, 233; threat of prosecution, 233–34; beginning of eye trouble, 234;

examined by Fortin, 234–35; death of Flaubert, 235; hatred for life, 235, 259; hostility to democracy, 235; the prolific writer (1881–90), 236–47; his syphilis, 236, 247, 252–54, 265–72; his subject matter, 195, 236–40; morbid fears in his work, 238–43; hallucinations, 239–42, 250–51; obsessions, 239, 259; distinguishes between the terrible and the horrible, 240; understanding of paranoia, 243, 255; fear of solitude, 242, 259; obsession with illegitimacy, 244–45; disastrous results of love, 244–45; theme of sexual abnormality, 245; his own sexual abnormality, 247, 259–65; his headaches, 248, 249, 252–53, 265; eye trouble, 248, 251–53, 254, 265; use of medication, 248, 265; trip to North Africa (1887–88), 249; amnesiac attacks, 249, 262; use of drugs, 254–55, 258, 265; schizophrenia, 255; his lawsuits, 256–57; and Gisèle d'Estoc, 260–62, 265; his swift decline, 256–57, 265–72; institutionalized (1892), 271–72; death (1893), 223, 272

Maupassant, Hervé de, Maupassant's brother, 219; committed to asylum (1889), 249; death (1889), 222–23, 227, 249–50

Maupassant, Laure Le Poittevin de, Maupassant's mother, 218; marital separation, 219; loneliness and grief, 220; superior to her husband, 221; indulges her child, 221; her poor health, 222–23, 230, 233; Graves' disease, 225–26; trip to Corsica (1880), 226; autocratic personality, 226–27; moves to Riviera, 235; sees Maupassant for last time, 269–70; death (1903), 222

Max, Dr. H.-E., 56
Max, Dr. Oscar, 54, 56
Maynial, Edouard, 254
Ménard, Louis, 9, 18, 42
Mendès, Catulle, 15
Mérimée, Prosper, 42

Meuriot, Dr. A., 271
Michaut, Dr. Paul, 197–99
Migraines, 230, 252–53
Mirès, Jules, 79
Misogyny, 15, 19–27, 81–90, 221, 227, 283
Monnier, Henri, 126
Moreau de Tours, Dr. Joseph: his medical teaching, 91–94; influence on the literati, 91, 93–94, 175
Morel, Dr. Auguste, 167
Morny, Auguste de, 284–85, 287, 309
Moulin Rouge, 76

Nadar [Félix Tournachon, called], 40, 41, 59
Naquet, Alfred, 310
Nardy, Auguste, 227
Neurasthenia, 105–6
Neveux, Pol, 217, 265
Neiss, Robert J., 220
Nieuwerkerke, Alfred-Emilien, 75
Noguchi, Dr. Hideyo, 59
Normandy, Georges, 224, 253, 254, 263, 265

Paresis. *See* General paralysis
Passy, Louis, 64, 77
Pater, Walter, 168
Penfield, Dr. Wilder, 211
Penson, Beatrix, 164
Pichois, Claude, 5, 47
Pillet, Dr. Maurice, 252
Pinchon, Robert, 217, 230, 231, 265
Poe, Edgar Allan, 26, 29, 40
Popelin, Claudius, 192
Porché, François, 9
Potain, Dr. Carl, 224, 230, 233, 234, 267, 288, 289, 291, 302
Pouchet, Dr. Georges, 192–93, 197–98
Poulet-Malassis, Auguste, 25, 31–33, 46, 48, 49, 54–57
Pound, Ezra, 168
Pradier, James, 124, 137
Primoli, Joseph, 224, 229, 265
Proust, Marcel, 195, 275, 311
Psychasthenia, 146, 210

Rank, Otto, 251

Regnault, Dr. Félix, 199–200, 202, 203
Reik, Theodor: interprets Flaubert's dreams, 116; on masochism, 145, 172
Requin, Dr. Achille-Pierre, 106
Richer, Dr. Paul, 195
Ricord, Dr. Philippe, 50, 85, 164
Rieu, Marie, 279, 283, 285
Robin, Dr. Albert-Edmond, 266, 267, 301
Rochefort, Henri, 309, 310
Rogier, Camille, 154
Romains, Jules, x
Rops, Félicien, 42, 56
Rougemont, E. de, 59
Ruff, Marcel, 3, 17, 35

Sabatier, Aglaé-Apollonie, 21–22
Sachs, Murray, 275, 277, 299, 303
Saint-Victor, Paul de, 80, 90
Salpêtrière, xii, 195, 196, 237, 303
Sand, George: 84; comments on Goncourt brothers, 76; friendship for Flaubert, 182, 198; offers to buy Croisset, 186; death of, 187
Sartre, Jean-Paul: on Baudelaire, 41, 42; on Flaubert, 116
Satyriasis, 262–65
Sauteiran de Saint-Clément, Zélie, 227
Schanne, Alexandre, 14, 31
Scherb, Dr. G., 106
Schlésinger, Elisa [Mme Maurice]: Flaubert's infatuation with, 117–19, 143, 145, 182
Schlésinger, Marie-Adèle, 118
Schopenhauerian pessimism, 237, 295, 307

Seymour, Lord Henry, 89
Sitwell, Osbert, 289
Slager, Dr. Ursula, 205
Starkie, Enid, 2, 5, 38, 44, 165
Steegmuller, Francis, 246–47, 256, 260, 270
Stekel, Wilhelm, 146
Stevens, Arthur, 57
Syphilis, symptoms of, 48–51, 107–9, 252, 292, 297

Tabes dorsalis, 291, 292, 297
Tassart, François: becomes Maupassant's valet, 248; records Maupassant's decline, 248–49, 261–62, 265–72
Thiébaut, Marcel, 85
Thomas, Louis, 231, 251
Toudouze, Gustave, 305
Tourneux, Dr. J., 191–92, 197
Toussenel, Alphonse, 36
Transsexuality, 213–14
Trélat, Dr. Ulysse, xii
Troubat, Jules, 25, 57
Turgenev, Ivan, 188, 192, 287, 288, 308
Turnell, Martin, 41

Venereal diseases, 153
Véron, Théodore, 17
Voivenel, Dr. Paul, 253

Wallace, Sir Richard, 89
Wallace, Dr. William, 50

Zola, Emile, 104–5, 150, 181, 192, 195, 213, 237, 254, 272, 275, 287, 296, 301, 302